GLOBALIZING CITIES

Studies in Urban and Social Change

Published by Blackwell in association with the *International Journal of Urban and Regional Research*. Series editors: Chris Pickvance, Margit Mayer and John Walton.

Published

Fragmented Societies
Enzo Mingione

Free Markets and Food Riots
John Walton and David Seddon

The Resources of Poverty
Mercedes González de la Rocha

Post-Fordism
Ash Amin (ed.)

The People's Home?
Social Rented Housing in Europe and America
Michael Harloe

Cities after Socialism
Urban and Regional Change and Conflict in Post-Socialist Societies
Gregory Andrusz, Michael Harloe and Ivan Szelenyi (eds)

Urban Poverty and the Underclass: A Reader
Enzo Mingione

Capital Culture
Gender at Work in the City
Linda McDowell

Contemporary Urban Japan
A Sociology of Consumption
John Clammer

Globalizing Cities
A New Spatial Order?
Peter Marcuse and Ronald van Kempen (eds)

The Social Control of Cities
Sophie Body-Gendot

Forthcoming

European Cities in a Global Age
A Comparative Perspective
Alan Harding (ed.)

Urban South Africa
Alan Mabin and Susan Parnell

Urban Social Movements and the State
Margit Mayer

GLOBALIZING CITIES

A NEW SPATIAL ORDER?

Edited by
Peter Marcuse and Ronald van Kempen

BLACKWELL
Publishers

Copyright © Blackwell Publishers Ltd 2000

Editorial matter and arrangement copyright © Peter Marcuse and
Ronald van Kempen 2000

First published 2000
Reprinted 2000

Blackwell Publishers Ltd
108 Cowley Road
Oxford OX4 1JF
UK

Blackwell Publishers Inc.
350 Main Street
Malden, Massachusetts 02148
USA

British Library Cataloguing in Publication Data

A CIP catalogue record for this book is available from the British Library.

Library of Congress Cataloging-in-Publication Data

Globalizing cities : a new spatial order? / edited by Peter Marcuse
   and Ronald van Kempen.
      p.   cm. — (Studies in urban and social change)
   Includes bibliographical references and index.
      ISBN 0–631–2189–2 (alk. paper). — ISBN 0–631–21290–6 (pbk. :
   alk. paper)
        1. Cities and towns. 2. Spatial behavior. 3. Polarization
   (Social sciences) 4. Human geography. I. Marcuse, Peter.
   II. Kempen, Ronald van. III. Series.
   HT119.G65   2000
   307.76—dc21   99-43570
                                                                        CIP

Typeset in 10½ on 12 pt Baskerville
By Ace Filmsetting Ltd, Frome, Somerset
Printed in Great Britain by MPG Books Ltd, Bodmin, Cornwall

This book is printed on acid-free paper

Contents

List of Figures

List of Maps

List of Tables

List of Contributors

Blair Badcock is Reader in the Department of Geographical and Environmental Studies at the University of Adelaide. Through his teaching and research he endeavours to bring an Australian perspective to bear in the field of urban and housing studies.

Robert A. Beauregard is Professor of Urban Policy at the New School for Social Research in New York City (USA). His current research focuses on the late 20th century city.

Luiz Cesar de Queiroz Ribeiro is Professor at the Institute for Urban and Regional Research and Planning at the Federal University of Rio de Janeiro. He currently serves as coordinator for the Center for Municipal Government and Urban Policy and is coordinator of a national research group on socio-spatial inequalities and urban governance. He has published several books on inequality, housing, globalization and urban policy.

Sanjoy Chakravorty is Associate Professor of Geography and Urban Studies at Temple University, Department of Geography and Urban Studies, in Philadelphia. His research focuses on issues of development and distribution.

William W. Goldsmith is Professor in the Department of City and Regional Planning at Cornell University and Director of its undergraduate program in Urban and Regional Studies. He has published widely on urbanization and

US urban policy and has worked in regional planning in the United States and Latin America.

Anne Haila is Professor of Urban Studies in the Department of Social Policy, University of Helsinki. She is currently researching the globalization of property markets and carrying out comparative research on cities.

Roger Keil is an Associate Professor in the Faculty of Environmental Studies at York University, Toronto. He has published extensively on urban politics, particularly in world cities, on urban ecological issues and environmental politics. He has been politically and professionally active in urbanist and environmental projects in Frankfurt, Los Angeles and Toronto. He is a founding member of the International Network for Urban Research and Action (Inura).

Christian Kesteloot is Associate Professor at the Institute for Social and Economic Geography at the Catholic University of Leuven (Belgium) and a lecturer at the Free University of Brussels. He has published widely on the relations between economic change and urban restructuring, ethnic minorities, and housing.

John Logan is Professor of Sociology and Public Policy at the University at Albany (SUNY). Much of his past research has dealt with racial and class segregation in the American metropolis. More recently he has been studying the historical roots of the contemporary situation, going back to the turn of the century in cities like New York and Chicago.

Peter Marcuse is Professor of Urban Planning at Columbia University in New York City. He has also taught at the University of California at Los Angeles, and has been President of the Los Angeles City Planning commission. A lawyer as well as planner, he has written widely on housing and planning issues, and from experiences gained as guest professor in East and West Germany, Australia, and South Africa.

Klaus Ronneberger holds a Masters Degree in Education (Dipl.Soz.Päd.), with a focus on cultural anthropology, European ethnography, sociology and political science. Ronneberger has been a researcher in the Institute for Social Research, Frankfurt am Main for many years and is currently a freelance writer. His major areas of research include urban consumption complexes, public space and surveillance, and neoliberalism.

Edward E. Telles is Professor in the Department of Sociology at the University of California, Los Angeles and is currently on leave to work at the Ford

Foundation in Rio de Janeiro where he is Program Officer in Human Rights. He has published widely on race relations and urbanization in Brazil and the United States.

Leo van Grunsven is Assistant Professor of Geography and International Economics in the Faculty of Geographical Sciences, Utrecht University, The Netherlands. From 1985 to 1990 he was Lecturer in the Department of Geography, National University of Singapore. His research interests are in development, regional economics and urban development in Asia. He has published extensively in these fields. He is the editor of "Regional Change in Industrializing Asia. Regional and local responses to changing competitiveness" (1998).

Ronald van Kempen is Associate Professor of Urban Geography at the Urban Research Centre Utrecht, Faculty of Geographical Sciences, Utrecht University, the Netherlands. His current research focuses on the links between spatial segregation, social exclusion and the development of cities.

Paul Waley is a Lecturer in geography at the University of Leeds. He has written extensively on Japanese cities and Tokyo in particular. His research interests range from historical change on the urban periphery to the relandscaping of rivers in contemporary Japanese cities. He has spent many years in Japan, writing for newspapers and working with local government.

Series Preface

In the past three decades there have been dramatic changes in the fortunes
of cities and regions, in beliefs about the role of markets and states in society,
and in the theories used by social scientists to account for these changes.
Many of the cities experiencing crisis in the 1970s have undergone revitalisa-
tion while others have continued to decline. In Europe and North America
new policies have introduced privatisation on a broad scale at the expense of
collective consumption, and the viability of the welfare state has been challenged. Eastern Europe has witnessed the collapse of state socialism and the
uneven implementation of a globally driven market economy. Meanwhile
the less developed nations have suffered punishing austerity programmes
that divide a few newly industrialising countries from a great many cases of
arrested and negative growth.

Social science theories have struggled to encompass these changes. The
earlier social organisational and ecological paradigms were criticised by
Marxian and Weberian theories, and these in turn have been disputed as all-
embracing narratives. The certainties of the past, such as class theory, are
gone and the future of urban and regional studies appears relatively open.

The aim of the series *Studies in Urban and Social Change* is to take forward
this agenda of issues and theoretical debates. The series is committed to a
number of aims but will not prejudge the development of the field. It encour-
ages theoretical works and research monographs on cities and regions. It
explores the spatial dimension of society including the role of agency and of
institutional contexts in shaping urban form. It addresses economic and po-

litical change from the household to the state. Cities and regions are understood within an international system, the features of which are revealed in comparative and historical analyses.

The series also serves the interests of university classroom and professional readers. It publishes topical accounts of important policy issues (e.g. global adjustment), reviews of debates (e.g. post-Fordism) and collections that explore various facets of major changes (e.g. cities after socialism or the new urban underclass). The series urges a synthesis of research and theory, teaching and practice. Engaging research monographs (e.g. on women and poverty in Mexico or urban culture in Japan) provide vivid teaching materials just as policy-oriented studies (e.g. of social housing or urban planning) test and redirect theory. The city is analysed from the top down (e.g. through the gendered culture of investment banks) and the bottom up (e.g. in challenging social movements). Taken together, the volumes in the series reflect the latest developments in urban and regional studies.

Subjects which fall within the scope of the series include: explanations for the rise and fall of cities and regions; economic restructuring and its spatial, class and gender impact; race and identity; convergence and divergence of the 'east' and 'west' in social and institutional paterns; new divisions of labour and forms of social exclusion; urban and environmental movements; international migration and capital flows; politics of the urban poor in developing countries; cross-national comparisons or housing, planning and development; debates on post-Fordism, the consumption sector and the 'new' urban poverty.

Studies in Urban and Social Change addresses an international and interdisciplinary audience of researchers, practitioners, students and urban enthusiasts. Above all, it endeavours to reach the public with compelling accounts of contemporary society.

Editorial Committee
John Walton, Chair
Margit Mayer
Chris Pickvance

May 1997

Preface

We have chosen the title of this book carefully. We call it "Globalizing Cities," not "Global Cities," because we treat both cities that do and cities that do not make it into the "global cities" category, as most commentators define them. But we also like the title because we view globalization as a process, not a state, and a process that affects all cities in the world, if to varying degrees and varying ways, not only those at the top of the "global hierarchy."

The subtitle: "A New Spatial Order?" is intended to frame the theme of the book, and to pose it honestly as a question. It plays on US President Bush's talk of a "new world order," after the collapse of the Soviet bloc, and is intended to look at the spatial order *within* cities, not among them.

The organization of this book is straightforward, if perhaps unusual:

- We start with a statement of the question with which we are concerned.
- We formulate a hypothesis as to its answer: that there is a new spatial order within cities, as the result of the process of globalization.
- We review the theory and the literature, essentially from Western Europe and the United States, providing the background for that hypothesis.
- We present the work of the distinguished contributors to this volume.
- We conclude that the opening hypothesis cannot be sustained, and present in our concluding chapter a modified version as the result of our review: that there are some common trends ascertainable as a result of globalization, but that neither in uniformity nor in scale do they justify the description: a new spatial order.

Thus, the Introduction and the Conclusion must be read together to see our own views of the subject matter of this book.

This book has had a long gestation period. Each of us has grappled with the issues raised here in a number of previous works centering on the way in which cities today are segregated, divided, quartered, partitioned. We assembled the contributors based on their interest in our issues, their extensive and diverse empirical work, and their openness to the kind of interchange we envisaged. We assumed the contributors would be familiar with the approaches of political economy, which we consider very fruitful, but we also assumed (correctly, it turned out!) that there would be substantial disagreement among them, both in perspective and in results. We had the opportunity to have a working session in Berlin and at the Bauhaus Dessau in May, 1996. Almost all the contributors were able to take part, and thus each was aware of the contributions of the others. We gratefully acknowledge the support of the Stiftung Bauhaus Dessau.

We have had significant correspondence with each of the contributors since then. We have however not tampered with any of the contributions contrary to their author's wishes, and each remains the responsibility of their own author.

We owe a debt of gratitude to the editors of this series, *Studies in Urban and Social Change*: John Walton, Chris Pickvance, and Margit Mayer. They supported the project from the outset, and helped us (forced, we sometimes felt, but with appreciation!) to sharpen and maintain its focus. In the process, it became clear that some of the contributions dealt centrally with the issue of the effects of globalization on the spatial structure within cities, and other took a longer-range and broader view of the question, dealing with the "partitioning effect" which is a central concern of the urban discussion today but looking at its manifestation in quite other circumstances. We have placed these parallel contributions in what is in effect a companion volume, to be published by Oxford University Press in early 2000.

Peter Marcuse would like to thank Columbia University's School of Architecture, Planning, and Preservation both for intellectual support and tolerance while he was engaged in the preparation of this volume, and his colleagues and students in the Planning Program there for intellectual stimulation throughout. Ronald van Kempen would like to thank the Urban Research Centre Utrecht (URU) of Utrecht University for the time they gave him for the work on this volume, the Centre for Research on In- and Exclusion (CRIE) for financial support and the Netherlands Graduate School of Housing and Urban Research (NETHUR) for organizational support.

Peter Marcuse, New York
Ronald van Kempen, Utrecht

1

Introduction

Peter Marcuse and Ronald van Kempen[1]

The Question

Is there something new, something different, about the spatial patterns of the cities of today and tomorrow which differentiates them from the cities of yesterday? That is the question to which this book is addressed. It asks it of cities around the world. New types of cities, called global cities by some, world cities or megacities by others, are described both in the scholarly and in the popular press. Indeed, internal spatial patterns seem to play a different role in cities today, and a very variable one: service-adapted patterns are different from manufacturing-based patterns, central cities have different patterns from those on the periphery, "edge cities" are different from traditional cities. Within cities, the ghettos are increasingly separated from the rest of the city, while the same holds true, though in a different way, for the exclusionary enclaves of the rich. Areas that are socially and spatially between these two extremes also separate themselves out from the rest of the city more and more. These are the evolving patterns we wish to examine in this book.

Of course cities are in a constant process of internal change. The center of cities decline or change form and functions, and new business districts spring up; immigrants cluster together and mix with others; ethnic and racial groups are segregated in ghettos and slums, or they escape to more livable neighborhoods; new cultural enclaves are formed, while old ones disappear; new forms of cities are created at the edges of metropolitan areas;

suburbanization never seems to end. Spatial divisions of themselves are nothing new, but they are not stable in their causes, in their appearance, in their scale, or in their effects.

There is today a growing consensus in the literature that significant changes in spatial divisions within cities have occurred very visibly since the early 1970s. Descriptive accounts of these changes have multiplied. So have accounts of changes in the national and international context that parallel and perhaps cause them: a process of globalization, changing forms of production, a declining state provision of welfare, differences in power relationships, developing technologies, all have their influence on urban patterns, within cities as well as among them (see, e.g., Fainstein et al., 1992; O'Loughlin and Friedrichs, 1996; Musterd and Ostendorf, 1998; Madanipour et al., 1998). But exactly how do these changes affect the spatial form of individual cities? Are the patterns of all cities convergent? On what do changes depend? Can (should) public policy influence them?

In this book, our focus is thus on one deceptively simple question: what is "new" about these cities of today, and in particular, what is new about the spatial arrangements within them? In brief, we ask the question:

Is there a new spatial order within cities?

We have tried to make this central question more concrete by formulating a set of subsidiary questions:

- Is there a clearly visible direct impact of globalization on the internal spatial pattern of cities? How (if at all) can the impact of globalization be separated from other macro-societal changes that are linked to globalization and/or parallel it?
- Is there indeed any generalizable city form that is characteristic of globalizing cities, be it radial, gentrified, edge city, or other? Or is it precisely that absence of conventional form that characterizes today's cities, as post-modern discussions of the Los Angeles model suggest?
- Do spatial cleavages that are indeed found in cities today reflect a dual city, a quartered city, a plural city? Are the separate residential parts further apart economically, socially, culturally, than in previous eras? The move of manufacturing to the suburbs and services to the central city goes back many decades: how can the effects of these developments be described?
- Is the old doughnut pattern, with the middle class in the white suburbs surrounding a lower class black inner city, obsolete in countries such as the United States? Is the reverse pattern, with an upper class inner city and working class suburbs, that has characterized many European cities, likewise obsolete? Or are today's patterns simply a continuation of older

and well-known market-driven mechanisms, with variations only in magnitude?

- Is "race" a critical factor in the definition of the spatial pattern of globalizing cities? If so, how and why? In all countries? Are patterns of immigrant location and separation/integration in the United States a forerunner of developments elsewhere?
- To what extent does, or can, public policy, at the local or national level, influence the internal spatial structure of cities?

We have raised these questions[2] with each of the contributors to this book. They have each provided valuable material towards some general answers; we have summarized our own understanding of what has been learned, and what remains unclear, in our Conclusion.

The volume begins with a general statement of our opening hypothesis in the next section of this Introduction. The following part of the Introduction is devoted to the factors that might be expected to produce a new spatial order within cities. This is followed by a general description of the different spatial forms we expected to find within cities. The core of the book is then devoted to case studies of diverse cities around the world. The cases provide evidence relevant to the validity of the hypothesis with which we began, although there is no pretense that they are representative enough or conclusive enough to validate or disprove it. They do clearly show the need at least for modifications, and we present a revised formulation of our hypothesis in our Conclusion, which presents our own summary and synthesis.

The Hypothesis

The hypothesis with which we begin can be formulated as follows.

There is a new spatial order of cities, commencing somewhere in the 1970s, in a period often described as one of a globalizing economy. While cities have always been divided along lines of culture, function, and status, the pattern today is a new, and in many ways deeper-going, combination of these divisions. Although it varies substantially from city to city by historical development of the built form, by national political and economic structures, by the relative weight of the contending forces involved in development, by the role of "race" and ethnicity, and by the place in the international economy, nevertheless there are basic features in common. They include a spatial concentration within cities of a new urban poverty on the one hand, and of specialized "high-level" internationally connected business activities on the other, with increasing spatial divisions not only between each of them but also among segments of the "middle class" in between.

Boundaries between divisions, reflected in social or physical walls among them, are increasing. The result is a pattern of separate clusters of residential space, creating protective citadels and enclaves on the one side and constraining ghettos on the other, in a hierarchical relationship to each other. The market produces and reproduces these divisions, but the state is deeply involved in their creation and perpetuation. The state can also ameliorate them, and will tend to do so under specific conditions. Present trends do not suggest it will do so in most places. The result is a converging pattern within cities radically different enough from earlier patterns to justify being called "a new spatial order."

Within this general hypothesis, there are the contours of specific, arguably new, socio-spatial formations (see also Marcuse, 1989; Van Kempen and Marcuse, 1997). They are mentioned briefly below and will be further elaborated later in this Introduction. Those formations include the following:

● Areas that can be considered as protected enclaves of the rich, the representatives of an extremely mobile top, operating at a more global level than ever before. These areas can be labeled as "citadels" or as "exclusionary enclaves" and generally consist of expensive apartments in favorable locations.
● Gentrified areas occupied by the yuppies, the professionals, the managers. They are surrounded by the older, often poorer, population. These areas are located in the inner parts of the older cities.
● Suburbs generally inhabited by the middle class, by households with children and substantial incomes.
● Tenement areas – with less expensive, often (but not always) rented dwellings – inhabited by the working class, the employed, unemployed and temporarily employed. The tenement city is not a homogeneous whole but is increasingly divided in itself. Neighborhoods are differentiated among each other by income, occupation, and ethnicity. In some cases the divisions are represented spatially by the hardening of the boundaries between them.
● Ethnic enclaves, often seen as a specific form of the tenement city. Here, ethnic minorities congregate for various reasons.
● A new type of ghetto, the so-called excluded ghetto, inhabited by the new urban poor, a fully and long-term excluded group at the bottom (Marcuse, 1998).

These ideas were formulated before we knew what the contributions to this volume would be. Since we know now, as this is going into print, what our conclusions are, a very brief summary here is appropriate:

The hypothesis accurately states certain common tendencies, but their manifestation in cities is the result of changes that are of longer historical origin, and dependent on multiple contingencies. In any given case, the variations may overwhelm the general, and the results are much subject to political control. While the general tendencies produce predictable socio-spatial patterns, very visibly affect some locations, and are increasing in importance, they are not so consistent or so different from prior patterns as to deserve being called "a new spatial order."

Each of these points is developed in our Conclusion.

Influences on the Spatial Order of Cities

It is not a very new idea that cities are part of a larger society, that their spatial form is inter-related with the economic, social, cultural, and political structures of the society within which they exist. Areas within the city are further influenced by developments and decisions on higher spatial levels. Sociologists and geographers now agree that patterns of segregation and concentration change as a consequence of the interaction of individual household decisions with a variety of structures and developments on different spatial levels. Societal processes – like economic restructuring on a global level – have their impact on local situations and developments (Sassen, 1990; Burgers and Engbersen, 1996, Van Kempen and Marcuse, 1997, Van Kempen and Özüekren, 1998) and on choice patterns of households (Clark and Dieleman, 1996).

We begin with a consideration of macro-social forces (see also Van Kempen and Marcuse, 1997).

The unclear impact of globalization

The causes of changes within cities can to a large extent be traced back to developments that take place on higher spatial levels, regionally and even more critically nationally and globally. The latter, with its concomitant national and regional implications, is today generally subsumed under the concept of globalization, a term that is often used, but not always well defined. Globalization can comprise many processes, such as the spatial integration of economic activities, movement of capital, migration of people, development of advanced technologies, and changing values and norms that spread among various parts of the world. We take it here to mean globalization in its present configuration, that is, a combination of new technology, increased trade and mobility, increased concentration of economic control, and reduced welfare-oriented regulatory action of nation states. Other forms of globalization have existed in the past, and today alternative forms of globalization could easily be envisaged, but we focus here on really existing globalization, globalization as it exists today (see also Marcuse, 1997a).[3]

Globalization clearly has much to do with mobility of goods, of capital, of persons. An important reason to expect spatial changes within cities is the changing nature of economic activities and the concomitant shift in location of components of the production process. One of the main changes in Western societies – but also in many Asian countries – has been, and still is, the declining importance of manufacturing, and the increasing significance of services. Many traditional production tasks in manufacturing have been mechanized, automated and computerized, making production more capi-tal-intensive and less dependent on manual labor. Other tasks have been shifted to other parts of the world, where labor is less expensive. The increas-ing ability to separate manual and non-manual components of the labor process has increased the division of labor in the production process, making on the one hand many lower – or unskilled people redundant, and on the other hand demanding more skills from others. The increase in the numbers of so-called flexible jobs gives an increasing number of people the opportu-nity to find work, but these people are not necessarily the same as those who were made redundant (see also Harvey, 1989; Badcock, this volume).

The power of capital is clear here. Capital's ability to bargain with labor is tremendously enhanced by its ability to seek out lower wage labor at all kinds of locations, sometimes very remote. Foreign capital may increasingly influence the spatial layout and physical appearance of areas within cities (Beauregard and Haila, this volume). Investors might seek to invest their capital not at home, but at places all over the world where profit is expected to be highest. Some areas profit, some others don't: uneven development is characteristic of capitalism.

The possible spatial implications of these changes are manifold. We can distinguish between spatial shifts in the production process itself and other spatial changes, e.g. in residential patterns that result from these shifts. For the shift in the production process itself, it is clear that some regions just lose employment, especially manufacturing jobs. At the same time, employment in the service sector increases in some, but not all, cities. It is important here to distinguish between higher-order and lower-order services. At the top of the service sector we find functions of control, in the field of management, finance, law, and politics. Spatial centralization of these kinds of job is in-creasingly important, despite new communication techniques and fast modes of transport. Centers of some cities keep, or even increase, their importance for these purposes. At the lower end we find unskilled and semi-skilled jobs in sectors like catering (salad bars and snack bars), surveillance, and cleaning. Although unskilled jobs are partly dependent on the existence of jobs in the higher echelons, they can also be found in many places, not only in central cities, but in every place where people concentrate (Sassen, 1988; 1991).

With respect to the effects of these shifts, two lines of reasoning can be discerned (see Bolt et al., 1998). The first follows Robert Reich's *The Work of Nations* (1991). He argues that local forms of social solidarity become less important because elites show an increasing international orientation and become less dependent on the services of lower status groups in neighborhoods. There is no need for the rich to live in close proximity to those of lesser wealth. If they even live in the same neighborhoods, the life world of the wealthy is clearly larger than their living neighborhood. Melvin Webber's (1964) old idea of "communities without propinquity" is important for those at the upper end of the economic spectrum today; the "urban realm" becomes "non-spatial." For the very poor, by the same token, their spatially defined neighborhoods, while in ways growing even more important for their residents, become more and more irrelevant to the functioning of the mainstream economy. The location of either with relation to the other recedes dramatically in importance. A logical result is an urban society that is increasingly socially and spatially disconnected, fragmented and polarized.[4]

The second line of reasoning focuses on globalization as leading to a kind of socio-economic symbiosis within an increasingly polarized society, which can be seen in a growing number of highly-educated, wealthy persons and households, but also in an increasing number of people in the lower segments of the economy (in dead-end jobs and chronically unemployed). Saskia Sassen (1984, 1986, 1988, 1991) can be seen as the main proponent of this argument. The crux in this line of reasoning is that rich and poor, those included in and those excluded from the (formal) economy are dependent on each other. One group has the money for products and services that the other group can provide. The emphasis on symbiotic relationships might end up with a society that is both more polarized and more interdependent and with spatial patterns characterized by a spatial mix of different groups.

Although globalization is a process that obviously has broad impact, there are important questions concerning the specifically intra-city spatial effects of this process. Globalization is not automatically translated into spatial patterns, even in the case of a growing social polarization. Symbiosis between groups might or might not lead to urban areas that include neighborhoods where people with different incomes, ethnicities, skills and education live together. It might also very well lead to different consequences for different groups, leading some to form enclaves, others to be confined to ghettos. Reasoning from megatrends through social interdependence to spatial patterns should be done with great care.

Patterns of migration and other demographic developments

Working people often seek to improve their position by moving. Emigration to areas where a better life can be expected is a process as old as the world. In more recent times, the migration to Western Europe from Southern Europe and other countries around the Mediterranean and the migration within the United States from South to North are examples of large migration flows that are principally motivated by perceptions of work opportunity (see, e.g., Özüekren and Van Kempen, 1997). Also, on a smaller spatial scale, migration for reasons of job-seeking are frequent. Processes of urbanization, suburbanization, desuburbanization and re-urbanization are sometimes motivated by the creation of attractive residential areas, but often have to do with economic opportunities, including the relocation of work.

Not all migration flows are labor motivated. Internationally, political oppression and wars in many countries have pressed people to emigrate, often, where colonies have become independent, to the land of the colonizer, both before and after independence. Illegal migration flows add to the number of "official" immigrants in many countries, often having a disproportionate effect in specific cities and neighborhoods because of chain migration (Burgers, 1998). Not all these migration flows are urban oriented, but many of them were and still are. Migrants increased the demand for housing, often resulting in fiercer competition between households, especially lower-income households, leading not only to overcrowding in receiving neighborhoods but also to price changes and inflationary pressures throughout the housing market. Consequently, conflicts among groups, between those who had already lived in the neighborhood for decades or even generations and newcomers from other countries, are still manifold in all kinds of urban areas.

Population movement from central cities to suburbs is a common phenomenon in most developed countries. The movement is not class-neutral: it is higher income households that move out, largely in search for better or more cost-efficient housing opportunities and for jobs likewise moving out of central cities. In developing countries the same pattern may be observed; the continuing growth of cities in developing countries, which seems to contrast to the pattern in the more developed world, in fact reveals the same class-specific mobility patterns, but coupled with a rural-to-urban movement that swells the concentration of poorer people in the central cities in quantitatively much greater proportions than in more developed countries. Differences between cities do however exist: not all cities can be characterized by a growing number of poor and a declining number of higher-income households, and both rural-to-urban migration and displacement can lead to residential locations for poor people far from the center of cities.

Demographic developments within cities can have enormous influences on local housing demand and therefore on the spatial patterns of households. A sharp rise, for example, in the number of large families may boost the demand for large dwellings. If they are only available in some parts of the city, a concentration of large families may result there. If these large families are mainly immigrant families, we may end up with a spatial concentration of ethnic families. Rates of divorce, increasing numbers of single parent households, the tendency for young people to stay at home longer, the process of people living longer, are other demographic and socio-cultural processes that affect the housing market opportunities of households.

"Race" and racism

The importance of "race" and racism for the development of the spatial structure of cities is not always clear. Their importance in the US experience, however, cannot be exaggerated. A number of recent works make this point eloquently (see Massey and Denton, 1993; Goldsmith and Blakely, 1992). Central city "decline", suburban and edge city growth, the changing nature of the ghetto, and the increase in fortified enclaves in US cities are inextricably linked to patterns of racial relations (Marcuse, 1997a). The fact that most African Americans in the United States live in neighborhoods that are racially stamped illustrates this point, especially when we realize that many of them do not live there as a matter of choice. Where the black ghetto was still seen before World War II as analogous to an ethnic enclave, as a place of cultural and economic and social solidarity, today it is more often seen as a place of social disorganization, restricting opportunity by its very spatial limitations (Wilson, 1987; Marcuse, 1998).

Indications of similar racist tendencies exist in many other countries, where opposition to immigration and immigrants has led to xenophobic political policies and even more visible direct hostilities, including physical attacks on immigrants. Turkish residents in Western Europe, for instance, have often met hostility based variously on immigrant status, culture, religion, and language (see Van Kempen and Bolt, 1997; Özüekren and Van Kempen, 1997). Until now, however, this has generally not led to the relegation of those who are not accepted in European urban societies to only a very small number of neighborhoods that can be considered as the worst places in town where nobody else lives (Peach, 1981).[5]

The changing role of the public sector

In some countries the welfare role of the state has always been very small: its support for the poor and provision of subsidies for the needy has always been narrowly limited. In other countries there has been an elaborate welfare state, especially since World War II. The main principles of the welfare state have always been twofold: an elaborate system to support those who are in a weak position on the labor market, which for instance meant (more or less structural) financial support in situations of unemployment and illness, and support for the elderly. The second principle is the existence of a system of subsidies in all kinds of fields, like housing, recreation, and social work. Especially since the middle of the 1980s, the welfare activities of states have been declining or retreating. Declining incomes, especially of those who are dependent on some form of state allowance, have been the direct effects of cut-backs in government expenditure. Declining subsidies further diminished the opportunities of all kinds of households on different markets, among them the housing market.

To elaborate on these briefly:

Government cut-backs directly affect the incomes of those who are dependent on the state, such as the unemployed, the elderly, and the handicapped.

Declining incomes directly influence the housing market opportunities of households because they are relegated to those dwellings they can afford to pay. When these dwellings are spatially concentrated in certain areas of the cities, increased spatial divisions may result, characterized by an increasing concentration of relatively poor households in areas with low-rent (and often low-quality) dwellings and a growing segregation of different income groups. Spatial divisions thus become sharper as public sector policies lead to an increasing polarization of incomes.

Processes of concentration and segregation may be further exacerbated by the declining welfare-oriented role of the state in housing. Traditionally, especially in Western European welfare states, social housing has been a very important factor in the housing market (see, e.g., Dieleman, 1994; Van Kempen and Priemus, 1999). Sometimes the social rented sector was designed to be available even to middle- and higher-income households, who entered it either because they liked it (social housing was often good quality), or because they had difficulties finding a place in the owner-occupied sector. Anyway, in countries like the Netherlands and Sweden, at least until the beginning of the 1990s, social housing could not be characterized as marginalized or residualized (see Meusen and Van Kempen, 1995; Özüekren and Magnusson, 1997; Van Kempen, 1997). This is an important difference with social housing in Britain, where the effects of the "Right to Buy" have been described as causing a residualization of the social rented sector (e.g., Robinson and O'Sullivan, 1983; Hamnett, 1984; Bentham, 1986; Forrest and Murie, 1990). In the United States, the construction of public housing has often led to increased segregation (e.g., Bauman 1998).

In a declining welfare state, declining subsidies for social housing and greater reliance on market forces lead to higher prices for new dwellings. Lower-income households then have reduced access to new dwellings. When individual housing allowances also decline, the choice of possibilities for low-income households diminish even further, relegating them to an ever shrinking number of neighborhoods where they still can afford to pay for their housing. Meanwhile, earlier low-income neighborhoods may be invaded by higher-income households, because they are the ones that can afford to pay for dwellings in those areas, in the processes known as gentrification.

The decline of the welfare state does not automatically lead to increasing concentration and segregation. Plans of local government to diversify the housing stock in poor neighborhoods with more market-oriented housing may reduce possibilities for relatively poor households, but at the same time decrease segregation (Van Kempen and Priemus, 1997). And where social housing has been a factor in increasing segregation, a greater reliance on market forces may very well lead to increasing diversification of the population of neighborhoods, temporarily or more structural, even though it leads to a net worsening of the housing situation of the poor, as may be the result of current policies of privatization in public housing in the United States.

The decline of the welfare state does not mean that all policies with regard to the city have disappeared. Although less government money is usually available than in the previous decade, numerous plans are being developed and carried out to improve parts of the cities. In the Netherlands, for example, the government has recently introduced a policy of urban restructuring. One of the main aims of this policy is to restructure neighborhoods with a concentration of low-rent dwellings: in these areas a large number of these low-rent dwellings will be demolished (and replaced by more expensive rented dwellings or owner-occupied ones), upgraded or sold, in order to reduce the spatial concentration of low-income households and to increase the attractiveness of the area for higher-income households (see Van Kempen and Priemus, 1997). Another example is Australia, where state-managed revitalization of the inner cities has, in combination with gentrification, resulted in the reclaiming of these areas by middle-income households (see Badcock, this volume).

Changing patterns of choice

Especially in many western societies, the standard life course of people and households has changed in the last two or three decades. Claire Stapleton already indicated in 1980 that the standard course from birth adolescent couple–family with children–old couple–widow/er is no longer dominant, certainly in Western societies. Part of the declining importance of this standard life-course has to do with the declining importance of traditional values and norms, obedience, and docility and dependence on the church, parents, and husbands, and on the economic end with the increasing participation of women in the paid labor force. Emancipation, individualism can be seen as the driving forces behind an increasing importance of individual choice in all aspects of life, including the life course, the house, and the area in which to live.

One of the main changes in this respect is the postponement of family formation. The longer phase preceding child-bearing can be characterized by an enormous flexibility: people change jobs, partners and dwelling places. Especially in an economy where flexible jobs are on the increase, individuals are more or less forced to be flexible with regard to work places and living arrangements. When this flexibility is translated to the neighborhood level, it is easy to conclude that there must be areas that show a high turnover of (especially young) people. These areas have a specific function for starters in the housing market. Generally they are not the best areas in town, but they are important for many in this phase of flexibility, who do not object to living temporarily in a neighborhood with significant perceived environmental or social drawbacks.

Flexibility may even be a central concept in the period after family formation. The idea that families settled down in a certain area, with aiming to stay there for the rest of their lives will not hold for everyone in the present period. Again, labor market opportunities may cause a family to move, but also the wish to live in larger houses or a better neighborhood be at the root of the move to another place. Even the usually relatively immobile owner-occupiers are expected to become more mobile.

Old people, finally, also have more choice now than ever before. After the children have left home, the empty-nesters may start a completely new life. The American snowbirds are a case in point; in Europe, similarly, some Western European elderly move to the Mediterranean, at least for a part of the year. Others move from their single-family, owner-occupied house to expensive apartments or condominiums, made possible by complex financial arrangements with banks or life insurance companies. For the elderly, some neighborhoods become more, others less, attractive.

But changing patterns made possible by such increases in choice are not available to everyone, nor in all places, nor is the range of opened choices uniform. In Western societies expanded choice has mainly to do with a growing economy; in Eastern Europe growing opportunities have to do with political changes, and in both cases they are very unevenly distributed. Those with low and very low incomes and low education may face declining opportunities, because of fewer labor-market opportunities (as a consequence of the changing economic structure), and because of the declining welfare states (which specifically results in the declining supply of affordable housing), and because of the differential impact of new political structures.

Spatial Divisions in the New Spatial Order

The discussion here builds on the earlier conceptualization of a quartered city comprising a luxury city, a city of the gentry, a suburban city, a tenement city, and an abandoned city, but it seeks to pinpoint within those general "quarters" specific types of neighborhoods that may be expected to be found in specific locations as the types of neighborhoods most likely to be produced, expanded, or contracted by the new societal forces described above.

It is difficult, if not impossible, to give an overview of all the changes in all cities all over the world, and we do not make that attempt here; in our conclusion we expand on what is said here, taking into account the lessons taught by the other contributions to this volume. What is presented here is a set of ideal types. Their relevance to particular cities is of course one of the main themes of this book.

The locations of the elite

Thirty years ago, and earlier, the residences of the rich and powerful, if they were in the city, were separate buildings: mansions or high-rises with penthouses and luxury services. They might cluster in neighborhoods, but their neighborhoods were not defined and isolated for protection as such. That pattern continues, but in addition a newer pattern seems to be developing, one for which John Friedmann selected the appropriate name of "citadel" (Friedmann and Wolff, 1982). Citadels are enclosed, protected, insulated areas of upper-income residence, often, particularly if located downtown, combined with office and commercial uses. Battery Park City in New York City, Pudong in Shanghai, La Défense in France, Renaissance Center in Detroit, are classic examples; the latter virtually has a moat around it, a high wall on one side, a river on the other, with entrances that can be controlled and a castle-on-a-hill relationship to the surrounding blighted and abandoned central city. Sigurd Grava (1991, p. 11) describes Battery Park City in understated terms:

"The major issue, in the opinion of most urban analysts, is the current exclusivity or isolation of the development. This is the case in a physical as well as social sense. Battery Park City today is an enclave [sic], a refined space that is not easily accessible nor particularly inviting to outsiders. The West Street chasm [its only land border] is enough to deter all but the most purposeful passers by . . . For those who do make it across, there are only a few attractions . . . The outsiders can sit in the Winter Garden for a while or stare at the incredibly luxurious yachts, but the recreational possibilities are soon exhausted. . . . The restaurants and bars tend to be at the plush end of the scale. The residential areas are perceived as expensive dormitories or fancy shelters for downtown bankers . . . . . . This is not necessarily a problem for those who wish to work and live in an exclusive, isolated, and protected environment . . . "

Citadel formation is in some ways an extension of prior (and continuing) gentrification (see below), but goes well beyond it. Gentrification by and large took place at the borders of the old downtowns, and was of the hardworking professionals, managers, technical people associated with the growing upper-income service sector. The citadels offer some housing for them also, but they include as well the top: board members and inheritors of wealth, ultimately belonging to a different class than those who work for them. They do not need to make the effort of gentrification, and edge cities (below) are not for them either.

The locations of the new gentry

Gentrified neighborhoods and areas of potential gentrification near downtowns are particularly affected by the changing productive structure of the economy.

More high-level jobs in the service sector imply more households with high incomes, much of which may go to housing. The gentrified city is the part occupied by the professionals, the managers, the higher technicians. They are the yuppies, the cosmopolitans (Merton, 1968), the careerists (Bell, 1968). They live alone, or in two-person households, at least for a part of their lives. Gentrification is by the same token likely to increase displacement of the poor from gentrified areas, for the areas of gentrification generally consist of older buildings, left vacant by poorer households after a process of displacement and rising prices.

Gentrified neighborhoods are not necessarily located in older cities; their essential characteristics are to be found in some suburbs, and their social characteristics in some exclusionary enclaves. But the difference is that, in the case of gentrification, the new population is in most cases surrounded by and mixed with the older population. Of course this can be a temporary phenomenon: poor households may be just there, "waiting" to be blown out by those who have more financial possibilities. It is an interesting question when the following stage would then be an enclave, surrounded by a wall, erected as a consequence of neighborhood action, or when the social mix may show a longer endurance. It is in these areas that Sassen's theoretical notions about the interdependence of groups at opposite ends of the economic spectrum can be seen in practice (Sassen, 1991 and 1994).

Sometimes gentrification is a result of local policy when local government decides to support housing expansion for the well-to-do. It may be preceded by improvement strategies with the aim of increasing the appeal of inner-city living for the new middle class. This could be in the form of attractive housing, but also by way of offering new places of entertainment (a concert hall, a theater) or a shopping mall in places in or adjacent to parts of the central business district, for example on disused tracts of land in harbor areas or former industrial sites.

Suburbs

The typical picture of a suburb includes owner-occupied single-family houses with "decent home-owning people" (Greer, 1962), gardens, green environments, nice places for children to play, quiet, and safety. The residential function is far more important than anything else. The suburban environments are usually inhabited by the middle class, family households with incomes sufficient to pay market prices for their dwellings. Most who live there do so by choice. Because they consider their present situation as the top of their housing career, they do not contemplate further moves, or at most horizontal ones if job location changes.

For some, a suburban location may be a place to live only as long as the children are in the house. They may consider moving (back) to the city thereafter; they are potential gentrifiers. And still some others may be attracted to more distant suburbs – ex-urbs –, or in some countries to the countryside. In general, however, suburbs do not show many changes in their population structure, both because mobility rates are relatively low and because vacancies in the housing stock are generally filled by people of the same lifestyle and income. Only the age structure then changes. But the balance between stability and change may be changing. In prosperous economies, households may indeed increasingly choose to move on, to find an even better place, bigger, more expensive, located in even quieter environments, away from the city. Whether for better or not, more families (at least in the United States) move every year, not to get more desirable housing, but because of job changes. There is now a clear tendency in some countries to look at suburbs as just another area to live for only a relatively small number of years. Expanding opportunities have their influence here.

Another major change with respect to suburban environments is the development of, what Marcuse (1997b) called the "totalizing suburb." Joel Garreau (1991) coined the term "edge city" for the formation, and the word has come into common usage and is used here, although in a broader and more analytically-defined sense than in Garreau (see Beauregard, 1997). This is a suburb in which business activities, employment centers, commercial and cultural facilities are brought together with the residential function. These suburbs are not primarily residential any more: more jobs than bedrooms (Garreau). Although ultimate economic dependence on the central city may still exist, in terms of daily life and daily activities people do not have to leave their suburban environment. The phenomenon is certainly to some extent a consequence of the increasing polarization of central cities, with a parallel increase in the distaste of some of higher income to continue to live near those increasingly excluded from economic growth; to what extent is not clear yet.

Suburbs do not include those with controlling positions in trade, industry, or finance. Their centers remain in or close to the central business districts. Neither do the new cities include the very poor. Their residents are in almost all respects indistinguishable from those of the typical suburb. Racially, edge cities are predominantly white (Marcuse, 1997) and therefore reinforce the class and racial partitioning of the metropolitan area. It is clear that edge cities compete with the existing (large) cities: the central city no longer is the dominant site in the metropolis for jobs, offices, restaurants, shops and cinemas. Literature on the development of edge cities in Europe is scarce, if existing at all, although developments on the outskirts of Frankfurt, for instance, might well qualify (see Keil and Ronneberger, this volume).

Suburban environments are found not only outside cities, but also within them. Almost every city has neighborhoods in which middle class families with children live, with all the social and cultural characteristics of suburbs, differing from the traditional suburb only in the built form (denser or multi-story housing instead of free-standing single-family houses) and tenure. And tenure differences are not that great: condominium and cooperative forms provide the equivalent of ownership, as may long-term leases. The changing spatial consequence here may be more in the form of social and cultural institutions than residential: the Disneyfication of Times Square can be viewed as the progressive suburbanization of a downtown.

Traditional working class areas

Traditional working class areas (the tenement city) are occupied by the blue- and white-collar working class, the (temporarily) unemployed, and those on benefits. The tenement city is the part of the city with less expensive private dwellings and social housing. In some cases, tenement areas are simply a transitional residence on the way up, particularly for the young; in others, people will be relegated to live there for the rest of their lives. In most cases these areas have mixed occupancy, with those whose employment is increasingly unstable (including many in the informal labor market and some at its criminal end) next to the stably employed, the secure elderly, and the hopefully upwardly-mobile. Tensions and hostilities between different categories of inhabitants can thus be part of every-day life. Social and economic change is likely to be the most enduring characteristic of these areas, moving from an autochthonous homogenous character to either ethnic mixture or ethnic concentration. Characteristic of the current period, such areas are not only threatened with instability but also shrinking in absolute extent under the pressure of abandonment on the one side (see below) and gentrification on the other.

Physical characteristics play a major role here. Three different types of areas can be discerned in most western European cities:

- The areas built before World War II, usually located in a belt of more or less deteriorated older, relatively inexpensive housing near the center of the city. We call them the old restructuring areas, because they are generally subject to all kinds of renovation activities.
- The early post-World War II social housing areas, typically located in a ring just outside the old restructuring areas.
- The high-rise areas of post-war construction, sometimes – but not always – spatially detached from the city.

Pre-war tenement areas – Dwellings dating from the second half of the 19th century and the first three decades of the 20th century can often be regarded as the worst part of the urban housing stock. They are often small, lacking basic facilities, like a bathroom; rents are generally relatively low. They are characterized by a mixture of housing types, and their occupants are people with low incomes: the unemployed, the starters on the housing market, students, immigrants, elderly, single-parent families. The enormous differentiation in lifestyles between these categories now and then causes tension, racial problems, social isolation, and fear to go outside at night (see, e.g., Van Kempen, 1997).

Partial or complete gentrification is an increasing phenomenon in such areas. Higher-income households may be attracted by the lively atmosphere of these areas, or by restructuring processes that lead to a more differentiated housing stock, either because of the implementation of local government plans or because of gentrification and spontaneous renovation by the inhabitants themselves. This might result in new elite enclaves in redeveloped parts inside or next to deteriorating neighborhoods and housing inhabited by the poor and elderly. Contrasts in social status and wealth in spatial proximity create a special kind of dual city where the poor and rich live together in the same areas, but use very different spaces: the rich go to the streets with the luxury shops, the poor visit the street bazaars; the rich use private cars, the poor public transport; and they have different places of work.

Early post-war tenement areas – In some countries the areas built just after World War II contain a large number of affordable social rented housing, built to cope with the enormous housing shortages resulting from the War. At the time they were aimed at housing middle class families of moderate income. Since they were built some developments have changed the areas from attractive family neighborhoods to areas in which many people do not want to live. New housing areas with more attractive housing have pulled households who could afford to move and to pay higher prices for their dwellings out of these areas. Because of the initial low quality of the structures, they are often deteriorating today. New households (young people, immigrants, perhaps former guest workers), usually with lower income, move in (Van Kempen and Van Weesep, 1997), making those areas less attractive for older residents and for other new housing applicants.

The future of these areas, directly affected by changing demographics and the ebb and flow of immigration, is largely dependent on government action. Without any intervention they will end up as the neighborhoods where only those without any other choice will end. On the other hand, intervention that includes demolishing or upgrading part of the existing stock may result in attracting those middle class households for which the areas were originally built.[6]

High-rise areas – In Western European countries, high-rise housing areas typically date from the period 1965–1975. They were built because the post-World War II housing shortage continued and it had now become technically possible to build high-rise structures relatively cheaply. In many countries these areas initially housed middle class families, and in many cities they still have this function. In other cases high-rises from this period has become a marginalized housing sector, housing only those who do not have another choice. The French "grands ensembles" are a case in point (Blanc, 1993; De Villanova, 1997).

Ethnic enclaves can often be seen as a specific type of working class areas. An ethnic enclave contains people, self-defined by ethnicity, religion or otherwise, who congregate in order to protect or enhance their (economic, social, political, and/or social) well-being (for a formal definition, see Marcuse, 1997a). They should be clearly distinguished from ghettos: the confinement of the ghetto's residents is desired by the dominant interests of society. An enclave is not solely a US phenomenon; enclaves can be found all over the world. Two older classic sociological studies illustrate how a particular culture is maintained within a concentrated area. The first (Dahya, 1974) describes a Pakistani community in Bradford, England. Many of the people who left Pakistan and immigrated to this city ended up in the neighborhoods where many Pakistani were already present. In this enclave there was a high degree of mutual support. People helped one another to find work and a place to live. On the labor market, informal contacts were activated to get jobs for the newly arrived migrants, albeit temporary jobs in some cases. On the housing market, the informal contacts ensured that newcomers were able to move in with friends or relatives – in some cases with vague acquaintances – at least temporarily. The second study (Suttles, 1974) describes a neighborhood in Chicago where Italian culture is pervasive. Local residents do their shopping exclusively in Italian stores in the same neighborhood. People help each other fix up their homes. Nearly all the Italians living in the neighborhood go to the same church (which is modeled after a church in Naples) and frequent the same parks. They wear the same kind of clothes and speak the same dialect. This is a classic example of a community. These are ethnic enclaves, quite different from, for instance, the racial ghettos of the United States or the townships of apartheid South Africa.[7]

Ghettos of exclusion

The pattern of changing land uses within the city is a centuries-old pattern; in the industrial period of capitalism, slum formation took place not only in areas of traditional residence for poor people, but also in higher-income neighborhoods whose location became increasingly undesirable for those who could afford better. Hitherto, however, new uses replaced the older ones, new populations moved in where earlier ones moved out. That is no longer always the case. Certainly in the United States entire sections of cities have been abandoned by the owners of their properties and by their residents, and then by their governments. The South Bronx in New York City was perhaps the best-known single example, but others existed in cities throughout that country. Whether there are indications of a similar pattern in other countries is a matter much debated (see, e.g., Peach, 1996).

The excluded ghetto is the prototypical, if extreme, form of the abandoned city: that part of the city that has, viewed from the outside, only a negative relationship to the social, political, and economic life of the rest. It has of course its own structure and organization, its own economy, largely informal but also formal, and indeed some of its residents are regularly connected to the economy and social and political life of the rest of the city. But the majority are not, and there are regularly tensions within the excluded ghetto between those who are connected and those who are not. The new ghetto is thus not Kenneth Clarke's ghetto of hope, expectation, and protest, but Wilson's ghetto of despair, oppression and impairment (Marcuse, 1998). It is in an abandoned part of the city, abandoned not by the people who live there but by those who are in control of the wider city (Wilson, 1987; 1996).

A ghetto in general may be defined as *a spatially concentrated area used to separate involuntarily and to limit a particular racially, ethnically or religiously defined population group held to be, and treated as, inferior by the dominant society.* But a new urban ghetto is developing, under the polarizing impact of current economic changes; we call it the excluded ghetto. It may be defined as *a ghetto in which race or ethnicity is combined with class in a spatially concentrated area whose residents are excluded from the economic life of the surrounding society, which does not profit significantly from its existence.*

Drawing on the US experience, the residents of the abandoned city, particularly in the new ghetto of the excluded, play a different role from those of the old ghetto in many respects. Primary is the convergence of class with race, poverty with minority status. Older forms of the ghetto were also racially defined, but remained an integral part of the mainstream economy, with residents of different classes and with a variety of prospects on the labor market. Their residents, when unemployed, were part of a reserve of workers, the "reserve army of the unemployed," who had expectations of reentering the mainstream labor force when conjunctural conditions changed. That holds less and less in the new ghettos.

Final Remarks

The picture that has been sketched in the preceding sections leads us to expect a new spatial order within cities, with cities increasingly partitioned spatially as a result of the factors earlier described as macro-societal, among which globalization is prominent. Although most inhabitants of the city do cross the borders of different partitions, from home to work, from home to recreational facilities, etc., the general tendency is inward and towards separation. The causes of this process are different for different areas. In the luxury city, those who live in them have created their environments for their own purposes, and deliberately separated them from the rest of the city. In the exclusionary enclaves of the well-to-do, people surround themselves more and more with walls, neighborhood watches and cameras. This is a "free" choice, but based on fear for crime, violence and a vague idea of "the other" (who is often black). In the suburbs, including the "edge cities," people are less and less forced to cross city borders, because more and more facilities are to be found within their limited new spaces, separated and as independent as possible of the older central city. And again: no blacks, at least no poor blacks (see also Marcuse, 1997b). In working class areas, flux and instability is widespread, with centrifugal forces strongly suggesting a continuing trend towards socio-spatial separation. And in the new ghetto of exclusion, the inhabitants are under duress: dominant interests neither want nor care about them, and the greater the separation the better. The partitioning of city space implies that the social dividing lines between population groups, between black and white, rich and poor, gentry and working class, have a spatial translation that might very well accentuate estrangement, prejudice, misunderstanding. Cities have always shown functional, cultural and status divisions, but the differentiation is increasing in new ways and is hardening, we hypothesize, sometimes literally in the form of walls that function to protect the richer from the poorer.

The developments mentioned under the heading of "macro-social forces" above are partly independent of each other, but partly intimately connected and mutually reinforcing. Spatial arrangements are both a product of these developments and a contributing cause. The complications of this interplay make urban sociological and geographical explanatory research so difficult (but also so interesting). Unraveling these forces is thus a real challenge, but to our minds an important one, because of what it might reveal about how nations, cities, regions, and perhaps even neighborhoods, can best cope with the influences of macro-societal factors. The pessimistic view that the world as it is, and our cities as they are, are the best that can be hoped for, because "there is no alternative," we believe to be a misreading of present events. The important question is how to get the best out of the interaction between macro-social developments, public policies, and individual opportunities. To make this possible, the concrete mechanisms by which national and international forces produce specific spatial changes within cities need to be teased out (Marcuse, 1997a). Because these mechanisms are in most cases still unclear, we see the present work as part of an important inquiry for anyone interested in improving life in our cities. It is an inquiry which will of necessity be going on for many years in the future. We hope the pieces in this book will make a small contribution to that inquiry.

Notes

1   Parts of this Chapter have been published in the *American Behavioral Scientist* of November 1997 (Van Kempen and Marcuse, 1997).

2   It should be noted that we are explicitly *not* dealing with the fashionable question of the relative position of individual cities in a world hierarchy of cities.

3   The definition adopted here is consistent with those used by, e.g., Saskia Sassen and Manuel Castells, although neither disaggregate as is suggested here, and the latter tends to place greater stress on the role of informational technologies as critical to globalization.

4   But we have to be careful here: the polarization and fragmentation might be between the (very) rich and the (very) poor, it is rather unclear what will happen with the middle groups, with those with incomes neither very high and nor very low. Cities generally have a majority in this middle range (Marcuse, 1989) and it has still to be discovered how their social and spatial proximity to those above and those below will develop. Disaggregating the "middle" into different sub-groups, as Marcuse (1989) suggests, is a first step.

5   Although big differences exist between European countries and cities. For example: Turks in Belgian cities are worse off than Turks in Dutch cities, if we compare the overall quality of their housing (Van Kempen, 1997; Kesteloot et al., 1997).

6   But this will definitely not happen automatically, as Van Kempen and Priemus (1997) have pointed out in a paper in which the new restructuring process in the Netherlands has been described and evaluated.

7   Of course, we should be wary of adopting an overly romantic image of the concept of community from the cases described in these studies. Undoubtedly, not all such neighborhoods are ideal places to live. Regarding countries such as the United States and France, Wacquant (1996, p. 126) warns that "one must be careful not to romanticize conditions in the proletarian neighborhoods and segregated enclaves [sic] of yesteryear."

2

The Unavoidable Continuities of the City

Robert A. Beauregard and Anne Haila[1]

Observers of Western societies generally agree that profound economic, political, social and cultural forces have transformed these societies during the latter decades of the 20th century. Some (Jameson, 1991) have characterized this historical shift as a movement from modernism to postmodernism; others (Piore and Sabel, 1984) have preferred to emphasize the economic and use Fordism and post-Fordism as labels. Regardless, and despite differences of opinion as to what has actually changed and what this means, the current historical period can hardly be equated with the 1950s and the decades that preceded them.

Not surprisingly, urban theorists (Ellin, 1996; Harvey, 1989; Knight, 1986; Robins, 1991; Savage and Warde, 1993; Zukin, 1991, 1995) have discovered a "new" city that reflects and embodies the novel forces operating in the United States and Western Europe. Emissaries from the "LA School" (Davis, 1990; Dear 1991; Dear and Flusty, 1998; Soja, 1990, 1997) offer Los Angeles as the quintessential postmodern city, urban form's future rather than its past. Soja (1997, p. 193), for example, claims that the "space economies of postwar urbanism" have been "radically altered" such that the form of the city has "exploded to an unprecedented scale, scope, and complexity."

From another direction, Sassen (1991) and others argue for the existence of new types of global cities that concentrate worldwide corporate and financial control functions. Such cities represent post-Fordist capitalism and its unique spatial dynamics. Neil Smith also sees a new urbanism. In what he labels the revanchist city, the intersection of global capitalism and the pursuit of identity produces new political struggles around urban spaces. The revanchist city is "a modest novelty but a significant one nonetheless" (Smith, 1997, p. 117).

Postmodern urbanists are particularly committed to the existence of a new urban form. They portray the contemporary city as fragmented, partitioned, and precarious and, as a result, less legible than its modernist precursor. Enclaves of global finance co-exist with "Third World" neighborhoods, peripheralization has accelerated even as concentration continues, new immigrant communities proliferate, and landscapes of consumption invade once thriving production sites. Buffeted by global forces and no longer protected by the national state, the postmodern city is in competition with urban regions around the world for an increasingly mobile capital. The hierarchical spaces of the modernist city have been replaced by a pastiche of disarticulated spaces.

No one would dispute that the city of the late 20th century differs spatially from the city of the early to mid-20th century. The multiple business centers, transformed waterfronts, gentrified neighborhoods, and hollowed-out zones of manufacturing distinguish the contemporary US city from its precursors. Western European cities exhibit some, but not all, of the same characteristics (Kunzmann, 1996). Yet US cities also continue to have downtowns, neighborhoods segregated by race and class, and sharp distinctions among functional areas. Despite the emergence of suburbs, central cities in most Western European countries still function as dominant cores for their regions.

Old processes continue to operate and sometimes, though not inevitably, produce new urban forms (Fishman, 1987, pp. 73–102, 182–207). These rearrangements and novel elements, moreover, exist interspersed with and layered upon the remnants of prior events and conditions. The partitioning of land uses, in particular, whether due to land value differentials, planning controls, social affiliations, or localization economies, continues to occur. The past is transformed; it is not obliterated (Ladd, 1997).

In sum, we are not convinced that a "postmodern" city has displaced the modern city. The form of the city has changed, but not enough to support claims for an undiluted postmodern or even post-Fordist spatiality. Novelty is always a rhetorical move and history ever-present. Thus, we see a more complex patterning of old and new, of continuing trends and new forces. It cannot be otherwise.

Even if the processes that characterize cities have changed, those processes do not necessarily create novel spatial patterns in the built environment. New urban forces, for example the globalization of corporate control functions, might have little or no impact on spatial form but simply, as in this instance, intensify the concentration of office functions in the core areas of cities with strong international linkages. Even when novel forces do connect with the physical city, they are unlikely to do so in unmediated ways. The spatial form of the city is never a clear and perfect reflection of urban processes.

Spatial form, then, is a product of these forces, but specific spatial outcomes are not so easy to predict (Knox, 1991). First, new and old processes join together in complex and over-determined ways and do so in particular places at particular points in the history of these places (Beauregard, 1989). The consequences are not easily traced back to one or a single cluster of forces operating together across time and space. Second, the actors (for example, property developers, financiers, architects) who control the built environment are not simply puppets dancing to the tune of socio-economic and political logics but rather relatively autonomous agents. Third, the spatial form of the city inhibits rapid and large-scale transformations. Capital is "frozen" in fixed structures and people have political and social commitments to places that cannot easily be dismissed. The relatively fixed form of the city enables and constrains current and future investments, modes of living, and cultural meanings. Consequently, new processes enter a world that is resistant yet malleable. Together, these forces operate to dampen the possibilities for sudden transformations in spatial form.

In this chapter, we explore how this enduring history and the ever-present continuities of the city stem from the simultaneity of past and current influences. Drawing mainly on examples from cities in industrialized countries such as the United States and those of Western Europe, and with references also to Asia, we discuss the possible connections between the spatial order of the contemporary city and the socio-economic and political forces that operate there.

We begin with two phenomena that are often cited as indicative of the change of spatial form associated with the postmodern or post-Fordist city: hollowed-out manufacturing zones (mainly in older US cities) and consumption-oriented waterfronts (found both in the US and Western Europe). We then turn to edge cities, the multiple nuclei that have come to characterize metropolitan regions, particularly US ones, in the late 20th century. Edge cities, we argue, are not wholly new. Rather, they are the product of forces that have been operating on the city since the last century. Finally, we consider changes in real estate dynamics – the delocalization and deepening commodification of real property – and the implications that these new phenomena have for urban form.

The Shrinkage of Urban Manufacturing

In the US and Western European countries after World War II, the manufacturing sectors in many industrial cities collapsed. As far back as the late

19th century, manufacturing firms had been decentralizing in the US. It was not until the 1970s, though, and particularly in the US, that the shrinkage of urban manufacturing had a significant impact on urban form, creating vast areas of abandoned factories, empty lots, environmentally polluted land, and blighted properties (Jakle and Wilson, 1992). The restructuring of advanced industrial economies away from basic manufacturing such as steel production, textiles, shoe-making and heavy machinery and to services such as health care, education, accounting and banking (Beauregard and Deitrick, 1995) combined with decentralization and technological change in manufacturing processes to produce a stark transformation (Bluestone and Harrison, 1982).

Cities like Detroit, Pittsburgh, Chicago, and St Louis in the United States, Liverpool and Manchester in England, Glasgow in Scotland, and Bilbao in Spain experienced blight and dereliction in their once-thriving industrial areas. During the 1980s, for example, Bilbao lost over one-half its industrial employment and in London manufacturing jobs dropped from approximately 20 percent of the total to about 10 percent (DeMaziere and Wilson, 1995, pp. 79, 145). Between 1950 and 1980, Philadelphia lost 3,762 manufacturing establishments and manufacturing employment fell by 60 percent. Job loss and establishment closings resulted in empty industrial buildings and, where factories had been spatially concentrated, derelict areas. A survey carried out in England found that the area of dereliction had increased from 17,000 hectares to 45,700 hectares from 1974 to 1982 (Syms, 1994, p. 64).

The shrinkage of the manufacturing sector left behind hollowed-out industrial landscapes and the new economic base compensated for neither the properties nor the jobs that were lost. Only in a few cases were these spaces reclaimed: transformed urban waterfronts, a few inner-city neighborhoods where gentrification occurred, rare instances of industrial redevelopment, and linear swaths where highways replaced factories. The contemporary landscape of industrial investment and disinvestment in European and US cities is thus quite different than it was prior to and just after World War II.

By contrast, the once robust industrial districts (and residential neighborhoods adjacent to business districts) of booming Asian cities like Singapore have been replaced by office buildings housing producer services and by retail malls. Industry did not collapse. Instead it was pushed to the outskirts of these cities.

While the existence of such large areas of derelict urban space – absent wars or natural disasters – is new, the processes that brought it about are not. Technological change, decentralization and deconcentration, and product obsolescence have been integral to capitalist economies since the early 19th century. Even the development of manufacturing outside of North America, Western Europe and Japan – the share of manufacturing employment in capitalist countries (including Latin America and parts of Asian and Africa) fell from 75.6 percent in 1974 to 65.8 percent in 1986–87 (Peet, 1991, p. 163) – can be explained as part of a long-term rearrangement of global economic space and a continued search by capitalists for low-wage production sites. Hollowed-out manufacturing zones are a new spatial phenomenon, certainly, but they originated in a juxtaposition, albeit unique, of pre-existing forces.

Transformed Waterfronts

In the port cities of the early 20th century, the waterfront consisted of wharves, warehouses and shipping-related activities, fishing boats, and various industrial uses ranging from scrap metal yards to power plants and steel mills (Hoyle, et al., 1988). Once the centers of commercial cities and, later, industrial cities (Gordon, 1978), by the 1960s the wharves that lined the bays and rivers of many older cities were abandoned and decayed. Warehouses were empty, much dockside land was vacant or under-utilized, and major highways had cordoned off the waterfronts from the rest of the city. By the 1980s, these areas had been revitalized with housing, marinas, aquariums, retail shops, museums, public promenades and even office space. The forces that produced these new landscapes of consumption (Zukin, 1991) were both familiar and unusual.

These ports were victims not only of relentless technological advances in transportation – particularly the expansion of trucking and air freight in the postwar period – but also of the industrial decentralization that was affecting cities generally. Even ports that managed to do well downsized in the process. The shipping industry became more concentrated spatially and was transformed by the use of pre-loaded containers. Containerization enabled ships to be loaded and unloaded faster with a much smaller number of dock workers. The increased capitalization of the shipping industry meant that fewer berths were needed. Ocean cruises were also less in demand by leisure travelers, and berths for cruise ships declined. In addition, the economy shifted away from the basic manufacturing, such as steel production, that once required waterfront locations. The direct consequence was deterioration and abandonment.

In itself, this was a significant change in spatial form. What makes it even more relevant for the contemporary city is the transformation of these decayed waterfront areas into sites of upscale housing, public parks, festival marketplaces, entertainment, and tourism (Harvey, 1987; Relph, 1987; Zukin, 1995). Baltimore's Harborplace, Quincy Market in Boston, Fishermen's Wharf in San Francisco, and Penn's Landing in Philadelphia are just four examples (Frieden and Sagalyn, 1989). Cape Town, Lille, Toronto, Rotterdam, Oslo, and London have similar developments. In Singapore, more recently, old

Chinese shops along the river have been succeeded by restaurants and entertainment areas – Boat Quay and Clarke Quay – for tourists and the global workers of transnational corporations.

Anyone knowledgeable about these new waterfronts will recognize that even though they all appeared after the 1950s, they did so at different times. San Francisco's Fishermen's Wharf predated Cape Town's 1980s waterfront development by at least two decades, for example. This observation simply reinforces the point that global forces operating on the contemporary city neither do so simultaneously nor have similar impacts in different cities and countries, differences attributable to the particularities of place and history. More importantly for our argument, the restructuring of shipping that led to this spatial transformation was a consequence of forces that have operated in capitalist societies for some time, the most obvious being technological innovations in transportation and foreign competition.

Unlike hollowed-out manufacturing zones that were land-locked, these waterfront sites were redeveloped. Good highway transportation (a problem that burdened inland industrial sites), proximity to central business districts, and a cultural valuing of waterfronts in terms of recreation and contact with nature all contributed to the greater attractiveness of abandoned waterfronts for investors and for the governments that encouraged and subsidized them.

Edge Cities

One of the most frequently mentioned spatial components of the contemporary urban scene is "edge cities", the nodes of office activities, retail stores and apartment buildings that now dot metropolitan areas, particularly in the United States, and which compete with the former central business districts for office tenants, restaurant patrons, shoppers, and movie-goers. Edge cities can be found outside such diverse cities as Phoenix, Toronto and Helsinki among others. Linked with decentralization and deconcentration, they are often touted as a unique addition to the urbanization process.

In the United States, households have been relocating from central cities to adjacent communities since the late 1800s and industry has been relocating outside the cities since at least the 1920s (Jackson, 1985; Walker, 1978). Although not always accompanied by deconcentration, decentralization has been one of the enduring (albeit inconsistent) processes shaping the modern city. Driven by obsolete buildings and infrastructure, poor schools, high taxes, strong unions, congestion, and high land prices among other factors and facilitated by successive advances in transportation that have made commuting and freight hauling less expensive and by municipal fragmentation that has enabled local control over taxes, racial composition, and land uses; cities have spread horizontally since the early 19th century. Although most pronounced in the US, the metropolis is now the dominant spatial form in Canada, Japan, South Africa and Europe (Angotti, 1993).

Despite decentralization, central cities maintained economic and cultural dominance in their regions through to the 1950s in the United States. Thus one could easily characterize the form of the early post-World War II city in terms of a dominant center of highest density development, peak land values, and highest-order functions surrounded by suburban areas of low-density residential development, scattered employment opportunities in manufacturing, and emerging retail concentrations in shopping malls.

Beginning in the 1970s, an ostensibly new phenomenon appeared in the US to change the form of the city in regions ranging from Dallas and Los Angeles to Washington, DC. This new element was the edge city (Beauregard, 1995, 1998; Garreau, 1991; Muller, 1976) and the new urban form was the multi-nodal metropolis. In the early 1990s, one commentator (Garreau, 1991) identified 123 edge cities and 78 emerging edge cities spread across all regions of the United States.

Edge cities were new because they concentrated in the suburbs high-order economic functions (such as corporate administration, financial, and business services) that had previously been confined to the downtowns of central cities. They are agglomerations of residential and retail developments but with the significant addition of office complexes. No longer does the central city contain the overwhelming majority of high-end office space and no longer is it the sole site in the metropolis for jobs in advanced services. Edge cities represent a new form for the contemporary city: a multi-nodal rather than a monocentric spatial pattern.

The edge city, though, is not simply a US phenomenon. In the early 1980s, Finland's largest corporation, Neste, a producer of oil products, built its headquarters just beyond the city limits in the town of Espoo where the Helsinki University of Technology had been located a few years earlier. A second major Finnish corporation, Nokia, followed. In Switzerland, peripheral clusters of office functions have emerged outside Zurich (Lehrer, 1994) and in South Africa, Sandton has become an edge city as office activities have fled downtown Johannesburg.

The element added to decentralization that created these edge cities is the deconcentration and peripheral reagglomeration of corporate business services brought about by a combination of the demand for business in the suburbs (resulting from previous decentralization of manufacturing), improvements in communication technology that enabled business service firms to disperse their operations geographically, the extension of limited-access highways and light rail lines, and new trends in business organization.

The deconcentration of business services from central cities and subsequent reconcentration in suburban office nodes is pivotal to the idea of the edge city. On this basis, proponents claim that edge cities compete with the once-central cities for dominance in the region. The data are not entirely supportive, however. One study (Schwartz, 1992) of financial, business and professional services in the metropolitan areas of New York, Los Angeles, and Chicago found that outer cities are neither self-sufficient nor economically autonomous from their central cities. Rather, a majority of suburban companies remain dependent on the central city for financial and professional services and this reliance increases with the size of the company.

The authors (Bingham and Kimble, 1995) of a study of seven metropolitan areas in Ohio also reflect on whether edge cities are replacing central cities. They argue that even though edge cities might be more self-sufficient than their central cities, they perform specialized functions that are signifi cantly different from the functions performed by the older downtowns. Moreover, few of the edge cities specialize in retail activities and a number have substantial manufacturing bases. These edge cities are very much the products of real estate speculation. In the United States in particular, changes in investment tax laws and rapid appreciation in property values during the 1980s led financial institutions to relax lending requirements. Investment capital was chasing investment opportunities (a point we will discuss below). Consequently, property developers searched out growth opportunities in suburban areas. The result was a proliferation of office parks, multi-use structures, retail malls, and housing developments that previously might not have been financed or built on the periphery. The ability to undertake large development schemes, an ability facilitated by "loose" real estate financial practices, was crucial for the emergence of edge cities.

Often overlooked is that many of these same forces also led to renewed investment in the downtowns. The central business districts of most US central cities and some Western European central cities (for example, London) also experienced major new office, retail, and residential developments. Residential gentrification frequently accompanied this commercial renewal. The property investment boom of the 1980s was not solely an edge city phenomenon. Consequently, the evidence suggests both a continuation of agglomeration forces and their transformation, thereby enabling multi-nodal metropolitan regions.

Of note, edge cities in the United States reinforce the class and racial partitioning of metropolitan areas. They are more likely than not to be places with numerous common-interest developments (often taking the form of gated communities) where middle-income and upper-income households have partially seceded from local governments (McKenzie, 1994). Racially, minorities are more likely to be found employed as service workers than as residents (Beauregard, 1995).

Thus, while the multi-nucleated spatial form that edge cities represent seems novel, that novelty is more superficial than fundamental. This is particularly apparent when edge cities are set in an historical context that starts before the 1970s. Prior to this time, a few major cities in the United States already had "satellite" cities: Beverly Hills outside Los Angeles and White Plains north of New York City are two examples. As early as 1937, one researcher (Ogburn, 1937, pp. 51–55) identified 20 satellite cities in the north and west regions of the United States. Quincy in the Boston metropolitan area, Wilkinsburg near Pittsburgh, and Cranston south of Providence (RI) were three of them. These cities had specialized local economies and high proportions of workers in clerical occupations. The edge city discussion also ignores the industrial cities that have existed since the early decades of the 20th century, places like Homestead (PA) with its US Steel plant, River Rouge (MI) with its Ford automotive assembly plant, and Camden (NJ), then headquarters of Campbell Soup, RCA Victor, and the American Shipbuilding Company. Such industrial satellites are now appearing in Asia, for example Shenzhen just across the border from Hong Kong and Johor Bahru (Malaysia) next to Singapore.

Seen in this way, edge cities are not a wholly new urban phenomenon. What is new is the suburban concentration of corporate services; that is, their dispersal from the business districts of central cities and re-agglomeration in the periphery. Even this, however, has to be qualified. In the 1960s, large corporations such as IBM, Pepsi Cola, and Connecticut General had already established headquarters in office campuses outside the central city. This was well before anyone recognized the existence of edge cities and the multi-nucleated metropolis.

Delocalized Property

Two qualities of the real estate sector appear frequently in descriptions of the postmodern or post-Fordist city. One is its increasing delocalization (or despatialization) and the other its deepening commodification.

First, numerous theorists (Logan, 1993; Sassen, 1991, pp. 185–188; Savitch, 1995) have commented on delocalization. They point to the rise to global prominence in the 1980s of property developers such as Olympia & York, architectural firms such as I.M. Pei, real estate brokers such as Jones Lang & Wootton, real estate investors such as Tishman Speyer Properties, and construction contractors such as Kugami Gumi. All operate transnationally (Thrift, 1987; Fainstein, 1994; Hines, 1988).

The ownership of urban real estate, particularly prime commercial properties, has become increasing non-local and international. Many Class A office buildings, upscale shopping malls, expensive resorts, luxury apartment buildings, and opulent estates are built by transnational investors, architects, developers, and contractors, and bought and sold in international markets. Singaporean and other overseas Chinese, for example, have invested in properties in China and construction companies from Hong Kong are involved in projects in numerous Chinese cities such as Shanghai, Beijing, and Shenzhen. Along Orchard Road, Singapore's main tourist and shopping center, properties are owned by investors from Japan, Kuwait, and Brunei (Yoong, 1990). One consequence of international ownership is the emergence of a new politics of global cities, a politics centered on real estate (Haila, 1997).

An editorial in a Philadelphia newspaper claimed that 40 percent of the 65 largest downtown office buildings there were owned by firms or institutions headquartered outside the city (Gyourko and Summers, 1995). Data (Budd, 1992, p. 274) on direct property investment from overseas to the United Kingdom indicate that investment averaged £88 million on an annual basis between 1980 and 1985. From 1986 to 1989, the yearly average soared to £960 million. McMahon (1990) claims that foreign investment in US real estate grew by 25 percent each year between 1982 and 1988.

The National Realty Committee's (1989, p. 139) array of government data shows that the foreign direct investment position in US real estate in current dollars went from $600 million in 1973 to $24.5 billion in 1987. In order to put this in perspective, the National Realty Committee also noted that in 1986 foreign investors owned approximately one percent of US real estate.

In terms of individual cities, Coldwell Banker's (1987) survey in 1987 found that 209 major office towers in 16 cities were owned by international investors, with nearly 60 percent of this total owned by Canadian and Japanese investors and another 20 percent by investors from the United Kingdom, West Germany, and the Netherlands. Los Angeles led the way with 46 percent of its space foreign-owned, followed by Houston (39 percent), Minneapolis (32 percent), and New York City–Manhattan (21 percent). The highest dollar value of foreign investment was in New York and Los Angeles. Together, they had over 50 percent of the total.

International financial capital's ability to delocalize property above pre-World War II levels is related to the financial innovations that occurred during the 1980s (Harvey, 1989), a decade of leveraged buy-outs, junk bonds, and corporate mergers that over-laid production for profit. Financial instruments such as Real Estate Investment Trusts (REITs) that enable individual properties from diverse locales to be bundled into single investment instruments, the rise of large institutional lenders (for example, pension funds and insurance companies), and the never-ending concentration of development capacity and ownership in larger and larger organizations also contributed to this delocalization.

Simultaneously, real estate has become more deeply commodified (that is, further separated from its social functions) and valued more and more for its performance as a financial asset (Haila, 1991; Lindahl, 1995). Opportunities for profit making through financial maneuverings expanded relative to those related to the production of goods and services. Developers built, investors bought, and financial institutions made loans because they expected a rapid appreciation in value. The income-generation potential of the property became disconnected from the investment decision. Real property thus became more like a stock or a municipal bond than like a business whose income stream mainly determined its profitability. Linking deepening commodification to globalization is the displacement of institutional investors, such as insurance companies and pension funds, from dominance in property markets by foreign corporations and joint ownership involving foreign investors.

The result is a widening gap between the use-value of a property and its market value. Indicative of this changing relationship is the sudden lack of correlation between commercial real estate loans and residential mortgage loans in the US beginning in the late 1970s and going through the end of the 1980s (Beauregard, 1994, p. 728). Prior to this time, commercial loans had lagged but basically followed the cyclical pattern of residential mortgages. During this ten year period, however, when the value of residential loans contracted in response to downturns in the business cycle, the value of commercial real estate loans continued to expand and, in fact, lost (albeit temporarily) its cyclical nature. Commercial lenders pursued appreciation while savings & loan associations, the major source of residential mortgages, adhered to the discipline of housing demand. The result was commercial overbuilding and a property bust.

Given the pivotal importance of real estate development and finance to the built environment of the city, its increasing delocalization and deepening commodification would seem to portend a significant impact on urban form. On the one hand, the distancing of owners from their properties along with the proliferation of ownership shares is likely to weaken the connection that owners or property managers have to the place in which the property resides. On the other hand, the de-emphasis of the property's utility in investment calculations would seem to portend a short-term rather than long-term perspective, with the short-term perspective less worried about the property's competitiveness within the local market.

Despite this logic, preliminary analysis uncovers few discernible spatial consequences. Four aspects of delocalized property are relevant to this point: (1) the greater potential for large-scale development projects, (2) changes in the ownership pattern of industrial property, (3) property value inflation caused by global portfolios, and (4) real estate cycles and the architectural fabric of the city.

First, the presence of large international real estate developers and investors increases the probability that big development projects will be undertaken in more and different cities. These actors apply their size, worldwide experience, and numerous organizational and governmental contacts in a variety of places. Three examples come to mind: the Docklands project in

London and Battery Park City in New York with Olympia & York (the developer) as a major catalyst in both instances (Fainstein, 1994) and Potsdammer Platz in Berlin. The latter is a multi-billion dollar office, retail, and housing project directed by three transnational corporations and involving architects, developers, and investors from around the world. To give a more specific example, the Jin Mao project in Shanghai had a US architect and interior designer, a quality surveyor from Hong Kong, and contractors from Shanghai, Japan, France, and Hong Kong. Structural and heating and ventilation systems were supplied by firms from Japan, Germany, and France. Without this international involvement, these projects would unlikely have reached their current sizes.

Such large development projects are not solely the products of the existence of big transnational actors but also a consequence of the image of prosperity and centrality that they represent. Especially pertinent here is the recent concentration of skyscrapers in the central business districts of East Asian cities such as Singapore, Hong Kong, and Kuala Lumpur, among others (Haila, 1998). Through real estate development, these cities search for the international recognition that will satisfy the needs of multinational corporations. Confidence-inspiring, visible signs such as lofty skylines are important in East Asia, a region that in many respects still adheres to non-Western values. Although upstart technology firms or law offices in the West can locate in loft buildings in gentrified neighborhoods, in the East such firms in old Chinese shop houses would hardly inspire confidence.

A balanced assessment, though, needs to point out that in many countries large property development projects have been carried out without international involvement. Internal improvements in many countries in the 1800s were made in the absence of international actors. Canals early in the century and railroads later were constructed in the United States with national capital and national ownership. The interstate highway system in the US, built mainly in the 1950s and 1960s, was also prior to the heightened delocalization of the property sector. Clearly, large development projects can occur in the absence of global actors and the financial instruments that have come to characterize the property sector.

Second, the development and ownership of industrial properties has been transformed in the last few decades (Ball and Pratt, 1994). Most industrial properties were once purpose built by the owner and subsequent user. Today, industrial space is more likely to be built by developers acting speculatively, leasing to users, and managing the properties as part of their portfolios. One study (Pratt, 1994, p. 46) done in urban areas of the United Kingdom found that while in 1973 about one-third of the industrial property was rented, that had changed to one-half in 1979. This shift in ownership is occurring both in the UK and the US and is one of the forces behind the proliferation of industrial and technology parks.

At the same time, industrial space is different in form and location than it was prior to World War II. Inner-city industrial districts have shrunk or been abandoned, industrial parks are more numerous, factories are one or two stories at most rather than multi-storied, and manufacturing plants are more likely to be surrounded by parking lots than housing and to be located near major highways. Nevertheless, it is not clear that one can attribute this solely to delocalization and the rise of large developers and investors or to the deepening commodification of property. More important seems to be the shifts from heavy to light industry, from vertical to a horizontal organization of the shop floor, and from railroads to trucks for shipping.

Third, increasing delocalization and deepening commodification produce a global portfolio effect that inflates the value of international-quality properties in the local real estate market. The price of local real estate is influenced by price levels in other markets. For example, when Japanese real estate investors went to New York City in the 1980s, *The Economist* (April 18, 1987) estimated that they were willing to pay up to five percent above prevailing market values. Such inflation was due to the strong yen, the economic surplus in Japan, and the high real estate prices in Tokyo. When Finnish construction companies in the 1980s drew significant profits from projects in the Soviet Union and Saudi Arabia, they invested these profits in Finnish cities and the result was both a construction boom and price inflation.

Interestingly, the inflated property values were soon devalued by the bust in the property market and a worldwide recession in the late 1980s and early 1990s as well as the discipline of the local demand for office and commercial space. Changes in international exchange rates which drove down the value of the yen and high vacancy rates in the New York City office market led to the Japanese selling at a loss many of the properties they had purchased in Manhattan during the earlier euphoria. The Docklands project in London was virtually halted by the international financial problems of Olympia & York. The speculative frenzy resulted in a banking crisis in the US in the late 1980s and numerous real estate properties went "belly-up" and were sold for a fraction of their original portfolio value.

Finally, delocalized property might impact spatial form through the temporal rhythms of property investment (Lindahl, 1995). In order to balance shifts in values across different markets, large national and international investors diversify their portfolios with properties from cities around the country and the world. In certain market niches, the diverse rhythms of investment that characterize cities are thereby dampened as investors act countercyclically. Properties are built or remodeled at different times than they would have been in the absence of delocalized and deeply commodified markets, thus coming under different planning and architectural influences. Theoretically, parts of the city should differ in appearance than would normally have been the case.

This claim for a shift in spatial form related to delocalized property, however, is impossible to verify. It depends on measuring a counter-factual. Moreover, even if such portfolio investments are large, they are still concentrated only in certain real estate markets in certain cities. Consequently, they are unlikely to influence real estate cycles in significant ways and thus unlikely to have a significant impact on the urban fabric.

With the exception of large-scale development projects, then, delocalization and deepening commodification have anemic and indirect effects on spatial form. Nevertheless, these forces are complicit in the hollowing-out of manufacturing districts, the transformation of waterfronts, and edge cities. The demise of urban manufacturing was exacerbated by industrial park development, itself fueled by the shift in ownership of industrial property. The adaptive re-use of waterfronts would not have proceeded without an inclination and ability to produce large-scale projects and transnational actors able to diffuse the development format across the international landscape. Edge cities, finally, had their growth spurt in the 1980s when speculation reigned in property markets and investors disengaged from traditional financial constraints.

In sum, although the linkage between increasing delocalization and deepening commodification of real property and major transformations of urban spatial form is problematic, numerous connections do operate. These new ways of doing business, however, are still variations on old themes – capitalism as usual.

Conclusion

In order to speak of the contemporary city as postmodern or post-Fordist without attaching a plethora of qualifications, one would have to represent it as a sharp break from the past. Clearly, this is not the case. The contemporary city is still under the influence of processes – decentralization, agglomeration, property market dynamics – associated with the modern or Fordist city, and its form the result of overlapping historical events and forces.

Decentralization, advances in communication and transportation, and local governmental competition for investment, forces that operated prior to World War II, contributed to the hollowing-out of industrial zones and furthered the demise of commercial and industrial waterfronts and their make-over to landscapes of consumption. Edge cities stand as illustrations of the long-term tension between decentralization/deconcentration and centralization/agglomeration. In each instance, the new spatial elements of the contemporary city owe their existence not just to novel social, economic, and political arrangements but to the interaction of the old and the new, the enduring and the emerging. As regards edge cities, the multi-nucleated met-ropolis, viewed in a larger historical perspective, does not seem as strikingly unique as some claim. Equally important, not all of the new processes have brought significant changes in the city's overall spatial form. This is the case with delocalization.

In sum, the contemporary city hardly reflects postmodernism or post-Fordism in a one-to-one correspondence. This attests not only to the still-relevant and underlying capitalist logic of urban development and the ever-so-slowly changing nature of social relationships, but also to the fixity of the built environment, a fixity not only of investment but also of identification and commitment.

One cannot but expect that the spatial form of the city will change more slowly than social relations, economic practices, and political arrangements. People and institutions have invested dearly in the city as it is. The value of their investments depends on relationships continuing relatively unchanged. Such continuity is supported institutionally through laws and regulations governing how land-use activities are to be arranged and properties exchanged. Cities are also cultural products (Jacobs, 1996). People identify with their neighborhoods and business owners commit to locations for other than purely economic reasons. They resist sudden, disruptive changes. Even disasters that obliterate large portions of a city are treated less as opportunities to create new spatial arrangements than as challenges to rebuild in the image of the past (Rosen, 1986). Only when growth is rapid or decay overwhelming can we expect that things might be different, and then we are often disappointed.

The spatial form of the city does not and will never correspond perfectly to the processes that constitute the city. Past trends continue, prior investments and social commitments slow the pace of spatial change, and the logic of capitalism (despite recent transformations) operates within property markets to reinforce the forms and relations of development. Consequently, unequivocal claims to a new type of city are at best naive and at worst theoretically unsophisticated. The spatial form of the contemporary city, like that of the cities that have preceded it and the cities that will follow, is always historically incomplete.

Note

1 This chapter is a slightly revised version of our "The unavoidable incompleteness of the city" which appeared in the *American Behavioral Scientist* of November 1997. The title has been changed to emphasize the historical thrust of the argument.

3

From the Metropolis to Globalization: The Dialectics of Race and Urban Form

William W. Goldsmith

The European city is threatened by change. The danger results in part from a peculiarity of the US city and its spatial form. This chapter is about that spatial form, how it spreads a pernicious influence through social and economic connections, and how those connections work internationally. The chapter focuses on the United States, but it ultimately traces a (global) connection to Europe.[1]

European cities are the envy of the world. They enjoy prosperity and harmony, especially in contrast to cities elsewhere, cities that are so often stressed either by poverty or by ethnic conflict.[2] This urban well-being is in good part a consequence of the ebb and flow of the global economy. Europe for decades has stood in a privileged position, influential throughout the world in economics and politics, and its city centers have profited from the wealth of hinterlands near and far.[3] The shape of these cities is distinctive and congenial and their governance is reasonably competent and compassionate.[4] They have exercised abilities to incorporate new residents and accommodate change, providing transportation, housing, and safety even for many who elsewhere would be pushed to the margins.[5]

Today, however, the urban prosperity and harmony of Europe are threatened. They are threatened by shifts in the global economy – as others in this volume demonstrate in detail.[6] But the character of European cities is also now threatened by a particular influence originating in a very strange way, as a consequence of the peculiar geographic pattern of the US city.

Usually, as others in this volume show, we expect global economic forces to impress their influence on the city, not the other way around. That is, we expect the push and pull of market competition and corporate power, ever more sensitive to overseas causes, to bring about industrial change, generate the economics of land use, arrange and rearrange residential neighborhoods, and finally, affect the way people are housed, transported, and served. Indeed, in an earlier study Edward Blakely and I found the global economy to constitute one of the roots of the US urban dilemma, producing in US cities a pair of *Separate Societies* (1992), as our book on the subject is titled.[7]

In contrast, the reasoning below turns the usual argument on its head. We will see that the pattern of urban form itself brings about social and economic change. More particularly, the peculiar physical patterning of the US city partially causes many of the problems the European city is just beginning to experience. Because this is an unusual argument, I offer an outline in this introduction, elaborating and providing evidence in the sections to follow.

In the post-war period until quite recently, it is especially notable that the European city has avoided the racial-caste character of US cities.[8] It has also avoided their poverty and squalor. But now, as we near the end of the 20th century, the vibrant centers, good transit, adequate housing, and decent social services of Europe's cities are threatened not only by cutbacks, but in some cities also by a new urban geography. As governments and employers cut benefits and protections, workers turn against darker skinned immigrants. Class struggle tends to take on the persona of "race" struggle, allowing governments to ignore further the demands of workers and residents.[9] I contend that these threats to Europe result in good part from a very particular set of American influences – not as direct copies, but through hidden influences. To understand these influences, we must focus attention on the American city and American politics and economics, the main subjects of this paper. There are six parts to the argument.

First, racial segregation is an essential feature and a leading cause of the bizarre spatial form the US metropolis has taken in this century, especially since World War II. Second, the social separation resulting from this spatial pattern has powerfully and detrimentally affected US politics not just at the municipal level, but also nationally. Third and partly because of these political effects, US leaders and the public have accepted deep social inequalities as though they were God-given, and they have embraced an exaggerated belief in the efficacy and fairness of the market. Fourth, because of the dominant position of the United States in international economics and politics, this market model has been exported worldwide. Fifth, the broad force of this market model itself has combined with the ideology of advertising and the media and practical influence from American corporations to put US-like pressure on cities elsewhere. Finally with the sixth part we turn fully around the vicious circle: For various reasons connected with the enlargement of the world economy and increased international migration, we find that neighborhood conflict and class struggle in big cities throughout Europe take on more and more the features of "race" and ethnic struggle, including segregation, as has long been the case in the United States.

This chain of reasoning is intrinsically interesting. Its logic suggests fascinating topics for research, challenging ideas, and peculiar historical twists, as well as troublesome questions for theory. Equally important, these issues have practical consequences.

The United States has occupied the dominant position in the world economy over the past 50 years. Racial inequality and discrimination have exerted unique and powerful effects on US politics and economics.[10] One expects *a priori* to find some linkage between the politics that come from racial segregation and global economics. Urban residential segregation lies at the core of racial politics in the United States, so segregation, also, is part of the story. This is where the argument begins.

Background

Students of urban affairs frequently remind us that international trade, exchange rates, flows of funds and patterns of innovation affect spatial form. In particular, they explain how the dramatic changes in international economic and industrial structure that have transformed commerce and politics in so much of the world in recent decades have also transformed the physical pattern of cities. Although many questions arise about the extent, the form, and especially the time lag for these transformations, it is indisputable that there are such effects. What this chapter argues, however, is that there are also important effects in the other direction. That is, peculiarities of urban spatial form can influence the contours of the global economy. In particular, *patterns of residential racial segregation in US cities have had pernicious effects on cities outside the United States.* These post-war urban geographies in the United States have not simply reflected but have actually contributed to the troublesome "globalization" of the 1980s and 1990s.

Now, some might agree immediately but reluctantly by saying, "well, of course, in social reality all causes and effects are mutual, and influences run in both (or all) directions." "By such bi-directional or multi-directional logic," they might add, "we would expect that the social and economic worlds (of globalization) and the physical worlds (of city geography) would be mutually influential." Nevertheless, they would warn that the effects in the second direction, from city spatial-form to international economy, would necessarily be minimal, even trivial, like a butterfly's flight affecting the wind. Surely, these are good reasons for caution. After all, most urban theorists and researchers are nervous in general about assigning much weight to the social or economic power of the physical form, and properly so. Not so long ago hard-thinking planners and urban scholars found it necessary to reject the popular but simple-minded social physics that suggested we could eradicate urban poverty by tearing down old buildings or destroying old neighborhoods.[11] Nevertheless, however true it may be that slum neighborhoods do not cause poverty, it does not necessarily follow that pervasive distortions in residential patterns have no important social, economic, and political consequences.

Indeed, the argument of this chapter may be open to even broader challenge because it is potentially more inclusive than the old error-laden theory from social physics. An even more extensive view of physical form looks not simply at the social, economic, and political effects of a particular building or project or neighborhood, but also at the effects of the overall pattern of spatial segregation in cities and metropolitan areas. The argument also has a much longer reach, for it claims not just local, or even national, but also international effects. These are indeed very strong claims. Still, although it is difficult to subject these claims to strong statistical testing, the chapter will show that they are well rooted in the historical facts.

Apartheid in America

Racial exclusion and residential segregation are essential, perhaps *the* essential qualities of the US metropolis in the last half of the 20th century. The standard, one almost must say approved, condition for African Americans in US cities is to live in neighborhoods that are racially homogeneous. Numerous surveys have demonstrated that black people do not wish to be segregated any more than do people belonging to any other group; statistics show that income differences explain very little of black segregation. In fact, African Americans are kept to restricted ghettos simply because white people, via numerous mechanisms of prejudice and privilege, do not allow blacks to live or live comfortably in white neighborhoods. It may be difficult for many liberal white Americans to swallow this pill, but the bad taste must be admitted – all evidence points to the primacy of overwhelming and effective racial discrimination in the development of cities and suburbs in the United States.[12]

The first important thing to remember here, because it is so often forgotten when related subjects are brought forth, is that – with the exception of a very small proportion of the black population who live in integrated neighborhoods – to live in highly segregated conditions is simply a fact of life. Nothing else is expected. For many Americans, nothing else can be imagined. The second thing to keep in mind is this – *no other group in US history has been similarly segregated* except American Indians, who have been segregated formally, by law, on reservations. Various white ethnic and immigrant groups have bunched together in neighborhoods, sometimes unwillingly and under oppressive circumstances, but their degrees of separation from others were relatively minor. Even Asians and Hispanic populations, among whom recent immigrants today *are* vigorously segregated, are by all measures segregated much less than African Americans.[13] Waters (1990) deconstructs the popular but undocumented argument that ethnic-Americans had it as bad as African Americans. She shows how such claims are based on false histories invented by ethnics as racist defenses against affirmative action.

Segregation, Politics, and the State

The racially segregated nature of the city in the United States has poisoned American politics. Extensive and intense isolation of one group from another can distort, damage and ultimately poison any chance for coalition and cooperation. As Lubiano (1997) says in her introduction to *The House that Race Built*:

"The idea of race and the operation of racism are . . . the means by which a state and a political economy largely inimical to most of the US citizenry achieve the consent of the governed. They act as a distorting prism that allows that citizenry to imagine itself functioning as a moral and just people while ignoring the widespread devastation directed at black Americans particularly, but at a much larger number of people generally."

More specifically, as Susan J. Smith (1993) writes of Britain, "the process of residential differentiation and, crucially, the imagery of 'racial segregation,' have played key roles in the social reproduction of 'race' categories and in sustaining material inequalities between 'black' and 'white.'" (p. 128)

In *The Uses of Disorder: Personal Identity and City Life* (1970), Richard Sennett argues from the perspective of social psychology to show that isolation of people in separated neighborhoods and suburbs can lead not just to lack of sympathy, but to mis-information and misunderstanding. When groups learn about one another only by means of distant, indirect, vicarious experience – through what they read or hear, or much worse, through what they see on television – they have shallow understanding, based only on superficialities. Living in separate neighborhoods, they are unable to learn to develop, to be tolerant, to work things through, to compromise. As Manuel Castells (1994, p. 22) says, "the exclusion of the other is not separable from the suppression of civil liberties and a mobilization against alien cultures."

Current racial segregation causes white suburban residents to be not just ignorant of but actually afraid of the city. They see it quite literally as a case of the "other," the alien, the hostile and the dangerous. In the social climate of the 1990s and amidst the growing number of gated communities, it is worth recalling that suburbanites' antipathy toward city people and their neighborhoods long predates the drug violence that today suffocates so many people with fear, inner-city residents included.[14]

Today, influential politicians and business leaders are almost exclusively drawn from among the suburban population.[15] Sennett (1970) refers to what he calls a permanent state of adolescence among these white suburbanites. He can be taken to mean that the leaders of the United States have never quite grown up – that their discomfort and inability to experience diversity, work through conflict, and arrange for compromise doom them, and their adversaries, to a permanent, psychological underdevelopment. Without much stretch in logic, we can see that these shortcomings might doom the rest of us to unrepresentative government. This may not be a bad explanation for the current state of national affairs, for such "conservative" absurdities as large and growing budgets for prisons but parsimony for public schools.[16]

Research on municipal and metropolitan governmental affairs demonstrates in detail how segregation has poisoned politics, and numerous studies document the rarity in US cities of cooperation across racial lines. Coalitions between blacks and whites are not simply rare, but they depend, argues Sonenshein (1993), on convergent political ideologies and willing leadership (particularly among whites) rather than simply on shared material interests. "Racial attitudes structure political choices. A racial conservative is highly unlikely to join a biracial coalition, especially if one of the coalition's explicit goals is African American political incorporation. Shifting interests are unlikely to shake that basic view of the world." (p. 56)

Most white Americans are highly conservative when it comes to racial matters. They have grown up in isolation, separated from others, and have developed their attitudes and behaviors toward African Americans in the absence of rich and productive interaction. They are nurtured on simplified myths of difference, danger and hostility.[17]

Damaging prejudices exist as well inside (Western) European countries, and they cross European borders. One does not expect instant sympathy among the English regarding some problem afflicting Germans or French or Italians, or vice versa, for the groups live in separate territories, grow up with separate cultures, and learn myths about the strange habits of foreigners. They develop knee-jerk animosities that are little based on fact and greatly influenced by prejudice. These are conservative prejudices, not easily amenable to change, not leaning toward tolerance. The difference in Europe is that most of these prejudices, damaging as they may be, have historically operated across borders, bounded by lines of national sovereignty, so they have had small immediate effect on the progress of national social legislation.[18]

To explain the special and unusual cases in which American cross-race politics *has* worked even to a limited extent, we must turn to situations in which blacks and whites *live nearby* one another. In Los Angeles in the 1960s, African Americans with relatively high incomes and extensive schooling lived in the predominantly white Tenth District, from which Tom Bradley, later to become the city's (first black) mayor, was elected to the City Council. In the Tenth, white political reformers and black entrants to the middle class formed a biracial alliance. The district was "a bridge between two worlds." "Black and white liberal activists worked together day by day, developing an understanding of each other's abilities and personalities." A key white activist remembers that blacks and whites who lived and worked together avoided "misunderstandings and serious disagreements and collisions . . . [thus avoiding] errors that other political campaigns may make just because they don't . . . have the people who know the differences among people." (Sohenshein, 1993, pp. 55–56)

After the South Central rebellion of 1992, and the election of a white, conservative mayor, presumably no one would argue that Los Angeles reflects deep racial harmony and cooperation. And no one can claim that Los Angeles is *not* highly segregated, given the powerful statistical evidence of racial segregation and the dismaying histories of white conspiracies to erect and maintain barriers against integration in Los Angeles.[19] The point is that political collaboration, the little there was, resulted only as a result of the daily interaction of black and white residents, who shared their lives in a *relatively* unsegregated district.

Moving from the municipal and metropolitan to the national level, it would be difficult to dispute the central influence that "race" has always had on American politics. As Michael Goldfield (1990) argues, white supremacy was essential to the development of American capitalism. Southern planters used slavery, crop liens and debt bondage in share cropping. Northern industrialists kept wages down with cheap cotton, racial strike breaking, and ethnic hierarchies. With minor exceptions – in the early Populist movement, organizing by the Knights of Labor in the 1880s and 1890s, the IWW in the first two decades of the present century, and the Communist Party in the 1930s – labor unions and labor-based political parties in the United States generally excluded blacks and ethnics. Although one expects to find the most liberal attitudes among prominent reformers, in fact there is considerable evidence that even the New Deal welfare state was racially biased. Lest these words be regarded as notes on ancient history, recall that not until 1967 did the Supreme Court rule against the numerous state laws then still prohibiting inter-racial marriages.[20]

To sum up: The general failures at building cross-racial coalitions in cities played and still play a major role in reinforcing the racism that exists at the deep core of US national politics. Big-city racial hostilities were developed and then sustained more and more by residential segregation as the nation urbanized throughout the 20th century. These hostilities have affected the formation of social movements, the selection of candidates, the conduct of elections, and the design and implementation of policies of all kinds.[21]

All Roads Lead to the Market

This racial tilt of US politics has led to many difficulties. It has long led to reinforcement of the traditional American reliance on "free" markets, rather than on cooperation, planning and the regulation of markets.[22] Most recently this tilt has predisposed American leaders to develop a preposterously exaggerated enthusiasm for market deregulation.[23] In the absence of strict regulation, markets (as opposed to planning, public intervention, legislation, and redistribution) generate high degrees of inequality of income. (This tendency of markets to reward some players handsomely but others barely is recognized by economists of all political colors.) Each person's or family's well-being is based almost entirely on the ability-to-pay, derived mainly from market-earned incomes, from either paid employment or, in a few fortunate cases, inheritance.[24] In the United States, these inequalities are tolerated more than elsewhere in good part because they conform so closely to racial hierarchies.[25] The truncated nature of political discussion finds people of color kept at bay and their interests denied, thus limiting serious consideration of the various alternatives to markets and preventing their adoption. Without intervention from outside the market, this alignment of poverty and political weakness is self-reinforcing in a grim, downward spiral. Not only do people of color suffer the consequences, but so do all others who slip into market failure.

Over the past century and a half, the experience outside the United States is quite different. Most industrialized countries have responded to pressures from workers and their families by establishing rather broad guarantees of economic equality. The wealthy nations of Western Europe and Canada administer national health care programs and guarantee vacations typically four to six weeks per year in addition to eight or ten national holidays and generous sick leave. They also provide housing subsidies (or "social" housing) to large proportions of their residents and support comprehensive systems of public transit inside cities and among them.[26] American capitalists alone have successfully resisted pressures for broad social guarantees, so that poor Americans must cope with the inadequacies of the bottom of the market in private health care and housing and most Americans must suffer from short vacations and poor public transportation. Why?

Some explanations for US exceptionalism are well known. Most commonly it is argued that the frontier was an escape for oppressed workers, providing them an alternative to the need for working class organizations. Furthermore, the frontier served as an alternative to the city, giving workers a means of sustaining high private wages, thus negating the need for social supports.[27] However true these arguments may be, and there is ample room for dispute, the racial factor is central to any theory of difference for America: White workers have organized less successfully for social benefits. Instead, they have been able to shift much of the burden of inequality and poverty to people of color. The politics of whites have been truncated as well because they have *believed* they could shift the burden to blacks and also because whites derive status and pleasure directly from the experience of racial dominance itself.[28] This psychological and practical ability to shift the burden has been generated, reinforced, and protected by the ignorance bred of isolation and segregation.

If whites and blacks had lived together in the same neighborhoods, segmented mainly and less drastically by income as is true of whites, then history might have been different, and that would negate the entire argument. Then whites might have observed more directly individuals' differential successes and failures with the economy, and they or their acquaintances would personally have suffered more of the consequences. Instead, in real history, whites observed failure at a safe distance, which made it easy to excuse the society and blame the victims.

The Washington Consensus

The anti-social character of US politics has begun to spread to other countries. Indeed, many have remarked on the worldwide marketing of the US model of individualism, deregulation, free trade, and privatization that threatens to cut into the guarantees of social democracy nearly everywhere. This has come to be called the Washington Consensus.[29] The most obvious routes for this free-market influence run directly and legally from Wall Street to the US Treasury, then to the World Bank and the International Monetary Fund (IMF), then to the rest of the world. These Washington-based and US-dominated "multilateral institutions" operate prodigious and technically proficient propaganda campaigns to assure the ascendancy of the market approach to economic management and political life.[30]

The World Bank and IMF derive most of their power as bankers who can withhold funds, their own and those of other lenders. They influence domestic policies through their insistence on "structural adjustment" and similar austerity programs not only in the Third World but in many rich industrial countries.[31] The World Bank and the IMF insist as a condition for life-sustaining loans that countries "get the prices right" by allowing supply and demand to operate unchallenged by government intervention. This often plays into the hands of monopoly or other unfair foreign competition and regularly promotes the worsening of income distributions. The World Bank and the IMF push countries to reduce public services and to charge more for them. And they push relentlessly for countries to privatize everywhere that it is possible.[32]

It would be a mistake to attribute the world-wide diffusion of pro-market hysteria to an organized conspiracy. Rather, the sweeping service cutbacks and planetary market enthusiasm find a welcoming climate because of the prior and general spread of US-based corporate attitudes, preferences, management styles, and activities, and because of the need to successfully compete against firms not regulated elsewhere.[33] These patterns of universal corporate behavior exist in good part as a result of expectations developed domestically, on the unregulated US scene. Because of their experience in the United States, corporations insist that their "markets" everywhere be "unregulated" and that the rules that protect their competitive domination be assured, not just at home but abroad. In fact, accompanying the Washington Consensus on economic management, we find another US ideological export, rhetoric on the value of democracy, putatively running 180 degrees in the opposite direction, but in fact often reinforcing the pro-market rules to the detriment of real democracy.[34]

The Global Escape to the Suburbs

My chain of reasoning began with American apartheid, which has led to truncated politics in the United States. Those damaged politics led to worship of the market, which has led to market-based political systems worldwide. The final link can now be forged: The dynamism of worldwide market deregulation leads to new pressures on the European metropolis. If Western Europe is, in the words of Manuel Castells (1994, p. 22), a "fragile island of prosperity, peace, democracy, culture, science, welfare and civil rights," then its cities are now threatened with social stratification, with exaggerated segregation by incomes, and especially by ethnic and racial segregation. Increased social stratification, in turn, fuels costly new suburban sprawl. There are of course many variants of pressures tending in the same direction. The syndrome begins to display some of the internal dynamics of the US metropolitan model, with national variations, as in the impoverished immigrant peripheries of Paris, Lyon and Marseilles.[35] But how do pressures descend from world markets to the European city?

To take the most obvious instance first, there is the celebrated influence of Hollywood and of US television programming, including much of the news. Either because they show better entertainment, or more likely because they are better funded, the American movie and television industries are dominant worldwide, issuing direct messages, indirect messages, and advertising. They spread not only the false, pastoral, romantic image of the suburb, but lately also the equally false, demonic, barbarian image of the city. Aside from the divisive and distorted racial imagery in these false pictures, there is also the transfer of preferences for high material consumption. How much social and psychological damage this misleading information causes is difficult to say with precision. But the overall effect is very likely to be negative in its nurturing of hostile racial stereotypes, its denigration of the inner city, and its celebration of the suburb.[36]

How do these damages connect with market deregulation? They connect directly, as we can observe when other governments object to the spread of these images. For example, when political bodies decide they want to interfere with markets – as when the French government tries to keep out Hollywood movies – they are beaten back by a panoply of structures erected to protect unrestricted competition. These structures include free-trade agreements, such as the North American Free Trade Agreement (NAFTA), the General Agreement on Tariffs and Trade (GATT), the new World Trade Organization, and compensatory award clauses in commercial treaties, etc.[37] Such damages connect indirectly, as deregulation stimulates international economic transfers. These transfers in turn stimulate sales of movies and TV shows and lead (through normal market operations) to dominance by the stronger and more developed (US) competitors.

There are less noticed influences from the internationalizing of affairs through the expansion of market-based rules. As markets expand to encompass more of social life, non-market welfare guarantees such as national health care or broad housing subsidies are reduced. These reductions began in Western Europe in the 1980s largely as a result of the pressures felt as a result of diminished restrictions against overseas competitors.[38] After non-market guarantees and subsidies are reduced, then social inequalities increase. Take the case of urban transportation. Under circumstances in which the public sector is shortchanged, funds for public mass transit decline precisely as the need grows. At the same time, incomes rise in those households who can afford to commute in individual automobiles. Pressures to build roads and manage automobile traffic thus explode, just as the capacity to provide mass transit declines, and the vicious cycle so well known in US cities takes hold. Traffic chokes city streets and arterial connectors, suburbs grow, and complaints pile up.[39] Suburbanites strengthen their hand in public affairs, and the pattern of expenditures, subsidies, taxes, and individual preferences for auto mobility smother the collective benefits of transit in cities. These trends are abetted by the actively pursued self-interest of industries that manufacture and maintain autos, construct roads, and refine oil.[40]

As neighborhoods inside the city become identified with particular ethnic groups of (poorer) people, these suburbanizing tendencies reinforce themselves with the pernicious weight of national, ethnic and racial bias. Services decline, public authorities permit lax standards of housing and welfare, commercial interests transfer their loyalties, real estate markets shift, and the relative advantages of suburban relief are compounded. Small businesses decline in poor neighborhoods but expand in areas of wealth; major employers move their offices to follow the skilled population. By the same logic applied in the United States, this segregated spatial form in Western European cities can be expected to degrade politics, further reducing protections for citizens and workers, so that the deleterious cycle will be reinforced.

In the largest European cities resistance to this model may be pronounced, and in many smaller ones the pressures may be barely felt, the tendencies hardly evident. National budgets for central-city vitality can fight the trend. The French government, for example, throws huge quantities of public funding at Paris, which strengthens a historic pattern that has subsidized the upper middle class in the city and put workers' residences at the periphery, the worst of them by now occupied by immigrants.[41] But as the pressures expand to cut public expenditures, there are likely to be reversions even here – witness the 1995 French decision to scale back drastically its plans for expansion of the Metro system.

Race and Class in the Global City

Just as "globalized" workers in European cities have lost benefits and protections, more of them have become darker skinned, since many are immigrants enabled or forced to move as markets expand.[42] Class struggle has begun to intertwine with racial conflict. These historical developments allow governments to ignore further the demands of (increasingly minority) workers and residents.

Here, of course, it becomes difficult to distinguish any longer between two phenomena – the effects of city form on economic organization, on the one hand, and the effects of the overall economy (and its world-wide extensions) on city form, on the other hand. One can thus see US exceptionalism in a very broad light. The US colonial situation was internal: the southern slave-holding states were like the overseas colonies of Western Europe. As slavery, reconstruction, and Jim Crow were attacked and partially defeated in the Southern colonies, the subject population fled, seeking freedoms, livelihoods, and new opportunities in the North. From that basic structural divide comes the story we have just reviewed, of the pervasive effects of racism and racial politics on the development, including the urban development, of the United States, with all its circular and destructive logic. A parallel phenomenon now involves Europe with its ex-colonial people of color, as physical boundaries of nations fall to the axes of cheap transportation and instant communication, and as both people and goods tend to move with fewer restraints. Globalization and the market economy are indeed colorizing European cities, just as local control over resources and politics shifts in favor of elites and corporations, causing the attendant conflict, resistance, hostility, and violence.

Combined with the techno-economic pressures put on cities by suburbanization and national budgetary shortfalls, there are also the spread of the drug wars, the widespread availability of murderous weaponry, and a more generalized level of violence. To the extent that newly "dangerous classes" are segregated into ghettos either in city centers or on the outskirts, the US city form tends to be reproduced elsewhere.

Notes

1   An earlier version of this chapter appeared in the *American Behavioral Scientist* of November 1997 (Goldsmith, 1997). Karen Westmont provided excellent and extensive research assistance for the revisions.

2   Castells (1994) correctly points out that all (Western) Europe, not only its cities, is a site of great privileges in today's troubled world.

3   In fact, the European city has profited over a much longer period. Beginning with the early emergence of the city from the Dark Ages, Western European ruling classes took profits from overseas trade and exploited domestic workforces to establish splendid private residences, churches, municipal buildings, and urban (later to become thoroughly public) spaces. See Bairoch (1991, 1988) and Braudel (1985).

4   These cities themselves – as physical structures *and* as social spaces – have long served and remain still today as enormously attractive magnets for tourism by the "middle classes" from all other parts of the world. It is a peculiar contradiction that Americans, who so neglect their city centers and so heavily subsidize the outskirts of the metropolis, take so much pleasure in visiting dense European city centers.

5   To take the example of Rome: even in the worst peripheral neighborhoods – the miserably designed Corviale high-rise project is one – residents find frequent and reliable access to city bus lines, some local shopping, schools, and programs for the elderly. The people who live in these places do not suffer the deep sense of isolation and despair that afflict so many of those who live in the worst parts of US cities. For further discussion of the US case, see, e.g. Wilson (1996).

6   These kinds of pressures sprang vividly into view when television newscasts showed refugees from Kosovo in small Italian cities, with public debate balancing local capacity for housing, schooling, and other public services against the emergency needs of the suffering immigrants. Similar pressures in Sweden force progressive, anti-racist politicians to cope with the tensions involved in the segregation of darker-skinned immigrants and their unassimilated children. See incidents described in newspaper articles by Allen-Mills (11/1/1998) and Williams (10/31/1998).

7   *Separate Societies* argues that rapid expansion of the international economy has led to a rearrangement of industry, resulting in a pattern that has left many city

people stranded without jobs and city governments unable to collect sufficient taxes. New funds are required to provide the public services needed by the additional unemployed or increasingly poorly paid workforce. These municipal fiscal shortcomings in turn make the city still less attractive for re-investors, thus aggravating the cycle. This circular causation of decline is further reinforced by, and especially reinforces, racial discrimination and segregation.

8   For an excellent comparison of US and French cities see Wacquant (1993). For (up to date statistical) studies of segregation in cities in Britain, the Netherlands, Belgium, Sweden, Germany, and Austria see Van Kempen and Özüekren (1998), *passim.*

9   Some papers in the special issue of *Urban Studies* (1998) on ethnic segregation, edited by Van Kempen and Özüekren, show that European cities provide much better conditions, compared to US cities, for minority residents (by "race", ethnicity, or foreign origin) relative to conditions for native citizens. Still, these papers also suggest considerable uncertainty about future social policy and urban results. It is difficult to summarize across very different situations, and (as Van Kempen and Van Weesep point out) statistical indices of segregation are highly sensitive to scale and other factors. Still, a reading of the entire special issue leads one to a sense of a growing concern with racial bias and danger to the proper functioning of the city.

10 Only in South Africa and in some ways Brazil do conditions parallel the stark ones produced by the US colorline, but since those two countries are also subject to the widespread poverty of Third World status, the US case stands alone. See Seidman (1994), Degler (1971) and Goldsmith (1994).

11 The same environmental determinism was sometimes employed in reverse, as in the case of the newly planned city of Brasília. There, as throughout the early modern movement, the planners and designers believed the city's physical form would help usher in more modern, egalitarian, and democratic social practices, not only in the city itself, but in the whole country. See Goldsmith (1998) at pages 1207–1208 and Holston (1989), *passim.*

12 An enormous literature documents the depth of this segregation and discrimination. The standard source is now Massey and Denton (1993), which compiles exhaustive evidence of racial segregation and examines the social forces behind it. Also see Goldsmith (1974), Farley (1996), Wacquant (1997), and Hanchett (1998). On the notion of "white privilege", see the seminal papers by McIntosh (1988, 1990). For discrimination arising more from institutional – rather than personal – causes, see Jackson (1985), Federal (1989), Munnell et al. (1992), Carr and Megbolugbe (1993), Yinger (1995), Baar (1981), and the *South Burlington* case (1975, 1983).

13 In addition to the works cited in the previous footnote, see Philpott's *The Slum and The Ghetto* (1978). Due to the complex social definitions of the "race" of Hispanic people, US Census categories rarely enable researchers to distinguish between light-skinned and dark-skinned Hispanics. Special, detailed demographic studies, however, suggest that light-skinned Hispanics suffer little segregation, after accounting for income, while dark-skinned Hispanics are victimized much like non-Hispanic blacks. See Massey and Denton (1993, 113–114) Massey and Bitterman (1985), Denton and Massey (1989) and Massey (1978).

14 Blakely and Snyder (1995) refer to "fortification," Marcuse (1997a and 1997b) refers to "citadels," and Christopherson (1994) refers to "fortress city," as they document how thoroughly the better-off people in US cities have isolated and insulated themselves in the 1980s and 1990s.

15 Formal representation of cities in the Congress has declined more quickly than has central city population as a proportion of the national population. While central city population fell only moderately, from 31 percent in the 1970s to 28 percent in the 1990s, the number of representatives in the House from districts with central-city-majority populations fell more, from 103 to only 84. The main change, however, has been decline in rural membership and growth of the suburbs. In spite of advantages from disproportionate seniority, such city membership on the (key) House Banking, Housing, and Urban Affairs Committee fell from 37 percent in 1983–4 to only 24 percent in 1993–4, while suburban membership rose from 21 percent to 54 percent. (Wolman and Marckini, 1998). In the US Senate, rural power remains intact. As Stephens (1996) explains, "Because small states are generally less urban, the Senate heavily underrepresents central cities and ethnic minorities and massively overrepresents suburban and rural/small-town residents . . ." Stephens concludes that the "institutional lock" in the Senate held by 26 states comprising less than 18 percent of the national population appears to cause bias in the distribution of federal grants.

16 Prison budgets have exploded along with prison populations in the United States since 1980. The number of prisoners rose from 320,000 to 992,000 from 1980 to 1994, according to the Justice Policy Institute's 1997 report using data from the US Justice Department as cited in Jet Magazine (1997). As noted by Davis (1995), since California's penal system has become the third-largest in the world after China and the United States, its prison–industrial complex threatens to become the dominate political force in the state. According to Skolnick (1995), " . . . most Americans have come to assume that lengthy imprisonment, determinate sentencing, mandatory minimum sentencing, and severe habitual offender laws offer safety along with retribution. Recent statistics from California . . . demonstrate the shortcomings of this assumption. Despite the 600 percent increase in the state's prison population and the 400 percent rise in its prison budget over the past decade, California's violent crime rate has increased by 40 percent." For the arguments of this paper, note that these huge increases in "crime", prisoners and budgets accompany the disproportionate criminalizing of the African American population, almost entirely for victimless use of drugs or for commerce in drugs. As researchers of various political or ideological stripes find, this terrible domestic consequence of the wrong-headed US-sponsored War on Drugs finds its match in the equally terrible consequences for supplier countries, especially in Central America and South America. See Kohl (1996) pages 3–4, Farthing (1997) and Sanabria (1997).

17 Note two indirect but telling indications of continuing political pressures to promote privileges of whites. Trent Lott, the majority leader in the 105th and 106th US Senates, seeks and finds support from the openly racist Council of Conservative Citizens (Herbert, 1999). US Supreme Court Chief Justice William Rehnquist in an incautious document written when he was a law clerk, revealed his support for the open discrimination embodied in the separate-but-equal

doctrine of 1896 in Plessy v. Ferguson (Rosen, 1999).

18   The domestic case in (Western) Europe is like a double-edged sword. In some cases minority groups are too small and weak to have affected either politics or budgets. In others, working class parties have maintained class solidarity above racial conflict. Unfortunately, in other cases nativist movements offer an ugly challenge. Where inequality as well as prejudice crosses national boundaries, even in the absence of the "race" factor, social damages can be profound.

19   On the astonishing history of deliberate racial discrimination by Los Angeles' early academic and civic leaders, see Davis (1990). Robert Millikan, a founder of both the California Institute of Technology and of the California military-industrial complex, sought a white-dominated pattern of growth. Millikan was happy that the Los Angeles population was "twice as Anglo-Saxon as that existing in New York, Chicago or any of the great cities of this country." (p. 56)

20   Numerous instruments of public policy prohibited or inhibited non-white residents from moving into white areas. See Goldsmith (1974) and Jackson (1985). Today, although such formal rules against racial integration would be illegal, many barriers still operate against minorities or prevent the mixing of households with different incomes. For example, the universal form of the Federal National Mortgage Association (FNMA) allows appraisers to adjust loan amounts by rating neighborhood for internal "compatibility" and by deciding whether the house is "compatible to [the] neighborhood." See FNMA Form RE-414W (12/89). Federal Reserve Bank statisticians found significant racial discrimination in mortgage lending. Their study [see Munnell et al. (1992), and also Carr and Megbolugbe (1993)] found white families denied mortgages only 11 percent of the time while comparable minority families (including Hispanic) were denied 17 percent of the time. Further raising the barrier to ownership, homes in low-income areas are assessed at higher rates than others (Baar, 1981), thereby raising taxes and offering the inescapable presumption of assessors' biases against non-white neighborhoods. By using "audits" to prove differential treatment of black and Hispanic auditors who were seeking to buy or rent housing, Yinger (1995) found extensive discrimination by brokers and agents in real estate offices. Compared to whites shown houses, minority households were told that nothing is available 5–10 percent of the time, and they were shown fewer units 19–23 percent of the time.

21   I have purposefully cited interpretations and evidence provided by white scholars and writers in this century. African American scholars, from W.E.B. Du Bois (1903) to John Henrik Clarke (1976), to mention only two of the most prominent and well-respected, provide abundant evidence of the pervasive and malicious violence of racism in all aspects of life. Also see Marable (1991).

22   For a thorough discussion of how politicians in the United States use "race" to obscure issues of income or class inequalities, see Silver (1993) especially page 345.

23   Knowing that markets generate inequality and acknowledging the fact are sometimes two very different things. For a discussion of the World Bank's refusal to acknowledge how markets create inequality, see Goldsmith (1977). Recent arguments emphasize the benefits of planning – rather than free markets – even in celebrated instances of "market-led" development. See e.g. Amsden (1997); Singh

(1994) and Amsden (1993) on Asia; and Amsden, Kochanowicz, and Taylor on Eastern Europe (1994).

24 To some extent, the evidence from Europe post-1980, where deregulation has proceeded apace, especially in Thatcherite Britain, must be counted as the effect of the American experience, not as a parallel development.

25 As Goldsmith and Blakely (1992) put it on page 54, "African Americans are increasingly isolated from mainstream American jobs, education, culture, and economic life, as are Puerto Ricans, Chicanos, Central Americans, women who manage families alone, and slum dwellers. These groups form the base for the evolution of new patterns of urban poverty."

26 For international comparisons of income distributions, see Atkinson et al. (1995, 1995). On European–US differences in public transportation, see Pucher and Lefèvre (1996). On social services, see Anderson (1996). Even compensation of top executives is hugely more skewed in US than in European firms. In 1998, e.g., while top US firms paid an average of $1.1 million, German firms (with higher costs of living) paid $398,000. (*New York Times*, January 17, 1999, Business Section, p. 1).

27 For application of American exceptionalism to current biases in the distribution of services, see Quadagno (1998), Lipset (1996), and Halpern and Morris (1997).

28 Peggy McIntosh (1988, 1990) wrote of "white privilege" to describe the many ways in which whites, compared to blacks, unconsciously enjoy advantages in everyday life as do men versus women, but my argument here goes further to assert that some whites consciously enjoy the advantage itself. Similarly, Massey and Denton (1993, p. 213) argue that whites want an absence of discrimination in principle but not in practice.

29 The term "*Washington Consensus*" suggests for some an overbearing and arrogant imposition of US power (originating more on Wall Street than in Washington, but carried there via the Treasury Department). The term seems to be used without self-consciousness by its self-described promoters. Williamson (1994, pages 22 and 26–28), e.g., who supplies a set of rules for the consensus, writes that the "Chicago boys" economics team that re-fashioned the Chilean economy under the Pinochet dictatorship, "implemented the Washington Consensus long before the concept was conceived . . . " (p. 22). Oddly, Washington sometimes accompanies its pressure to expand markets with parallel pressure to expand democracy. See for example, Kohl (1999).

30 The most sustained effort in recent years was the World Bank's to promote the idea that the best, for them the only, route to development for poor countries would employ markets functioning entirely on their own, without public intervention. See, e.g., World Bank (1993) and critiques cited above by Singh, Amsden, and others. Celarier (1998) writes in *Euromoney* magazine of 18 years of a "mantra of free markets." According to the *Institutional Investor* , "Despite their failures (. . .) this coterie of insiders [Treasury Secretary Robert Rubin, IMF managing director Michael Camdessus, World Bank president James Wolfensohn and Federal Reserve Chairman Alan Greenspan] still believes it is the world's best hope to devise an answer to the mess." (Muehring, 1998, p. 74)

31 Structural Adjustment Programs (SAPs) are the latest versions of international economic strictures dictating austerity in public budgets. In the many countries

where the World Bank, the IMF, and local banking/conservative/public authorities have imposed SAPs, the short-run results for the – mostly poor – population has been a tragic shortfall in incomes, social services, and supply of basic goods. For examples, see Stein and Nafzier (1990), Ruderman (1990), Bello, Cunningham and Rau (1994), and Beneria and Mendoza (1995). Even the international institutions themselves have acknowledged this problem, subsequently trying to impose SAPs "with a human face." See, e.g., the UNICEF study, Cornia et al. (1987) and more recent World Bank admissions of difficulties with SAPs. Also see Fitch (1977).

32 This sort of austerity program is familiar to students of urban politics and budgets, especially in the United States and Britain. In the 1970s and 1980s, authorities often responded to municipal "fiscal crises" with draconian austerity programs, such as those spawned by the Big MAC (Municipal Assistance Corporation) in New York City. See Shefter (1985, 1992). Of New York City's budget cuts, Jack Newfield (1976) said, "Every day I get a phone call, or a press release or meet someone who tells a small, personal horror story of the budget cuts."

33 A *New York Times* journalist, R. Cohen (1997) refers to the "velvet hegemony" of the US corporate style. For an articulate summary of the effects of free-market economies, see Larudee's (1993) discussion of NAFTA's approximation of a non-regulated economy and its resulting shift of earnings from labor to capital. The gap between European and US corporate compensation to top executives is now shrinking, partly through the effects of mergers, as US corporate style dominates and as individual European-employed executives take the opportunity to escape their national restraints on greed (*New York Times*, January 17, 1999, Business Section, p. 1 ff).

34 Notably, the academic world of the 1990s is having a run on the idea of "democracy," or "democratic theory," involving at its best a politics with transparency, accountability, and participation (see, e.g., Putnam, 1995, and Putnam et al., 1993, and critical responses by Lemann (1996) and Tarrow (1996)). Too often authorities use superficial coatings of democratic forms to disguise power grabs by powerful economic groups. In an unusually blunt exercise, Crozier, Huntington, and Watanuki (1975) forthrightly argued the counter-case to the Trilateral Commission, that an excess of democracy would threaten market capitalism.

35 See the insightful analysis by Wacquant (1993).

36 See Goldsen's (1978) analysis of the "working over" that American television programming does to its viewers. Recently, Pasquier (1993) has documented that the industrial nature of the Hollywood "salt mine" torpor of doing business is overwhelming the public service ethic of French TV. See related work mentioned below by Dorfman and Mattelart (1975). More generally, Cohen (1997) writes that although the French compete with the United States to offer the world their "universal model" of "Liberty, Equality, Fraternity," still the French ethos in not praising wealth and personal enrichment is a "feeble dike to the global tide." Although there are many excellent works on the biases in the media, Jones (1996) captures perhaps best the ideas of both the racism and the ghettoization of the central city.

37 For an interesting discussion in the context of GATT of cultural protectionism by European governments from the US point of view, see Van Elteren (1996). On the invasion of images and corporate culture, Cohen (1977) writes about the negative reaction of French business to an American-styled high-technology firm in their midst. The effectiveness of the US commercial culture has been documented by – among others – Dorfman and Mattelart (1975).

38 On the damage of free markets, Larudee (1993) explains how NAFTA imitates free-market mechanisms to shift earnings from labor to capital.

39 For a full treatment of the inherently contradictory nature of auto-based urban growth, see Vietorisz, Goldsmith and Grengs (1998). Also see Vasconcellos (1997).

40 For comparisons of US and European transportation and public transport, see Pucher (1995a, 1995b) and Pucher and Lefèvre (1996).

41 The national government pays 40 percent of Paris' budget, thereby allowing lower taxes in Paris itself relative to the ratios of services/tax in surrounding localities. See Greenhouse (1992). In contrast to most US cities, the poor live in the periphery of Paris. See Wacquant (1993).

42 At the end of the 1980s, Sutcliffe (1994) finds that non-natives make up an average of 2.5 percent of Western European populations, with France having more than six percent and Spain, Portugal, Ireland and Greece each having less than one percent. Sutcliffe comments that governments in Europe – and the US – react with anti-immigration policies, thereby encouraging the expression of racist attitudes.

4

From Colonial City to Globalizing City?
The Far-from-complete Spatial
Transformation of Calcutta

Sanjoy Chakravorty[1]

Like the proverbial Hindi deity, Calcutta has had many names: "city of palaces" (in the 19th century), "city of dreadful night" (Kipling's description at the turn of this century), "city of joy" (in the dreadful book and movie of recent years), "dying city" (by the late Rajiv Gandhi, Prime Minister of India 1984–89); its recent rulers have proclaimed that they would like the city to be known as the "gateway to the Asian tigers" (in media promoting the investment virtues of the city and the state). In postmodern parlance these many names reflect the many histories and realities of the city – its colonial past, industrial decline, and hope for resurgence in the present and near future. Interestingly, these names also hint at the many geographies of the city – its palaces and hovels, wealth and poverty – and, analyzed chronologically, the names offer some insight into the spatial structure of the city.

This paper, like the others in the book, focuses on intra-urban (or intra-metropolitan) distribution of wealth and poverty, using Calcutta as an Indian case study. The editors of this book asked an intriguing question: "Is there a new spatial order within cities?" This is really a two-part question: one, is there something new about the spatial structure of cities today and tomorrow, something fundamentally different from the same cities in the past; and, two, is this a generalizable model *worldwide*? For much of this paper I will try to answer the first part with reference to Calcutta, leaving enough signposts along the way to be able to deal with the second question at the end.

I, and I believe others in this volume, use a somewhat different analytical framework from the one suggested by the editors. This should not be surprising since the default model and hypothesis appear to be have been proposed, to a large extent, with the "western" city and economy in mind, especially its American variant. This default framework uses the new industrial divide, or the transition to a post-Fordist economy as the fundamental element defining the past and present structure of urban areas. The argument, very simply put, is that industrialization- and manufacturing-led economic growth created the "old" urban structure; deindustrialization- or service-sector-led global economic expansion is in the process of creating a "new" urban structure.

There are a number of reasons why this model cannot begin to apply to "Third World" contexts in general, and its cities in particular. The so-called Third World encompasses a great diversity of development levels, political–economic structures and histories, and levels of integration into the global economy; their city (and country) sizes are diverse, their city functions are rarely comparable to developed nation city functions, their public sector is much more active in urban land markets, the CBD is more important as the locus of employment, rent gradients are more unilinear and steep moving away from the CBD – all factors leading to distinct monocentric cities as opposed to the clearly established polycentric cities of the west. Above all, deindustrialization in the west actually implies its opposite in the Third World, i.e., increased industrialization, presumably in its urban centers. In fact, a more appropriate argument is that there is no singular "Third World" and that perhaps none of the many different political–economic–historical systems that make up the "Third World" bear any resemblance to the system described in the opening hypothesis. This case history is not the place to debate these arguments and questions; the focus is on the Calcutta story as a case history and should not to be used to draw generalizations about India or the Third World. Some of the more serious shortcomings of the editors' hypothesis will be pointed out along the way.

It is clear that the two-stage Fordist/post-Fordist model cannot adequately describe the economic and urban development of India, particularly its colonial cities (and perhaps some other once-colonized third world nations and cities). Rather, a three-stage model may be more appropriate, where the three stages are:

1 colonial economy during the first global period;
2 post-colonial (or command) economy during the nationalist period; and
3 post-command/reform economy, during the second global period.

The relationship between colonization and urban development in the colonized countries has been discussed quite exhaustively (see King, 1976). Many of these cities, usually ports, were created specifically for colonial extraction: i.e., to act as points of transshipment of commodities from the colonized region and processed goods to it, and as seats of administration. Their primary links were to the international economy rather than to the regional economy.[2]

In the post-colonial or nationalist phase the idea of "development" as opposed to exploitation came to the fore; key ideas such as import-substituting industry, big push, infant industry protection, balanced growth, self sufficiency, etc., dictated the policies of the relatively inward-looking newly formed nation-states. And now, a combination of the failures of import-substituting industrialization in the south and the demand for new markets and production centers in the north, have forced many developing nations *back* to the global market. Post-Fordism does not describe this period as accurately as the term mixed-Fordism does, for large-scale capital-intensive production still has to take place somewhere – in the current global shift, in an ironic turn of events, it is the developing nations which are home to Fordist industry. I argue that these three stages are characterized by distinct modes and relations of production and investment, policy and goals, and consequently they also characterize distinct spatial forms. In the next section I will briefly outline this three-stage history of Calcutta (with the last stage still in its formative phase), and show how the spatial order has been shaped by the dominant ideology of production.

However, the Calcutta story would be poorly understood without mention of two factors that, though not unique to itself, are rather different from developed nation contexts. First, I must highlight the importance of the size and function of the "informal" sector in Calcutta's economy: by most estimates this collection of urban workers comprises 40 percent or more of the Calcutta labor force, in occupations from garbage collection, material transport, home delivery of consumer products, to small crafts and manufacturing (leather products, printing, etc.). The notion of formal "flexible production and accumulation" (see Storper and Walker, 1989) that some scholars argue is reshaping urban space in the developed world has long been an aspect of the conditions of production in Third World cities like Calcutta. One subsector of this informal economy is of particular interest in analyzing the spatial distribution of income and wealth: the domestic servants, ubiquitous in upper- and upper-middle class residences, have lived and continue to live in close proximity to their employers. I will argue that it is essential to have an understanding of the spatial distribution of the informal sector, particularly the domestic service element, and its relationship to capital and technology, to understand the geography of poverty and affluence in Calcutta.

A Brief History of Calcutta Metropolis

Calcutta is the capital of the state of West Bengal, and the primate city of Eastern India, with a hinterland of over 220 million, mostly poor rural population (comprising the states of Bihar, Orissa, Assam, etc.). Calcutta's metropolitan population of about 11 million (it varies with the definition used) is almost ten times higher than that of the second largest urban agglomeration in eastern India – Patna, in Bihar, with a population of about 1.1 million. This is by far the highest primacy ratio of any Indian region. To put it in context, it would be similar to a situation in the United States where after New York with 18 million people, if the second largest metropolis (Los Angeles) had a population of 1.8 million. As shown in Map 4.1, the city is located on the east bank of the river Hughli, considered the "wrong" side because the partition of India at independence in 1947 left much of the hinterland on the west of the river. The city's size and shape have obviously changed over the 300 years of its existence. The size shown in all the graphics here conform to the city's pre-1984 boundaries.[3] The city of Calcutta is small – 104 sq. kms. (excluding the most recent additions) – and extremely congested (the density at the business core is around 95,000 persons/sq. km., reputedly the highest in the world: United Nations, 1993). In the following paragraphs I describe the growth of Calcutta, the city and the metropolis, over the last three hundred years into its present size.

Colonial economy: Calcutta in ascendance

In 1690 an English merchant named Job Charnok arranged to lease three villages (named Kolikata, Gobindapur, and Sutanuti) by the river Hughli in order to set up a trading post. In 1698 Fort William was established by the river for defensive purposes, and a large open area was cleared around the fort for military engagements. The fort and the open area (called Maidan) formed the core of the city that emerged rather rapidly. The English traders' territorial expansion soon brought them into conflict with the local rulers, and a decisive battle in 1757 at Plassey (about 120 kms. north of Calcutta) left the victorious traders in sole control of the Bengal region. In 1763 a large area made up of Bengal (including present day Bangladesh), Bihar, and Orissa, was placed under the control of Fort William, or the territorial domain of Calcutta. In 1780 work began on building a marine yard and dock in Kidderpore, but the effort was abandoned temporarily and taken up later. By this time Calcutta had become a significant trading and administrative center, and in 1794 the Governor General of Bengal Province, Lord Cornwallis, decided the official delineation of the city boundaries.[4]

In 1835 industry began in the Calcutta region, but not in the city: the first jute mill was established in Rishra, a suburb (for lack of a better term).[5] Jute, used for making bags, carpets, and low cost clothing, became the mainstay of the region's economy till the middle of the 20th century. Other jute mills were established (usually) along the west bank of the river, towards the north

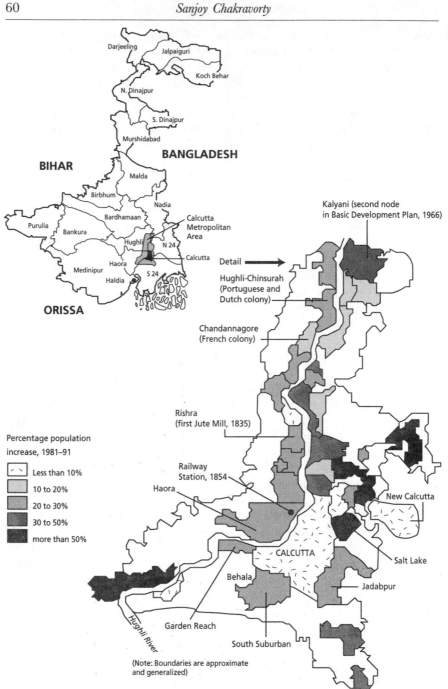

Map 4.1　Calcutta City and Metropolis: regional and historical context

of the city. Thus, industry in Calcutta began in the suburbs and continued to locate in the suburbs through another 100 years of colonial rule and 50 years of independence. In 1854 Haora station was built on the "correct" side or west of the river, and in 1880 steamships began arriving at the now complete Kidderpore docks. By the end of the 19th century Calcutta was a powerful metropolitan center, and the British capital in India (often called the second city of the British empire) – a city of palaces and hovels. In 1912 the capital was shifted to Delhi, and a period of stagnation began for Calcutta and Bengal. Some engineering industry (medium scale metal and iron works) owned largely by British people did start locating in the industrial belt along the river,[6] but the world demand for jute products was on the decline (interrupted only by increased demand during the two world wars).

The command economy: Calcutta in decline

Independence in 1947 was especially traumatic for Calcutta. First, religious strife led to a massive migration of Hindus from the newly formed East Pakistan to the city; there was some Muslim out-migration, but in smaller numbers. Second, a significant portion of Calcutta's hinterland (mainly the jute growing region) now became part of another, hostile country. Despite these problems the city was in an enviable position by Indian standards: until the mid-1950s West Bengal was the leading industrial state in the country with established economic infrastructure and manufacturing industry (automobiles, chemicals, consumer non-durables, etc.), and the highest per capita income levels in the country (which has since declined to rank seventh). It was also clear, however, that the city and the region were in decline. Delhi had long replaced Calcutta as the political capital, and now Mumbai began replacing it as the economic capital of India. Hastening this decline was the Freight Equalization Policy of 1956 which equalized prices of "essential" items like steel and coal nationwide, while prices of private-sector produced items (like textiles) were not controlled. The eastern region, the center of coal and steel production, was hardest hit.

The post-colonial economy's fundamental thrust was toward import substituting industrialization. In keeping with the dominant development paradigm of the time (see Harrod, 1948; Lewis, 1954; Domar, 1957), the emphasis was on industrialization-led economic growth, infant industry protection, and heavy state involvement in the ownership of key industrial infrastructure sectors like power generation, iron and steel, etc. (Ahluwalia, 1985). This heavy Fordist industry tended not to be located in the existing core cities (like Calcutta, Mumbai, Delhi, or Madras [now Chennai]), but in smaller urban areas, lower in the urban hierarchy (like Ahmedabad, Pune, etc.), or in newly created potential "growth centers" (like Durgapur, Raurkella, etc.)[7], or (in the case of small scale manufacturing) in the suburban industrial belts around the old colonial cities. The core cities continued to serve as centers of regional and/or national administration (with increasingly large bureaucracies in the public sector, and expanding offices of the private sector), trade and commerce, small scale industry, and services in general. That is, the economic functions of the colonial cities in general, and Calcutta in particular, did not fundamentally change after independence; they had largely been non-industrial and service oriented to begin with, and they continued to play these roles.

In Calcutta, however, unlike the other major cities in India, the hinterland remained generally unindustrialized (with the states of Bihar and Orissa at the bottom of every development index), and very little new industry moved into the agglomeration around the city. This situation was exacerbated by political developments from the early 1960s when centrist, leftist, and radical forces fought for control of the State.[8] Between 1967 and 1971 the State was in political turmoil, with a succession of coalition governments unable to bring order, and in a literally bloody fight the centrist and leftist forces combined to crush the radical, revolutionary movement (see Mallick, 1993). This period (1970–72) was also marked by a second large migration wave – this time of refugees from the newly formed Bangladesh, then at war with Pakistan.

The centrists (Congress Party) ruled with a massive majority till 1977, but were unable to stem the steady decline of the city, the State, or the region. From 1977 the leftists have been in power; they have concentrated their efforts on rural development, particularly in quite successful land redistribution policies (see Kohli, 1987). Calcutta in the meantime has faced what may be called benign neglect. The city and metropolis have seen capital flight to the west and north, the degradation of ageing infrastructure, a scramble for upper-middle class housing construction, and increasing corruption and inefficiency at all levels of municipal authority.

Liberalization and globalization: Calcutta reinvented

If the above description paints a gloomy picture of Calcutta and eastern India while the rest of the country was increasingly prosperous, it is incomplete. As the following account indicates, the overall accomplishments of the command economy were quite mixed:

Between 1950 and 1990, (Indian) national output increased 4.6 times, the volume of industrial output 12 times, food-grains production 3.5 times, pig iron and steel 10 times, electricity 43 times, motor vehicles 70 times . . . the crude death rate declined from 27 per thousand of population to 12, and infant mortality from 170 per thousand to 89 . . . life expectancy at birth increased from 41 to 61 years . . . However, on the flip side, the number of persons below subsistence level now equals the country's total population in 1951, and the number of job seekers has increased 100 times . . . about one third of the country suffers from malnutrition . . . 60 percent of the country's population does not have access to safe drinking water, 48 percent are illiterate . . . There is a clear trend of widening regional disparities . . . The ratio of per capita income (of Punjab to that of Bihar) has increased from 1.9 in 1960–61 to 3.4 in 1989–90 . . . the coefficient of variation (of per capita incomes) has increased from 0.22 in 1960–61 to 0.33 in 1988–89 . . . (Swamy, 1994, pp.18–21).

The figures above portray the dualistic nature of Indian development: industrial growth whose benefits have not trickled down, and at the same time have exacerbated regional imbalances. The figures also underline the notion that, starting from a very small industrial base at independence (one designed for colonial extraction), Indian industry has matured in some sectors. Nevertheless, India's economic performance has been much poorer than the NICs of East and Southeast Asia, and somewhat comparable nations like Brazil and China. There seemed to be general agreement that India was a "shackled giant," bound by a nexus of controls, subsidies, and licenses which led to a vicious cycle of stagnation, high cost, and inefficiency (Ahluwalia, 1985).

India had, in the past, sometimes been forced to "open the economy" when faced with serious balance of payments crises (Lal, 1995). But with the ascension of Rajiv Gandhi to the Prime-ministership in 1984 the beginnings of a hegemonic intellectual change appears to have taken place. Mr Gandhi's inclination to open India was clear, but had to be tempered to suit his party's populist mission and was eventually overtaken by an arms import scandal (see Corbridge, 1991; Kohli, 1987). There were important but small steps taken then. The reforms announced in July 1991, apparently triggered again by a foreign exchange crisis, went much further by making it easier for foreign capital to enter the country by largely removing entry barriers such as industrial licensing and equity participation limits. Foreign investment was welcomed in 31 high priority sectors, and in additional key infrastructure areas such as power, petroleum, telecommunication, air transport, ports and shipping.

When I first wrote this paper, in early 1996, the reforms seemed to have succeeded in breathing new life into the Indian economy. By 1995, four years after the initiation of reforms, foreign exchange reserves were at $20 billion, up from $1 billion at the time of crisis; industrial growth was up to 8 percent compared to 0.6 percent in 1991–92 (Government of India, 1995). The volume of the proposed investments (about Rs 4170 billion in early 1995) was about four times the size of the Indian budget: Rs 1122 billion for 1994–95.[9] But by late 1998 economic growth was at a standstill and it had become apparent that only a small proportion of the proposed new investments (especially foreign investments) were being implemented on the ground.

For West Bengal the liberalization process appeared to have been heaven-sent.[10] Of all the new investment *proposed* after the beginning of the structural reform process, almost 60 percent was concentrated in five states (Gujarat, Karnataka, Maharashtra, Tamil Nadu, and West Bengal), all leading urban states with large cities; whereas backward states like Bihar and Madhya Pradesh had less than one percent each. Gujarat appeared to be the leading investment magnet, with West Bengal a close second. But by 1998 a clearer picture has emerged: Gujarat is still by far the leading investment destination, but West Bengal is far behind – with less than 5 percent of the total *real* investment it is nowhere near the leading states. The picture is a little better as far as FDI is concerned, but only marginally so.[11] The spatial distribution of the new investment in West Bengal is also illuminating. About 35 percent of the small scale investment (up to $150 million each) is in the Calcutta metropolitan area; a substantial proportion of this investment is in the city in the service sector (office complexes, theme parks, transportation), and a large proportion is in manufacturing in the industrial suburbs. The bulk of both the small and large scale investments, however, are targeted for two ports (both south of the city and currently outside the area defined as the Calcutta Metropolitan Area): these are a new port at Kulpi (about 30 km from the city), and the industrial complex in Haldia (about 50 km. from the city). The latter with about a quarter of all small scale investments, and two-thirds of all large scale investments, is in the process of becoming a major industrial enclave.

Closer to the city two recent developments are noteworthy (for details see Chakravorty and Gupta, 1996). First, the Calcutta Metropolitan Development Authority (CMDA) is implementing the Government of India's Mega City Programme – Calcutta is one of five agglomerations (Mumbai, Chennai, Bangalore, and Hyderabad are the others) that are receiving special funding for the first time for infrastructure improvements. In keeping with the new liberalization philosophy, these new projects are to have significant cost recovery or surplus generation components. The CMDA, in response, has moved away from its acknowledged expertise in slum improvement to housing, new area development, and building commercial facilities.[12] Much of these new investments (estimated to be over 80 percent of the metropolitan total) are targeted to the city and its immediate surroundings, where it is clear that the city is congested and overbuilt, and has experienced serious out-migration over the preceding three decades.

The second development relates to the creation of new towns adjoining and to the east of Calcutta city. One of these, named New Calcutta (see Map 4.1), is designed to house 500,000 people (78 percent of whom will be middle- and upper-income earners), among high-technology oriented office complexes, and open spaces. Despite some environmental concerns – the designated area has considerable amounts of protected wetlands – work on the ground has begun despite some unexpected difficulties in land acquisition; the State Housing Board, which is now in charge of the project, expects to sell housing units from 2000.[13]

The Spatial Structure of Calcutta

The colonial city

At inception, the colonizers (then merely traders) sought to establish terms of trade favorable to the home country; later, after gaining complete territorial control, they used the colonized regions as sources of raw material to be processed in industrial England, and as captive markets for the processed products. The colonial city was a center of administration, a port, and an European residential enclave. This city's structure (as shown in Map 4.2) was deeply divided – the important spatial divide being that between the colonizers (living in high amenity, well serviced areas) and the natives (living in unplanned, congested, poorly serviced areas). Describing a model of the South Asian colonial city Dutt (1993, p. 361) writes:

The European town . . . had spacious bungalows, elegant apartment houses, planned streets, trees on both sides of the streets, . . . , clubs for afternoon and evening get-togethers . . . The open space was reserved for . . . Western recreational facilities, such as race and golf courses, soccer and cricket. When domestic water supply, electric connections, and sewage links were available or technically possible, the European town residents utilized them fully, whereas their use was quite restricted to the native town.

Calcutta city, then, started growing around an empty core (the fort and Maidan), with the English town growing south and south-west of Park Street (see Map 4.2), an area of Eurasian and mixed-marriage residences (i.e., an Anglo Indian enclave) immediately to its north, and the area further north and east being occupied by the natives (working as merchants and traders, and as clerks for the British administrative system). However, it would be wrong to presume that this spatial division by race and class was strictly enforced.[14] The first wave of poor migrants to the city did not come to work in factories (because none existed), but to service the lavish lifestyles of the British. They settled in small slums within the English town, "or how else could the rich get servants, cooks, darwans, chowkidars, cleaners, gardeners, dhobis and the rest? Labour was abundant and cheap and it paid to keep the slums within the city, in fact nearer the mansions" (Munshi, 1975, p. 111). Bardhan Roy (1994) argues that the domestic services were needed from early morning to late at night, and as a result the dwellings of the poorest could be seen within walking distance of most

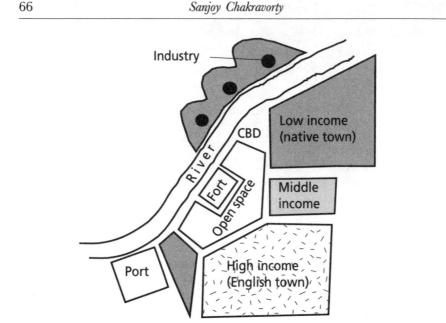

Map 4.2 The spatial structure of colonial Calcutta

luxurious areas of the city. I shall show later that this basic structure, created in the 18th century, still dominates the spatial pattern of work and home in the city.

The second wave of migrants came seeking employment in the engineering units and jute and textile mills that began west of the river from the middle of the 19th century, and to work for large transportation projects (Haora station in 1854, Sealdah station in 1856, the Calcutta tramways, and the Kidderpore docks). All of these activities (except the tramways) took place on the fringes of, or outside the city boundaries of the time; the new slum areas, as a result, began growing in these fringe areas.[15] Not surprisingly, the low income occupations were somewhat linguistically segregated: Bengalis in the clerical professions, Biharis as rickshaw pullers, porters, and factory labor, Oriyas in domestic service, and plumbing, gas, and electrical works. Their slums also tended to retain occupational and linguistic identities, as did Muslim slums (specializing in labor for soap and leather factories on the eastern and southern fringes). This structure within the city was replicated in miniature in the riverside industrial suburbs; these had small high-amenity areas (large estates as living space during the work-week for the British owners and managers), surrounded by a small middle-income area, and low income areas where the factory labor lived.

The post-colonial city

With the achievement of independence in 1947, the spatial divisions of the colonial city (demarcated by class and race barriers) were largely retained, with the native upper class (capital and land owners, political leaders and top government officials) now occupying the privileged space once reserved for the colonizers. The refugee inflow from East Pakistan, however, introduced an unexpected spatial twist. As Goswami (1990, p. 92) writes:

The influx of refugees really brought the city's elite face-to-face with the urban problems that were brewing for a long time. In the first place, unlike previous migrants, who were clearly subalterns, the typical displaced families were vocal and considered it a political right to be gainfully re-settled in the city. They belonged to the same culture background as the city's intelligentsia, and demanded to be heard. Second, they settled in areas that were perilously close to affluent South Calcutta neighborhoods: Behala and Chetla bordered Alipur, Kasba and Dhakuria were just next to Baligunj and Gariahat, Jadabpur was not too far from the mansions of Southern Avenue, and the brown and white sahibs could no longer go to play golf without seeing the slums in Tollygunj. The new urban poor could not be put out of sight in the unmentionable parts of north Calcutta.[16]

The inherited (colonial) space was divided into quarters, or ghettoes: British, mixed-race, and native town bordering the center (with slums interspersed in every quarter). The new (post-colonial) space retained much of this inheritance with the race divisions being replaced by class divisions. In addition, population pressure forced the city to grow outward, with the farthest areas being occupied by the low income population. As depicted in Map 4.3, the quartered structure of the colonial city was replaced by concentric half-circles, with income declining with distance from the center. However, as also suggested in Map 4.3, the area north of the empty core is missing the middle-income ring. This area, adjacent to the CBD and Burrabazaar (a large wholesale market), was the native town during the colonial period; its infrastructure deficiencies have increased over time, and the absence of planning and investment here is evident in its congested lanes and by-lanes, open drainage, and generally miserable living conditions. As expected, this area (north Calcutta) does not house the elite or the upper income population.[17]

The spatial distribution of the low income population at two time periods (1965 and 1983) is shown in Maps 4.4 and 4.5. In general, the two maps are similar – the significant difference is in the proliferation of slum areas in the far south (Jadabpur) in the latter period. This is not surprising, since as suggested earlier, north Calcutta has been completely congested for some time; any growth in poor areas has had to take place in the south (which is also a refugee stronghold, and a bastion of leftist politics). Two additional points should be noted: first, many slums have located on the least desirable

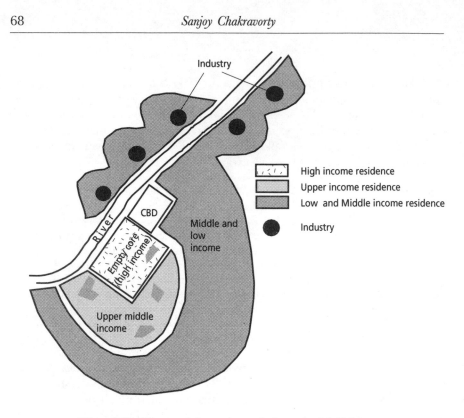

Map 4.3 The spatial structure of post-colonial Calcutta

public land (along railway tracks, and open sewerage and drainage lines); and second, the location of Calcutta's poorest, its pavement dwellers (or homeless population), is in many ways the opposite of that of the slum population. An extensive survey of the pavement dwellers was done in 1971 during the Census of India. This survey, and one carried out by the CMDA in 1987 found about 50–55,000 homeless persons in the city, and about four times that number in the metropolis (Mukherjee and Racine, 1986; Bandyopadhyay, 1990). The city homeless were (and still are) concentrated in the CBD, Burrabazaar, and Chowrangee, and are also found in the high income areas of Park Street and Alipur. As expected, there are few pavement dwellers in the slums.[18]

Some residential segregation by occupation, religion, caste, and ethnicity continued into the post-colonial period. Two points should be noted in this regard. First, the ghettoes are not large (i.e., unlike in the United States where the black population in cities like Detroit and Philadelphia is concentrated in large contiguous areas). For instance, one can find (in east Calcutta)

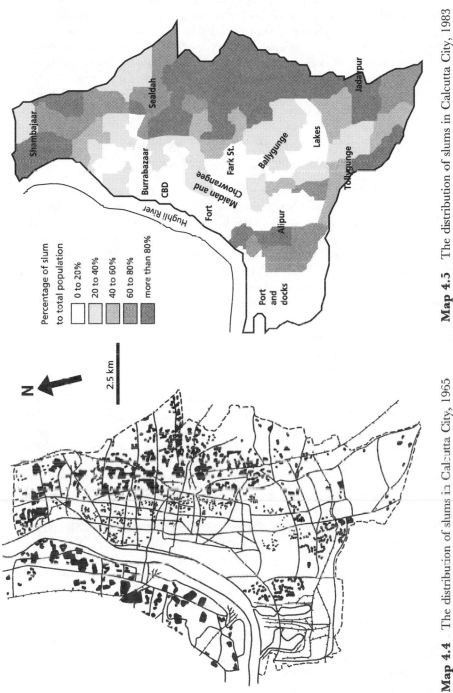

Map 4.4 The distribution of slums in Calcutta City, 1965 **Map 4.5** The distribution of slums in Calcutta City, 1983

Source: Map 4.4 Adapted from Basic Development Plan, CMPO, 1966; Map 4.5 Adapted from CMDA Bustee Improvement Sector Document in Bardhan Roy, 1994

Percentage of slum to total population

- 0 to 20%
- 20 to 40%
- 40 to 60%
- 60 to 80%
- more than 80%

N

2.5 km

Shambajaar

Sealdah

Jadavpur

Burrabazaar

CBD

Fort

Park St.

Maidan and Chowrangee

Ballygunge

Lakes

Alipur

Tollygunge

Port and docks

Hughli River

a low caste Hindu leather-worker bustee of say 15,000 people adjacent to an equally large Muslim leather-worker or tailor bustee. Second, this pattern of spatial separation is not confined to the poor: the business elite, which is generally non-Bengali, occupies the center; of special interest are the Marwaris (a group of very prosperous entrepreneurs from Rajasthan) who tend to live in enclaves in the Burrabazaar and Park Street areas. Professional South Indians tend to reside around the Lakes, and professional Bengalis live in south Calcutta.

The post-reform city

India's structural reform is a relatively recent event. Some spatial changes in the seven post-reform years are noticeable, but, at this moment, it is difficult to foresee the post-reform spatial structure with certainty. First, there is no guarantee that the reform process will continue in its present form, though it increasingly seems that a significant change has taken place in a society traditionally slow to change. The aftermath of the 1996 and 1998 elections suggest that regardless of the ideology of the group in power, the reforms will continue, and that it may be impossible to return to the centralized nation-alist development ideology of the recent past. Second, our singular interest in economic outcomes in spatial terms may blind us to a perhaps more signifi-cant transformation in Indian society, where there is increasing (and more acceptable) social, cultural, and technological polarization.[19] The reforms are significant (just as independence was) in more than economic terms. It has raised a number of unresolved intellectual and political questions about na-tionalism, regionalism, governance, decentralization, inequality, and secular-ism. The resolution of these questions may influence the spatial structure of urban society as deeply as do the economic actions of domestic and global actors. Therefore, given the absence of structural stability, and the lack of hard data for the post-reform period, I have to rely on declared intentions and plans, and my often idiosyncratic personal observations to formulate the following speculative analysis.

The most significant new spatial component of the reforms in Calcutta are its new town projects, particularly New Calcutta (see Map 4.1). New Town projects in the Calcutta metropolis have a long history. In the late 1960s, following the recommendations of the Basic Development plan, one was created at Kalyani (see Map 4.1) at great expense and to resounding failure. Kalyani was a planned city where the state government would have re-located, but for the fact that the government employees refused to move. The city still has paved streets overgrown with weeds, and street lamps that were never lit – a perfect example of a planning disaster. Salt Lake, a new town closer to the city, was begun in the mid 1970s. This upper-income enclave is considered successful – it has a population of around 150,000 now, and is expected to grow to 250,000. Salt Lake has no slums; its residents' biggest and most persistent complaint concerns the difficulty of obtaining affordable and reliable domestic servants (the old bourgeois complaint that "good help is so hard to find"). Many state government offices have relocated to the Salt Lake township (the Chief Minister has moved his residence there from south Calcutta), and many of the region's electronic production units are also located there.

New Calcutta can be expected to be successful for the same reasons that Salt Lake has been successful: it is close enough to Calcutta city for a relatively easy commute (for employment or services), and as a planned development it will bypass the city's ills — poor infrastructure, slums, and poverty. This new town will have 100,000 dwelling units (spread over 8.4 sq. km.), 1.5 sq. km. for a new business district and commercial complexes, 2.2 sq. km. for "modern, pollution free industries", and 13.1 sq. km. of water bodies and green areas (including a golf course).[20] A strong selling point of this new town is to be its proximity to Calcutta's recently expanded international airport — clearly the planners want this development to contain new (rather than relocated) industry, of the type that is high-tech and/or global in nature.

Can New Calcutta succeed without slums, or will its success depend on its ability to keep out slums? I believe that the answer to this question will partly lie in the degree of capital-labor substitution in the sphere of domestic production. Day (1992) discusses the capital-labor relationship in an analysis of housework in north America in the 20th century. She argues for a progressive model in which increasing industrialization led to higher wages, more women in the work force, and the availability of domestic appliances like the range, refrigerator, washer, dryer, and vacuum cleaner. As the supply of servants (usually recent immigrant women) fell, the wealthiest households continued to hire servants, but the middle-income groups did without, and substituted capital for labor. In India, the most visible signs of liberalization are colas, fast food, and domestic appliances — specifically the washer, dryer, and microwave oven (the refrigerator has been around for some time, and the vacuum cleaner is available, but generally considered unnecessary). New Calcutta is clearly designed for professional upper-income earners, the group most likely to adopt these household labor saving devices. If that happens, New Calcutta will look like a "modern" city, what is sometimes called a postmodern city in the US context (Charlotte, NC, for example) — clean, spacious, and free of visible poverty.[21]

A second major development is the growth of heavy industrial investment in Haldia (about 50 straight km. from Calcutta), and the so-far less successful Falta Export Processing Zone located between the two. As of July 1998 expected capital investments (largely in petrochemicals) in this port-city was about $4 billion (my calculations). If expectations are met, and it seems likely that they will be, Haldia will become a rather large industrial city.[22] This city appears to be modeled after the Fordist growth centers like Durgapur and Bhilai, which, revealingly, are made up of "colonies" named after specific corporations; e.g., AVB colony, MAMC colony. That is, like most other planned developments in India, the city design will keep the informal sector and the poor spatially separated from the middle- and upper-income formal sector workers. As argued above, keeping the poor out may now be technologically feasible, but separating the dynamic and essential informal sector may be the seed of failure as a growth center, even if Haldia succeeds as an industrial enclave.

Where Does the Calcutta Story Fit?

Calcutta's spatial structure cannot be separated from its political-economic history. This history has been influenced strongly by global and local events. On the one hand, Calcutta's genesis and early morphology was defined by the global force of colonialism: "chance selected, chance directed" the city grew as a center of colonial exchange and administration in inhospitable urban terrain – a silting river, salt marshes all around it, unstable soils unable to carry heavy loads, in a very poor rice-growing hinterland. It never acquired a strong industrial base; its predominant industrial commodity, jute, was made technologically obsolete not long into this century, and the city's global trading links withered with the downfall of its primary product. On the other hand, the more influential events of the 20th century, as far as the city is concerned, have been local or regional in character. While independence may be viewed as a global event (the end of the colonial system), the impact on Calcutta was in its lost hinterland, and the flood of refugees. In this Calcutta is different from even the other comparable Indian colonial cities, Mumbai and Chennai, not to speak of colonial cities worldwide. Thereafter local politics, policies and events (Freight Equalization, communist infighting, the refugee influx from the independence of Bangladesh) have held center-stage.

Now the city has been reintroduced, willy-nilly, to the global system of production and exchange. The question raised here is what will happen, or is happening, to the internal structure of the city as a result of its *re*integration into the global economy. I believe that the answer will depend substantially on the degree of integration of the local economy in the global market. It appears unlikely that Calcutta will soon become a "world city" in Hall's (1966) terms, or that it is on the way to becoming a "global city" in Sassen's (1994) terms; that is, one cannot expect Calcutta to become either a global center of production (aircraft, ships, military hardware) or services (banking, insurance). The declared goals of the state's leaders are more modest – to become a center of large scale production of petrochemicals, leather, pharmaceutical, metallurgical, and engineering items within the Southeast Asia region, and to compete globally in the electronics field (mainly computer software and hardware). The local state wants to evenly distribute the location of production facilities, but clearly expects such units to converge around the infrastructure advantages in and around Calcutta (in Haldia, Falta EPZ, Kulpi, and the city's industrial suburbs).[23]

There are several possible spatial outcomes. First, the city and state may utterly fail to integrate in the global economy ("a loser city"); this may imply spatial status quo and possibly increasingly miserable conditions for the city's poor. At the moment of writing this appears to be the outcome for the foreseeable future. Second, both goals (in the Fordist manufacturing and post-Fordist service arenas) may be successfully realized, leading to a spatial scenario as outlined in Map 4.6: high-tech, high-income planned enclaves on the eastern edge of the city, and planned industrial enclaves further south, resulting in the creation of a considerably larger agglomerative field, or metro-region. Intermediate outcomes are also possible, whereby the city succeeds as a center of Fordist production, but fails in post-Fordist terms, or vice versa. (Truth be told, my feeling is that the city would rather be a Fordist

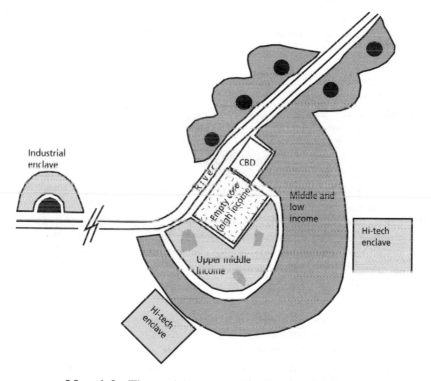

Map 4.6 The spatial structure of post-reform Calcutta

success, if it could choose only one area of success.) And, given the city's history as a refugee haven, one should not rule out the possibility of events beyond the control of the local state (like war, famine, and natural disaster). Remember that Calcutta is the city of last resort for a largely rural population of over 300 million people (including Bangladesh). Through all these possibilities, except the disaster scenarios, the core city is unlikely to change much in terms of the spatial distribution of wealth and poverty.

Does the Calcutta story fit a model? I am not sure. The city is quite different from its colonial counterparts – the more segregated, hierarchical, monolingual Chennai, or the dynamic, polyglot, recently chauvinistic Mumbai. Calcutta's leftist political leaders do not demolish bustees in high income areas (though, in a desperate move to clean up the city's image they have started conducting street sweeps to round up pavement hawkers – a fascinating story in itself). [24] The city has the reputation of being more hospitable to refugees and migrants than any other in India. The Hindu-Sikh and Hindu-Muslim riots of the 1980s and early 1990s barely touched the city. Perhaps globalization will change all that, with increased hardening of spatial boundaries between income, language, caste, and religious groups. Certainly the bourgeois planning apparatus has worked and continues to work for the benefit of the upper classes. If the liberalization process continues, and is accompanied by a larger role for urban planning (as in planned developments in New Calcutta and Haldia), and the adoption of labor saving household devices, one could see increased spatial separation between rich and poor in the new enclaves. Barring a dramatic economic turnaround, however, the city proper is likely to retain much of its present structure – perhaps not quite unique, but certainly one that cannot easily be fit into a model.

Notes

1   The author would like to thank the American Institute of Indian Studies for funding the fieldwork that led to this paper.

2   Salman Rushdie (1991, p. 11) writes about the Bombay (now Mumbai) of his childhood, splattered with advertisements for foreign products. He also writes of the very popular Hindi film song of the time, sung by Mr. Raj Kapoor, the everyman hero. Rushdie translates the song ("Mera joota hai Japani.." in Hindi) as follows:

O, my shoes are Japanese
These trousers English, if you please
On my head, red Russian hat –
My heart's Indian for all that.

Indeed, colonialism's "gift" to India (especially Indian cities) was the foreign brand name (Unilever, IBM, Shell, Goodyear, and, of course, Coca-Cola).

3 Before the 1985 civic elections the municipality of Calcutta was expanded to include the units of Jadabpur, South Suburban, and Garden Reach (shown in Map 4.1). The number of wards in the city increased from 100 to 144, and the population increased by about 1 million.

4 Estimates of Calcutta's population during this period are available in Mitra (1990): 10,000 in 1701; 140,000 in 1801; and 950,000 in 1901.

5 It is interesting to note that Calcutta was not the first colonial establishment in the region. Some municipalities which are currently in the suburbs actually predated the establishment of Calcutta. For instance Chinsurah, Hughli, and Chandannagore were outposts of Portuguese, Dutch, and French traders respectively, established before Job Charnok's Calcutta lease, but were eventually brought under British authority.

6 These industries often had Indian nationals in senior management positions, but capital ownership was almost exclusively in the hands of British nationals or Anglo-Indians. Mitra (1990, p. 114) argues that "this exclusive monopoly of European capital in Calcutta continued till 1947."

7 There were two primary reasons for this spatial pattern of investments. One, regional inequality was perceived as a serious threat to the Indian multi-language and multi-religion polity; decentralizing industry out of the core metropolitan regions into growth centers near raw material sources was argued to be efficient and equitable. Two, the core metropolitan regions were already perceived to be congested and unmanageable; any more investment in these regions would exacerbate the problems of visible concentrated poverty and congestion-created inefficiency.

8 The centrist force was the Congress Party, the leader of India's freedom struggle, and the party in power at the State and Central government. The leftist force, the Communist Party of India (Marxist) or CPM, has been the party in power in the State since 1977. The radical force, the Naxalites, were exterminated in urban areas, but sporadically resurface with actions in rural areas.

9 In August 1998 US $1 = Rs 42 (approximately).

10 The leftist government in West Bengal was initially skeptical and resistant to liberalization. However, since mid- 1994, it has revamped its industrial policy, brought in a high profile Member of Parliament to head its Industrial Development Corporation, sent the Chief Minister on investment seeking visits to Europe and North America, and helped repeal the Freight Equalization Policy.

11 These data have been taken from my ongoing research into the spatial distribution of new investment in India. The preliminary findings are in a working paper (Chakravorty, 1998). The source of the raw data is the Center for Monitoring the Indian Economy.

12 Slum (or bustee) improvement had been a significant success story of the CMDA (Pugh, 1989). In earlier development plans it had spent up to 25 percent of its budget on slum improvement, with less than 14 percent spent on housing etc. Under the Mega City Programme slum improvement is budgeted about 1.7 percent, while housing, new area development, and commercial facilities are budgeted over 46 percent.

13 Another new town, this one named Second Calcutta, on the south-eastern border of the city, is being shepherded by the minister for Urban Development.

This project appears to be a non-starter: the area chosen is too large, and the environmental problems are more serious than in New Calcutta.

14   It is interesting to note that high-level recommendations to formally recognize this three-fold division of the city were made twice: by the Chief Magistrate in 1833, and later by Baron Dowlean in 1860 (Munshi, 1986 and Banerjee, 1986).

15   The term 'bustee' is often used interchangeably with slum. Bandyopadhyay (1990, p. 86) points out that there are legal differences between the terms. A slum is an area with "conditions injurious to public health or safety . . . "; a bustee, on the other hand is defined by the physical nature and dimensions of contiguous dwelling structures. Generally, a bustee is an inferior slum. There are at least 2,000 bustees in Calcutta city, and in the metropolitan area the total bustee population was estimated to be 3 million.

16   See Maps 4.1 and 4.4 to locate most of the neighborhoods mentioned here. The Lakes in the figure is the upper income "Southern Avenue" area. Baligunj is Ballygunje and so on. I have used more current, phonetic spellings for place names throughout this document: Haora instead of Howrah, Hughli instead of Hooghly, etc.

17   North Calcutta does include some impressive mansions: Rabindranath Tagore's house and the Marble Palace, for example. These are remnants of an era when some native elites preferred, for political reasons, not to settle in the English town.

18   The pavement dwellers tend to be the most recent migrants (over 65 percent had moved to the city in the last six years) with the lowest skill levels (about 45 percent are beggars or casual-day laborers). They are not refugees, but tend to be villagers from the agricultural hinterland (see Mukherjee, 1975). These, the truly disadvantaged, lack the resources to even be slum dwellers in Calcutta.

19   There is a long standing (and some argue, false) dichotomy in India. *Bharat* (which is the native name for the country) is the "real" country and lives in its villages; *India* is its "foreign" element, residing in its cities. This view was/is held by many influential people, including the late Prime Minister Charan Singh.

20   These figures are taken from New Calcutta promotional literature and media.

21   The provision of 7,000 housing units in "service villages" in New Calcutta raises interesting questions. The Minister of Housing explained to me that these would house the displaced persons; it is possible, though, that some mini-slums are being thoughtfully incorporated, to avoid the "servant problem" of Salt Lake.

22   Here one finds interesting parallels with spatial restructuring in Sao Paulo, Brazil. Diniz (1994) and Storper (1991) have argued that despite "polarization reversal" within the state of Sao Paulo (using conventional definitions of the metropolis), an "agglomerative field" of around 150 kms. around the city is the dominant growth region in the country. That is, an expanded definition of the metropolis would show continued polarization of industry and population into it.

23   The information in this paragraph is culled from the state's Industrial Policy Statement of September, 1994, and promotional literature published by the West Bengal Industrial Development Corporation. The industrial location incentives offered by the state favor the backward, unindustrialized districts, but

the investment response, as shown earlier, is heavily lopsided toward south Bengal.

24 British Prime Minister John Major's January 1997 visit to the city prompted these unexpected street sweeps. The left leaders went against their decades-old reluctance to evict unlicensed hawkers and pedlars so as to show Mr Major a clean and efficient city, worthy of British investment. In a surprising twist, some of the prime movers of the sweeps have suffered embarrassing defeats in local intra-party elections. The story continues.

5

Rio de Janeiro: Emerging Dualization in a Historically Unequal City

Luiz Cesar de Queiroz Ribeiro and Edward E. Telles

Rio de Janeiro's elites are preparing the city to "enter a new era of competitiveness". They seek to direct investments to economic sectors that offer comparative advantages for world capital while constructing images showing the world that the Rio of violence and environmental degradation is a thing of the past (Prefeitura de Rio de Janeiro, 1995). However, the insertion of Brazil in global markets appears to increasingly subordinate it to the interest of world financial circuits and promote the loss of the state's capacity to control its own development. In a country noted for large scale social inequalities, capitalist development has been unable to integrate much of the Brazilian population and Rio's dominant classes have been incapable of creating a socially integrative project. Based on the new economic model, social fragmentation is likely to increase yet further.

Ironically, the current elite discourse for transforming Rio de Janeiro is similar to that at the turn of the century. The elite of the then largest city and capital of Brazil sought to show the world that the era of Rio as the city of disease was surpassed. Rio's iron-fisted Mayor, Pereira Passos, with the support of the federal government, led an urban reform campaign that consisted essentially of designing a center in the image of European cities and razing the downtown tenement buildings. This led to the consolidation of the now infamous favelas (shantytowns) as the new urban project displaced poor residents to distant suburbs and to the surrounding hillsides. In those "euphoric years of reform", the new urban elite, raised during the transition from a slave-export to a speculative economy, excluded the masses of its poor residents, mostly of African origin, from its urban project. Lacking a domestic model, they would construct the symbols of their class identity based on the cosmopolitan elites of European cities. For Rio's elites, the urban majority mattered only to the extent that it symbolized resistance to the project of bringing Rio de Janeiro into the international and civilized urban order.

Fortunately, Rio de Janeiro would experience rapid industrialization and economic growth from about 1945 to 1980, allowing unprecedented social inclusion and mobility. These decades would also transform Brazil from a rural export society to a complex urban industrial one. By the late 1970s, however, Rio de Janeiro would resume its earlier tendency to dualization, having entered a period of regressive deindustrialization.

Today, city elites enthusiastically announce a new phase of insertion into the global economy. However, the fate of the city and its people, when this finally occurs, is unclear. Will the city consolidate and further deepen its historical tendency toward dualization? Will Rio's economy and society be inexorably subordinated to global dynamics, making any of its own developmental projects untenable?

Industrialization and Urbanization

During the industrialization period, Brazil established a strong domestic market, resulting in a complex territorial division of labor and an integrated, dynamic urban network. Unlike most Latin American countries, where the largest city was far larger than the others, Brazil had 14 cities with populations over one million by 1980.

The expansion of the labor market created a large supply of urban jobs and the economically active population became an increasingly wage-earning one. Indeed, the dynamism of Brazilian industrialization meant that the 2.5 million wage jobs in 1950 (36 percent of the non-agricultural economically active population and 15 percent of the total economically active population) increased to almost 12 million by 1980 (40 percent of the non-agricultural economically active population and 28 percent of the total economically active population). Such dynamism allowed for a social process with a reasonable degree of occupational mobility and integration into urban industrial living, despite high and increasing income concentration.

Another dimension of the integration and mobility of Brazilian urbanization was the expansion of "home-owning". In metropolitan areas, less than 30 percent of households owned their homes and 64 percent rented in 1940. By 1980, these figures had changed to 57 percent and 34 percent respectively (the remainder refers to a category that refers to housing that is loaned or granted). Home ownership clearly represented the expansion of minimum citizens' rights in both real and symbolic terms. Home ownership allowed for access to consumer credit and the establishment of stable ties of sociability, which became the basis for establishing legitimate collective claims on urban services.

Yet, despite this integration and mobility, a vast, unstable, and heterogeneous contingent of poor urban workers would barely survive by working in informal sector jobs. The economic and social crisis of the 1980s greatly increased the size of the vulnerable population, although the potentially devastating effects were attenuated by a decrease in population growth, urban deconcentration, and a reorientation of social policy. Nonetheless, a portion of the urban population began to circulate from vulnerability to social exclusion. Whereas vulnerability refers to poverty and increasing job insecurity, signifying partial disconnection from employment, social exclusion meant complete isolation from the world of work.

Regressive Deindustrialization

The Brazilian economic crisis of the 1980s had actually begun in the 1970s in Rio de Janeiro with the deindustrialization of key sectors like steel and shipbuilding (Sulamis, 1990). Rio had never been able to attract the consumer goods sectors which led to the dynamic industrialization and strong local markets of São Paulo, which overtook Rio de Janeiro as Brazil's largest city in the 1950s. Rather, the economy of Rio had been dependent on the local tertiary sector, comprised of a small modern segment (finance, computers, commerce) and a large personal services sector.

Brazil's structural monetary adjustment policies beginning in the late 1980s have also had particularly dramatic consequences for Rio de Janeiro by reducing both the size of the public sector, which had employed about one million local workers, and real wages in the effort to control hyperinflation. Table 5.1 demonstrates Rio's declining economic dynamism during the period of deindustrialization. Growth is in traditional service sectors, marked by their low productivity and informality, and to a smaller extent, in the modern service sectors. (Note that these sectors are as indicated in Census publications. Personal services includes those that are not included under street peddling or household services).

Table 5.2 shows further evidence of the regressive effects of deindustrialization in Rio de Janeiro in the decrease of the proportions of salaried workers and the growth of the self-employed and the loss of public sector employees. The large majority of the self-employed are manual workers whereas only a small minority are professional consultants.

Table 5.1 Percent of employed persons in Rio de Janeiro by economic sector, 1981, 1990 and percent change

Sector	1981	1990	Percent Change
Manufacturing	20.7	19.3	− 6.8
Construction	7.7	5.4	− 29.9
Other Industrial Activities	2.4	2.0	− 20.0
Services and Trade	69.3	73.1	5.5
Street Peddling	2.8	3.6	28.6
Formal Trade	10.0	11.7	17.0
Household Services	8.6	7.4	− 14.0
Personal Services	14.4	17.9	24.3
Professional Services	6.9	7.2	4.3
Public Administration	9.6	6.1	− 9.7
Social Services	12.5	11.7	15.8

Source: Census of Brazil

Table 5.2 Distribution of employed population by position: Rio de Janeiro 1981 and 1990

	1981	1990
Employers	3.7	4.3
Employees	58.8	56.7
Public Employees	12.4	11.2
Self-Employed	15.5	19.5
Household Workers	8.8	7.5
Unremunerated	0.7	0.7

Source: Census of Brazil

Metropolitan Deconcentration and Socio-Spatial Polarization

The Rio de Janeiro metropolitan area is comprised of 9.7 million persons spread across 1255 sq. kms and 17 municipalities. Sixty percent of the metropolitan area population is in the city of Rio de Janeiro. Annual population growth rates in the metropolitan area have been steadily increasing since 1872, the year of the first Brazilian census, until the 1970s. Because of Brazil's rapid fertility decline and Rio's deindustrialization, the Rio metropolitan area grew only 1.1 percent between 1980 and 1991, the lowest population growth rate in Brazil. This is partly accounted for by the net out-migration of 580,000 persons, most of which went to medium sized cities in the state of Rio de Janeiro.

Decentralization of the metropolitan area also continued between 1970 and 1991, as the share of metropolitan area residents in the city of Rio de Janeiro went from 60.9 to 55.9 percent. Also, by 1991 Rio de Janeiro had the lowest fertility rate of all Brazilian states at just above replacement levels (Camarano, 1997). The outermost ring of suburbs grew the most during this period.

Maps 5.1, 5.2 and 5.3 show that the poor, the less schooled and non-whites are concentrated in the periphery. For example, the population of the Baixada Fluminense, the most populated and established municipality in the periphery, has low levels of schooling, is mostly poor, is largely illiterate and is roughly 60 percent non-white. By contrast, the central city is mostly non-poor, has almost no illiterates and is 80 percent white. The presence of a poor non-white population in the Center is largely accounted for by the favela population, which cannot be distinguished spatially with available data. Today, the Rio de Janeiro favela population is scattered throughout the metropolitan area and is estimated at 1.2 million or about 18 percent. Elites and the middle classes have congregated in the South Zone, known for beachfront communities like Copacabana, Ipanema and Leblon.

During the 1980–91 period, income concentration also increased. Nationally, Brazil gained the title of world champion in income inequality and Rio was emblematic of this (World Bank, 1997). While the poorest 50 percent of the economically active population in the metropolitan area had their share of total income reduced from 14.6 percent in 1981 to 12.8 percent in 1990, the richest ten percent increased their share from 46.5 percent to 48.6 percent. The percentage of employed persons earning less than one minimum salary increased from 17.7 to 21.3 percent in the Rio de Janeiro metropolitan areas while it remained stable at about 10 percent for the two periods in the São Paulo metropolitan area (Saboia, 1994).

Spatially, income also became more concentrated. By 1991, nine percent of the total number of families and 11 percent of the state's (metro area) population that resided in the center (Zona Sul/Niteroi) earned about 31 percent of total family income. Table 5.3 shows that although the percentage of poor persons increased throughout the city, the poor population in five of the seven districts in the outer rings increased more than the poor population in the center. However, income concentration in the center decreased during the period. The portion of all income earned for the metropolitan area of Rio de Janeiro by the center decreased. This seems to be the result of an increasing centralization of the very poor population.

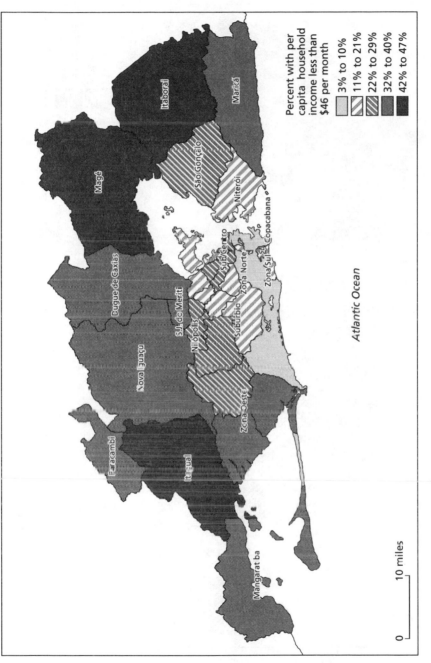

Map 5.1 Per capita income above $46 per month by district, metropolitan region of Rio de Janeiro, 1990
Source: IBGE, PNAD, 1991

Percent with per capita household income less than $46 per month

3% to 10%
11% to 21%
22% to 29%
32% to 40%
42% to 47%

Itaboraí
Maricá
São Gonçalo
Niterói
Copacabana
Magé
Duque de Caxias
Sub Centro
Zona Norte
Zona Sul
S.J. del Meriti
Nilópolis
Subúrbio
Nova Iguaçu
Zona Oeste
Paracambi
Itaguaí
Mangaratiba

Atlantic Ocean

0   10 miles

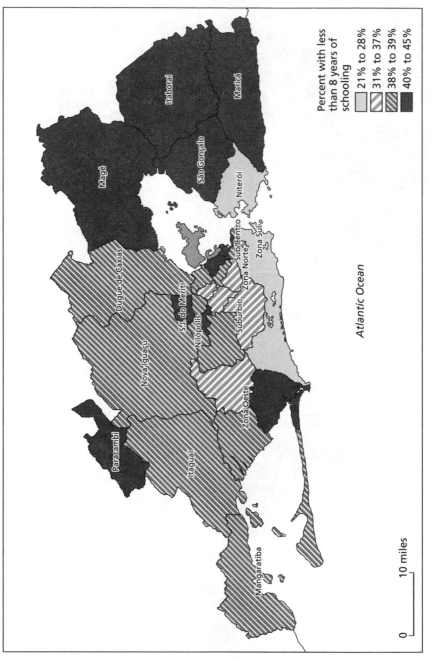

Map 5.2 Illiteracy by district, metropolitan region of Rio de Janeiro, 1990
Source: IBGE, PNAD, 1990

Percent with less than 8 years of schooling

- 21% to 28%
- 31% to 37%
- 38% to 39%
- 40% to 45%

Atlantic Ocean

Itaboraí

Maricá

Magé

São Gonçalo

Niterói

Duque de Caxias

Sub/Centro

Zona Sul

Zona Norte

S.J. do Meriti

Nilópolis

Subúrbio

Nova Iguaçu

Zona Oeste

Paracambi

Itaguaí

Mangaratiba

0   10 miles

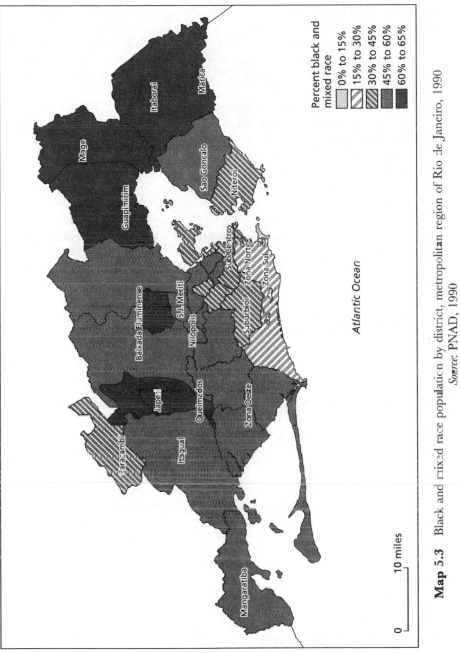

Percent black and mixed race

	0% to 15%
	15% to 30%
	30% to 45%
	45% to 60%
	60% to 65%

Itaboraí

Maricá

Magé

São Gonçalo

Niterói

Guapimirim

Sub-Centro

Zona Norte

Zona Sul

Baixada Fluminense

S.J. Meriti

Nilópolis

Suburbio I

Japeri

Queimados

Zona Oeste

Itaguaí

Paracambi

Mangaratiba

Atlantic Ocean

0   10 miles

Map 5.3 Black and mixed race population by district, metropolitan region of Rio de Janeiro, 1990

Source: PNAD, 1990

The very poor population (third column of Table 5.3) grew throughout the region but their much higher growth rates than for the poor overall in the Center suggests increasing polarization between the middle class and the indigent population in that area. Thus, spatial income concentration over the decade of regressive deindustrialization was characterized by a peripheralization of poverty along with increasing indigence in the traditionally elite city center.

Rio's favelas tend to be favored by persons without regular income precisely because of their proximity to the income sources in the central city, generally in irregular personal services work. Figure 5.1 shows that in the 1980s the favela population increased for the first time since at least 1950, despite continuing reductions in the overall rate of population growth. This is consistent with decreases in income and salaried employment during the period, suggesting that the prospect of even the most meager income attracted persons from more regular housing in the periphery to central city favelas. This factor is likely to have accounted for the greater polarization of the city center. The spatial proximity of the two ends of the social structure, coupled with middle class fear of the poor, has led to new form of social segregation in residence and leisure, exemplified by walled communities, streets patrolled by private police, shopping centers and residential enclaves.

Large Brazilian real estate companies have also intensified central city polarization, transforming the South Zone into an exclusive citadel, fortified by Rio's steep hills and an ominous public and private police presence. The

Table 5.3 Change in percent of Rio de Janeiro income earned by district and percent of poor and very poor population by district from 1980 to 1991

	Change % of income	% Poor	% Very Poor
Center (South Zone/Niteroi)	− 6.6	8.6	46.7
Ring 1:			
North Zone	− 9.5	1.6	31.8
Suburb District 1	3.3	19.4	26.4
Suburb District 2	5.7	9.5	89.9
Ring 2:			
West Zone	10.9	3.7	− 3.7
Nova Iguaçu	2.0	32.2	49.4
Baixada Fluminense	− 3.8	16.6	6.6
Ring 3 (SUBURB Municipalities)	7.8	12.0	24.8

Source: 1980 Census of Brazil

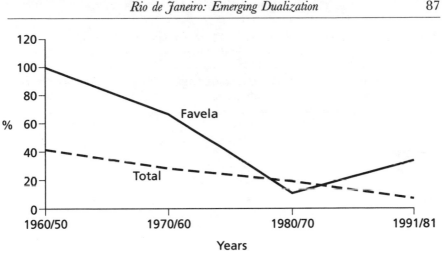

Figure 5.1 Percent growth between Census periods of total and favela population in the city of Rio de Janeiro, 1950–1991
Source: IPLAN RIO

termination of the housing finance system in the 1970s, the reduced income
of workers, and upper middle class desires to live in exclusive zones has
made elite housing by far the most viable sector of the real estate market
(Ribeiro and Cardoso, 1996)

The Role of Race

Brazilian blacks and mixed race persons number 70 million and constitute
the second largest African-origin population in the world, only after Nigeria.
Of the national population, the proportion identified as mixed race is
42 percent while blacks comprises 5 percent. Rio de Janeiro has a roughly
similar composition by color or race. Rio de Janeiro brings the race and class
divisions of Brazilian society into sharp relief because of substantial racial
inequality along with well-defined socio-spatial distinctions. Table 5.4 shows
that half (50.8 percent) of the poorest two-fifths (38.8 percent of its population) is of African origin (black and mixed race) compared to only five percent of the richest 6.7 percent. Thus, the poor in Rio de Janeiro are multiracial
while the middle-class is nearly all white. Notably, race is based on both
interviewer and self-classification in Brazil (Telles and Lim, 1998).

Compared to US cities like Chicago and Detroit where racial residential
segregation is extreme, segregation in Brazilian cities is moderate. Table 5.5
shows overall racial dissimilarity, the traditional segregation index, of 37

Table 5.4 Percent of non-white households by income and distribution of household income for population of Rio de Janeiro metropolitan area: 1980

Monthly dollar Household income	% of households with nonwhite heads	% income distribution of all households
1–225	50.8	38.8
225–375	42.6	22.2
375–750	31.0	21.2
750–1500	15.1	11.1
1500+	5.1	6.7
Total	37.8	100.0

Source: 1980 Census of Brazil

compared to much higher scores in the 1970s and 1980s for many large US cities. However, this index may underestimate the sense of segregation from the perspective of individuals, captured by the isolation index or the extent to which the African-origin population lives among itself. An isolation index of 50 for Rio de Janeiro means that 50 percent of neighbors for the average African-origin person are also non-white. This is similar to major US cities. Finally, the 1991 Census showed that 71 percent of favela residents were non-white. Thus the brown and black population is more likely to reside in favelas than poor whites.

The data on race in Brazil may underestimate racial segregation. A substantial number of low status persons that self-classify as white, which is the method by which the Census presumably collects race data, are perceived as

Table 5.5 Indices of racial dissimilarity by household income groups in Rio de Janeiro, 1980

Income (in US dollars)	Dissimilarity*
Overall	37
1–75	(45)
75–150	35
150–225	36
225–375	36
375–750	40
750–1500	53

* Overall index calculated for all individuals while other indexes calculated for household heads.
Source: Telles (1992)

non-white. These persons are likely to have some African origin but because race is based on appearance and is sometimes defined in relational terms, those at the lightest end of the color spectrum may define themselves as white (Telles and Lim, 1998).

The salience of both class and race in residential segregation and social tensions is illustrated by a 1992 incident where busloads of young people from Rio de Janeiro's poor communities arrived in unprecedented numbers in Rio's prestigious South Zone beaches. Their presence startled local residents, leading to reactions that revealed their prejudices and fears about the poor, mostly non-white youth of the socially distant shantytowns. The South Zone residents were quite conscious of and even haunted by the color differences, making this a racial as well as a class issue. The reactions of the middle-class residents ranged from declarations of fear about the "bands of poor dark people" to the preparations of martial arts clubs in the South Zone to defend against another "invasion" (Veja, 1992).

Although they had occurred in the past, this "sweep" (arrastão) was important because it was highly publicized, presumably to frighten local citizens about what might happen if Benedita da Silva, a black favela resident, were elected mayor of Rio de Janeiro. These events brought to light the tenuous relation between the predominantly black poor and the white middle class in Rio, a problem which had been conveniently neglected in the past because of the distance that had generally separated the two groups.

Although key studies in the 1950s, based mostly on impressionistic evidence, concluded that racial segregation was highly conditioned by social class, studies of the time also showed a consistent 30 to 40 percent of whites claimed that they would not be willing to accept blacks or mulattos as neighbors (Ianni and Cardoso, 1959; Bastide and Van den Berghe, 1957; Fernandes, 1955). Thus, although these studies set the tone for understanding racial segregation as based on class, they also provided evidence that racism also may explain some segregation. However, the interpretations of the studies at the time downplayed this factor.

Also, a study of São Paulo and Rio de Janeiro suggests some self-segregation for cultural or ethnic reasons. It shows that the African-origin population tends to be concentrated in certain poor neighborhoods, near other "co-ethnics" and generally near Afro-Brazilian cultural and religious institutions like samba schools and *terreiros de candomblé*. These neighborhoods often emerged around the cores of former slave neighborhoods (Rolnik, 1989). This suggests a pattern that resembles enclave formation, although increasing stigmatization of these places and their residents suggests increasing ghettoization.

The indexes of segregation (dissimilarity) in Table 5.5 show that residential segregation among color groups cannot be accounted for only by socioeconomic status. Rather, moderate residential segregation along color lines occurs among members of the same income group. This supports the argument that racism or ethnicity also contribute to racial segregation. Table 5.5 also shows a pattern of greater segregation with higher income groups. The Afro-Brazilian middle class is clearly more segregated from middle class whites than poor Afro-Brazilians are from poor whites. (Note that a segregation index is not calculated for the highest earning groups because the insufficient numbers of non-whites in this category precludes a mathematically reliable indicator.)

In order for racism to have much effect on segregation, there must be differential levels of housing discrimination (if not outright conspiracies to steer blacks into certain neighborhoods, as in the United States) among neighborhoods so that non-whites are kept out of certain neighborhoods, rather than simply random incidents of discrimination. There are plenty of examples of incidents suggesting discrimination in housing, such as the common complaint of middle class blacks that they are sometimes required to use the service elevator in residential apartment buildings. To our knowledge, there are no studies of how racism directly affects the Brazilian housing markets. Perhaps the fact that much of the population, especially the poor, live in unstable and irregular housing, has not allowed for the crystallization of racially separate housing markets (Ribeiro, 1993). However, even if stability were to exist, as it does for middle class housing, high racial segregation would require some motivation such as a strong association between property values and racial composition of neighborhoods, as in the US.

An important difference between Brazil and countries like the United States and South Africa is that the state never created legal racial segregation or classification laws. Relatedly, miscegenation was common and produced a large population of racially mixed persons with often ambiguous racial identities. The particular classification of persons by race, even in official data collection, is often inconsistent and omits commonly used racial categories. Given such a classification system, segregation into racially separate neighborhoods in Brazil would be difficult, if not impossible.

Unfortunately data have not become available with which to measure segregation since 1980. At this point, we can only speculate on the change. The regressive industrialization of the 1980s supports the hypothesis of increasing segregation by race and by class, in which greater class segregation also means greater race segregation. The economic crisis of the 1980s has increased the level of overall and racial income inequality (Bonelli and Sedlacek, 1989), both of which lead to greater racial segregation (Telles, 1992). At the more interpersonal level, race relations may have become more strained as blacks and browns often become the scapegoats for Brazilian society's increasing social and economic ills, thus making racial divisions more salient. Finally, the substantially higher fertility rates of the black and brown population (5.3 and 4.9) compared to the white population (3.4) in 1980 suggests that racial segregation is growing as the poor segment of the population becomes increasingly non-white.

Although the racism of Brazilian labor markets has led to large racial inequalities, racial identities in Brazil are not as consistent or strong as in the United States or South Africa. Afro-Brazilian activists claim that a racial democracy ideology, substantiated by the lack of race-based segregation or classification laws, have camouflaged the pernicious racism of Brazilian society. Recently, however, there are forces which bring public attention to Brazilian racism and promote race as a factor for uniting persons on the basis of a common culture and experience. The first of these is the influence of Afro-Brazilian social movements, which seek to raise black consciousness and change public opinion to recognize racism as a primary generator of inequality in Brazil. Relatedly, an increasingly globalized black culture and its strong reception by Afro-Brazilian youth (Sansone, 1993) has increased the salience of race, especially among urban youth. Through television, music and videos, a global black culture industry which brings images from Africa, the Caribbean and the United States, and an emerging local black media has penetrated Brazilian society (Sansone, 1993).

The Future of Rio de Janeiro: Fragmentation or Dualization?

The literature on globalization's effects on urban socio-spatial structure and political organization have focused on the so-called global cities (Mollenkopf and Castells, 1991; Sassen, 1991). Analyses of New York, London and Tokyo have noted a shrinking of middle professional categories, including skilled manual workers, as a result of industrialization substituted by the growth of new productive services. Analysts predict an increasingly divided city, including the dual city (Mollenkopf and Castells, 1991), the quartered city (Marcuse, 1989), and divided cities (Fainstein, Gordon and Harloe, 1992).

However, others dispute this. Because global activities may represent only a small part of urban employment, they claim that the thesis that globalization necessarily leads to socio-spatial dualization needs to be relativized (Preteceille, 1988; 1994a). For example, the transformation of the Paris economy has not led toward a binary opposition between rich and poor in the Parisian social or spatial structure, even though the physical and aesthetic contrasts of the most visible neighborhoods, in the popular and media imagination, increased. On the one hand, the exclusive spaces of wealthy social categories are evident, on the other, the diversity of the social structure and the complexity of its spatial distribution continue to grow.

Recent work (Storper, 1994; Preteceille, 1994a, 1994b) has called attention to the absence of a majority model of globalization. It shows the existence of two micro-processes that are distinct because of their social, economic, political and urban impacts. If, in effect, the hegemony of the urban economy were to be commanded by financial capital, as Rio's elites plan, the city would become merely an export platform, agglomerating businesses through a global communication networks that link it to other global cities. In this case, only part of the urban structure assumes the role of agglomerative capital for business, creating strong tendencies for the dualization of the socio-spatial structure. If, on the contrary, industrial capital commands the insertion of the city in the global economy, this opens up possibilities for policies that create favorable contexts for a learning economy (Storper, 1991).

Another much discussed subject in the literature is about the fragmentative tendencies of social identities created by polarization and socio-spatial segregation. In the past, we have had examples of situations in which socio-spatial segregation obstructed the formation of a working class, to the extent that such segregation consolidated identities that were territorially fragmented, as Katznelson (1981) showed for the United States. Other research results have shown the opposite: socio-spatial segregation promoted the formation of identities among the Parisian working class (Brunet, 1979; Fourcaut, 1986). Contemporary studies of New York (Mollenkopf and Castells, 1991) suggest that socio-spatial inequalities reinforce tendencies toward fragmentation of social identities, which results in the contrast between a capacity for creating social cohesion at the high end of the social structure and the dispersion of the remaining social groups by ethnicity or occupation. For this reason, power can be increasingly controlled by an elite that acts together with local governments in large urban restructuring projects in the city center, further augmenting social segregation.

The analysis of economic and socio-spatial changes in the metropolitan area of Rio de Janeiro suggest that globalization may reinforce tendencies toward dualization and fragmentation that have been present in Rio's regressive deindustrialization. In examining patterns of association, the comparison of Figure 5.5 with Figures 5.1 and 5.2 show two distinct socio-spatial patterns in organizing and mobilizing which are highly correlated with education and income. The poor segments and those with low levels of schooling are most common in neighborhood community and religious associations while they participate little in unions, professional associations and political parties. By contrast, those with high income and education are more organized in unions, professional associations, cultural and sports associations, and political parties. Associationalism in the metropolitan area is therefore segmented into corporate organizations and in community-religious organizations, the first being organized around the world of work and politics and the other around popular and more diffuse organizations.

The associative fragmentation constitutes a context for the increasing symbolic fragmentation of the lower classes, destroying the values and symbols that were previously references for the formation of class and neighborhood-based collective action. In the old model of social-spatial segregation, the favelas were unified territories of identity and culture, founded on social homogeneity which sheltered a large contingent of salaried workers. On the other hand, the periphery began to be occupied in the 1940s and 1950s, attracting those salaried workers that obtained employment with stability and lower remuneration, thus creating the conditions for becoming home-owners. The favelas and the periphery at that historic moment in Rio were culturally and territorially united with relevant roles in the construction of collective identities as workers or poor. Because of the associative importance of the favelas and the periphery, many of these areas became objects in struggles over political power, which gave these places a strong organizational vitality and identity.

In the new model of socio-spatial segregation, favelas and the periphery are characterized by the decline of the old associative fabric and by the expansion of criminal and perverse forms of sociability. Such a change reinforces the dissemination of a culture of fear that reconfigures the socio-spatial meaning of the favelas and the periphery. They stop being seen as territories of positive values and poor and black residents become increasing stigmatized to the extent that they are associated with these places.

The concentration of Afro-Brazilians among favela residents and the poor has led to an association between blacks and favelas, increasing the distance between the elites and the masses or between the center and periphery. Afro-Brazilians disproportionately suffer from the lack of adequate housing, excessive crime and violence largely brought about by a rapidly growing drug trade abuse by police and government officials, lack of basic infrastructure, and an absence of basic human rights. However, many analysts claim that racial identity is not a core element of personal identity in contemporary Brazil to the extent it is in the United States. Rather, racial identities are often ambiguous and variant, depending on the social context. The lack of extreme residential segregation prevented the clear separation by race of social spaces, institutions and culture as in the United States but has led to a class-race ghetto with its own culture, symbols and values (Vianna, 1997). The lack of strong racial identities among blacks may be changing among younger persons as both global and local media present positive images of blackness and an emerging black movement gains legitimacy. Also, the increasing social tension that accompanies dualization may be undermining the cross-race and class relations in Brazil that commonly occur in some contexts (Sansone, 1998). Relatedly, the concentration of blacks and browns in the favelas and periphery may also be contributing to making racial divisions more rigid.

The intensification of desalarization and poverty and the consolidation of the urban survival economy create tendencies that maintain or increase an incomplete class structure. Globalization in Rio de Janeiro might thus create greater distance between those integrated in the new economic order and the excluded. The result could be that the symbols and values of Rio's elite and middle classes lose their historical connection with those of the poor, thus weakening inter-class solidarity regarding the city's destiny.

6

Singapore: the Changing Residential Landscape in a Winner City

Leo van Grunsven

In no other metropolitan area in the Southeast- and East-Asian region, have the residential landscape and pattern changed more profoundly during the past decades as in Singapore. Some of the changes are unique to the small city state (only 640 sq.km.), others have been or are currently occurring in other rapidly growing and changing metropolitan areas elsewhere in the Southeast- and East-Asian region — though as yet less profoundly. Similarly, some of the forces which have shaped the changes in Singapore's urban and residential fabric are unique to the city state, others are commonly shared by the Southeast- and East-Asian metropolitan areas.

The new administration which took office in 1959, when Singapore was granted self-rule by the colonial power (the British), inherited a partitioned city shaped by and during almost 150 years of colonial rule. The basic contours of partitioning had been laid down during the two to three decades after the founding of the city in 1819, while significant new elements emerged in the urban fabric during the decade immediately after World War II. This legacy gradually gave way, during the 1960s and 1970s, to a more "inclusive" or integrated residential pattern, a de-partitioned urban fabric, simultaneously with profound structural changes in the housing market and concomitant physical changes in the residential landscape. However, it will be argued in this contribution that — roughly from the mid-1980s — tendencies towards partitioning in the residential fabric have been on the increase again, though in a form different from the one prevailing during the "pre-integration" period.

Some of the forces which have shaped the nature of recent residential change in Singapore are closely linked to the overall theme of this book. By now, none of the large metropolitan areas in the Southeast- and East-Asian region has been left untouched by the process of internationalization or globalization of economic activity, which is a significant feature of the phase of global capitalism after the Fordist crisis (i.e. from the 1960s onwards). Singapore stands out among other metropolitan areas in the region, and particularly among many of the "western" cases discussed elsewhere in this book. While a number of the theses brought forward in the introductory sections of this book apply to the Singapore case, parts of the framework adopted have less – indeed little – relevance in this case. It will specifically be argued that the types of "divisioning" of the economic structure of society and of the metropolitan space which is seen as characteristic of the post-Fordist phase of capitalism do not necessarily hold outside the realm of the "traditional" core areas of the world economy. The Singapore case also demonstrates that government intervention, and its underlying philosophies, may play a significant role in reshaping the spatial or residential order of cities.

The Residential Landscape on the Eve of Urban Transformation

During the last century, Singapore developed as an entrepôt port, linking its immediate hinterland and large parts of Southeast and East Asia to Western Europe. Economic activities, directly and indirectly linked to this entrepôt function dominated the Singapore economy for much of the colonial period. The small indigenous population in Singapore at the time of its founding and the decades thereafter, comprising mainly Malays, could not supply the labor necessary for the activities linked to the entrepôt function. This problem was solved through attracting migrants from other parts of Asia. China, the Indian sub-continent and to a lesser extent the Malay Peninsula became the main sources of migrant labor. Indian migrants were absorbed in the colonial administration and in the construction sector, while the Chinese immigrants were absorbed in the entrepôt economy and a range of other commercial activities. Because of the diverse origin of migrants, the population of Singapore rapidly became ethnically heterogeneous. It still is today. Four main groups are distinguished, namely the Chinese, the Malays, the Indians, and Others. Since the end of the 1950s the proportion of each of these groups in the total population has more or less remained stable: Chinese 76 percent, Malays 15 percent, Indians six percent, and Others three percent (Department of Statistics, Singapore, 1995).

From the outset, the British adopted a policy of residentially segregating the different ethnic groups and allocated different sections of the city to each of them. The spatial pattern laid down by the British reflected the differential roles of each of the immigrant/ethnic groups in the colonial economy and was perpetuated during the 19th and the first half of this century by a compartmentalization of the economy and labor market along ethnic lines (Hassan, 1971; Hodder, 1953; Neville 1965, 1966, 1969; Pang, 1974). An important characteristic of this was the virtual monopolization by the Chinese of those sectors of the economy which reflected the function of Singapore as "middle man" in colonial trade. This translated in the residential pattern in a central location. After the establishment of two large "Chinatowns", one to the north and the other to the south of the Singapore River, with the characteristic shophouse-architecture, the city centers (the area which is currently the CBD; see Map 6.1) became the virtual exclusive domain of the Chinese. New Chinese migrants kept converging on these central locations, leading to an ever-stronger concentration in this part of the city in the course of the first half of this century. A substantial segment of the Indian population also was located at rather central locations. Two clusters came to be established on the edge of the central city, one directly to the north (a cluster known as "Little India") and one directly to the south. These clusters of the Indian minority remained throughout the colonial period.

The Malays hardly had access to the relatively high-earning jobs in the commerce and banking sectors. In colonial times they occupied a position which has been characterized by a number of authors (Betts, 1975; Hassan, 1971; Neville, 1965, 1966, 1969) as peripheral to the mainstream of life, in economic, social, and political terms. This also translated into a peripheralization in geographical terms. Thus, the Malays were virtually absent from the central parts of the city. They came to occupy a number of small clusters across the city and one large cluster in the eastern part of the city (Hodder, 1953; Neville, 1965, 1969). This cluster, known as Geylang Serai/Eunos, has historically been an important area of Malay settlement in Singapore.

With the growth of the population and the expansion of the urban area, the Chinese gradually became the dominant group in large parts of the city. Though in the 1950s and 1960s ethnic segregation became most manifest at the micro-spatial scale, at the meso- and macro-spatial scale the above elements remained very visible in the residential structure. The continued undisputed position of the Malays at the bottom of the urban socio-economic ladder during the 1960s kept being reinforced by a peripheral position in terms of residential location. Malay clustering in the Geylang Serai/Eunos area remained quite visible as this ethnic group constituted the majority of the population here. Significantly, this Malay cluster coincided with one of the largest concentrations of irregular (i.e., squatter-like) settlements found in Singapore in the 1960s (Van Grunsven, 1990).

Singapore's population had reached about one million directly after World

Map 6.1 Location of New Towns and public housing estates, private housing estates and condominium projects
Source: Compiled by the author from HDB Annual Reports; Singapore Street Guide; URA construction data

War II. Out of these, about 700,000 lived in the urban area. In the immediate post-war period (1947–1957), Singapore experienced an exceptionally high population growth (on average 4.4 percent per annum). By 1957 total population had grown by half a million, and the urban population by 300,000. Accommodating about one-third of the urban population towards the end of the 1950s, the absorption capacity of the centrally located shophouse tenement areas had reached its upper-limit. Throughout the 1950s, new housing construction remained far below what was needed to accommodate population growth. In addition, newly constructed dwellings were increasingly unaffordable by large sections of the population. The 1950s saw a rapid increase of the urban low-income group and of urban poverty, due to the fact that the entrepôt economy was increasingly unable to absorb the annual additions to the labor force and to other mechanisms of exclusion to the formal economy and labor market.

These circumstances combined led to a rapid growth of irregular housing during the 1950s and early 1960s. The number of urban dwellers in such housing increased from about 100,000 (or 14.5 percent of the urban population) in the second half of the 1940s (the shift to irregular housing during the first half of the 1940s, particularly of the Chinese, was largely a response to the Japanese Occupation), to about 250,000 (or 27 percent of the urban population) around the middle of the 1950s. In the 1960s extensive areas of irregular housing (mostly of wooden construction) were found throughout the urban area, occupying sites which had been left vacant in the process of urban expansion. Generally, despite self-construction and being the areas where a significant part of the urban low-income groups and the poor found accommodation, living conditions in these areas were better than in the central city tenement areas, as the latter were far more overcrowded.

A contrasting picture provided the expanding areas of private housing occupied by the middle class, mainly consisting of row-houses and semi-detached dwellings. An even greater contrast provided the upper class/elite suburbs, which by the end of the 1950s occupied extensive areas to the north-west, west and east of the central city area. Typically, housing had been constructed here in rather low density, often detached houses and bungalows set in frequently large compounds. The suburb to the north-east of the central city area included the original "European Quarter", established during the period 1890–1920. Until the end of the colonial period, the typical bungalow-compound complexes in this Quarter, built in an architectural style imported by the British from the Indian subcontinent, housed the colonial administrative and business elite. After the end of colonial rule, these complexes were taken over by the local business elite. The Chinese-style bungalows were more typical of the other suburbs, having become the domain of the immigrant Chinese business elite. As will we see later in this chapter, these elite suburbs also have undergone substantial change in the process of urban expansion, transformation and redevelopment over the past decades. However, sections of the former European Quarter have survived in more or less their original form until today (although the use of the bungalow-compound complexes has often changed). In the original Chinese elite suburbs, the original type of housing may still be observed, interspersed between recent (re-)development projects.

Economic Change: the City-state under Globalization

As already well documented in the by now rather extensive literature (see, e.g., Chiu et al., 1997, Perry et al., 1997; Rodan, 1989), the development of the Singapore economy in the post-colonial period (or, rather the post-independence period, from 1965 onwards) shows four dominant, and interlinked, characteristics: continuous high economic growth, structural transformation of the economy and of economic sectors, a profound role of international capital and the significant role of government in the economy.

Some figures may illustrate the main trends in the Singapore economy over the past three decades. Over the period 1965–1980, GDP grew at an

Table 6.1 Singapore: key indicators of economic performance

| | Gross Domestic Product | | Gross National Product | |
	At 1990 Market prices (S$Million)	Annual Change	At Current Prices (S$Million)	Per Capita (S$)
1965	7,718.2	–	3,052.3	1,618
1970	14,177.2	–	5,861.1	2,825
1975	22,329.0	–	13,566.5	5,903
1980	33,581.6	–	24,188.5	9,941
1985	45,344.9	– 1.6	40,330.4	14,741
1986	46,388.0	2.3	40,212.9	14,712
1987	50,899.9	9.7	43,140.6	15,547
1988	56,821.1	11.6	51,505.5	18,097
1989	62,288.8	9.6	59,788.8	20,400
1990	67,878.9	9.0	68,306.0	22,645
1991	72,860.9	7.3	75,328.2	24,379
1992	77,393.8	6.2	82,433.8	25,939
1993	85,473.2	10.4	93,466.0	28,676
1994	94,063.6	10.1	108,239.7	32,181
1995	102,299.1	8.8	121,486.8	35,036

Source: Department of Statistics (1996)

Table 6.2 Singapore: sectoral structure of the economy (percentage distribution)

| | Gross Domestic Product at Current Market Prices | | | | | | |
	Manufac-turing	Utilities	Con-struction	Commerce	Transport & Comm-unications	Financial & Business Services	Other Services
1965	15.2	2.2	6.5	27.2	11.5	16.6	17.6
1970	20.2	2.6	6.9	27.4	10.7	16.6	12.9
1975	23.3	1.8	7.9	24.8	10.8	18.2	11.1
1980	28.1	2.1	6.2	20.8	13.5	19.0	8.8
1985	22.0	1.9	10.0	15.9	12.6	25.6	11.0
1990	27.2	1.8	5.2	17.9	12.2	25.0	10.3
1995	24.9	1.5	6.7	18.6	11.1	26.9	10.0

Source: Department of Statistics (1996)

average annual rate of 9.1 percent. In quite a number of years, double-digit growth was achieved. This slowed to an annual average of about seven percent during the first half of the 1980s, the prelude to the economic recession which hit the city state in 1985 (when the economy showed negative growth). However, this recession was only of short duration. After 1986, the economy showed robust growth again, with some years in which double digit growth was achieved. With the rapid expansion of the economy, tremendous increases in per capita income also were achieved. As Table 6.1 shows, per capita GNP reached S$10,000 in 1980, from a low S$1,618 in 1965. Over the period 1980–1995, per capita income more than tripled, to reach S$35,000 in 1995, the second highest after Japan in the Asia-Pacific region. Singaporeans on average enjoy incomes and a standard of living far above those enjoyed by the population in the surrounding countries. We will return to this point below.

The structural changes which have taken place in the Singapore economy over the past three decades, concerns first a transition from an entrepôt economy to a "low-tech" manufacturing and trading economy during the 1960s and 1970s (revealed by a significant increase of the share of manufacturing in GDP), and from a manufacturing and trading economy to a "high-tech" manufacturing, financial, and business services economy over the past decade. In Table 6.2, this is revealed by a drop of the share of manufacturing in GDP and a significant increase of the share of financial and business services in GDP in the period from 1980 to 1995. "High-tech" instead of "low-tech" manufacturing indicates a significant transformation within the manufacturing sector. This brings us to a brief consideration of the more specific phases of development of the Singapore economy, linked to the role of government and of international capital.

At the time of independence, Singapore was faced with high unemployment (some 10 percent of the economically active population at the end of the 1950s), an economy highly dependent on entrepôt trade, a small manufacturing base and local capital reluctant to invest in manufacturing, as well as the imminent closure of the British military bases on the island, and the lack of a hinterland. The government therefore adopted a strategy aimed at industrializing by attracting export production internationalized by capital from the core economies of the world in search of lower-cost production sites. Thus, the government deliberately chose an alliance with foreign capital. To achieve this, it put much effort into creating a suitable infrastructure (e.g. industrial estates) and a low-cost business environment which was highly conducive and attractive to foreign business. To this end, it established a strong grip on labor relations.

This indeed attracted foreign manufacturing activities as Singapore's labor costs were low. Singapore rapidly developed into an offshore production and export base for international capital: cumulative foreign manufacturing investment grew steadily from S$1 billion in 1970 to S$7 billion in 1980. In the early 1980s, foreign-controlled companies commanded about 70 percent of total cumulative investment, and about three quarters of total output, exports and value-added in the manufacturing sector.

In line with the emerging New International Division of Labor, most manufacturing activities internationalized to Singapore during the 1960s and 1970s concerned labor-intensive, low value-added production. This suited the government very well as foreign capital created employment. In fact, by the end of the 1970s a tight labor market arose. It became necessary to recruit substantial numbers of foreign workers (on a temporary, three-year basis; after these three years they lose their working permit and with it also their permit to stay in the country). In 1980 the government adopted a strategy of industrial restructuring, presented as the Second Industrial Revolution. The strategy aimed at restructuring the manufacturing sector towards productivity-driven growth and higher value-added activities. To this end, it implemented a three-year wage correction policy so that wage increases would reflect the tight labor market. There was also a renewed emphasis on education and training, encouragement of automation, mechanization and computerization, a more selective investment promotion policy, and increased emphasis on R&D.

At this juncture, the strategy met with little response from international capital. The steep increase in labor and other business costs in fact led to a rapid erosion of international competitiveness, causing a stagnation of foreign direct investment. The chain of responses in the economy as a whole led in 1985 to a steep recession. Although measures were immediately adopted to restore international competitiveness, halting industrial restructuring, the strategy was by no means abandoned. On the contrary, in terms of economic strategy the mid-1980s marks a watershed. The report *The Singapore Economy: New Directions*, conceived by Singapore's economic planners – in consultation with the private sector – following the economic recession, proposed not only the measures to be taken immediately to restore Singapore's international competitiveness, but also the changes needed in the economy to maintain high economic growth in the long run.

The core of the vision and associated strategic thrusts concerns Singapore's move beyond a manufacturing and export base for international and domestic capital to a future position as a Total Business Centre. This vision was reinforced during the second half of the 1980s by increasing pressure on resources, on labor and other business costs, by the strength of the Singapore dollar, and increasing competition from surrounding countries. Besides high value-added manufacturing, the Total Business Centre vision targeted the service sector, especially financial and business services, and non-production activities in the value chain (R&D, logistics, regional offices or headquarters) of (foreign) industrial enterprises operating in Singapore and elsewhere in the Asian region. On the other hand, it was envisaged that low value-added, labor-intensive, production would be relocated out of Singapore by foreign and domestic firms. The government could encourage and guide this process through a proper framework.

The Strategic Economic Plan published in 1991 reiterated the overall vision, the more specific strategies, and the necessary measures, and elaborated on the enabling and guiding role of government as being to provide the institutional and infrastructure framework for the achievement of the strategic thrusts. It reformulated relocation of production out of Singapore to the broader thrust of making Singapore invest abroad, both internationally and regionally, creating a "Second Wing." Thus, besides continuing to receive foreign investment, Singapore should also become a foreign investor, in both other countries in the region and the core areas of the world economy. The Total Business Centre idea was reformulated into the goal of developing into a International Business Hub. Indeed, in many areas Singapore was to assume a position of regional "hub", the catchword of the planners in the early 1990s. Major strategic programs, elaborating the Strategic Economic Plan, reflect these goals.

The strategies have not remained without success. They targeted white-collar activities, work in MNCs, and financial and business services, at a time when the internationalization of these to Pacific Asia gained momentum. Singapore provided the right conditions to effectively compete with other metropolitan areas in the region (e.g. Hong Kong) to attract these activities. International business responded much better to the strategies at this stage than it had in the early 1980s, as the idea fitted their plans for regional expansion, and the operational and geographical strategies pursued in the region. The trends in e.g., sectoral structure of the economy, stock and composition of foreign investment, growth and composition of foreign companies, and the rapidly changing nature of the activities performed by foreign capital, warrant the observation that over the past ten years the Singapore economy has moved away rapidly from the role it assumed during the 1970s under the NIDL, to a role in the current global and emerging regional division of labor in line with the "new" competitive advantages corresponding with the strategies pursued.

Restructuring, employment and incomes

Since many of the statements on new patterns or divisions in cities link the "urban" with the dynamics of "class configuration", impacted by the aspect of work/employment and income, it is necessary to briefly consider the trends in the area of labor, linked to the economic restructuring outlined above. The period 1965–85 was marked by rapid expansion of employment and a shift of labor towards the manufacturing sector, which rapidly increased its share in total employment. The labor market became characterized by high labor-force participation rates (of both males and females), very low unemployment, and, as noted earlier, an increasing number of foreign workers.

Overall employment has continued to expand throughout the 1980s and first half of the 1990s. Significantly, throughout the second half of the 1980s and the early 1990s, employment in manufacturing expanded substantially, after significant lay-offs during the recession. Only from 1993, this sector started to record slight negative employment growth. By the mid-1990s the overall employment structure had clearly shifted from the manufacturing towards the services sector. Although economic/industrial restructuring has led to a substantial contraction of labor-intensive activities, this has not led to labor redundancy. Unemployment, which rose significantly during the economic recession of the mid-1980s, dropped rapidly again after 1986 and has remained at a very low level since (about 2.5 percent). A clear feature of employment trends in manufacturing (and the economy overall) in the phase of restructuring is the compensation of job losses in labor-intensive and less technologically-based activities by the creation of jobs in higher value-added and more technologically-based activities. Thus, lower-qualified jobs have been replaced by higher-qualified jobs.

Another linked aspect of employment shift in the manufacturing sector concerns the occupational distribution. An analysis of the annual growth rates as well as the relative distribution of occupational divisions, grouped into three categories (high, middle and low)[1] over the period 1983 to 1994 clearly reveals that after 1986 the "high" occupational category has shown a

Table 6.3 Resident private households by monthly household income* from work and ethnic group of head

Monthly income (S$)	Total 1980	Total 1990	Total 1995	Chin. 1980	Chin. 1990	Chin. 1995	Malay 1980	Malay 1990	Malay 1995	Indian 1980	Indian 1990	Indian 1995
Below 1,000	57.6	16.0	11.6	56.9	15.7	11.6	67.7	17.0	10.5	61.6	16.7	12.7
1,000–1,499	16.7	13.6	8.8	17.1	12.8	8.2	17.5	18.7	12.8	15.3	14.4	9.2
1,500–1,999	9.6	13.5	9.3	9.9	12.7	8.6	8.5	18.3	14.1	8.8	14.2	10.1
2,000–2,999	8.6	20.1	17.7	9.1	19.6	16.8	4.8	23.4	24.2	8.1	21.6	17.7
3,000–3,999	3.5	13.0	14.1	3.6	13.3	13.7	0.9	11.6	16.3	3.0	13.0	16.0
4,000–4,999	1.7	8.2	10.5	1.6	8.6	10.7	0.3	5.6	9.5	1.3	7.4	10.9
5,000 and over	2.3	15.6	28.0	1.8	17.3	30.4	0.3	5.4	12.7	1.9	12.7	23.4

* Although these incomes are nominal incomes, price inflation has always been very low in Singapore; therefore the figures are comparable between the years.

Source: Department of Statistics (1997).

higher growth rate than the "low" category (Ministry of Labor, 1995). The negative growth of the latter in the early 1990s, in combination with the growth trend of the other divisions, has resulted in a clear shift of the occupational structure towards the "high" divisions. Thus, upgrading of the occupational structure is quite evident. This trend in the employment structure has occurred also in the financial and business services sector, indeed in the economy as a whole.

To the extent that labor became redundant (those unemployable in higher qualified jobs), this has involved mainly the flexible segment of foreign workers, most of whom could easily be "removed" from the labor force by terminating their contracts and revoking their work permits, thus compelling them to leave the country. This is an additional reason why economic restructuring has not resulted in the emergence of a "class" of economically active which has become superfluous.

The growth of employment *vis-à-vis* the availability of labor, government policy, combined with the structural shifts outlined above, have resulted in significant changes in the salaries commanded by labor. The percentage of workers earning less than S$600 a month (still amounting to more than half of the total in 1983) declined very significantly between 1983 and 1994, while the percentage earning S$1,500 and above increased very significantly (Ministry of Labor, 1995). The shift in the salary structure was most profound in the manufacturing sector.

Class configuration

As a result of the developments outlined above, the class configuration in Singapore has changed substantially. Once dominated by low-income groups, the dominant trend in the socio-economic structure has been the emergence of a middle class society. The trends in household income and the distribution of income may serve to reveal and demonstrate the dynamics of class in Singapore. Income data are shown in Table 6.3. The following observations may be made:

- with greater affluence, there were more households at higher income levels in the mid-1990s than in 1980;
- there has been a shift of households towards the middle-income ranges around the average;
- these trends hold true for each of the ethnic groups, though to a differential extent (Chinese households have gained relatively more than Indian and Malay households);
- although income distribution became somewhat less unequal between 1980 and 1994, lower income households (the bottom 20 percent) had an income share of only 4.7 percent in 1994, while the top 20 percent of

households commanded almost half of total household income. However, the absolute gain is not concentrated in particular deciles in the
income distribution; also the bottom 20 percent gained, not only in
nominal terms but also in real terms given the low inflation and the trend
in the consumer price index;
- looking at the quintile groups of each of the ethnic groups, gains can be
  seen in each of the subgroups.

Thus, the class configuration in Singapore appears to have evolved in the
following way:

- No group can be identified which shows signs of gradually becoming
  more marginalized and impoverished. Rather the opposite is true. While
  there still is a sizeable group of lower-income households, this group has
  become smaller and has still managed to achieve income gains.
- The upper class is a small, although expanding, group. It includes a
  number of extremely wealthy families. The upper class is strongly dominated by Chinese.
- A growing middle class, which is rather heterogeneous in income, ethnic,
  and household characteristics, as well as occupational characteristics. If
  subdivided in a lower-, middle-, and upper-middle class, the latter remains smallest.

Changes in the residential fabric over the past decades in part reflect this
evolution of the class structure. Before turning to this, it is necessary first to
consider the evolution of the housing market and the actors involved.

The Dynamics of the Urban Housing Market and the Agents of Change

The urban housing situation and market in Singapore has shown rather
exceptional trends and characteristics since the early 1960s. Unlike in metropolitan areas elsewhere in the region, there is now hardly any housing deprivation in Singapore. A remarkable feature of the housing stock is the extent
to which it is provided, regulated and managed by the government, while
more than 90 percent is owner-occupied. Singapore no longer has a segment
of rental or owner-occupied dwellings in irregular settlements (Toh Mun
Heng and Tay Boon Nga, 1994; Cheng Lim Keak, 1995). The sector of
private housing, with rental and owner-occupied subsegments, is small in
relative terms. Yet it is a dynamic sector, with substantial growth in absolute
terms over the past ten years, and substantial changes in composition. While
a substantial part of the stock of inner-city shophouses has been demolished,

new luxury housing has been and is continuously added. As this new private housing has sprung up in many parts of the city, it is a highly visible segment of the housing market. While the latter is the result of the operation of private agents in the housing market, the trends and characteristics mentioned earlier are due to the government's high level of intervention. Below we shall first address the role of government, being the main force shaping the urban housing market over the past few decades.

The role of government and housing policies

The government has assumed a dominant role in the provision of urban housing through its agent, the Housing and Development Board (HDB), established in 1960. This was inspired by a range of factors, the most significant ones being:

- the necessity to alleviate housing shortage in the 1960s;
- political expediency, elements of which are the necessity to politically legitimize the regime in the face of controls imposed on labor (deemed necessary for the economic strategies pursued), and the desire to politically control the population by incorporating a large section into a housing system provided, managed, and controlled by the state (Van Grunsven, 1991) and by engineering alterations in the "inherited" residential patterns (to be elaborated below);
- the desire to achieve a different overall population distribution in the city (given the extremely high residential densities in the urban core, referred to earlier);
- economic reasons (to facilitate urban physical restructuring according to the demands of strategies in the economic field);
- and to remove elements from the city, perceived a "urban blight" not befitting "modern Singapore".

The HDB's building program aims to provide housing for large sections of the population. (According to the income and family composition criteria, some 90 percent of households – the lower classes and most of the middle classes – are eligible for public housing.) This construction work has resulted in a ten-fold increase of the public housing stock between the mid-1960s and the mid-1990s. As Figure 6.1 shows, this involves an increase from about 70,000 units in 1965 to almost 700,000 units in 1995. The type of dwelling constructed in the public sector has changed considerably over time. During the 1960s the emphasis was on one-, two- and three-room units. Nearly half of the dwellings constructed in the period 1966–1970 consisted of one-room units. After 1975 the share of small dwellings in new construction has decreased steadily while the share of three-room – and more recently four- and five-room – units has increased significantly. Presently, the four-room unit is the most important dwelling type in the construction program, followed by the five-room unit. Consequently, the composition of the housing stock in the public sector has changed considerably over the years.

The smallest dwellings became difficult to let, due to changing patterns of demand and intra-public sector residential mobility, combined with the specific policies pursued by HDB, and thus there was an increase in the number of permanent vacancies in this segment of the public housing sector during the 1980s. Many were demolished. We will return to this later.

Public housing in Singapore has been developed uniformly in a high-rise high-density form (for an overview of public housing characteristics in Singapore, see Perry et al., 1997; Wong and Yeh, 1985; Teo Siew Eng, 1986, 1989; Tai Ching Ling, 1988). In terms of scale of development a distinction can be made between the rather small-scale housing estates and the large-scale New Towns. The latter each comprise 20,000 to 65,000 dwelling units on 500–1,000 hectares of land, with a population size varying from 150,000 to 350,000. Thus far, 16 New Towns have been developed or are currently

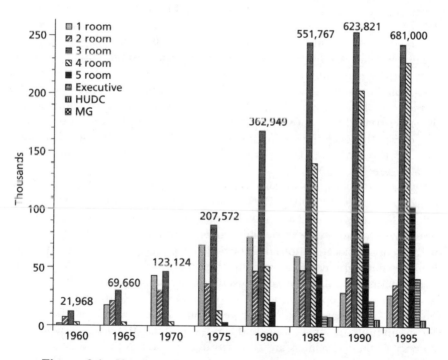

Figure 6.1 Number and composition of public housing units under management of HDB, 1960–1995
Source: HDB Annual Reports

under development. Map 6.1 shows the location of these New Towns.

At the levels of the individual dwelling, the housing blocks, neighborhood and the estates or New Towns, a clear evolution in design and planning can be observed over the years. Gradually the emphasis in construction has shifted from quantity alone to quantity and quality. During the 1960s and the first half of the 1970s the central concern was to construct as many units as possible within the shortest possible time. The quality of the life in the high-rise housing estates and New Towns received relatively little attention. From the middle of the 1970s attention to the overall living environment has steadily grown. Though the basic concepts have remained unchanged, and the high-rise high-density form of public housing has been stringently ad- hered to, planning and design in subsequent building programs provide much- improved housing and living environments.

The earliest housing estates and New Towns (e.g. Toa Payoh, Queenstown and Bukit Merah) were constructed relatively close to the city center. Public housing construction at rather central locations has continued throughout the 1970s and 1980s though in the form of increasingly smaller scale projects and through infilling (and redevelopment) rather than development of land previously not used for residential purposes. From the second half of the 1970s, a continuous outward shift of the location of new large-scale projects may be observed, at increasingly larger distances from the central city.

The element of differentiation, particularly spatial differentiation, needs some further elaboration since it is of central concern to the topic under discussion. Gradually a clear spatial differentiation has emerged in the public housing sector, not only in terms of the quality of the living environment but also in terms of the composition of the housing stock in estates/New Towns. Of course, the evolution as to the types of dwelling constructed already points in this direction. Thus period of construction is the main underlying variable here.

By the mid-1980s, the implications as to the spatial differentiation of the housing stock were as follows. Firstly, most of the one- and two-room flats, as well as the three-room flats (i.e. the oldest housing stock) were centrally located. Also, these types of dwelling units constituted a very large segment of the centrally located housing stock in the public sector. These types of dwellings have gradually "moved" to the bottom end of the public housing hierarchy (indeed, of the urban housing hierarchy as a whole). Dwellings in New Towns, developed during the second half of the 1970s and first half of the 1980s and located in a "suburban" zone, consist mostly of three- and four-room units, or three-, four- and five-room units. Also, the overwhelming majority of these dwellings are concentrated in these New Towns.

The emphasis of construction in the recently developed New Towns or those which are still being developed is on four- and five-room and executive flats. Currently, the older New Towns no longer have the original dwelling mix. As a large number of housing blocks with one- and two-room units were demolished from the mid-1980s onwards, new blocks with larger dwellings have been constructed on the vacant land. This is part of the rejuvenation and upgrading/redevelopment exercise which was initiated after the mid-1980s in response to changing demand and mobility patterns. We will return to this below when we revisit the residential landscape in the next section.

Added to these dimensions of spatial differentiation may be a third, overlapping, one: ownership/tenure. According to tenure, two subsectors may be distinguished in public housing, namely the rental subsector and the purchase or owner-occupation subsector. Most of the smaller one- and two-room flats are rented while most of the other types of flats are owner-occupied, sold by HDB to first-time buyers under the "Home-ownership for the People Scheme" or bought by second and subsequent occupants under the resale of flats arrangements.[2] Since the discontinuation of the construction of one- and two-room units (around 1975), only dwellings to be sold to the clientele have been added to the housing stock. Many rental three-room flats have also gradually been transferred to the owner-occupation subsector. The substantial reduction of the one- and two-room stock added to this change, and the tenure arrangements of the total public-sector housing stock has changed drastically: while at the end of the 1960s more than 80 percent still consisted of rented dwellings, by the mid-1990s almost ninety percent were owner-occupied.

Table 6.4 serves to demonstrate how much Singapore's urban housing market has become dominated by public housing. While this in large part concerns the role of government as *provider* of housing, it also pertains to the virtual elimination of two types of urban housing which were still very significant in the early 1970s, namely the inner-city stock of shophouses and the stock of "attap-/zinc roofed" dwellings, often found in irregular, squatter-settlement-like housing areas. The near eradication of these types of housing highlights another aspect of the highly interventionist role of government and brings us to a consideration of some other elements of government policy in the field of housing and residential patterns relevant to the discussion in this chapter.

From the 1960s clearance of squatter-settlement-like areas has been pursued vigorously, to the extent that these have now almost disappeared from the urban landscape. The affected population has generally been offered public housing. In the 1970s and much of the 1980s a similar approach was followed in respect of the inner-city shophouses. The government considered it necessary to make land at central locations available for infrastructure development, new construction, and urban renewal, in order to meet the demands of the modern economy. From the mid-1980s this approach made way for a new emphasis on heritage conservation, preservation, and restoration. Thus,

Table 6.4 Type of dwelling, 1970, 1980 and 1990

Type of Dwelling	Number 1970	Number 1980	Number 1990	Percentage 1970	Percentage 1980	Percentage 1990
Bungalows	10,711	9,962	9,495	3.5	2.1	1.4
Semi-detached Bungalows	7,465	12,114	15,041	2.4	2.6	2.2
Terrace Houses	21,500	21,462	24,241	7.0	4.6	3.5
HDB Dwellings and other public flats	120,138	337,198	575,443	39.3	72.2	83.3
Condominiums and Private Flats	10,008	16,321	39,693	3.3	3.5	5.7
Shophouses	19,806	13,453	9,315	6.5	2.9	1.4
Attap-/Zinc-roofed Houses	104,188	50,313	5,697	34.1	10.8	0.8
Others						
Total	305,833	467,142	690,561	100.0	100.0	100.0

Source: Toh Mun Heng and Tay Boon Nga (1995)

the remaining stock is currently being restored to its original state. However, the specific approach adopted and the planned functional changes still involve the relocation of most of the original residents away from the shophouse districts into public housing areas.

The clearance of squatter-settlement-like areas and the relocation of the population into public housing also served another element of government policy, namely residential integration of all the ethnic groups. The government adopted this policy at the end of the 1960s as it became increasingly faced with a number of issues associated with the position and residential pattern of its largest ethnic minority, the Malays. Clearance and resettlement, voluntary and forced incorporation of households of the minority ethnic groups in public housing, combined with control over the allocation of such housing, were largely used to achieve the rehousing of substantial enclaves of ethnic minorities, involving not only Malays but also Indians.

Specifically, in 1969 the decision was taken to remove spatial concentrations of Malays and to disperse the community across the city (Van Grunsven, 1990). It should be noted in this context that there was a clear political relevance to the significant concentrations of Malays, given the electoral system based on districts. The Malays constituted the majority of the electorate in a number of electoral districts in the Geylang Serai/Eunos area. De-clustering could change this. This strategy fitted in a much larger system of control developed by the People's Action Party (PAP) in order to limit the articulation of particularistic interests, demands, or dissatisfaction (on either a communal or a class basis) by groups considered by the PAP as threatening or destabilizing (Van Grunsven, 1990). The PAP was clearly not interested in the emergence and further development of a pluralist political structure in Singapore. The main underlying factor here was the new development strategy which the PAP government was forced to adopt after independence in 1965. The success of this new strategy, export-oriented industrialization through foreign investment, depended heavily on a sufficiently attractive investment climate. In this respect political and social stability was considered essential. Thus, the PAP became heavily concerned with efforts to limit political pluralism (Van Grunsven, 1990).[3]

It was the belief of the government that the necessary changes in the society would take place in response to changes in the physical environment (Betts, 1975). Through large scale relocation, ethnically mixed residential environments in public housing estates could be developed. Such environments were seen as the ideal physical context to increase inter-ethnic contact and understanding. The sort of stereotyping which had prevented communal socio-cultural integration earlier on would gradually disappear.

The removal of significant segments of the population from their traditional housing environments, their incorporation in a new housing system and physical integration were also considered desirable to bring about the type of socio-cultural change, as well as the adoption of new values necessary to put the country on the path to rapid economic modernization and swift transition towards a modern urban-industrial society. From this perspective the incorporation of the minority groups (especially the Malays) was considered particularly relevant, as a mechanism both for their socio-economic integration in mainstream life and to alter their attitude towards an "acquisitive mentality." The perceived advantage of the government policies outlined above as catalysts of change provided additional legitimacy to the removal of concentrations of Malays through clearance and resettlement in public housing (see Van Grunsven, 1990).

The private sector and property developers as agents of change

The large-scale public housing program left little opportunity for a significant expansion of the private housing sector. Another factor was the price of private-sector housing, which was relatively high due to the high cost of land. Thus private-sector housing was beyond the reach of most urban households. The private sector consists of a range of dwelling types: bungalows, semi-detached and row houses, private flats and condominium housing. It constitutes only ten percent of the urban housing market.

While the share of this sector in the total housing market has remained comparatively stable, there has been a steady expansion in absolute terms, as noted earlier. Since the mid-1980s, many new property projects, particularly high-rise condominiums, have been completed and launched. These condominiums, catering to the increased demand from the growing upper-middle and lower-upper class, have become a very visible element in the residential landscape, in part because of their concentration in particular parts of the city. Areas adjacent to the central city, the eastern corridor stretching to Bedok, and a western corridor stretching to Clementi, as shown in Map 6.1, have been very popular for condominium development. However, due to shortage of land and high land prices in these areas, more recently new projects have increasingly been developed in more outlying areas, adjacent to and in between New Towns. While there is a growing demand from relatively well-to-do households, the market is still rather constrained by high prices. Prices have particularly escalated in the private sector. Overall, residential property prices have risen 2.7 times since 1990; private residential property prices have risen by 3.2 times! This reflects not only the forces of demand and supply, but also substantial property speculation.

The Residential Landscape Revisited

Over the past thirty years the rapid process of housing change, under the aegis of the agents discussed above, has led to fundamental changes in the

Table 6.5 Key indicators of housing, 1970–1995

Year	Resident Private Households ('000)	Type of Housing				Home Ownership			
		% Private Houses	% HDB Flats	% Private Flats	% Others	% Overall	% Private Houses/ Flats	% HDB Flats	% Others
1970	374.8	14.4	33.5	5.1	47.0	29.4	38.8	20.9	34.0
1980	472.7	8.5	68.5	2.3	20.7	58.8	72.3	60.6	46.0
1990	661.7	7.0	84.6	4.1	4.3	87.5	85.1	89.4	56.5
1995	773.5	6.1	88.2	4.0	1.7	90.3	90.0	90.6	74.0

Source: Department of Statistics (1995)

housing and residential patterns of the population. Two aspects of these changes are depicted in Table 6.5. The 2.8 million people living in this metropolis presently enjoy a level of housing consumption unparalleled in the Southeast Asian region. The large-scale shift of the population to public housing has also led to significant changes in the aspect of *spatial* residential patterning or division. The rapidly improving economic environment, expressed at household level in substantial improvement in living standard, together with specific government policies and developments in the private sector of the housing market have provided a rare dynamic to the patterning. Two elements will be discussed below, the ethnic and the socio-economic factor.

From segregation to residential integration

The question whether dispersal of the ethnic minority groups, particularly the Malay community, and residential integration have been achieved may be considered by first looking at the related objective of their incorporation in the public housing sector. The changes between 1970 and 1982 as to the distribution of households of each of the ethnic groups by type of dwelling indicate that the objective of incorporation had been reached. For example, in this period the percentage of Malay households living in an HDB flat increased from 23 percent to 77 percent. The latter percentage was higher than for any of the other ethnic groups. In 1985 the proportion of Malays among the population living in an HDB flat was equal to that among the population at large (Li, 1989; Wong and Yeh, 1985).

However, the pattern of incorporation of Malay households into public housing was different to that of the Chinese. In the early 1980s a much larger proportion of the Malay households living in public housing were found in the smaller rented dwellings (Humphrey, 1985). The different pattern of in-mobility can be explained by their different socio-economic characteristics.

In the allocation of new public housing units to its regular clientele, the Housing and Development Board had adopted the "first-come-first-served" system. A substantial number of new housing projects was under development at any one time. In addition, in each project a mix of different types of dwelling units was made available, catering to different income groups. At any point in time the stock of newly completed dwelling units to be allocated would be quite diverse in terms of type and location. Thus, in the case of voluntary relocation the "first-come-first-served" system was considered to be sufficiently effective to achieve dispersal and integration.

It was mentioned earlier that a significant segment of the Malay community was living in "squatter" areas. Implementation of the integration policy meant that these areas became priorities for clearance. Care was taken not to rehouse households from the same clearance area "en bloc", but to disperse them over a number of housing projects. However, dispersal through clearance and resettlement was limited by the prevailing supply of vacant dwellings. Yet between 1970 and the mid-1980s substantial de-clustering of the minority communities (especially the Malays), and desegregation of the ethnic groups have occurred, at least at the macro-level.

At the level of the neighborhood and precincts, residential integration of the different ethnic groups has been established (the Malays mostly assuming a minority position). At the micro-scale – individual high-rise blocks in public housing estates – the pattern of ethnic distribution showed two distinct features. First, ethnic mixing at block level was the rule rather than the exception. No block was found to be occupied entirely by one ethnic group. However, households of minority groups tended to group together at the same floor within individual high-rise blocks (Straits Times, March 1988). Apparently the allocation mechanism has been less effective at this level. The minority groups have been able to use the imperfections in the system to effectuate their preference to live next to a family of the same ethnic group. Evidence of this preference has been provided by Chiew Seen Kong (1976, 1983).

One consequence of the pattern at the micro-level has been, that inter-ethnic interaction has remained rather limited (Van Grunsven, 1990; Tai Ching Ling, 1988; Wong and Yeh, 1985). Thus, the dominant orientation of members of each of the ethnic groups towards members of the own group was hardly modified. This brings us to the question of the longer-term stability of residential integration.

Maintaining dispersal and residential integration

While the measures which have been in force from the end of the 1960s have been effective in *achieving* residential integration, they appear to have been less effective in *maintaining* it. During the second half of the 1980s evidence of a trend towards re-clustering of minority groups surfaced. The recent developments in the Singaporean context seem to provide additional empirical evidence that household movements in the housing market which are less subject to control by either the measures originally devised to achieve residential integration or the existing housing distribution mechanisms sooner or later tend to result in spontaneous regrouping of ethnic minorities.

Towards the end of the 1980s evidence of the following elements in the pattern of change emerged:

- a tendency towards less residential integration at the meso- and macro-levels;
- a tendency towards a greater degree of concentration of the minority

groups (particularly the Malays) in particular parts of the city;
- a tendency for the Malays to re-cluster in a number of blocks in a few public housing estates. These estates are generally those where representation of Malays was already "above average" in 1980 (Cheng Lim Keak, 1995, Straits Times several issues).

The main factor responsible for the emergence of these tendencies is the operation of the *resale market* in public housing which until recently has been comparatively uncontrolled.

Though subject to a number of restrictions, households owning a HDB-flat were allowed to sell on the open market after five years of occupancy. Already during the 1980s a large number of households "filtered up" in the public sector by applying for larger flats and selling their present homes in the open market, by moving from a rental flat to a larger purchased flat (either a newly constructed one or one bought in the resale market), or by selling and purchasing in the resale market (Van Grunsven, 1990). As noted earlier, the pattern of incorporation of the Malays in the public housing sector was significantly different from that of the Chinese, due to their less favorable socio-economic position. During the 1980s the economic participation of the Malays increased steadily and the community became gradually incorporated in the industrial economy (Mattar, 1984). But, while large segments of the Malay population have been able to improve their socio-economic position during this period, the pace of improvement was not as fast as that of other ethnic groups, particularly the Chinese (Van Grunsven, 1990).

Consequently, during the 1980s the Malays started to participate increasingly in upward mobility within the public housing sector. Between 1980 and 1990 the proportion of Malay households living in HDB dwellings increased from 72 percent to 97 percent. In 1980 30.3 percent of Malay households lived in a one- or two-room flat. This percentage decreased substantially to 6.4 percent in 1990. As Malay households renting one- or two-room flats upgraded and bought their own flats, the proportion living in three-room flats and four-room or larger flats increased from 32.9 percent in 1980 to 49.1 percent in 1990, and from 8.8 percent in 1980 to 41.7 percent in 1990 respectively (Toh Mun Heng and Tay Boon Nga, 1994; Cheng Lim Keak, 1995). A large share of Malay mobility has involved movement from the rental sector to a three-room flat bought in the resale market. In order to be able to buy a flat in the resale market, the prospective buyer has to satisfy both the general criteria which govern access to the public housing sector and the more specific criteria which govern eligibility for a particular type of flat. They pertain to citizenship, household size and household income (Van Grunsven, 1990). The fact that ethnicity and location have not been among the criteria has enabled households in each of the ethnic groups to buy a resale flat in a location particularly favored by them. Unrestricted movement of households from one public housing area to another has resulted in a process of succession of the majority group by the minority group (i.e. Chinese households by Malay households).

The failure to maintain dispersal or residential integration has hardly provoked a discussion among policy makers about the underlying causes of re-clustering, nor about the merits or demerits of the government policy which had been pursued for more than 20 years. Indeed, the basic tenets of the policy of residential integration, implying dispersal of minority groups, have remained unquestioned. They have even been reaffirmed by the government after the trend towards re-clustering came to light (Straits Times, several issues, January 1989). Thus the government has attributed the failure to maintain dispersal mainly to "imperfections" in regulation and control associated with the hitherto employed housing market measures and claimed that the mechanisms through which re-clustering has emerged simply indicated deficiencies in the system of control. It is hardly surprising therefore that in early 1989 the government intervened in re-clustering.

The government has responded by increased regulation of household movement aimed at preventing the renewed development of enclaves and stopping the process of neighborhoods becoming ethnically more homogeneous again. Specifically, for reasons which may be clear from the foregoing, this intervention took the administratively convenient form of tightening control through devising a new set of public housing allocation rules, aimed at blocking the mechanisms which enabled a movement towards a more segregated state. The new set of rules involved specific limits to the proportion of flats each ethnic group is allowed to occupy in each neighborhood, and in each block in the public housing estates. The limits on individual blocks have been set three percentage points higher than the limits on neighborhoods to allow some variation in ethnic proportion from block to block (Cheng Lim Keak, 1995; Van Grunsven, 1992; Straits Times, several issues).

The ethnic limits have been introduced as an additional criterion in the allocation of new flats in newly completed neighborhoods and housing blocks in the public housing estates and New Towns. When the limit for a particular ethnic group is reached under the "first-come-first-served" system, allocation to that group will be stopped. As far as the existing stock is concerned, as at February 1989, 35 out of the total of 125 neighborhoods, and 1,177 out of the 4,825 housing blocks, did not conform to the ethnic limits (Straits Times, March 1989). The latter figure provides some illustration of the abovementioned tendencies at the micro-scale.

Households were not forced to move from or to existing neighborhoods and/or blocks which did not conform to the ethnic limits. However, transactions in the resale market became subject to restrictions implied by the ethnic limits. This means that each proposed transaction is checked against the existing ethnic distribution (in the neighborhood and block concerned) on the one hand and the ethnic limits on the other hand. The general principle is that the group which has already exceeded its limit in a particular neighborhood or block is not allowed to "grow" at that location until the neighborhood and/or block proportion for that group falls below the limit (Straits Times, March 1989; Van Grunsven, 1992). Thus, under the new rules in a neighborhood/block with too many Chinese a Chinese owner can sell his flat to a buyer from any ethnic group, but non-Chinese owners can sell to non-Chinese buyers only. The ethnic limits also apply to the rental subsector.

Clearly, the government has adopted the view that the effectuation of housing and locational preferences should be sacrificed for the higher goal of residential integration. It has publicly justified this by arguing that a balanced social and ethnic mix in housing estates leads to harmonious living and better understanding among the races.

It is interesting to note here that it is not to be expected that the ethnic limits will affect or significantly alter residential patterns at the micro-scale. This is not to argue that, therefore, the imposition of ethnic limits should be accompanied by mechanisms which can assure ethnic distribution at the micro-level according to a predetermined pattern. This would require total control. While this is feasible in the Singapore context, the government itself has so far refrained from such extreme intervention. This is understandable if we perceive that, to the government, the issue is secondary to the political aspects of ethnic dispersal and residential integration versus segregation. In relation to the re-clustering tendencies and government responses, the Minister for National Development pronounced that: " . . . living in separate enclaves, community leaders will develop narrow views of society's interests. The enclaves will become the seedbeds for communal agitation. We will witness the unraveling of what we have knit so carefully since independence." (Straits Times, January 1989).

Socio-economic status in the residential pattern: evolution

The socio-economic element in spatial residential patterning that started in the early 1960s – specifically the residential divides – was also substantially reshaped during the 1960s and 1970s. This was due to the changes in the housing market outlined earlier. As was the case with respect to the ethnic element, more recently – during the 1980s and early 1990s – a specific dynamic has characterized this element, such as to prompt the government into action over outcomes which it considered either undesirable or politically expedient to address.

The story of socio-economic residential patterning that lasted from 1960 until the end of the 1970s briefly goes as follows. The government interventions in the housing market resulted in the gradual dissolution of concentrations of lower-income groups (Van Grunsven, 1990; Humphrey, 1985; Cheng Lim Keak, 1995). As the lower-income groups, together with the middle class, became increasingly incorporated in the public housing sector, the practice of spatial mixing of dwelling types, as well as of rented and owner-occupied housing adopted by HDB ensured that substantial socio-economic mixing occurred at neighborhood, estate and New Town levels. In general, public housing areas showed little differentiation in socio-economic profile of the residents, both internally between neighborhoods and at a macro-level between public housing estates and New Towns. At the latter level a clear divide emerged between the public housing areas and areas dominated by private housing, i.e. areas with predominantly low-rise terrace houses, more luxurious semi-detached houses and bungalows on the one hand and private apartment complexes on the other hand. These became the domain of the local upper class (the business and professional elite), the growing expatriate community and the local upper-middle class.

The dynamics during the 1980s and early 1990s involved a number of processes and resultant developments. Increases in standard of living led to both newly formed households and those already resident in public housing having higher housing aspirations. Many people living in the public housing areas developed during the 1960s and early 1970s decided to shift to a new, larger, and better (and for many previous tenants an owner-occupied) flat in the New Towns. Residential mobility within the public sector of the filtering-up type grew to a large volume in the course of the 1980s (Van Grunsven, 1986, 1990).

By the end of the 1980s such mobility had become evident in respect of the New Towns developed during the 1970s, but the impact was more severe and most apparent in the public housing estates and New Towns of the 1960s. The population base was affected and demographic characteristics were altered in more than one way. The absolute population declined substantially as the vacancy rate in the rental stock increased rapidly. This was reinforced by the thinning out of non-mobile households living in three-room owner-occupied flats. As younger people moved out, households' age profile rose (Straits Times, May 8, 1989). More important in the context of the discussion here, in the overwhelming majority of the occupancy mutations the socio-economic status (measured by occupational group and income of working members) of the incoming households was lower than that of the outgoing households. Thus, to some extent socio-economic downgrading occurred as well. Because of the smaller and older population, consumption started to decline. This affected the base necessary for shops, businesses and other facilities to operate successfully. Also, public facilities and social amenities became underutilized, leading to deterioration. This affected the overall living environment even further.

At the same time, further spatial residential division in socio-economic terms was engendered by the rise of spatial concentrations of households in the upper-middle and lower-upper classes (with dual income-earners in professional occupations), linked to the growing number of condominium complexes. These effectively introduced gated communities, with residents enjoying rather luxurious housing and a range of exclusive amenities, well cordoned off by fences and guarded barriers restricting access by outsiders. The significance of these complexes should be seen not only in terms of deepening the spatial socio-economic divisions in Singapore. A significant demonstration effect is derived from the visibility of these complexes in the city; they have come to be regarded by sections of the population which are somewhat less well off yet aspiring to socio-economic improvement, as epitomes of individual success. They have become a reference point by which these sections in the 1990s can define their housing and living environment aspirations.

Towards the end of the 1980s the government took the view that the outcomes of the dynamics outlined here had to be addressed through new approaches and policies if the socio-economic residential fabric was to be maintained (i.e., if spatial socio-economic divisions were not to deepen even further), and if it were to avoid the severe political costs which would no doubt result from leaving housing and living environment aspirations unanswered.

The public housing areas of the 1960s and 1970s: policy responses

From the above developments and the basic tenets underlying housing and residential policy which were to be upheld, the government formulated a number of challenges:

- How to redress the physical, economic, and social impact of an increasing vacancy rate of rental dwellings, population decline, ageing and socio-economic downgrading in the 1960s New Towns, and to restore the socio-economic balance *vis-à-vis* newer New Towns.
- How to prevent similar developments occurring in the New Towns of the 1970s and to put a brake on residential mobility.
- How at the same time to address potential sources of dissatisfaction and effectively manage housing and living environment aspirations, increasing with growing affluence.

To meet these challenges, the government and housing authority adopted a number of new policies and programs. First, many of the tenants of the one-room units constructed during the 1960s were resettled in public-sector housing during the second half of the 1980s, and their old homes demolished. Demolition and redevelopment (i.e., construction of new, larger and better-designed, flats) have become very visible in for example Toa Payoh, one of the New Towns (Table 6.6). Through the replacement of one-room rental flats with four-room, five-room and executive owner-occupied flats, households of higher socio-economic status than the longer resident households have been attracted to this New Town again.

Table 6.6 Composition of the housing stock in Toa Payoh New Town, 1985 and 1995 (absolute numbers)

		1-room	*2-room*	*3-room*	*4-room*	*5-room*	*Exec*	*Total*
1985	rental	11,368	5,416	81	–	–	–	16,865
	owner-occupied	–	258	15,342	2,607	768	–	18,975
1995	rental	1,755	3,837	136	30	–	–	5,758
	owner-occupied	–	259	17,776	5,732	3,034	1,020	27,821

Source: HDB Annual Reports

Second, at the end of the 1980s physical rejuvenation of the older estates and New Towns was given the much broader meaning of upgrading the total housing, living, and social environment. In mid-1989 the government announced a massive upgrading program, encompassing all estates and New Towns constructed before 1980. Under this program, to be carried out over a period of 15 to 20 years starting in 1991, a total of S$15 billion would be invested in housing and environmental upgrading. The aim is to revitalize these public housing areas and upgrade the total environment to a standard comparable to or even better than the standard found in the HDB's newest New Towns, thus giving these areas a more upmarket, high-quality environment and narrowing the gap between public housing estates and condominium complexes in terms of living environment. (For a comprehensive discussion, see HDB Annual Reports and Teo Siew Eng and Kong, 1997).

The key components of the upgrading program are:

- Improvements of the inside of the flats. These include better sanitary fittings and the addition of an extended kitchen/dining area and extra bathroom or toilet for flats which have only one bathroom/toilet.
- Improvements at block level, such as upgraded corridors, staircases, facade design emphasizing individuality, improved lift lobbies and enclosure of lobbies and entrances to limit access, and improve security.
- At neighborhood or precinct level, breaking up these units into distinct groupings of five to seven blocks only, and allowing each to have a distinct appearance as well as resident-controlled access within them. In addition, at this level new amenities will be added, such as multi-storey

car parks, walkways between blocks, landscaped gardens and children's playgrounds. It is possible that these groupings adopt a new, distinct area name, to ensure individual identity.

After a pilot and demonstration phase, the Main Upgrading Program (MUP) entered the steady phase in 1995. The program will be carried out in batches of six neighborhoods. For each neighborhood, the government will absorb 80–90 percent of the total costs involved. As noted above, the MUP will take many years to complete. To bring the benefits of upgrading to more estates faster, the Interim Upgrading Program (IUP) was introduced in 1993. While the MUP will initially concentrate on neighborhoods 18 years or older, the IUP will be carried out in neighborhoods between 10 and 17 years of age and improvements will be concentrated only on the housing blocks and neighborhood surroundings.

The deeper underlying aims of redevelopment and the upgrading program seem to involve more than was stated above. First, over the past decades the construction sector has made a not insignificant contribution to economic growth (Van Grunsven, 1990). However, in the course of the 1980s the slowdown in population growth and new household formation have had a negative impact on the scale of new residential construction. Non-residential construction has also slowed down substantially during the second half of the 1980s due to the fact that the unprecedented investment in non-residential buildings during the first half of the 1980s had resulted in an oversupply of offices, shops and other non-residential floor-space. The overall result has been a slump in the construction sector. Thus, in part economic considerations may have led the government to formulate the large-scale upgrading program.

Second, there is the question whether the physical and living environment of many public housing estates and older New Towns is conducive to social interaction, neighborliness and community spirit. This has been a constant source of concern to the government and the housing authority. Whatever the "hidden agenda" and the potential for achievement, the policies and programs discussed above seem to offer the prospect of spatial divisions in the residential pattern in socio-economic terms not being deepened, indeed maintaining or re-engineering spatial balance in this aspect.

Conclusion

It is clear that a new spatial order has arisen in Singapore since the 1960s. However, this new spatial order has not been constant. On the one hand, a movement in the direction of "re-divisioning", or a broader (i.e. more refined) divisioning, with new, more or less permanent elements in the patterning (especially in the socio-economic aspect) can be discerned. On the other hand, we have seen that a trend towards more divisioning is followed by a trend in the opposite direction. It may be compared to the swing of a pendulum. The permanent finer division – the forward swing of the pendulum – is very much related to the autonomous force of economic change, how this is reflected in the dynamics of class structure (resulting from household changes in standard of living or level of affluence), changing housing aspirations, as well as socio-cultural inclinations. However, the operation of specific agents in the housing market has played a significant role as well. While part of the dynamic has been influenced by the operations of private agents, it is particularly the role of government which should be highlighted here. Not only does the spatial order established during the 1960s and 1970s to a large extent reflect the government's pursuit of specific policies guided by specific goals and tenets, the backward swing of the pendulum also reflects the intervention of government in autonomous dynamics in an attempt to redress outcomes which are considered incongruous with the basic tenets underlying government policy.

Considering the range of factors and processes indicated in the overall framework as the main forces leading to spatial change within cities, some appear to be applicable in the Singapore context. But many do not or have operated in a different way, leading to different outcomes. This should not come as a surprise, considering the fact that Singapore has been very much on the winning side as to the manifold processes of economic change (at many levels) which characterize the post-Fordist stage of capitalist development. Issues of exclusion, increased polarization, and deepening cultural or racial cleavages have little validity here. This implies that the residential divisions, segregation and decay associated with these do not have much validity here either.

The foregoing discussion supports the view that Singapore stands out among other metropolitan areas in the region and particularly among many of the Western cases discussed elsewhere in this book, in that where changes in its spatial order and underlying forces can be linked to globalization or internationalization as part of the post-Fordist phase of capitalism, the outcomes are at variance with other cases. It demonstrates that the types of partitioning of the economic structure of society and of the metropolitan space which is seen as characteristic of the post-Fordist phase of capitalism do not necessarily hold outside the realm of the traditional core areas of the world economy. Whether Singapore – and also other metropolitan areas in the developing Asian Pacific Rim region – at some stage in the future will be confronted with changes and issues like those highlighted in the rest of this book as yet remains a matter of speculation.

Notes

1   The high occupational category consists of legislators, senior officials and managers, professionals, technicians, and associate professionals; the middle category consists of clerical workers; and the low category consists of service and sales workers, production/plant/machine operators, cleaners, and laborers.

2   For a discussion on home-ownership in Singapore's public housing, see e.g. HDB Annual Reports, Chua Beng Huat (1996); Lin Kuo Ching and Amina Tyabji (1991) and Van Grunsven (1990).

3   It also served a second purpose, namely the promotion of greater inter-ethnic understanding and interaction, considered a vital element of nation building in a multi-ethnic society. The third purpose concerned the promotion of the process of social change (particularly among the Malay community) which was considered necessary to achieve modernization (Van Grunsven, 1990; Tai Ching Ling, 1988) as well as the integration of the minority ethnic groups in the emerging new mainstream economy.

7

Tokyo: Patterns of Familiarity and Partitions of Difference[1]

Paul Waley

Among the recurrent impressions that strike the visitor to Tokyo are its clutter and lack of urban plan accompanied by an apparently contradictory sense of social order. As in other Pacific Asian capitals, the clutter can be related to the different layers in the built form of the urban structure subsisting one on the other like geological strata. On top, there is Metropolitan Tokyo, center of finance capital, city of high-rise office blocks and international hotels, its high-order urban functions a reflection of primate status. Below, cut off by highways and railway lines, are the variegated expanses and shared spaces of trade, manufacture, and habitation, manifestations of local-level adaptability as much as they are of a lack of central planning (Abeyasekere, 1987; McGee and Yeung, 1993). Through much of the post-war period Tokyo has experienced a gradual expansion and then a rapid explosion of mushroom clusters of higher-order functions combined with a retreat and a rearguard action from the barricades of the backstreet factories, community buildings, shopping streets, and serried houses of the inner-city areas.

This chapter starts out with a brief survey of the post-war historical and geographical expression of the close alliance between industrial capital and the state, charting Tokyo's growing centrality within the Japanese urban system. At the thematic center of this chapter's concerns lie the tensions between corporate expansion through urban space on the one hand and change at the local level on the other, set against the frenetic events of the 1980s and 1990s, when average land prices in Tokyo rose fourfold only to fall back to near their starting point. The effects on Tokyo's inhabitants of this remorseless process of change are assessed, as are the sometimes contradictory attempts to contain corporate encroachment.[2] The final part of this chapter juxtaposes some of the familiar interpretations of the socio-spatial effects of urban restructuring – disenfranchisement and pauperization, gentrification and internationalization – with patterns discernible in the Tokyo conurbation.

It would be hard to deny that the relatively equitable distribution of wealth in Japan during much of the post-war period of economic growth has played an important part in minimizing spatial concentrations of poverty in her large cities. At the same time, it is necessary to avoid the dangers of a simplistic cultural-determinist response. Sub-standard living and travelling conditions and very high consumer prices might easily have created conditions of profound social malaise, coupled as they were in the 1980s by a deteriorating quality of urban life at the very time when fast-growing corporate investment was directed toward the exploitation of urban land. Indeed, for a time in the late 1980s, it was widely predicted that a widening wealth gap between owners of land and those without, the haves and have-nots, was creating the conditions for social unrest (Do Rosario, 1990).

I will argue that central-government policies exacerbated problems caused by the use of urban space as a vehicle for corporate expansion but that a continued, if somewhat diminished sense of social order, tapped and co-ordinated by urban managers, served even if in a wayward and contradictory way to mitigate the impact. In so doing, I will place in narrative opposition the story of rampant corporate advance through the urban territory and the many lesser tales of confused activity at the local level. The resulting picture sets Tokyo somewhat at variance with other cities discussed in this volume. I will argue in response to the initial proposition posed by Peter Marcuse and Ronald van Kempen that what we have seen develop is not so much a new spatial order as an accentuation of pre-existing trends, first of expansion in Tokyo's higher-order functions within the conurbation, secondly of urban sprawl within the Kantô region of east Japan, and thirdly of the region as a whole within the country. Holding operations mounted at a local level have probably done no more than slow down this process, while social dislocation is unlikely to form spatial patterns of concentration and poverty unlikely to be spatialized for the foreseeable future.

Sprawl and Primacy: the Tokyo Conurbation in the Post-war Period

By the 1930s, Tokyo's dominance over other Japanese cities was already firmly established, and with it, the dominance of oligopolistic corporate interests. But the process had begun long before then, for even before the defeat of the shogun in 1868 at the hands of imperial forces, the old social and spatial boundaries between the military-political capital and the city of the merchants had grown increasingly blurred. From the late 19th century on, the state increasingly identified for itself a supervisory role in urban management, occasionally making land available and a limited infrastructure, and forging alliances with merchant-industrialist entrepreneurs. The latter exploited their power and proximity to government and invested heavily in the city, shaping it in their interests and profiting as a consequence. Housing conditions remained poor throughout most of the first half of the 20th century, even as employment opportunities increased and the city spread voraciously out into neighboring areas.

The process of urban expansion within the Kantô plain and its surrounding hills has been given substance by a series of dispersal plans, whose purported aim has been to take pressure off the city but the consequence of which has been, paradoxically, to accelerate the process of urban sprawl.[3] One of the most far-reaching of these plans was a measure introduced in 1959 designed to remove from the 23-ward area large factories, university campuses, and other such 'inefficient' users of land. As a result, factories moved out and universities relocated campuses to distant suburbs, their place being taken by apartment blocks and office developments, all of them using urban space more intensively (Ishida, 1992). The creation of a vast metropolitan region has been further enhanced by a number of other measures. Among these is the construction within a 30 to 50 kilometre radius of several large 'new towns' with populations in the hundred-thousands and by the designation in 1985 of a number of existing urban centers as "satellite business cities" (Map 7.1).[4] Ishida suggests that, rather than absorbing excess capacity from Tokyo, these subsidiary centers have accrued new and supplementary functions. Tokyo's leaders were, in Douglass' words, "alleviating existing land use conflicts by expanding Tokyo's area rather than making more difficult choices" (1988, p. 449).

These trends have been reinforced by the outcome of policies implemented in central parts of the conurbation. In 1983, six sub-centers (*fuku toshin*) were designated, with the aim of making Tokyo a multi-core city (Map 7.2). Planning controls were eased, as they were in the new satellite cities, so as to allow for more intense exploitation of land. To the six sub-centers (which included the office, retail, and entertainment districts surrounding some of the world's busiest railway junctions, Shinjuku, Shibuya, Ikebukuro) was added a seventh in 1986 on land reclaimed from the bay. This was the Waterfront Sub-center (*rinkaibu fuku toshin*), which itself was but one of many large-scale bay-side projects, projects which continued – indeed, brought to an apogee – a long tradition of land reclamation from coastal waters and of urban projects (most of them never realized) in Tokyo Bay (Bourdier, 1993).

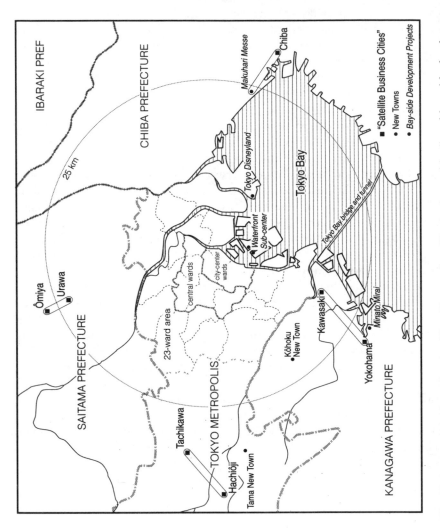

Map 7.1 The Tokyo conurbation, showing New Towns, "satellite business cities," and bay-side development projects

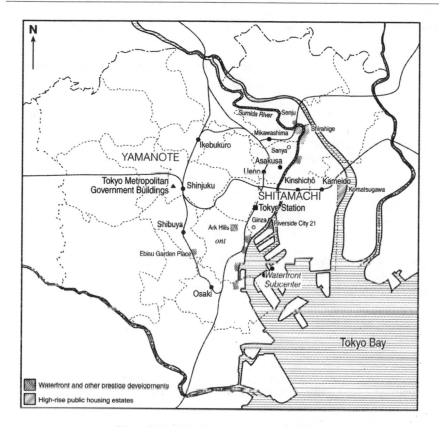

Map 7.2   The 23-ward area of Tokyo

The exploitation of the bay-side area was matched in central Tokyo by a number of private-sector developments, some of them on land sold off by the government, involving the construction of high-rise office buildings, hotels, and conference and cultural facilities. Taken together, these plans and developments acted to enlarge the expanse of city-center space devoted to higher-order urban functions.

This process of intensification of business functions at the center and generalized extension at the periphery is reflected in the changing patterns of population, which show a hollowing out at the center, stagnation in the older metropolitan area, but growth in the conurbation (Table 7.1).[5] The population haemorrhage was most dramatic of all in the three city-center wards in the second half of the 1980s (a fall of about 59,000, almost 20 per cent), but it was considerable in all the central wards (TMG, 1996a, p. 205; Map 7.3).

Table 7.1 Population of Tokyo, its region, and Japan (absolute figures (abs) in millions, percentages as part of total population in Japan)

	1975	*1980*	*1985*	*1990*	*1995*
Japan					
absolute figures in millions	111.94	117.06	121.05	123.61	125.57
National capital region*					
absolute figures in millions	33.62	35.70	37.62	39.40	40.40
percentages	30.0%	30.5%	31.1%	31.9%	32.2%
Tokyo region**					
absolute figures in millions	27.04	28.70	30.27	31.80	32.57
percentages	24.2%	24.5%	25.0%	25.7%	25.9%
Saitama prefecture (abs)	4.82	5.42	5.86	6.40	6.76
Chiba prefecture (abs)	4.15	4.73	5.15	5.55	5.80
Kanagawa prefecture (abs)	6.40	6.92	7.43	7.98	8.25
Tokyo metropolis (abs)	11.67	11.62	11.83	11.85	11.77
23 Ward area (abs)	8.65	8.35	8.35	8.16	7.97

* National capital region (shutoken) composed of the following prefectures: Ibaragi, Tochigi, Gunma, Saitama, Chiba, Kanagawa, Yamanashi and Tokyo metropolis.
** Tokyo region (Tôkyô ken): Saitama, Chiba, Kanagawa and Tokyo metropolis.
Source: Kokudochô (1996, p. 17)

The highest growth rate in the first half of the 1990s was, tellingly, in a radius of 30 to 50 kilometres from the city center (Kokudochô, 1996, p. 18).

At the root of this irresistible trend toward the ever greater centrality of the Tokyo conurbation within the country lies the functional stranglehold that Japan's capital city holds. It is the financial, political, and industrial center.[6] Critically, it is also the center for information dissemination, for cultural production, for education and research, and for all the service industries that have grown on the back of the computer revolution. Fujita Kuniko has described it as the "City of London, Silicon Valley, and the Third Italy all wrapped up into one dynamic region" (Fujita and Hill, 1993, p. 9).

It is important to note too that, despite a partial decline, the Tokyo region remains Japan's industrial heartland. Three key indices for manufacturing – the number of enterprises, number of workers, and factory-gate output – have remained unchanged or declined only slightly in Tokyo and the six eastern prefectures since 1980. In Tokyo's three adjacent prefectures, the figures for each index reached a peak as recently as 1988 (Kokudochô, 1996,

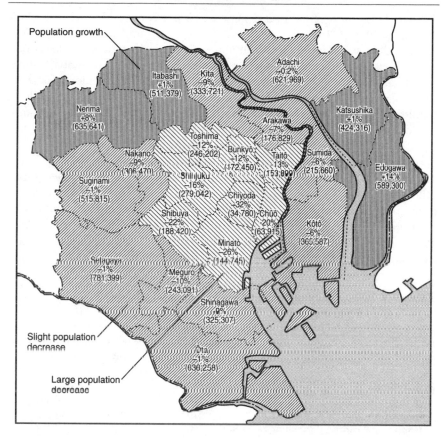

Map 7.3 Population of Tokyo wards in 1995 and population change, 1985–
1995

p. 98). Within this picture of continued industrial concentration in the Tokyo
conurbation, the second half of the 1980s saw a slow retreat of manufacturing industry in inner city areas, as economies created by concentration and
lower transport costs as well as affection for a neighborhood with which
multiple ties existed could no longer outweigh the costs and diseconomies of
operating on such expensive land. Small-scale manufacturers suffered particularly from the rise in the value of the yen against the dollar in 1986 and
1987 (Patrick and Rohlen, 1987). In Ôta Ward, where industrial output
totalled the same as that of a middle-ranking prefecture, there was a significant shift in land use away from industry (7.3 per cent between 1981 to
1990). In the inner city ward of Sumida the number of people employed in
manufacturing fell by almost a quarter between 1975 and 1985 to just under

48,000. This compared with a decline of 15 per cent for Tokyo as a whole (Sumida, 1989, p. 156).

The 1980s saw a rapid growth in office space particularly in the latter part of the decade, as the city's economy adopted new roles in the global control of capital and absorbed the new businesses needed to provide support for these higher-order services. This was reflected in the changing profile of employment, with a particularly sharp increase in the number of people working in the finance and insurance and real-estate sectors (TMG, 1993, p. 184). By 1987, companies in Tokyo offering information-related services accounted for half the national share in terms of annual turnover (TMG, 1989, p. 108). Eighty per cent of foreign-owned companies had their Japan offices in Tokyo (Kokudochô, 1991, p. 38). Office-building starts in terms of floor space rose from 154 hectares in 1981 to 485 hectares in 1988, with enormous growth in stock, especially in the three city-center wards (TMG, 1991, p. 70). Even so, empty office space remained at an astonishingly low rate of around 0.3 per cent in Tokyo (Kokudochô, 1991, p. 34).

Table 7.2 Selected examples of land use change in eight central and inner Tokyo wards*, 1986–1991, in hectares

Land use	1986 ha	1991 ha	% change
Public land			
government facilities	404	401	– 0.76
education and culture facilities	981	993	1.17
health and medical facilities	97	98	1,08
utilities and public provision	62	61	– 1.40
Commercial			
office buildings	783	1017	29.91
commercial facilities	154	155	0.67
hotels and lodging houses	180	175	– 2.76
sports and entertainment	67	78	17.38
Residential			
detached single-occupancy housing	1694	1463	– 13.62
multi-occupancy housing	1225	1288	5.15
Industrial			
industrial buildings	111	88	– 20.54
mixed industrial/residential	118	100	– 14.89
warehouse and distribution	213	199	– 6.58

* Chiyoda, Chûô, Minato, Shibuya, Shinjuku, Toshima, Bunkyô, Taitô wards.
Note: This table includes figures for all categories of "built land" (*takuchi*), categories used for assessment of land tax. The figures refer to plot size, not to floor space of buildings.
Source: TMG (1996a, p. 65)

Table 7.3 Relative change in use of floor space in Tokyo, 1980–1990

Three city-centre wards*	1980 %	1990 %
Housing	27.52	25.60
Offices	46.69	55.79
Shops	8.22	6.60
Factories	2.50	1.44
Warehouses	6.03	4.49
Other	6.04	6.08
*Eight central wards***		
Housing	49.94	46.97
Offices	30.73	36.22
Shops	7.34	6.40
Factories	2.44	1.56
Warehouses	4.25	3.24
Other	5.30	5.61

* Chiyoda, Chûô, Minato wards.
** Chiyoda, Chûô, Minato, Shibuya, Shinjuku, Toshima, Bunkyô, Taitô wards.
Source: TMG (1991, p. 141)

The process of land-use change is captured in some revealing figures for the city's eight central wards (Tables 7.2 and 7.3). In terms purely of land use rather than floor space, there was a 30 per cent shift to office buildings in the five years from 1986 to 1991. Despite a significant decline in single-occupancy dwellings, a considerable amount of land in central areas remained dedicated to housing (and there was indeed a limited increase in the number of apartment blocks). Land use characteristic of the Japanese inner city – mixed function, storage and distribution, and industrial – receded before the advance of the office building.

The *gourmandise* of the center has inevitably led to scarcity elsewhere. Already in the 1930s, Japan's growing military involvement on the Asian continent had enhanced Tokyo's centrality to the detriment of Osaka (Hill and Fujita, 1995). In more recent times, the continuing process of industrial restructuring has downgraded the importance of the older industrial cities like Osaka, Nagoya, Kitakyushu, and other strongholds of heavy industry (Rimmer, 1986). The reinforcement of Tokyo's role as business center in the 1980s can be seen, as Douglass has pointed out, in its relationship with the capital cities of prefectures – localized control centers and homes to a growing number of employees sent out by head offices to man local outposts

(1988, p. 441). But above all else, it has been the casting of their net overseas by Japan's leading post-war industrial and trading corporations – their transformation into (Japanese-style) transnational corporations – that has propelled Tokyo onto a different plain from other Japanese cities.

Tokyo in the 1980s: City as Corporate Playground

Urban restructuring and the role of capital

The 1980s, and in particular the second half of the decade, was a period of exceptional change, indeed upheaval, exceptional even in the turbulent history of twentieth-century Tokyo. Driving these changes were three closely interlocked developments. First, as a result of a coincidence of economic circumstances, Tokyo property became a favoured outlet for speculative investment. Secondly, a number of restrictions on planning and construction were lifted, and political blessing was given to the use of urban land as a vehicle of corporate investment. And thirdly, an ideological imprimatur was placed on the restructuring of Tokyo through the burnishing for the Japanese capital of a new image as international city.

The insertion of Japanese capital and the Japanese capital into a global urban system conspired to set off a spark in central Tokyo in the mid 1980s that very rapidly led to a conflagration as property-price inflation spread first out from the city center through the capital and then to Japan's other major cities (Table 7.4). Spectacular though the rise was, it has been almost negated by subsequent falls in property values. By 1996, land prices in the 23-ward area had returned roughly to the level of ten years earlier, having fallen by a half in the case of residential land and by 75 per cent for commercial land from their peak values of 1988–91 (TMG, 1996a, p. 31).

As we have already noted, by 1974 half of the land in the three city-center wards not owned by government was in the hands of private corporations. During the second half of the 1980s, there was a notable increase in the amount of land held by corporations, as well as a concomitant process of consolidation. By 1989, four-fifths of all Tokyo land owned by corporations was in the hands of a minority of large land-holders (Oizumi, 1994, p. 206). They were therefore well placed not only to take advantage but actively to manipulate the market in order to exploit the situation to their greater benefit (Douglass, 1993, p. 87).

A word needs to be said at this point about the nature of Japan's leading corporations, not least in order to explain the commonality of purpose with which they took investment decisions. Many of their number had countered the rising value of the yen and the growing shortage of labour by investing overseas, increasingly in the Pacific Asian region. The big names of Japanese

Table 7.4 Changes in price of commercial and residential land* in Tokyo, 1985–1996 (thousand yen per square meter)

Wards	1985	1990	1995	1996
Chiyoda (central Tokyo)				
commercial	4,334	17,512	6,336	4,716
residential	1,706	9,080	2,878	2,174
Shinjuku (central-inner)				
commercial	5,031	16,085	5,172	3,881
residential	578	2,024	836	700
Sumida (inner city)				
commercial	711	3,474	1,291	969
residential	278	610	421	480
Nerima (suburban)				
commercial	849	3,088	1,013	888
residential	282	773	459	446

* Categories used for valuation and assessment purposes for land tax (*kotei shisan zei*).
Source: TMG (1996a, pp. 143/4)

manufacturing were followed by some of their larger component suppliers and by independent middle-ranking companies. The city banks and general construction companies also extended their activities worldwide during this period. However, although international in their operations, Japanese corporations never became international in terms of ownership, management, or employee structures (Machimura, 1994, p. 84). They remained Japanese-owned and Japanese-based companies with an upper echelon of Japanese executives. They were transnational companies with worldwide networks but driven by a Tokyo-oriented decision-making framework.

Falling interest rates at home (down to an official discount rate of 2.5 per cent in 1987) made land one of the most attractive berths for excess liquidity. The large Japanese corporations found themselves either flush with repatriated profits or with the proceeds resulting from cheaper import. But, rather than raise salaries, lower prices, or pay out higher share dividends, which tended to be low relative to share price, they chose one of two routes. The first was investment in real estate, in which choice they were encouraged by a tax system that exempted land from capital gains tax so long as it was held and not sold (Noguchi, 1994, p. 310).[7] The second was the raising of funds on the stock exchange, an action facilitated by deregulation of the financial markets, and the profitable deposit of these funds in bank accounts that paid higher rates of interest (Noguchi, 1994, p. 297). Meanwhile, the banks found themselves awash with liquidity and shorn of their favourite corporate clients, for whom the stock exchange was now a cheaper source of funds. Desperate for custom, the banks diverted parts of their assets to real estate companies or to subsidiaries specially created for the purpose of investment in property development. By 1989 banks of all categories were directing almost ¥41 trillion, a sum well over half the national budget, into real estate (Hayakawa and Hirayama, 1991, p. 161; Oizumi, 1994, p. 205). From here funds made their way into the accounts of land developers and property speculators, many of whom used gangster groups to consolidate plots.

In continuing, as they were, a long tradition of activity in urban land markets, speculators were creating conditions which, as Wegener has shown, responded to their own self-fulfilling expectations (1994, p. 101). Land was treated as a commodity like any other, with supply seemingly unproblematic. There were small plots to be bought up and amalgamated, relaxations in plot-to-floor-space regulations to be taken advantage of, former factory and warehouse sites and government land to be bought up and built on, and new land reclaimed from the bay to be developed. With a growing gap between inflated demand for property and its supply in new office space and with speculators operating in the expectation of ever-rising prices, conditions were in place for the creation of what was soon to become known as the bubble economy. The city had become the crucial frontier for capital, and land in Tokyo a machine for making money (Machimura, 1992, p. 122).

Urban restructuring and changes in government policy

The urban restructuring occasioned by this surge in investment in land was underpinned by the traditionally close ties between politicians and corporate interests. It coincided with a period of relative political stability both at the central and metropolitan government levels. Under the prime ministership of Nakasone Yasuhiro in the mid-1980s, the Japanese government introduced a consistently more right-wing line throughout its policies. The Soviet threat was deployed as an argument to justify increases in defence spending. At home, there was a new emphasis on traditionalistic, indeed nationalistic moral values, especially in education policy. In the arena of economic affairs, a political climate was engendered favorable to corporate interests, epitomized by a loosening of government regulatory controls on various areas of activity, including urban development. Many of these policies bore a resemblance to those being introduced at about the same time in Britain and the US. Three in particular dominated political discourse for much of the 1980s: the use of private enterprise, the expansion of domestic demand, and internationalization.

The first of these was generally referred to in Japanese as *minkatsu*, short for *minkan katsuryoku no katsuryô*, and meaning something like the "active use of the dynamism of private enterprise". Although it involved both an element of deregulation and of privatisation, it was envisaged as a more eclectic operation when it was launched in 1983 than either of these terms suggests. It became an official invitation for private corporations to involve themselves in urban development projects through participation in *dai san sekutaa* (third sector), joint private-public companies (O'Leary and Machimura, 1995).

Hayakawa and Hirayama call *minkatsu* "a mechanism for reorganizing urban space in pursuit of economic growth" and see it as consisting of relaxation of zoning, disposal of public land, and measures advantageous to private landowners (1991, p. 152). The deregulation that this entailed often had a pivotal bearing, involving as it did changes to the ratio of floor space to plot size in inner-city and inner suburban areas and directly facilitating the construction of office buildings in a particularly sensitive belt of land. Meanwhile, it was the sale through competitive bidding of government land in key sites in Tokyo, many of them connected with the privatization of the Japan National Railways, that stimulated the market into its period of fastest growth (Hayakawa and Hirayama, 1991, p. 152).

The expansion of domestic demand (*naiju kakudai*) became from the mid 1980s an important component of Japanese economic policy, a means of both reducing reliance on exports and boosting corporate profits at home. Justified as a response to foreign (meaning US) pressure (*gaiatsu*), its implementation was envisaged through the execution of large-scale infrastructure projects such as the New Kansai International Airport and the bridge across Tokyo Bay. The process was driven in part through the Strategic Impediments Initiative round of talks between the US and Japanese governments designed to pare away at structural barriers to trade.

Internationalization (*kokusaika*) was a catch-phrase rather than a policy and was used by both central and metropolitan governments as an injunction to build more office space. The argument repeatedly advanced was that a dearth of accommodation suitable for the international companies beating at Tokyo's door was forcing up office rents and retarding the progress of the city on the international arena. Internationalization carried with it a host of other implications, including the need for Japan to extend its influence in foreign and defence related policies and activities.

During the same period, Suzuki Shunichi was in the middle of his long tenure as metropolitan governor. A former Interior Ministry official who had cut his teeth as organizer of the Tokyo Olympics of 1964, Suzuki had turned around the metropolitan finances and was enjoying broad support from right-wing and centrist parties. As the TMG's resource base grew ever more substantial, Suzuki made "world city Tokyo" part of his vision for the city (Machimura, 1994, p. 124). He also embarked on his two most ambitious

projects. The first was the construction of a massive new complex of buildings for the metropolitan government in the largest of Tokyo's sub-centers,
Shinjuku (Coaldrake, 1996). The second was the upgrading of the Teleport
plan for artificial islands on the bay of Tokyo into Tokyo's seventh sub-
center.

Ideological restructuring of urban space

Through government white papers, Tokyo planning documents, international conferences, and a host of other media sources and outlets, the mes-
sage was conveyed that Tokyo must be and was being internationalized. "As
Japan's ties with the international community grow ever stronger, Japan's
metropolis of Tokyo, which serves as a junction point in the international
flow of persons and information, is increasingly counted upon to play a still
greater international role" (TMG, 1990a, p. 8). In this way, Tokyo the city
became an asset to be advertized on the international market place, a resource to be exploited (Fujita and Hill, 1993, p. 9).

It is only recently that Tokyo has projected itself onto the imagination of
people around the world. Even in the 1970s, when the Japanese economy
had already grown to occupy second position in terms of size of GDP, Tokyo
was considered largely in the negative terms of ugliness, noise, and crowds.
The images were of masked policemen on point duty and commuters being
squeezed onto trains by station staff. By the early 1980s, however, the picture
began to change. A number of books appeared written both by Japanese and
foreigners projecting a collage of more engaging and nuanced cameos of the
city. New and more frankly appreciative *aperçus* of Tokyo's urban culture
linked the city to the replacement of modernist modalities and ideologies by
their supposedly postmodernist successors.[8]

Four clusters of images dominated the ideological idiom of urban change
in the Tokyo of the 1980s. The first of these four is expressed in terms such
as flux and fluidity (Bognar, 1990). This set of images was linked both to
qualities of social life – gregariousness, nomadism – and extended into the
realm of technology through images of cyberspace and virtual space. Tokyo,
it was suggested, was an information center in which the invisible and intangible world of instantaneous communication triumphed over the material
world. A related set of images and ideas emphasized Tokyo as an arena in
which activity rather than physical form defines the urban experience, one in
which historical legacies are transmitted through intangible processes such as
the collective memory rather than the built environment. Each of these sets
of images can be seen as a standing on its head, an inversion, of a previously
held image. The third image, that of "Tokyo the anarchic city, the city
without master plan", was transformed in the 1980s into Tokyo the village
city, the city of a myriad microcosms, and the city of a hidden order.[9] A

fourth and final act of reconstitution saw Tokyo cast as an international city, a global city, the financial peer of New York and London and yet with pretensions to be ranked alongside Paris as one on of the world's great cultural centers. The services of renowned architects and designers like Bellini, Foster, and Starck were an important component in conferring an international cachet. Their works added to the prestige of their clients and contributed to the lustre of the city as a whole.[10]

None of the directions of the 1980s was presented to the residents of the city as a policy option to be debated and possibly discarded. They were portrayed as inevitable (the result of "outside pressure"), as desirable (part of progressive moves toward "internationalization"), as locally appropriate (through reference to the city's history), and as beneficial to residents (through the use of slogans such as "My Town Tokyo"). Through the slogan "My Town Tokyo", the city's governor had been able not only to extend the appetite for "my home" and "my car", concepts that had already entered the Japanese vernacular, into a wider domain but also to encourage at least some of the residents of the city in a belief that they were sharing in the kudos created by Tokyo's new international image. Enough pride was generated to retain political support despite the damage caused to the lives of those who found themselves in the way, either metaphorically or literally, of the bulldozers of developers and speculators. In many ways, many of the residents of Tokyo felt comfortable with themselves, with the city, and with their country, basking in its new global centrality.

Urban Restructuring and the Changing Face of Tokyo

Atomized households and fragmented landscapes

The central effect, ironic but ineluctable, of the restructuring of Tokyo in the 1980s was that living conditions grew worse for many of the inhabitants of the region at the very time when business corporations were profiting and expanding as never before and the state was benefiting as a result of higher tax revenues. The tensions that resulted from this state of affairs were considerable, especially in those areas where urban restructuring (reconstruction and readjustment of land use generally but not necessarily favouring corporate interests) was at its most intense, that is to say within central areas and in the belt of urban land surrounding it.

Its effects were particularly pernicious because they were divisive, profiting some but damaging others, and therefore having an atomizing, isolating impact on urban households. Some reaped rich rewards from their land holdings, particularly individuals able to hide from the tax collector's gaze behind facades of non-profit-making institutions. Politicians were among those who profited, not least because of their proximity to a state apparatus that was itself deeply implicated. For many who owned land, however, the changing situation promised a bonanza, but few were able or indeed willing to capitalize, and for some, the decision about whether to sell and move created deep inter-generational family tensions. In many cases, life for those unwilling to sell was made miserable by gangsters acting on behalf of property developers and using tactics varying from threats to physical violence. Harrowing but well substantiated stories – for example, of local shopkeepers being bulldozed out of home and workplace – became the common currency of newspaper reports and television documentaries in the years from about 1986 to 1991 (Smith, 1987; Do Rosario, 1990).

The tax system was generally seen as unhelpful at best and damaging at worst. Property valuation for tax purposes ensured that a rise in the price of property in one place soon spread through a district, affecting all its landowning residents (Honma, 1986, p. 248). Even though valuation rates failed to keep up with market prices, the rate of inheritance tax on land assets was considered to be punitively high by many private landowners, but so too was capital gains tax on the sale of land. Caught between a rock and a hard place, landowning families in urban areas often resorted either to the disposal of small parcels of their land, thereby further splintering an already fragmented pattern of tenure, or to the creation of a corporate entity as owner of their property, thus exacerbating the corporatization of urban land (Ôtani, 1988; Nakabayashi, 1990, p. 58).

The expanding city center and the construction of prestige high-rise compounds

The impact of urban restructuring varied at the level of the individual household, with a resultant pattern too intricate to be easily represented in spatial terms across the city. Nevertheless, some consistency of effect is evident at the larger scale, permitting a level of generalization. Urban restructuring, as we will see in this section, had a variegated pattern of effects in city-center, central, and inner-city wards, while reaction, both on a governmental and unofficial level, was contradictory and restrained but at the same time not insignificant.

In central wards, the office-building spree gnawed away at remaining areas of low-rise housing and small-scale commerce. There is a contrast here to be drawn between the three city-center wards – Chiyoda, Chûô, and Minato – with their concentration of government buildings and headquarters of large corporations and the other central wards – Shinjuku, Shibuya, Bunkyô, Taitô, and Toshima – in which Tokyo's sub-centers are surrounded by land use characteristic of the inner city. In the three city-center wards the office-building spree gnawed away at the last few remaining interstitial pockets of low-rise housing and small-scale commerce, pockets that had yet to be affected (as a result, in many cases, of land-owning anomalies) during earlier periods of property boom and construction. In the other central wards away from main roads and railway stations, large tracts both of single-dwelling and multi-occupancy housing remained. Where this housing was low rise, it tended to consist of low-income wooden rental housing, residual housing of the professional classes, and (mainly in Shibuya and the outer parts of Minato wards) up-market rental housing for the foreign business community, for whom a large detached dwelling near the city center was deemed *de rigueur* regardless of cost. Where it was medium rise, it was likely to be middle-income employee housing, dating from the 1950s and 1960s, social housing from the same era, or more recent, up market, *bijou*-style tenancies, often used for business purposes. Where it was high rise, some of it came in the form of compulsory adjuncts to new developments, and some of it as up-market tenancies often diverted for office use. Along the main streets, nearly all remaining traditional-style shop-houses were knocked down and replaced either by "pencil buildings", gaining maximum permitted height from a restricted plot of land, or larger residential buildings, normally of about nine storeys, built on amalgamated road-side plots.

Within this complicated jigsaw of a central area, with its many ambivalent trends and anomalous terrains, the three factors examined above – excess liquidity diverted to real estate, relaxation of planning controls, and the new ideology of Tokyo World City – conspired to instigate a number of prestig-ious, high-rise, and ostensibly mixed-function development projects. These made themselves manifest, some sooner, some later, in the new clusters of skyscrapers. Among the more prominent examples are the Ark Hills devel-opment in Minato Ward and the Ebisu Garden Place complex on the site of an old brewery in Shibuya Ward, a fine instance of *fin-de-siècle* Tokyo pas-tiche, with a pseudo-*château* French restaurant, a high-rise hotel, and a mix-ture of social and private housing (Map 7.2).

Several of the more high-profile mixed-function developments were un-dertaken along Tokyo Bay and the city's main river, the Sumida. Outstand-ing among these was the plan to construct the city's seventh sub-center on landfill in the bay, situated directly out from the center of Tokyo (Machimura, 1994). The size of this project set it apart from others undertaken at this time. So too did the close, almost personal control, exercised in its formative stage by the governor of Tokyo, Suzuki Shunichi, made possible in part through the metropolitan government's ownership of much of the land and in part through Suzuki's virtually unassailable political position. Private sec-tor participation was effectively bound in through involvement in key con-sultative committees and the creation of a joint public-private consortium in which the TMG had a controlling stake. As plans unfolded, the size and symbolic significance of the project drew the attention of the deputy prime minister and political fixer Kanemaru Shin as well as other politicians. By

1988, when the blueprints were at their most grandiose, the project involved the development of an area of a little under 500 hectares, where over 100,000 would work and 60,000 live. The estimated cost of ¥4 trillion ($38 billion at 1996 rates), soon raised to ¥8 trillion, was to be shared with private enterprise, and key money and income from rents was to mean no outlay from the public purse (Aita, 1995). The TMG was forced to scale down its plans, partly as a result of its own hubris in fixing for the year 1994 a massive global exhibition to celebrate the project's completion, partly because of the political controversy eventually caused by the desultory consideration given to the provision of housing and urban amenities, and partly as a result of the onset in 1991 of Japan's most profound post-war economic slump.

Several other prestige city-center developments grew out of former shunting yards along railway lines. These developments were large but mutually disconnected compounds whose multi-storey edifices bore no relation to the more modest buildings that surrounded them. Although a number of them were located near the bay and the river, there was little more than a perfunctory attempt to create a thematic or scenic link with the water.

The inner city and the survival of mixed-function zones

The real battle against the consequences of urban restructuring was waged in Tokyo's inner city, much of which remained predominantly multi-functional, with a mixture of traditionally operated wholesalers, petty retailers, and small-scale manufacturers often living above the place of work, while other parts became increasingly the domain of the higher-order functions of a rapidly expanding city center. These inner-city areas, characterized by dense population, lax controls on building type and land-use function, and a complicated pattern of property rights, are a prominent feature not only of Tokyo but still more of Osaka, Nagoya, and Japan's other large industrial cities. They came into existence during the decades of rapid industrialisation that affected Japan for most of this century up to the 1970s. Without effective planning controls, growth patterns were disorderly. Small manufacturing plants were built cheek by jowl with flimsy, wooden row-housing. Although the fire bombing of Tokyo and other Japanese cities in 1944 and 1945 destroyed much of this original fabric, the same disorderly pattern characterized rebuilding activity.

The subsequent decades of growth and prosperity affected these areas in a haphazard way, leaving a residue of wooden rental lodgings, flanked by newer apartment buildings, and a substantial number of shops, factories, and low-level distribution and service facilities. There remained nonetheless a recognisable belt – referred to either as "inner city" or as mixed-function zone – around the central part of Tokyo, taking in both large parts of central wards such as Taitô, Bunkyô, Toshima, Shinjuku, and Shibuya and extending

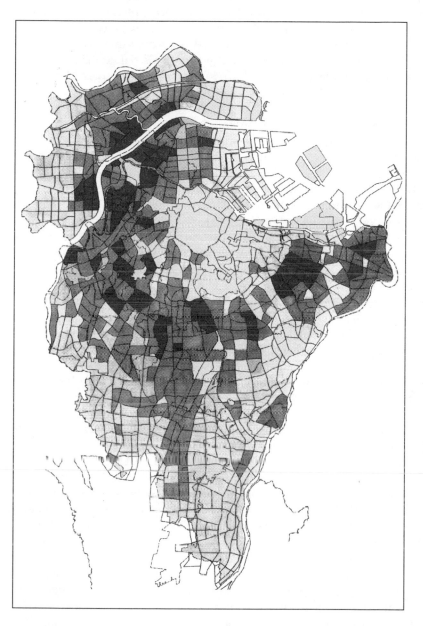

Map 7.4 Tokyo Metropolitan Government map showing areas of maximum congestion in terms of population density and inadequacy of housing and infrastructure and areas of lesser but still significant degrees of congestion

out into the surrounding areas (Map 7.4). This belt can broadly speaking be divided into two. In the east, north, and south, it is characterized by what is still a significant number of small-scale manufacturing plants and traditional-sector storage, wholesale, and office facilities and is known among urban managers and academic writers as a mixed residential-industrial zone (*jûkô konzai chiiki*). Along the western part of the belt, industrial establishments are a far less prominent feature. Here, low-rise housing shares space with small-scale commercial outlets and business offices following patterns described above.

Within these inner-city areas, opposition to the symptoms of urban re-structuring was muted. In some districts, local residents were involved in campaigns against the construction of so-called one-room mansions. These apartment blocks, for use by single people (normally male company employees), became an increasingly common feature of inner-city areas during the 1980s and were seen by long-term residents as inimical to the interests of the established community (Machimura, 1994, p. 212). In other districts, industrialists campaigned against the construction of apartment blocks, fearing that a re-classification of their neighborhood as a residential zone would lead to growing complaints and limit their freedom to operate.

These campaigns, however, lacked a central focus – a change of the law, for example – or a *cause célèbre* that might galvanize people. In broader terms, there was a lack of definition in the eyes of the public as to the causes of the problem of land-price inflation. At no point was there any phenomenon comparable to the mounting of citizens' protest groups in the late 1960s and early 1970s to campaign against pollution. The edge had been taken off those campaigns by limited responses from corporate interests and pledges of reform (some of them realized) from local and central government. Changing alliances within the state itself, especially at the local level, betokened an appreciation of the need to adopt new strategies. The confrontation of the earlier era gave way to a co-opting of causes and co-management with local government.

It was out of these changes that a coalition was struck between local government officials and community leaders, and with them, local residents. In the eastern and southern inner-city wards of Tokyo, local governments pursued a number of policies designed to maintain a multi-functional use of land. In pursuing these policies, they received the active support of place-based associations of local residents, industrialists, and traders. Local-level coalitions of interest worked best in inner-city and adjacent suburban areas where affective ties to place and community remained the strongest but where corporate-led urban restructuring hit communities the hardest. Here, the interests of local residents and the local government coalesced around the maintenance of a stable population and a continuance of commercial and industrial enterprise.[11] Here too, an engagement between local government and residents was generally facilitated through the existence of a densely woven net of social imbrication. Whether they took the form of territorially anchored neighborhood associations (*chôkai*) or territorially based business groupings such as shopkeepers' associations or school-based PTAs, local organisations could be seen as representing a viable if somewhat inchoate framework for resistance against the inroads of corporate interests and the commodification of urban space (Bestor, 1989). Nevertheless, in the wider context of the socially divisive nature of galloping land-price inflation, the extent of overall effectiveness of local-level coalitions remained open to question.

It is not surprising that inner city areas should have been considered by local government officials and other urban managers as particularly vulnerable at a time of rapidly rising land prices. Concern revolved around two inter-related dangers: that of a draining of economic dynamism – the closure of shops and factories – and consequent collapse of communities on the one hand and the dangers posed to residents in a disaster. The fear was specifically that a residual population of aged residents living in precarious wooden dwellings would render these neighborhoods particularly vulnerable in case of a disaster (a fear borne out by the high casualty rates among the elderly following the Kobe earthquake of 1995).[12]

In reacting to the increasing fragility of inner-city areas, government found itself caught within several contradictions, none of which were resolved. Central government was responsible for a number of the policy directions that were exacerbating these problems. With its relaxation of controls on floor-space to plot-size ratios (a move which had a major effect in inner-city areas), government was clearly signalling its support for the construction of more business space outside the city center. Following a similar logic, government continued a policy of comprehensive redevelopment that involved the purchase of land (often vacated a decade or two earlier by departing factories) and the construction of uni-functional high-rise housing estates This was seen as having the twin advantage of creating a city better equipped to withstand earthquake and fire and of helping curb the falling population levels of inner-city areas. Large swathes of inner-city land in the east and northeast of the city were purchased, cleared, and used for the construction of high-rise apartment blocks varying from ten to thirty floors (over 4,000 dwellings in West Shirahige and 114 hectares of high-rise housing in Komatsugawa – see Map 7.2). Nevertheless, the policy of constructing large public housing estates was already throwing up problems by the 1980s. The buildings and their occupants were ageing contemporaneously. Refurbishment projects were extremely expensive, and some of the expense was passed on in the form of increased rents even though many tenants were living on pensions.

At the same time as all this was going on, advisory councils to both the central government and the TMG were stressing the importance of the maintenance of mixed-function inner-city areas. The policies that central and metropolitan authorities adopted involved a variety of measures designed to preserve communities and maintain the multi-functional nature of inner-city areas, promoting their industries and facilitating through grants the reconstruction of housing in fireproof material. Ward governments in inner-city areas pursued measures to subsidize rents and extend credit for young people moving in or wishing to remain ward residents. In several wards, they put in place programmes to support local industries. Sumida Ward, for example, on the east bank of the city's main river, opened a center for the promotion of small industry, where it ran training courses and industrial fairs. On the whole, however, these measures merely scratched at the surface of the problem. Piecemeal in their nature, they were implemented at such a slow pace that little substantial change was effected.

Behind these developments in the inner-city areas of Tokyo, the *jûkô konzai chiiki* of mixed residential and industrial land use, lay a planning irony. On the one hand, urban administrators and many community leaders were pressing for the maintenance of a mixture of functions. They argued that small-scale industry was an important generator of wealth and guarantor of a stable and economically vigorous community. They saw a need for a range of services to be on offer in the streets, primarily shops for local residents, but also bathhouses and other traditional neighborhood institutions. On the other hand, however, it was the same lax zoning regulations permitting factories and housing to exist side by side that facilitated the advance of office building and the gradual corporatization of parts of the inner city.

Sprawl and suburbanization

By 1990, a typical 57-square-metre apartment in the 23–ward area cost 12 times the average annual salary (TMG, 1990b, p. 4). Families were forced to buy their homes further and further from the city center, often only able to purchase by securing a two-generation mortgage. More and more people crowded onto trains to work in the growing number of offices in central areas, with the satellite business cities and new towns generally failing to attract business facilities and retain new residents as local employees (TMG, 1996a, p. 55). Average journey times rose to about 70 minutes, while congestion at peak hours remained around the 200-per cent level and sometimes higher (TMG, 1996b, p. 74). Commuting fathers left behind them wives and children whom they saw for ever briefer periods, as working men became more and more locked into their business lifestyle (Wegener, 1994, p. 103; Douglass, 1993, p. 104).

A further consequence of urban sprawl was the environmental damage caused. Regulations on urbanization left landowning farmers considerable leverage in decisions on the timing and extent of conversion of land from agricultural to urban use (Hebbert and Nakai, 1988). In many parts of the environs of the conurbation, especially in the hills to the west and east, suitable flatland had either been urbanized or was being held back. As a consequence, housing estates were built in wetlands or on hills whose soft loam soils were easily sliced, flattened, and compacted. It was only some years later that local officials, concerned residents, and planners began seriously to assess the long-term impact of urban sprawl on river flows and on local eco-systems.

In these ways urban restructuring in the city center and the increasing pace of concentration in the Tokyo conurbation affected the lives of people throughout the east of Japan as well as the quality of the environment in which they lived.

Patterns behind the Partitions

Prestige high-rise compounds, skyscraper clusters, public-private consortia, deteriorating infrastructure and sub-standard housing in inner-city areas, urban sprawl into surrounding territories: the terminology of urban restructuring in contemporary Japan is a fairly familiar one. Superficial familiarity should not, however, obscure certain fundamental differences: a lack of widespread areas of social deprivation and disenfranchisement, the absence of street-level fear and violence, an internationalization that has not extended significantly across the urban terrain, the absence of a widespread trend toward (re-)occupation of central and inner-city areas by the new urban young. It is to an examination of these dissimilarities (often concealed by coincidences of economic structure, systems, and cycles) that we turn now, in the specific context of the hypotheses advanced in the introductory chapter of this book.

The prevalence of an outward, street-level tranquillity should not lead the observer to infer that there is (to borrow Wacquant's term) no "territorial stigmatization" in Tokyo or other Japanese cities. On the contrary, there is a long history of official neglect and public ignorance of districts inhabited by *burakumin* (the former outcast community) or those occupied by the lodging houses of day labourers. Day labourers' districts like Sanya in Tokyo contain an ageing and abused population, a decrepit reserve army for the construction industry whose plight is treated with disdain by both government and the public at large. Strong, sometimes repressive, networks of control often involving gangster groups have generally contained dissatisfaction and restiveness in Sanya (Fowler, 1996). These areas, however, are written off the map of public consciousness as a result both of conscious stratagems and of conditioned patterns of thought. The location of *buraku* districts in Tokyo is not generally known (the same is not true in the cities of western Japan), with the result that many inhabitants of the conurbation appear to believe either that there are none or that much of northeast Tokyo is in some unspecified way tainted ground.[13] As for Tokyo's day-labourers' district, which is far smaller than the equivalent district in Osaka, its name no longer figures on published maps. In these and other ways such areas are marginalized, so that their existence is not considered relevant to wider discussions of urban society. This has proved more problematical in the Osaka conurbation and other cities of western Japan, where *buraku* communities are larger and more numerous.

The potential for marginalization is not limited to districts inhabited by those who historically have suffered discrimination. Within Tokyo's inner-city belt, several other urban areas with severely substandard housing and infrastructure and attendant problems exist. In some of these a slow process of renewal is being undertaken through the sort of measures discussed above to help small-scale industry and create urban territories resistant to fire. Others have been eradicated and replaced with slabs of high-rise housing. Harbingers of widespread social malaise though they may be, these housing complexes are still fairly new and clean and not generally considered central to a discourse of social problems and urban decay. This is not the tenement city to which Marcuse and Van Kempen refer in the Introduction.

In acknowledging the existence of difficulties faced by certain marginal groups, it is important to be aware of the overall framework of social order within which they exist. It is of course a cliché of the Japanese urban scene to state that it is generally speaking safe. Physical violence in public places is uncommon, with police and neighbourhood associations maintaining what elsewhere might be considered an unwarranted degree of supervision. Urban crime, principally blackmail and other forms of extortion, tends to be the prerogative of the corporate entity and its white-collar employees. Although the recession of the 1990s brought an inevitable but only partial deterioration, for most of the 1980s a buoyant economy as well as Japanese employment and training practices meant that finding a job was not a problem for young Japanese. For, at the end of the day, if urban pauperization and social exclusion have not been considered significant problems in Japan, this is attributable too to the many decades of stable economic growth that the country enjoyed, to a relative equity in income distribution, and not least to the very powerful forces working to create a social consensus around economic growth and to enshrine it in ideological legitimacy.

Another determining element in the interplay of socio-economic conditions and urban space is the extent of geographical concentration of international low-level migrants, enticed to Japan by high wages and plentiful work, especially during the construction boom of the 1980s. Migration to Japan is not a recent phenomenon. A large community of Korean origin exists from before World War II. Despite the fact that it is now made up of second, third, and fourth generations, many members of the Korean community retain Korean nationality and face both official barriers to integration and deep-rooted discriminatory behaviour at a non-official level. Although there are sizeable Korean communities in Kawasaki (between Tokyo and Yokohama) and in parts of inner-city Tokyo, the largest concentrations lie in the Osaka conurbation. The expansion of Japanese manufacturing as well as urban and infrastructure construction in the decades of rapid post-war growth was powered by internal migration from rural areas. The 1980s saw the export of manufacturing capacity, in particular to those very countries in Asia from which labour migration might have been expected (Connell, 1993). While demand for labour remained high in Japan, both in manufacturing and in the growing service sectors, the tendency was to fill it where possible with residual categories from the internal labour market, that is to say, students, housewives, and older people. These developments have gone some way to satisfying labour demand, especially in service industries like retailing, but the growing reluctance of young people to seek employment in the small-scale manufacturing sector as well as in construction and "entertainment" drew in growing numbers of migrant workers from abroad. Many of these arrived in Japan on student or tourist visas and ended up working illegally (Fielding and Mizuno, 1995). Despite some pressure from industry, the government retained strict controls, easing them only peripherally, in order to expand work-training schemes and the permitted quota of Latin Americans of Japanese descent.[14]

From this picture, confused though it may appear, arise several developments of relevance to our considerations. First, many migrants working illegally are women (principally from Southeast Asia but also from China and eastern Europe) employed in bars and other night-time "entertainment" establishments, and they are spread throughout the country. Similarly, immigrant men working in construction tend to be geographically scattered. However, employment in the small-scale manufacturing sector has meant that certain areas contain a higher level of low-level migrant workers than would otherwise be the case. In the Tokyo conurbation, migrant workers are to be found in inner-city areas and industrial zones of the periphery in the small-scale manufacturing sector – in foundries, metal-plating, the processing of fats and oils, and among suppliers of parts to the automobile industry (Connell, 1993, p. 13).

Many of the large entertainment districts surrounding main-line railway stations in Tokyo (as in Osaka and other large cities) have links with Korean and Chinese (or Chinese-Taiwanese) capital dating back to the immediate post-war period. Some of these districts, notably parts of Ueno, Ikebukuro, and Shinjuku, have become increasingly distinct as "ethnic" areas, with, for example, neon signs in Korean advertizing restaurants. Some of these changes

have been noted and welcomed as portraying an "ethnic-style" internationalisation of the city (especially where they involve Chinese and not Koreans,
as in the case of parts of Shinjuku). Elsewhere they have elicited a more
prickly reaction, especially among older residents (Wada, 1992, p. 61). Nevertheless, Tokyo has not seen the formation of immigrant quarters of the sort
found in many of the cities of the west, and this for a number of reasons,
principal among which are a combination of recent date of arrival and
tendency to geographic and occupational dispersal. Of equal importance is
an economic context of relatively low levels of unemployment even in recession, and a historical context of restricted links with Japan's former colonies.
In the long term, however, labour pressures both within and outside the
country caused not least by the rapid rise in the average age of Japan's
population are likely to bring about a more fluid situation, and the formation
of districts with a greater degree of ethnic distinctiveness seems probably, if
only in parts of the large conurbations.

If Tokyo has its own geographies of poverty and marginalization, so too it
has its own patterns of urban identity and attachment and its own geographies
of urban consumption. The ideological restructuring of the city discussed earlier has helped produce an urban territory rich in new associative meanings,
and these have been exploited and embroidered to create a highly refined,
urban, place-based geography of consumption. A young population of students
and office employees has thronged the entertainment districts for decades, but
since the 1980s they appear to have had more income at their disposal, not
least because of the postponement of house-buying and child-bearing decisions, often forced on them by high property prices. They have had more time
as a result of changing patterns of work and are better informed as a consequence of the growing sophistication of listing guides and other media.

Indeed, the 1980s saw the emergence of a section of the urban population
who are deeply involved in urban issues and belonging, approximately, to
one of three groups. Some are urban managers – town planners, architects,
landscape designers, professional environmentalists, all those who are involved directly in shaping the city. A second, larger group is made up of
cultural mediators of various kinds – journalists, photographers, editors, copy
writers, film makers, and other purveyors of written and visual images. The
professional activities of this group are inevitably broader, but to the extent
that the city has become a prestigious subject for cultural production, here
too there is a substantial involvement in forming images of the city. In this
sense, both groups have profited from the restructuring of the 1980s, and
continue to do so to the extent that the city remains a viable locale for
cultural as well as spatial production. They have not, however, benefited to
the same extent as a third category: that of the financial consultants, lawyers,
speculators, international traders and others who provide local services for
international business newly located in Tokyo.

If gentrification has any meaning within the Japanese context, then these are the groups who would be expected to have given spatial meaning to their interests and status (and in some cases, their wealth) by moving into re-evaluated urban areas, either to create personal capital or to reflect place-related cultural taste or both. With limited exceptions, however, this has not occurred. Some have not wanted to move, for example, members of families resident in Tokyo for two generations or longer, for whom attachment to locality might outweigh the kudos gained from a move to a more prestigious area. But for many more, there was simply nowhere to go. Land prices have been too high and "affordable" rented accommodation in suitable areas too expensive for all but the very wealthy or those on salary levels paid by international companies. What Tokyo has experienced is not gentrification, but the construction of a limited number of new high-rise prestige complexes in relatively central parts of the city. That these "luxury" housing projects have been a limited phenomenon is explained in part by the fact that property in Tokyo has not become a sought-after asset on international markets as it did long ago in New York, London, or Paris. Tokyo has not therefore experienced the problems of "delocalized property" as described by Beauregard and Haila in this volume. It has been limited too by the proportionately smaller number of super-rich, itself a result of different structures of corporate ownership and of reward for top management.

All this has militated against both the process of gentrification and that other process, so aptly described by Loïc Wacquant (1996), descent from communal solidarity at the margins to collapse into an asocial void detached from any affective ties to place as a social construct. The visitor to Tokyo – and this should not be forgotten – sees neither the iron gates and brick walls of the recently built luxury compounds of London, Los Angeles, or Manila, nor the battered swathes of urban territory with their disenfranchised populations that have become a feature of the major metropolises of both the industrialized north and much of the disadvantaged south.

The Tokyo Conurbation: Corporate Advance into Social Order

An accumulation of trends in the 1980s led to the appropriation of an urban area, Tokyo, to advance investment interests and the political vision to which they were allied. The deregulationary policies of the Nakasone government laid the groundwork, with the prime minister himself seeking to be cast in the role of a Japanese version of Ronald Reagan. The revaluation of the yen against the dollar beginning with the Seoul Plaza accord of 1985 accelerated the trend toward the relocation of industrial plant to other parts of Pacific Asia. The consequent coming-of-age of leading Japanese enterprises as transnational corporations intensified pressure to create a fitting urban back-drop, a corporate global city whose physical appearance matched the pretensions of its leading corporate establishments. These latter for their part – along with a host of other players of less elevated stature – were repatriating or generating at home assets that were directed into the property market, with consequences that were sketched above.

Corporate intervention in the city was so massive in the 1980s that it came to resemble a grotesque parody of the traditional vision of the city as locale of bustle and prosperity. And when the bubble burst and property prices plummeted, it was Tokyo's private citizens who often came off worse. The flood of bank loans that found its way into unwise property-based lending activities led to a massive bail-out launched by the government with public funds.[15]

The lack of a strategic vision for the conurbation and of a tradition of state intervention in planning has allowed corporate interests to dictate the priorities of urban restructuring. An orientation toward economic growth and urban expansion has not been fundamentally challenged. The male-oriented businessman vision has held a dominant position within public discourse, and as a consequence quality of life issues and urban amenities have tended to come secondary to policies designed to sustain urban expansion. It is no coincidence that an urban vision that takes into account women's experience and perceptions is absent, if not from all local-government projects, then certainly from most central-government decision-making on economic policies that affect urban life.

At the same time, many of the trends that accompanied the trajectory of urban restructuring in the West have been absent in Japan. There is little sense in Tokyo of a festering disenchantment among disenfranchised sections of the population. Violent crime is not a problem, and the streets are safe. Unemployment rates are low, and racial hostility has not provoked social tension. Gentrification is not a recognisable phenomenon; the newly wealthy do not deem it necessary to lock themselves in behind iron gates and high walls. Yet at the same time, nowhere in the world experienced quite the same shake-up as did Tokyo in the 1980s and 1990s. Nowhere did property prices behave in such a frenetic fashion. Nowhere was the potential for disruption so great. Nowhere were inner cities so threatened as a result of incursions by the forces of rampant capitalism.

The fundamental story of the modern urban experience in Japan is one of relatively unfettered corporate advance but of a strong social order able to absorb much of its impact. As we have seen, the freer intervention of capital forces on the face of the city leads to a physical environment that changes far more rapidly than in the West, with buildings torn down and replaced and urban areas spreading outward at a frenetic pace. But this is mitigated by a number of social controls on capital accumulation.

A number of factors have served to reinforce social order. First, income has been fairly evenly distributed within society in a context of relatively high economic growth rates throughout much of the post-war period. Not only that, but it has been more evenly spread in spatial terms across the city, with much smaller disparities in wealth between one part of Tokyo and another compared to the cities of the West. This has contributed to a surprising persistence in use of land and social practices even as the physical surroundings have changed.

Secondly, what might be called "metropolitan internationalization" has been of a limited nature. Tokyo has not become an international city to anything like the extent of other centers in capital's global control system. Japan's transnational companies have not become international in the upper echelons of their management structure. Catch a train in Tokyo and you are still unlikely to see more than the occasional foreigner. With the exception of long-established Korean and Taiwanese interests, property in Tokyo is in the hands of Japanese. Internationalization is an ideological catchphrase, strictly controlled and limited.

Thirdly, embracing these and other factors lies a web of ideological control. Discourse within Japan is cajoled away from contention and conflict by a whole series of controls exercized through education, the media, regulation of the economy, and more generally a socially encoded preference for consensus-building. Discrimination is concealed. Territorial marginalization is written off the map. Potentially divisive social forces are downplayed. The labour market remains basically closed to legal migrants. Regulation of the economy has served to limit foreign ownership.

Tokyo creates its own patterns which need to be understood in their own right, however many their points of overlap with North America or Europe, not to mention the cities of Pacific Asia. Certain concluding generalizations can however be made about the pattern of urban restructuring and socio-spatial change. First, short-term fluctuations in property prices occurred within a general continuation of trends toward concentration of activity in the east of Japan. Secondly, higher-level urban functions advanced significantly in the Tokyo conurbation during the 1980s as a consequence in part of global economic change and in part of local urban conditions and political strategies. Thirdly, urban restructuring has tended to favour consumer interests, both in terms of the city itself and of consumption groups such as young people; consequently, it has damaged production interests and the ability of residents to bring up families without retreating to the urban fringe.

Finally, the historical pattern of urban governance, with corporate interests favoured within a loose system of governmental control and overall social order, remains basically unchanged if not totally unchallenged. Indeed, already at this time of writing (in 1998) there are signs that the property market is picking up, boosted by low interest rates and further rounds of deregulation. With Japanese élites increasingly concerned by the growth of Shanghai and other Pacific Asian metropolises, we can expect more of that same pattern of urban governance, with a continued rapid growth trajectory and a maintenance of strong ideological control.

Notes

1 Research on which parts of this chapter are based was made possible by a grant from the Japan Foundation. A visit to Japan in 1995 was greatly facilitated through affiliation to the Tokyo Metropolitan University. Kawabata Naoshi and Watanabe Kiyomi in Tokyo have been of great help over the years. I would also like to thank Martin Purvis and Penny Francks in Leeds and Charles Cardozo for their helpful comments. An earlier version of this Chapter appeared in the *American Behavioral Scientist* of November 1997 (Waley, 1997).

2 Among a small number of recent works on the restructuring of Japanese cities in the 1980s, Machimura Takashi's study (1994) provides detailed insights set within a surely grounded theoretical framework. Mike Douglass brings a similar critical perspective to bear in discussing the growing gap between corporate wealth and individual welfare (1988; 1993). The various authors in Takahashi (1992) examine the process of social change in inner-city wards of Tokyo.

3 The legitimation of Tokyo's sprawl is, as Machimura Takashi (1994, p. 63) reminds us, encapsulated in the words commonly used to refer to the capital, from Tokyo through Dai Tokyo (Greater Tokyo, dating from the expansion of administrative boundaries in 1932) to Tokyo-to (the Tokyo Metropolis, created in 1943, and now the administrative prefectural boundary) to Tokyo-ken (the Tokyo region, which comprises the Tokyo Metropolis and its three surrounding prefectures and includes therefore virtually the whole conurbation). The conurbation itself occupies much (but by no means all) of the Tokyo Metropolis and its three neighboring prefectures, Kanagawa, Saitama, and Chiba.

4 Among the new towns are Tama (with a planned population of 300,000) and Kôhoku in Yokohama.

5 Although the proportion of the national population resident in Tokyo's 23-ward area has fallen from 6.9 per cent to 6.3 per cent in the ten years from 1985 to 1995, it has risen from 25.0 per cent to 25.9 per cent in the Tokyo metropolitan region (Kokudochô, 1996, p. 17).

6 In 1992, a legislative measure (the Capital Functions Relocation Act) was introduced that envisaged the eventual move of the nation's central political functions to a site yet to be decided but not less than 60 and not more than 300 kilometres from Tokyo. As Ishida observes, if the move does eventually take place, it is likely to lead to a downgrading in the importance of national political institutions, with the new city becoming a Japanese Washington to Tokyo's New York (1994, p. 8).

7 Not all of this activity was at home – in the US Japanese investment in property rose from $1.9 billion in 1985 to $16.5 billion in 1988 (Oizumi, 1994, p. 203).

8 For a discussion of the postmodern in the context of Japanese cities, see Berque

(1993, pp. 153 ff.). Field (1989) relates consumerism and place to the postmodern in a provocative commentary on one of the literary icons of urban Japan in the 1980s, Tanaka Yasuo's (1980) *Nantonaku kurisutaru* (Somehow, crystal).

9　*The Hidden Order* is the title of the English-language translation of a book by the Japanese architect Ashihara Yoshinobu, (*Kakureta chitsujo*, 1986). One of the principal ideas elaborated in the book is plainly reflected in the title; and indeed the same could be said of the anthology of essays entitled *Des villes nommées Tokyo* (Pons, 1984).

10　In 1985, the *Mainichi* newspaper sponsored a symposium on Shitamachi, to which foreign scholars and planners were invited. The proceedings were later published in a book which is full of suggestive thoughts on the Japanese experience and sense of urban life (Mainichi, 1986).

11　Machimura has described how this coalition of interests worked in a district in central Tokyo threatened by *ad hoc* and unplanned development (1994, p. 209–35).

12　In Tokyo's three central wards, there is almost double the national proportion of single persons aged 65 or over (Kokudochô, 1996, p. 36). Presumably some of these are well-heeled city-center dwellers, perhaps the owners of a block of flats built on the site of a family house.

13　The subject of *burakumin* remains highly sensitive. Historic divisions between organisations representing the *burakumin* have contributed to the difficulties experienced by foreign writers in representing their situation. For a survey of these divisions, see Neary (1997).

14　Government figures tend to understate the number of migrant workers in Japan, not least because of the difficulty in ascertaining the numbers who work while on tourist on student visas. The figures given range from government estimates of 300,000 who overstay their visa period to a total "immigrant" population of two million, although not all these are working (Fielding and Mizuno, 1995, p. 14; Connell, 1993, p. 12).

15　The operation cost the exchequer ¥685 billion ($6.52 billion), although the total cost to the taxpayer was thought likely to reach ¥1.3 trillion (Moffett, 1996).

8

Still a Global City: The Racial and Ethnic Segmentation of New York[1]

John R. Logan

The approaching turn of the next century invites us to ask: does New York exhibit the outlines of a new kind of city? Does it have a new mode of production and a corresponding pattern of social inequalities? New York's size and economic centrality, and especially its importance in an increasingly global economy, have prompted many observers to study it as a harbinger of the urban future. And of all the metaphors that have been used to characterize this city, the one that has had most resonance is that of the global city (Sassen, 1990).

Like London and Tokyo, New York is a world center for a reorganized financial industry, the growth pole of modern economies. Though such cities had long served key functions in international finance and trade, critical changes occurred in the 1970s and especially in the 1980s that generated new forms of centralization. Global cities "account for a disproportionate share of all financial transactions and one that has grown rapidly since the early 1980s [because] the more globalized the economy becomes, the higher the agglomeration of central functions in a relatively few sites" (Sassen, 1990, p. 5).

All researchers who have studied New York in recent years recognize this role (Mollenkopf and Castells, 1991; Fainstein, Gordon, and Harloe, 1992; Marcuse, 1989). Unique to Sassen, however, is her view that the "finance and specialized service industries have restructured the urban social and economic order" of global cities (p. 4). More precisely, these industries are held to contribute to increased class polarization. They do this directly, because they themselves employ many high-wage and low-wage workers but few in the middle range. They do it indirectly, because they support high-income gentrification which in turn gives rise to large numbers of low-wage service workers who support their expensive lifestyle. Though her earlier studies emphasized the ethnic and racial differentiation of the region stemming from immigration (Sassen, 1988), she now considers it theoretically subordinate to the stronger force of financial globalization.

In this chapter I argue that the impact of the global financial and service industries of the 1970s and 1980s on New York's occupational structure actually has been minor. New York is certainly in motion, but I believe that much of what observers today consider "new" is substantially an outgrowth of old patterns and not mainly a reflection of contemporary innovations. Deindustrialization, growth of the service economy, and transnational linkages are being felt now in New York, but they first appeared here at a much earlier time owing to the historic global role of the city (Buck and Fainstein, 1992). New York was already the predominant financial center of the country in 1900, and its position had been reinforced after World War II as a result of its firms' heavy participation in the emerging municipal bond market (Duncan and Lieberson, 1970).

The changes in this respect since 1970 have been relatively small. More important in the past forty years have been changes in labor relations associated with post-Fordism, including a decline of unionization, flexibilization, contracting out, and increasing reliance on low-wage labor pools. These shifts may have a distinctive appearance in New York due, on the one hand, to the entrenched power of labor in municipal and state politics and, on the other, to the high concentrations of vulnerable immigrant workers and competitive immigrant entrepreneurs that have always characterized this city. Class divisions are exaggerated by the especially deep divide between protected and unprotected workers, but the trends originating in the reorganization of the economy are essentially the same in New York as in Los Angeles and many smaller cities.

Finally, race and ethnicity lend a particular coloration to these economic cleavages in New York. The main line of demarcation separates African Americans and Latinos from whites, neither more nor less here than in other urban centers. What is unique about New York, a characteristic that derives directly from its global connections, is the depth and complexity of ethnic boundaries among non-whites. New York's diversity, like its function in the national and international economy, is deeply rooted in the city's history. But in this dimension of globalization the region has continued to develop rapidly since the 1950s.

My central thesis is that the key features of social inequality in New York are traceable not so much to the city's new function in the world economy (the global city in Sassen's sense of the term) as to its continuing and expanding function as a receptor of peoples. I develop this thesis in two steps. First I review the evidence of increasing income inequality in New York and examine whether it coincides with changes in the occupational structure associated with the expansion of financial and corporate functions. I then investigate the evolution of racial and ethnic segmentation of its labor and housing markets, beginning from the turn of the last century.

Inequality and Global Restructuring

The sense that there has been a recent change for the worse pervades many scholarly accounts as well as those found in the mass media. For example, the commentator Paul Goldberger (1989) has observed that "human anguish is surely more visible on the streets of New York than ever before. But the illness that afflicts the cityscape is not only a matter of human suffering. In a much broader sense, the city is only rarely these days a place of hope, or promise and glory."

Social scientists focus on evidence of income inequality, which is both high and increasing in New York. Stegman (1988) measured the income disparity between persons at the top and the bottom of the income distribution and in 1977 found a ratio of 15:1 in the average income of the top 10 percent to that of the bottom 10 percent. This ratio had increased to 20:1 in 1986. Rising income inequality has brought with it rising rates of poverty (Logan et al., 1992). The percentage of persons in New York City living below the poverty line was 18.5 percent in 1977 and 23.9 percent in 1985. Nearly one in four persons is in poverty today. These figures are much higher for certain parts of the population: families headed by an unmarried woman are particularly at risk. The number of such families in the city increased by about a third between 1975 and 1986, and the percentage of those families who lived in poverty rose from 47 percent to 67 percent in that period (Barbanel, 1989).

How are we to interpret these trends of the 1970s and 1980s? In particular, has New York's key role as an international financial and corporate center been a stimulus to increasing inequality? I think not, and I will argue this point on two grounds.

First, trends in inequality in New York mirrored what was happening in the nation at the same time. According to a report by the House Ways and Means Committee, the average income of the bottom fifth of the population dropped by 6.1 percent between 1979 and 1987 while the average income of the top fifth increased by 11.1 percent (Tolchin, 1989; see also Levy, 1987). Inequality and poverty in New York City have not been remarkably higher than in other large American cities; these appear, therefore, to be phenomena of urban America, not of the global city.

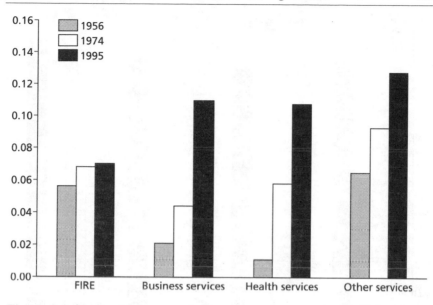

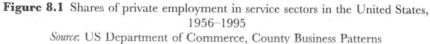

Figure 8.1 Shares of private employment in service sectors in the United States, 1956–1995

Source: US Department of Commerce, County Business Patterns

Second, changes in the labor force in New York – despite its special international position in the production of financial and business services – have also mirrored what was happening in the rest of the nation. In recent decades, in fact, growth in these industry sectors in the New York metropolis has lagged behind the national average. The relevant data for the period 1956–1995 are summarized in Figures 8.1 (for the nation) and 8.2 (for the New York metropolitan region). These data are from the annual series of *County Business Patterns*, published by the United States Department of the Census, which offers reliable information on private sector employment (but not including self-employed persons). This four-decade time series begins at about the point where manufacturing employment in the United States had peaked and the rise of the service economy had begun.

In this period, total employment more than doubled in the United States. Manufacturing employment was stagnant despite large increases (not shown) in manufacturing production; hence its share dropped sharply from 41 percent to 19 percent of total private employment. This is a substantial deindustrialization. At the same time, the nation experienced a shift to financial and business services. These sectors are at the core of a new form of production: the control of the flow of capital, the facilitation of interorganizational relationships, and the handling of information. As shown in Figure 8.1, the

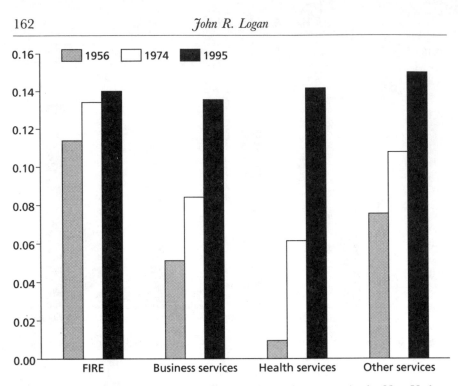

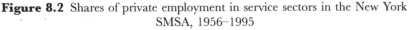

Figure 8.2 Shares of private employment in service sectors in the New York
SMSA, 1956–1995
Source: US Department of Commerce, County Business Patterns

FIRE sector (finance, insurance, and real estate) expanded greatly in absolute terms but very little in its share of employment, from under 6 percent to
7 percent. More substantial was the growth of business services (defined
broadly to include legal, accounting, engineering, and administrative services). This was a very small sector in 1956, accounting for only 2 percent of
employment; by 1995 it had grown to 11 percent. To some extent this
growth represents a reorganization of business enterprises: many industrial
and commercial enterprises that once had large white collar staffs have tended
instead to contract for these services from specialized firms. But it also reflects new corporate needs and information technologies.

Another service sector, health and medical services, grew equally fast in
this period and employed almost 11 million persons by 1995 – reaching
almost the same size as business services. Health services, too, can be thought
of as a new form of production, incorporating both high levels of technology
and large numbers of lower-skilled production workers. The continuing
national debate over the financing of health care reflects this shift in the
economy, due in part to the ageing of the population and made possible

by the expansion of private and (for older Americans and for those below the poverty line) public health insurance.

Finally, there was also growth in "other" services (including education and a wide range of consumer services such as personal services, repair services, membership organizations, etc.). Adding together all types of services, the proportion of private sector employees in services grew from just under 10 percent in 1956 to over 40 percent in 1995.

Let us turn now to the case of New York, summarized in Figure 8.2. The region's population grew slowly in this period, as did its total private employment. Manufacturing accounted for only a third of total employment in the metropolitan region in 1956. By 1993 it declined by half, and now represents barely a tenth of jobs. What is remarkable about New York, compared to the nation, is not the trend of deindustrialization but that in every year the region was less specialized in manufacturing than was the country as a whole. Regarding services, the following are the salient points.

First, both FIRE and business/professional services grew. Together they encompassed 16 percent of jobs in 1956, and that has now grown to 28 percent. As a major urban center, New York already was specialized in these functions in 1956 compared to the national economy, and it remains so today. Note, however, that the number of jobs in these two sectors grew much more rapidly in the nation than in New York. The share of such employment accounted for by New York dropped substantially (from 17.5 percent of the national total in 1956 to 5.3 percent in 1995). Although this region is special because of its role in national and international economic transactions, this unique role seems not to have had much impact on changes in the shape of its employment base in the last 40 years.

Secondly, it is also interesting to look separately at FIRE and business services. In both New York and the nation, there was some growth in the relative size of the FIRE sector between 1956 and 1973, but almost no change after 1973. It is business services that grew more robustly in the latter two decades. But while the New York region had more than double the national percentage in business services in 1956, and nearly double in 1973, by 1995 it was barely ahead of the national figure. In this respect change *since* the 1970s has had stronger effects on other American regions than on New York. Paradoxically, the most "global" metropolis is among those least affected by recent globalization.

Finally, the growth of "other services" in New York has been quite consistent with national trends. The health services industry in particular has become one of the region's largest employers, growing from 31,000 in 1956 to 618,000 in 1995. This growth was nearly equal to the decline in manufacturing during that period, and also nearly equal to the combined growth of FIRE and business/professional services – and greater in the period after 1974. If we were to assess the impact of an economic change entirely in terms of employment changes, the region's "medicalization" might well be its central feature.

We expect the economy to be the engine of change in society, and surely the impacts of deindustrialization and the concomitant rise in financial and business services have rippled through the nation. But there is little reason to believe that they have been especially strong in New York, despite its unique global functions, or that there has been any intensification of changes in occupational composition since the mid-1970s compared to the previous two decades.

Racial and Ethnic Diversity of a Global City

What has intensified in this period, and at breakneck speed, is the racial and ethnic diversity of the region. The global connections of New York have been most consequential not for the concentration of financial functions but rather for the influx of people from around the world. Immigration has shaped the region, because the entry of new groups – from Europe, from the American South and Puerto Rico, and then from Latin America and Asia – has been the main source of its growth.

Others concur in this outlook. A notable example is the analysis of New York by Mollenkopf and Castells (1991). These authors recognize an impact of globalization, in that they consider it to be the source of the "upper corporate stratum" that gives New York its "dual" character – which they describe as a cleavage between that relatively homogeneous stratum and everybody else. More important for them, the latter strata are divided along lines of race, immigration status, gender, economic activity, and neighborhood. They are the ethnically diverse female clerical working class, the disproportionately immigrant service sector, the white ethnic and native black public employees, the downgraded, largely Latino manufacturing sector, and a final category marginal to the formal economy and comprised disproportionately of native black and Puerto Rican young adults. What they have in common is "precisely their diversity, their heterogeneity, their externality" to the core (p. 403).

As applied to New York, the simple notion of duality thus disintegrates into a "plurality of peripheries," to use Castells' and Mollenkopf's term. This is a realistic approach, one that reflects a general characteristic of other major North American cities: the lines of cleavage, stemming from its economy and reflected in spatial segregation, are overlaid by divisions of race and ethnicity. This entire system of stratification – by occupation, race and ethnicity, and space – has evolved over time, fed by the influx of different waves of immigrants. The pattern we see today represents an accumulation of many historical layers of inequality. Recent changes in this pattern may in the main represent greater polarization, but more relevant to people's experience are the specific modes of incorporation of every distinct subgroup, which are hard to characterize simply as moving up or down.

This same observation applies to New York an earlier period when immigration from Europe was still in full force. Consider historical trends in population composition and in the social divisions between racial and ethnic groups. Table 8.1 provides comparable population data for 1920 for New York City, for 1960 for the metropolitan region (New York MSA), and for 1990 for the New York/New Jersey consolidated metropolitan area. These

Table 8.1 Composition of the New York population, 1920 1990 (in thousands)

	New York City 1920	New York SMSA 1960	New York CMSA 1990
Total population	5620	10694	17087
Non-Hispanic white total	5460 (97.1)	8653 (80.9)	10647 (62.3)
Italian	786 (14.0)	1126 (10.5)	2517 (14.7)
German	607 (10.8)	465 (4.3)	1437 (8.4)
Irish	695 (12.3)	452 (4.2)	1620 (9.4)
Russian	852 (15.2)	1148 (10.7)	534 (3.1)
Other white	2520 (44.8)	5462 (51.0)	4539 (26.5)
Black	152 (2.7)	1228 (11.4)	2886 (16.8)
African American		1120 (10.4)	2396 (14.0)
Afro-Caribbean		108 (1.0)	490 (2.9)
Hispanic	3 (0.1)	753 (7.0)	2704 (15.8)
Puerto Rican		631 (5.0)	1196 (6.9)
Dominican		13 (0.1)	403 (2.3)
Cuban		43 (0.4)	156 (0.9)
Mexican		8 (0.1)	95 (0.5)
Other		58 (0.5)	854 (4.9)
Asian	5 (0.1)	60 (0.5)	850 (4.9)
Chinese		36 (0.3)	317 (1.8)
Indian		4 (0.1)	187 (1.8)
Korean		na	117 (0.6)
Filipino		5 (0.1)	104 (0.6)
Japanese		7 (0.1)	40 (0.2)
Other		8 (0.1)	85 (0.5)

* *Note:* White ethnic groups are identified by foreign birth or parentage in 1910 and 1960, and by "first ancestry" in 1990.
Source: own calculations

changing boundaries are required because the "suburban population" was mainly within the city in 1920, but kept spreading over time across a wider swath of space.

In 1920 New York was one of the world's largest cities with nearly five million residents – double the size of Chicago, the country's second largest city. Its population was almost entirely white (with only about 100,000 non-white residents, about 2 percent). The ethnic divisions among whites ran deep, however. After all, the city was the main port of entry for immigrants. Two out of five New Yorkers were born abroad, and a nearly equal number were the children of immigrants. Less than a quarter were real "natives" (i.e., they had parents who themselves were born in the United States). The ethnic composition of natives, as compared to that of immigrants, directly reflected the waves of new arrivals. Most people of English or Scottish ancestry by this time were third generation or beyond. Those of German and Irish background tended to be United States born but with foreign-born parents. The most recent arrivals, such as Italians and Russians, were more likely to be born abroad.

How had the region changed by 1960? First, it doubled its 1920 population, but more importantly it changed its composition. While foreign immigration was small after World War I, waves of black migrants from the American South began in large numbers at that time, and these were joined by Puerto Rican migration after World War II. From a nearly all-white city in 1920, New York had become a racially mixed metropolis fifty years later. Out of the metropolitan population of over ten million, about two million were black and Hispanic. But although the minority presence was substantial and profound in its implications, almost all of these people were from two specific sources: they were either blacks of southern origin or Puerto Ricans. Only about 100,000 West Indian immigrants were included in the black population, and about the same number of non-Puerto Ricans among the Hispanic population. The Asian population was even smaller.

Despite the growing presence of African Americans and Puerto Ricans, the region remained predominantly settled by whites whose ethnic identity was directly linked to their country of origin. Even in 1960, half a century after the height of European immigration, 17 percent of the population was composed of white immigrants and another 28 percent were the children of such immigrants (Kantrowitz, 1969). The main nationality groups were – naturally – similar to those from before. The largest group were Russians, with more than a million members.[2] The second largest group, also with more than a million, were Italians, followed by Irish and Germans. Thus in studying intergroup relations at this time, it would be potentially as important to study ties and tensions among white ethnic groups as between whites and black or Puerto Rican minorities.

By 1990 the region's population had sprawled across an extended "Consolidated Metropolitan Statistical Area," including the cities of Newark and

Jersey City and their suburban surroundings. The principal change in composition has been another substantial shift in race and ethnicity, much more profound than had occurred by 1960. The non-Hispanic white share of the population declined dramatically, while other groups increased. Most striking are the increases associated with new waves of immigration, partly stimulated by changes in US immigration law beginning in 1965. Quotas that had previously favored Europeans were equalized across regions of the world, and policies to facilitate family reunification turned out to be of most benefit to persons from Latin America and Asia.

Still, the region has a white majority (more than 10 million of the 17 million total). I will argue below that white ethnicity continues to be a salient aspect of intergroup relations, although by this time less than a fourth of any European ancestry group is first or second generation immigrant. As counted by ancestry, rather than place of birth, the largest white group is Italians, with two and a half million, followed by Germans and Irish, and then Russians (for 1990 I have not included Poles in this latter category).

Among minorities, blacks are the largest category. Hispanics are the next largest category. Finally, the Asian population, which was minuscule in 1960, is now substantial. Besides their overall growth, the outstanding characteristic of these minorities in 1990 is their heterogeneity. Much of the growth among blacks has been comprised of immigrants from the Caribbean, who now make up about a sixth of the black population (Kasinitz, 1992). Similarly, although the biggest single Hispanic group is Puerto Ricans, the greatest increase has come from immigrants from other areas, especially Dominicans. (Other large categories, not shown in the table, are Salvadorans, Ecuadorans, and Colombians.) The biggest single Asian group, as before, is Chinese, but Indians, Koreans, and Filipinos are also present in large numbers.

Table 8.1 is designed specifically to provide a context for two hypotheses about the ethnic divisions of New York: First, that they are long-standing, based upon the attraction of the region to immigrants; this is the main reason for reaching as far back as 1920. I will argue that New York was never a melting pot. Second, that they are changing, and especially that they are becoming more complex, as people of different races and national origins enter the region. New York is a place of many minorities. To these I will add a third: that among minorities it is not only the underclass that suffers from ethnic boundaries. Particularly among African Americans, I will argue that even the "truly advantaged" have significantly different experiences than do comparable whites. In this chapter, I will review evidence relevant to these points, drawing on information about ethnic differentiation in the labor market and in residential communities. To clarify my point of view, it will be useful to distinguish it from other interpretations of intergroup relations in the city.

Never a melting pot

A key influence on interpretation of current divisions is our reading of how the old cleavages evolved. Social science has largely accepted an "optimistic" view of the white ethnic experience. The Irish, the Italians, the Jewish immigrants from Russia and East Europe are considered early success stories of social assimilation. By mid-century, Glazer and Moynihan (1963) could still recognize these groups as distinct communities, and they voiced doubts that the city was a melting pot in which ethnic identities had been purged. But they, like most social scientists, believed that white ethnics were being assimilated; they had grabbed – in Lieberson's (1980) terms – their piece of the pie; they were becoming progressively more "white" and less "ethnic."

I offer a different hypothesis: that white ethnicity has remained an essential element in the social structure of the city. Ethnic differences in origin and time of arrival were reflected in segregation within neighborhoods and workplaces after the turn of the century. We should remember that Italians and Slavs were perceived as racially distinct from the white Anglo stock that had comprised most of its 19th century population, and a virulently racist social movement was on the verge of cutting off further foreign immigration. And although it is common today to conceive of this period as one when poorly educated newcomers had better opportunities for advancement than is true today, we should be careful not to overstate those opportunities. New York was not a post-Fordist but a pre-Fordist city, which in some respects is the same thing: a high proportion of manufacturing jobs were unskilled or semi-skilled, and workers had few formal protections either through the state or from employers (Soja, 1991). Upward mobility has taken place for these groups since that time (so that, as we shall see, the income differences among white ethnic groups are modest). But upward mobility has not erased ethnic differences; the old cleavages among whites continue to structure their access to opportunity and resources. As I intend to show, differences remain in where whites of different origins live and work.

People gain security by their collective hold on particular positions in the labor market and in residential communities. Groups compete for space, for employment, and for position, and ethnicity is an important collective tool in this competition. We should expect them to relinquish this tool only slowly, if at all.

Many minorities

A potential pitfall in my emphasis on racism is the temptation to overstate its theoretical power. It has become common in the political rhetoric of minority groups to subsume all minorities in the category of "people of color," arguing implicitly or explicitly that blacks, Latinos, and Asians share a subordinate position in white America (Takaki, 1993; see Torres, 1995 for a discussion of parallels between the experience of Puerto Ricans and African Americans in New York. Torres is less sure, however, of the impact of new immigrant groups on minority solidarity).

This distinction between white and minority America is parallel to the duality between the corporate stratum and "everyone else" that Mollenkopf and Castells identify in New York (see above). But the latter authors at the same time stress the diversity of minorities. Evidence of emerging tensions among minority groups reinforces that approach. These are highlighted in several studies of the New York region, including especially Kasinitz's (1992) analysis of political tensions between African Americans and Afro-Caribbean immigrants (see also Mollenkopf, 1992, pp. 89–92, for a broader discussion of the political fragmentation of minority constituencies in the city). In California, Horton (1995) demonstrates similarly complex interethnic relationships in Monterey Park, the "first Chinese suburb." (For other examples of these issues, see the case studies reported by Lamphere, 1992). My view is that the common fate that can be perceived at a high level of abstraction obscures useful distinctions both among white ethnics and among non-white minorities. It also directs attention away from variations in the implications and manifestations of racism, variations among groups and across historical periods. Though it is *prudent* to retain racism as a theoretical tool, it would be *imprudent* to ignore the variety of group experiences.

One reason for treating minorities as a single category is the timing of the deindustrialization of the city, which began in the 1950s when blacks and Puerto Ricans were arriving in New York in large numbers and well before the mass immigration of other non-European groups. The prior assimilation of white ethnics – facilitated by opportunities in a secure, unionized, and expanding industrial workforce – is often taken for granted. It might be argued, then, that it is minorities who have suffered from deindustrialization, constituting a critical common experience.

A useful point in this regard has been made by Waldinger (1986–87). At its height, the manufacturing sector was largely white, but its decline has coincided with an exodus of whites from the New York population as a whole and especially from its manufacturing workforce. Paradoxically, then, even this declining industry has offered work opportunities for new groups. Waldinger notes that economic restructuring has been confronted by different minorities in a variety of ways. Broadly speaking, African Americans have become more dependent on public employment and Hispanics have moved into low-wage manufacturing, while Asians have managed to gain a foothold as owners of small businesses and less capital intensive manufacturing firms. Further, Waldinger suggests that these groups compete as solidarity factions against one another, so that one group's gain in a sector becomes an obstacle to another's success. To the extent that groups exhibit distinct and competing modes of adjustment to deindustrialization, we gain more from distinguishing among them than we would from stressing the majority–minority cleavage.

Not only the underclass

New racial and colonial issues were introduced by the large-scale movement of Southern blacks and Puerto Ricans into the city through 1960. Glazer and Moynihan recognized the marginalization of these minorities, but guessed that they too would experience a gradual, if delayed, assimilation into the urban mainstream, eventually replicating the incorporation of previous groups (1963). The evident failure of this expectation (see Glazer, 1997) has provoked a variety of explanations. Of these, the one most compatible with the assimilation model is the theory of the underclass neighborhood. In Wilson's (1987; 1996) view, the very success of minority incorporation – the emergence of a black middle class and its increasing access to better neighborhoods – has narrowed the class basis of traditional ghetto areas. At the same time, new external forces – deindustrialization of the economy and suburbanization of the remaining manufacturing base – have left many remaining ghetto residents jobless. Deindustrialization of the city, of course, began in the 1950s, and neither blacks nor Puerto Ricans ever participated in large proportions in the relatively high- wage, unionized sector of New York manufacturing. So the argument must be that they never got the chance that they otherwise would have had in this sector, not that they actually lost their niche in the labor market.

Wilson's emphasis on the underclass neighborhood presumes a partial incorporation of blacks into the mainstream, both socio-economically and residentially. Thus it attaches a small role to specifically racial divisions (though recognizing the historical reality of racism). Through the progress of civil rights reform, the black poor could have and would have been incorporated but for the recent and unexpected transformation of the urban economy. The black poor have become a special case in which a new kind of ghetto (quite unlike the ghetto of the 1920s and 1930s) reinforces a culture of poverty (lack of appropriate role models, inability of men to support families, the turn to illicit activities and welfare dependency) that is now itself a powerful obstacle to social progress. In this view, to put it metaphorically, the city is willing but unable to find a secure niche for the black poor.

I doubt this premise. To restate my view, I interpret the metropolis as a mechanism of shaping and reinforcing inequalities, at least as much as it is an engine of incorporation. We should expect that the collective identity of racial and ethnic groups will be used by others against them, at the same time that it is one of their key resources to sustain themselves. Suppose this is true, and that it applies even to competition between white ethnics (e.g., between Italians and Jews) decades after these groups "assimilated" into the urban world. Then how much more clearly should it apply to the case of groups whose identity is founded in a heritage of slavery and colonial rule? I am arguing that racism, construed broadly, was at the heart of urban inequality in 1900 and that the most prudent approach is to assume that it continues to be central today. More specifically, my premise, unlike Wilson's, is that racism affects black Americans of all social classes, not only the underclass (I agree in this respect with Massey and Denton, 1993).

Let us turn now to a review of how the New York region's many "minorities" – both white and non-white – have fit into local society, from early in this century until today. I will consider first their socio-economic standing, including not only the usual question of income differences but also what part they play in the economy – in what sector they work, and in what capacity. Then I will consider patterns of residential segregation.

Socio-economic Standing

An important study of socioeconomic inequalities among white ethnic groups at the turn of the century was conducted by Lieberson (1980; see also Laurie et al., 1981; Hershberg et al., 1981). He analyzed occupational distributions for non-Southern cities in 1900, showing that native whites had considerable occupational advantages over white immigrants. For example, white natives were over-represented on average by a factor of three in professional occupations. There were further gaps between earlier immigrant groups – Germans and Irish – and later immigrant groups. Germans and Irish were more likely to be professionals, bankers, or clerks; Russians and Italians were more likely to work in personal and domestic services. Lieberson found the older and newer immigrant groups were about equally represented in manufacturing. But Russians were concentrated in the garment trades, Italians as masons and cotton mill workers, Irish as plasterers and plumbers, and Germans as bakers, butchers, and cabinetmakers. These occupational niches suggest that the urban economy was highly differentiated by ethnicity.

More specific information for New York City is available from newly released individual files drawn from the 1920 Census. Table 8.2 displays the occupational composition of adult workers of various racial and ethnic origins. By comparison with other groups, native whites (those with US-born parents) were disproportionately concentrated in professional and sales/clerical occupations. Among persons of immigrant stock, this profile was most closely matched by the English and Irish, both of whom were over-represented in professional occupations (though not nearly so much as native whites). Russians and Italians were found instead in manufacturing industries, with more than half classed as operators and laborers. However, both

Russians and Italians stood out in terms of self-employment. Already in 1920 it is evident that self-employment was a strategy of upward mobility for selected immigrant groups, though not for the earlier-arriving English, Irish or Germans. The black population, it should be noted, was poorly represented in all these spheres; they were mainly concentrated in personal services, especially as servants in private households.

What has happened to these differences as seventy years have passed, new groups have entered the region, and the economy has shifted toward the

Table 8.2 Occupation by race and ethnicity, New York City 1920

	Self-employed	Professional	Sales/ Clerical	Operator/ Laborer
Native white	12.8	26.1	13.7	29.0
Foreign-born or second generation white				
England	9.4	16.2	9.4	37.8
Germany	18.7	4.7	6.9	35.6
Ireland	5.5	15.6	5.8	37.7
Italy	24.4	2.4	2.4	51.3
Russia/Poland	30.2	6.7	1.1	58.0
Black	8.0	2.4	1.2	22.8
Total	17.0	11.3	5.6	41.2

Source: own caluclations

new service sectors? Table 8.3 presents one indicator of the socio-economic standing of selected groups in the New York–New Jersey metropolis in 1990: the median household income. Not unexpectedly, for those who are familiar with national averages for the United States, whites have the highest median household income, followed closely by Asians. Blacks and Hispanics lag considerably. More interesting is the differentiation within these large categories:

1. Among whites, people of Russian and English ancestry stand out strongly with a median of $54–56,000, well above other European ancestry groups.
2. Among blacks, Afro-Caribbeans – despite relatively recent immigration – have an average income about $8000 higher than other blacks (termed African American in this table).

3. Hispanics have very low average incomes, even below those of African Americans. This is particularly true of Puerto Ricans and Dominicans. Other Hispanics, not listed separately in the table, have incomes equivalent to Afro-Caribbeans. These include Cubans, Mexicans, and South Americans.

4. Such variation is most pronounced among Asians. Despite their reputations as successful immigrants, Chinese and Koreans report incomes around $35,000 – only 10 percent higher than Afro-Caribbeans. But Indians are above the white average at $45,000. Smaller groups not shown in the table, like the Filipinos (who include many health professionals) and Japanese (many of whom are temporary residents linked to Japanese corporations in the region) have incomes nearly equivalent to whites of Russian ancestry.

This differentiation by ethnic categories implies that the simple pecking order among larger groups – white, Asian, black, Hispanic – requires a finer cut. We might rather think of Russians, Filipinos and Japanese at the top.

Table 8.3 Median household income for selected racial and ethnic groups, the New York CMSA in 1990

	Median income
Non-Hispanic white	$43,000
English	54,036
German	49,200
Irish	40,000
Italian	45,000
Russian	56,000
Non-Hispanic black	$20,000
African American	24,941
Afro-Caribbean	32,692
Hispanic	$25,447
Puerto Rican	22,000
Dominican	20,792
Asian	$40,800
Chinese	35,585
Indian	45,050
Korean	35,000

Source: own calculations

These are followed by Germans, Indians, and Italians; then Irish. Considerably lower, then, would be Chinese, Koreans, Afro-Caribbeans, and Cubans. Then, again considerably lower, would be African Americans, with Puerto Ricans and Dominicans at the very bottom of the list. This hierarchy is not simply a racial one, nor is it based on a distinction between earlier and later immigrant groups among whites, nor between established groups and those who arrived in large numbers after 1960.

Income is not the only dimension of incorporation in the labor force. Other important characteristics are business ownership or self-employment and access to public employment. Unlike income, these are not necessarily indicators of hierarchical position; what they indicate, rather, is the degree to which various groups fit into the economy in a different manner. Data on these indicators are provided in Logan et al. (1999). One striking pattern is the very high dependency on public employment by African Americans (found not only in New York, but in almost every major metropolitan area). This confirms the high reliance of this group on public jobs as stressed by Waldinger, and it represents a significant shift from earlier decades where white ethnics held those positions. Reliance on public employment adds another distinction between African Americans and Afro-Caribbeans (who have higher incomes but are less likely to obtain government jobs). It also helps discriminate between the situation of Puerto Ricans (who rank second only to African Americans in this respect) and Dominicans (nearly absent from the public sector), who have about the same household incomes. Presumably the higher proportion of citizens among African Americans and Puerto Ricans, compared to Afro-Caribbeans and Dominicans, contributes to this difference. Among these groups, probably public employment is an advantage, and it is likely that it has an important political component.

Business ownership and self-employment address the phenomenon of enclave economies that Alejandro Portes and others (Portes and Bach, 1985) have described as an alternative mode of incorporation for immigrant minorities. Cubans in Miami are the prototype for this model: a large ethnic community in which a high proportion of residents are employed by Cuban entrepreneurs. According to Portes, in such a case the entrance of immigrants into the labor market is facilitated, and people are more likely to be paid commensurate with their education and skills. For those with little access to good positions in the mainstream economy, then, a high level of business ownership and self-employment is said to be advantageous.

Whites and Asians have the higher average levels of self-employment than blacks or Hispanics, but again there are important variations within these large categories. Koreans and Russians are especially high. Irish and Chinese (despite the well known Chinatown economy in New York) lie closer to the other end of the continuum.

Blacks, regardless of ethnicity, are remarkably low in entrepreneurship, a feature of the black community that has long been described as a key source of weakness. Yet it would be unwise to focus solely on blacks in this regard – the entrepreneurial levels of Puerto Ricans, Mexicans, Dominicans, and even the Irish are in the same general range.

Contemporary disparities in socio-economic level are thus compounded by differences in groups' modes of integration into the economy. Some divisions among white ethnic groups that were apparent early in this century remain visible even now (this point is made also by Mollenkopf, 1992, pp. 59–60), and there is great variation among various black, Hispanic, and Asian national origin groups. It is somewhat misleading to speak of the situation of whites, as though there were now a single "assimilated" white experience. It is even more dubious to refer to a minority, or even a black, Hispanic, or Asian experience. The global city requires finer grain distinctions to reflect its racial and ethnic segmentation.

Residential Segregation

The final portion of this analysis addresses the issue of residential segregation. First, what is the overall level of segregation (measured by the standard Index of Dissimilarity)[3]? Has segregation declined during this century, and for whom? Second, what kinds of places do various groups live in? Do their communities constitute simply residential separation, or do they also embody spatial inequality?

Values of the segregation index for 1920 for New York City are presented in Table 8.1. These are based on approximately 1500 "sanitary districts," essentially equivalent to today's census tracts. The "native white" population is defined as whites born in the US of non-immigrant parents. White ethnic groups are defined by their country of birth or that of their parents. African Americans and Asians are defined by race. There is a clear distinction between earlier immigrant groups – Germans and Irish, who have fairly low levels of segregation from native whites – and later white immigrants – the Russians and Italians, who are highly segregated both from one another and from other groups. Indeed, a striking finding of this table is that Russians and Italians were actually more segregated from native whites than were blacks. Another way of thinking about segregation is to ask what kind of area the average group member lived in. In a city that was only 15 percent Russian (counting foreign-born or US-born of Russian parents), the average Russian lived in a district that was 42 percent Russian. In a city that was only 11 percent Italian, the average Italian lived in a district that was 44 percent Italian. By contrast, the earlier immigrant groups, such as English, Irish, and Germans, lived in districts where they were outnumbered by native white Americans.

Table 8.4 Residential segregation indices for New York City ethnic groups (first- and second-generation), 1920

	English	German	Irish	Italian	Russian	Black
Native white	.18	.28	.29	.63	.71	.72
English	–	.32	.31	.63	.63	.72
German		–	.39	.64	.68	.77
Irish			–	.62	.73	.71
Italian				–	.71	.80
Russian					–	.84
Black						–

Source: own calculations

Even more striking, the relatively small black population was almost entirely confined to neighborhoods such as San Juan Hill (on Manhattan's middle West Side) and Harlem (which was 75 percent black). Though blacks were only 3 percent of the population, the typical black person lived in an area that was 43 percent black.

The distributions of people underlying these index values can be understood in broad strokes by simple comparisons among the boroughs. Manhattan was the borough with the highest proportion of foreign-born immigrants. German and English immigrants were found in higher proportions in the outer boroughs of Queens, the Bronx, and Staten Island, however, while natives of Italian and Russian origin were least likely to be found in these outer boroughs. Such differences persisted into the 1960s, when Glazer and Moynihan (1963) still found many factors that operated "to keep much of New York life channeled within the bounds of the ethnic group"(p. 19). Most salient for Italians and Jews (for which Russian ancestry was used as a proxy) was continued residential segregation.

New York was not unique in this respect. Lieberson's (1963) study of ten northern cities (not including New York) in 1910 reported levels of segregation among white ethnic groups using the Index of Dissimilarity (ID) as a measure of segregation, based on city wards. Segregation from "native whites" for the English foreign-born was generally in the .10–.25 range. For Germans, it ranged mainly between .15 and .40. But values for Russians rose to between .50 and .65; and for Italians, most were in the .55–.75 range. Lieberson argued that such segregation among white ethnics had already declined sharply by 1950. Yet the averages for his ten cities show only a small overall decline in values of D from 1910, and for several groups these values remained markedly high. For Italians it was .46 in 1950. The average for Russian foreign-born was .60.

Another study (Kantrowitz, 1969) analyzes tract-level data for the New York SMSA in 1960 for persons of "foreign stock" (born abroad or the children of immigrants). Kantrowitz argues that there has in fact been more continuity than change in white ethnic segregation. For example, the segregation of Russians from members of several other white groups was similar in 1960 to what Lieberson had found in 1950 in other cities: from the Irish (.57), Germans (.52), and Italians (.60). This same argument has been made in a different way by those who have looked further back in the 19th century. Segregation of Germans and Irish in Philadelphia was already low (in the range of .30-.35) in 1880 because workers needed to live close to their jobs, which were highly dispersed at that time (Greenberg, 1981). Thus, the relatively low segregation indices for these groups in the 20th century may represent not a decline as they assimilated, but rather a continuation of an established pattern. Hershberg et al. (1981) show that segregation levels of Irish and Germans from native whites in Philadelphia were nearly unchanged between 1950 and 1970. Among later arrivals, segregation of Russians stayed above .50 throughout 1930–1970, while that of Italians declined from .58 to .48 in the same period.

To reflect the current situation, the values of the Index of Dissimilarity for 1990 are presented in Table 8.5 (calculated for the entire metropolis). The key findings here are:

1. There are fairly low levels of segregation among the older white ancestry groups (English, German, and Irish) – .30 or less – comparable to levels found in 1920. But segregation of the Italians from the English (.41) is somewhat higher than this, and Russians remain more segregated (though not quite as highly segregated as 70 years before) with scores of about .50 in relation to other white groups. Russians demonstrate an astonishing durability of residential separation.

   What does a segregation score of .90 or .40, like that of Italians from other white ethnics, represent? A close examination of locational patterns (reported in detail in Alba et al., 1997) reveals that we cannot assume that it implies the disappearance of ethnic neighborhoods. Fully 27 percent of Italian Americans in 1990 lived in neighborhoods in which they were the predominant ethnic group (defined as areas over 35 percent Italian ancestry, and with at least one core census tract over 40 percent Italian). While some traditionally Italian neighborhoods in the central city have shrunk noticeably from their prior size and importance, some new Italian neighborhoods are now emerging in the suburbs. These have a less "Italian" character (a smaller proportion of residents are foreign-born or speak Italian at home), but they represent remarkable community areas nonetheless.

2. There are generally much higher levels of segregation between white

ethnics and the non-European groups. Black segregation from whites in 1920 (around .75) had edged upward to about .80 by 1960. Puerto Rican segregation from whites was at this same level at that time. These values have risen even higher for blacks and Hispanics in 1990. But now the experiences of newer groups are added. Afro-Caribbeans and Dominicans have segregation scores of nearly .90 in relation to whites. And Asian segregation from whites is around .65.

3. Finally, the various minority groups are also highly segregated from one another. The emphasis in the segregation literature on the white-minority dimension fails to take account of the degree to which ethnic groups within each major minority category perceive themselves as distinctive, establish boundaries around themselves, and occupy their own spaces. For example, in 1960 the segregation of blacks and Puerto Ricans from one another (.70) as reported by Kantrowitz (1969) was nearly as high as either group's segregation from whites. In 1990, though the index value for African Americans and Puerto Ricans is down to .57, the value for African Americans and Dominicans is .71. All Asian groups are highly segregated from black and Hispanic groups. And there is even significant segregation within the large minority categories: among blacks (.43 between African Americans and Afro-Caribbeans), Hispanics (.50 between Puerto Ricans and Dominicans), and Asians (above .60 for the three groups listed). The unique identities of these national origin ethnic groups are clearly preserved and reflected in urban space. These results taken together undercut the viability of interpreting New York along a simple white–non-white dimension.

As a final step, I address the question of what kind of neighborhoods members of different groups live in, and why. This is an important issue because the quality of one's neighborhood – public facilities and shopping, access to employment, personal security, effectiveness of public schools – has so strong an impact on daily life (Logan and Molotch, 1987). The value of living in a racially integrated environment, as indicated in segregation indices, is somewhat abstract (and increasingly contested). By contrast, the inequalities in resources offered by different neighborhoods are quite concrete.

I use the median household income of the census tract where people live as a general purpose indicator of neighborhood quality. It is well documented that higher-income areas enjoy better shopping facilities, are more attractive to employers, experience lower crime rates, and have better schools than poorer areas. Table 8.6 (in the first column) summarizes the overall averages for persons of various racial and ethnic backgrounds. Not surprisingly, since whites have higher incomes than other groups, they also live in higher income neighborhoods (an average census tract income of $47,700). Asians live in somewhat poorer environments ($39,600), but blacks' and

Table 8.5 Segregation among selected racial and ethnic groups, New York metropolitan region (CMSA), 1990

	German	Irish	Italian	Russian	A-A	A-C	P.R.	Domin.	Chinese	Indian	Korean
English	.24	.30	.41	.49	.83	.85	.77	.88	.70	.67	.72
German	–	.19	.27	.49	.83	.85	.75	.87	.67	.62	.69
Irish		–	.26	.51	.83	.84	.73	.86	.66	.62	.68
Italian			–	.52	.83	.84	.73	.86	.64	.61	.68
Russian				–	.84	.83	.78	.88	.62	.65	.66
African American					–	.43	.57	.71	.85	.79	.89
Afro-Caribbean						–	.67	.75	.84	.76	.89
Puerto Rican							–	.50	.73	.71	.82
Dominican								–	.80	.77	.88
Chinese									–	.61	.63
Indian										–	.66
Korean											–

Note: White ethnic groups are defined by the "first ancestry" indicated on census questionnaires. Asians are classified on the basis of racial categories; African Americans (A-A) and Afro-Caribbeans (A-C) on the basis of race and national origin; and Hispanic groups on the basis of Hispanic identity and national origin questions.

Source: own calculations

Hispanics' neighborhoods are clearly poorer ($28,400 and $27,500, respectively). There also appears to be a hierarchy within each of these broad racial categories. Persons of English ancestry live in neighborhoods that are $5000 richer than those of Italians. Puerto Ricans and Dominicans both live in neighborhoods below the Hispanic average. And Indian and Korean areas stand out clearly above the Chinese.

The main question that arises from these differences in neighborhood character is whether they represent strictly racial and ethnic effects or are they no more than a reflection of the differences in socio-economic standing

Table 8.6 Average values of the median household income of tracts where group members live, and predicted values for an "affluent urban native" of each group (NY-NJ CMSA 1990)

	Average Value	*Predicted Value*
Non-Hispanic white	47,700	53,800
English	51,700	54,900
German	49,600	54,200
Irish	48,200	52,900
Italian	46,400	53,200
Russian	51,600	56,900
Non-Hispanic black	28,400	38,300
Hispanic	27,500	45,400
Puerto Rican	24,800	43,900
Dominican	22,800	44,700
Asian	39,600	48,000
Chinese	35,900	47,400
Indian	41,600	47,200
Korean	42,000	51,300

Note: The predicted values for Hispanics and Hispanic subgroups refer specifically to white Hispanics. These values are $3700 higher than the predicted values for black Hispanics. The predicted values are for a male, aged 25–64, living in a married-couple household in the central city. Affluent means that he is a homeowner, with a college education and over $100,00 income. Native means that he was born in the U.S. and speaks only English at home. The estimation equation for Hispanics also included the person's race, and figures in this column refer specifically to white Hispanics (a large share of Hispanics, especially Dominicans and Puerto Ricans, define themselves in the census as black or other non-white). The pattern of group differences would be similar but not exactly the same for other background profiles.

Source: own calculations

of each group that were noted above? The effects of personal characteristics other than race and ethnicity can be partialled out and held constant through the use of individual-level prediction equations in which the dependent variable is the income level of one's tract and determinants include one's income, education, and other relevant traits (this procedure is described in detail in Alba and Logan, 1992). Such equations have been estimated for 1990 for the New York region (Logan and Alba, 1996; see also Logan et al., 1996 for results based on the 1980 census). Table 8.6 summarizes these results by calculating the predicted value of neighborhood median income for group members with a specific array of personal traits that represent an "affluent urban native" American. Disparities in these predicted values are differences that can be attributed to group membership, not to other aspects of one's personal background.

In one respect the controls for background characteristics simplify the results. Sub-group differences among whites, Hispanics, and Asians remain but are smaller in magnitude than are the gaps in the overall, unadjusted averages. This means, for example, that although Puerto Ricans and Dominicans, or Chinese and Koreans, or British and Russians live in different neighborhoods (as indicated by the segregation scores reviewed above), they do live in more or less equal ones – if they have the same income, education, and other personal characteristics.

On the other hand, deep inequalities are revealed between the four larger racial/ethnic categories. The widest gap is between whites and blacks. The net disparity between these two, a gap of $15,500 in the neighborhood's average income, is only negligibly reduced from the gross difference of $19,300 shown in the first column of Table 8.6. Black white differences are also revealed in the effect of race among Hispanics: the predicted values for white Hispanics are $3700 higher than would be predicted for comparable black Hispanics. But even white Hispanics live in substantially worse neighborhoods than comparable non-Hispanic whites.

Predicted values for Asians are closer to whites. Indeed, for a slightly different profile – suburban rather than urban – Asian values would actually be higher than those for whites. This is because Asians in the central city, particularly Chinese, are highly concentrated in relatively low-income enclaves. Their suburban residential settlements, by contrast, are quite affluent.

These findings define the racial/ethnic hierarchy of the New York region. They are especially poignant in regard to the continuing handicap of blacks of all social classes. The wealthy and highly educated black residents referred to in Table 8.6 live in areas equivalent to those predicted for a white person with only a $45,000 income and high school education. Clearly it is not only the black underclass that feels the weight of a discriminatory housing market.

Yet a closer look at the equations underlying Table 8.6 (not shown) shows that the persisting color line in the metropolis is tempered by the divergence between native African Americans and black immigrants (as we have seen, mostly from the Caribbean). Blacks are the only group, contrasting with whites, Hispanics, and Asians, among whom immigrants achieve better residential outcomes than natives. In fact, middle class black immigrants live in neighborhoods with about the same socio-economic level as do middle class white natives (not shown in this table).

Continuities in the Global City

In response to the questions posed by the editors of this volume – has social inequality acquired a new or characteristic property in the late 20th century city? does it appear in a new form or with a new spatial configuration? – my emphasis has been on the continuity of social relations in this region. New York is *still* a global city, and its global character principally derives today as in the past from its role as a receiver of people. It creates global neighborhoods, segmenting the metropolitan space by race and ethnicity. These spatial patterns are durable, and they reflect an equally durable segmentation of the economy and labor force by the same dimensions of race and ethnicity.

This is not a region where unprecedented spatial or socio-economic divisions have been invented under the sway of a new world order and international economic function for the city. Of course there have been changes, but we must carefully identify the timing, content, and impact of these changes. I have argued that deindustrialization and the restructuring of metropolitan economies as centers of corporate, financial, and other services have taken place more recently and at a faster rate in the nation as a whole than in New York. New York's special role in the international financial products industry has evolved out of its historic position in the world economy and has had minor effects on the area's labor force and neighborhoods.

More important have been the waves of migration, which initially brought together a motley array of European peoples, then added Southern blacks and Puerto Ricans to this mix, and most recently have introduced an even more diverse collection of non-European immigrants in large numbers. One interpretation of this history is that white ethnics were easily incorporated and assimilated into mainstream society earlier in the century, when times were "better," facilitated by their racial homogeneity. This interpretation can be combined with divergent views of the fate of more recent arrivals: 1) they are all excluded from the mainstream by an overriding white–nonwhite divide; 2) Asians and Hispanics are moderately assimilated but blacks are excluded; or 3) minorities are increasingly incorporated into the mainstream consistent with their individual qualifications but a new black underclass has been created by a failure of occupational opportunities.

I have suggested that the underlying premise of all these versions of intergroup relations – the powerful assimilation dynamic demonstrated by the disappearance of white ethnicity – is overstated. My reading of the evolution of differences among white ethnic groups in New York is that the divisions among them have been maintained, at least in attenuated form, at the same time that many members of these groups achieved higher socioeconomic positions and left their original residential enclaves for better neighborhoods. The best evidence for this conclusion is the experience of people of Russian origin. Distinctive early in this century for their concentration in manufacturing, and their bifurcation into either self-employment or occupations as laborers, Russians are now unique among white ethnics in terms of high income and business ownership. Highly segregated from other white groups in 1910, they still maintain a distinctive residential profile. One might argue that this is an exceptional case – Russians after all are predominantly Jewish. The English, Germans, and Irish (all of whom arrived in large numbers earlier in the 19th century) now seem neither occupationally nor residentially distinctive. Don't these latter groups represent the real story of white ethnicity? I believe this is the wrong question to ask. What about the survival of Italian neighborhoods? Or if we look more closely at the labor force, the predominance of British and Greeks as well as Russians as business owners in the strategic financial and professional services sector? There is variation in white ethnic groups' experiences, and it is more useful to acknowledge this variety than to maintain that they are really the same. This approach draws attention to the constancy of competition among groups for a place in the metropolis, apparent already at the turn of the last century and continuing today even as new groups appear.

These comments should not be construed as a broad rejection of assimilation theory. The positive theoretical point that I wish to stress is that opportunities for mobility are consistent with the erection of group boundaries that give some people a special advantage or handicap. On the whole, education, work experience, language ability, and familiarity with the local environment improve socio-economic and residential opportunities, as presumed by the assimilation model. But people compete for position both as individuals (or families) and as members of racial and ethnic groups, and their resources at both levels (their individual traits and the collective standing of their groups) both affect the outcomes. This point is especially clear from the analysis of locational patterns. Members of every major racial/ethnic category live in better neighborhoods to the extent that they have higher incomes, can arrange to buy their homes, or manage to move to the suburbs. Yet having taken into account these individual characteristics, there remains a hierarchy of racial and ethnic groups such that, for example, affluent whites and Asians live in the most attractive neighborhoods, followed by comparable white Hispanics, and with blacks (both Hispanic and non-Hispanic) in significantly lower status communities. The disadvantage associated with black race, affecting blacks of all class backgrounds, is strong evidence against Wilson's (1987) non-racial interpretation of the underclass community.

Another weakness of assimilation theory is that one cannot identify a uniform disadvantage of being a new immigrant group, which is an important hypothesis of this theory. Instead, the impact of immigration is group-specific and depends on what aspect of incorporation is considered. Among blacks, Afro-Caribbeans (largely immigrants) have less access to public jobs but they earn higher incomes than African Americans, and the analyses of residential quality showed that black immigrants have an advantage in neighborhood location over black natives. Among Hispanics, Puerto Ricans earn almost as little as the mostly immigrant Dominicans despite their greater access to public employment, but locational analyses demonstrate that immigrant Hispanics who do not speak English well are greatly disadvantaged compared to natives. Finally among Asians there is no indication that recent immigration is either a handicap or an advantage.

Underlying these variations in the effects of immigration are sharp differences among subgroups within the general categories of blacks, Hispanics, and Asians. As Mollenkopf (1992, p. 68) has put it, "West Indian immigrants differ objectively from native-born blacks in economic and cultural terms and compete against them, just as Latinos do against blacks and Dominicans do against Puerto Ricans." These deviations rob the white–non-white dichotomy of some of its meaning: recall that Japanese and Filipinos earn about the same household income as Russians, considerably more than Italians or Germans. They also devalue black, Hispanic, and Asian as meaningful social categories. There is a different socio-economic and residential profile for African Americans than for Afro-Caribbeans, for Puerto Ricans than for Dominicans, for Chinese than for Filipinos. Comparing across categories, Afro-Caribbeans earn about the same as Koreans, and African Americans about the same as Mexicans.

This heterogeneity of group experiences defies a simple model. It is one thing to recognize and highlight the racial/ethnic segmentation of New York's labor and housing markets, quite another to offer theoretical tools to explain or to classify it. I have put forward several hypotheses that are consistent with the evidence reviewed here. First, ethnic segmentation is rooted in the history of the region. Divisions among white ethnics originating early in the century or in the last century have been only partly attenuated, and new fissures have been overlaid across these. Second, social categories that seemed useful in an earlier period – black, Hispanic, Asian – have become less meaningful as the numbers of these persons have grown and their origins have become more diverse. The deepest line of cleavage is between blacks and other New Yorkers, but even this one is being obscured by the newly important distinction between African Americans and Afro-Caribbeans. The divide between natives and immigrants, so consequential in the phase of

European immigration, has become group- and context-specific. Third, long-term economic restructuring has changed the environment in which intergroup competition occurs. Yet it seems unlikely that the recent development of the international financial industry and New York's special role can explain either the overall increase in class inequality or the racial/ethnic patterning of inequality. Rather than subscribe to a broad theory of economic globalization, the challenge is to understand the particularities of group identities and experiences, taking into account the background of each group and the conditions and timing of its entry into the metropolis.

Notes

1 An early version of this chapter was presented at the University of Toronto, February 9, 1996. The initial draft of this chapter was completed when the author was a Visiting Scholar at the Russell Sage Foundation. Some results reported here are based on work conducted jointly with Richard D. Alba, in a program of research supported by National Science Foundation grant SBR9507920.

2 I have combined people from the Soviet Union and Poland as "Russians" for 1960, in part because boundary changes in East Europe make it difficult to distinguish more clearly between what was "Russia" in 1920 and what was the Soviet Union or Poland in 1960. More important, they were both predominantly Jewish.

3 The Index of Dissimilarity is a measure of segregation that ranges from zero (indicating that two groups are distributed in the same proportions across geographical areas) to one (indicating that they are entirely separated from one another). Values of .60 and above are considered very high; values below .20 are considered quite modest.

9

Brussels: Post-Fordist Polarization in a Fordist Spatial Canvas

Christian Kesteloot

Like many Western cities, Brussels has experienced an economic upturn since the second half of the 1980s related to the growth of a global economy. However, unemployment, poverty, and the trapping of the poor in segregated areas of the city – all resulting from the worldwide crisis whose inception is usually related to the oil crisis in 1973 – were not reduced by this new era of economic growth. On the contrary, the growth of global capitalism goes hand in hand with increasing social inequality at regional and local level. It seems to be the price to pay in order to stay competitive in the global economic context.

The Brussels case is an interesting one: the capital of Europe houses institutions and persons who directly participate in the global economy. At the same time, like other Western European cities, it has several large ethnic communities from "guestworker" origins. Moreover, Brussels displays a very clear socio-spatial structure, with the poor in the inner city and the rich in the suburbs and an unimportant social housing sector. Thus, at first sight, all elements are present to consider the Brussels case as resembling the American global city. However, a close analysis of the urban developments since the end of World War II reveals this view to be too simplistic.

The link between globalization and growing inequality in cities which is central to this hypothesis was first asserted by Friedmann and Wolff (1982). Their analysis was further developed by Sassen (1991; 1994). According to their work, this link is based on a changing distribution of labor in global cities, namely those cities of which the socio-economic structure and development is determined by their role in the global economy, rather than by their national or regional dynamism. As decision centers for the world economy, these cities experience a shift in their division of labor with both the growth of a highly skilled upper class employed in the global economy (the transnational elite according to their terminology) and the concomitant increase of low-skilled and badly paid workers servicing this new upper class and their enterprises. Sassen documented these changes for New York, London and Tokyo (1991) and searched for similar phenomena in other cities in her later work (1994). However, this theory has been questioned on empirical grounds by Fainstein et al. (1992) and Hamnett (1994a; 1994b) and also on theoretical grounds (for an overview see Hamnett, 1998). The main arguments are directed towards the oversimplification of the social structure of the cities (e.g., Marcuse, 1989) and the underestimation of national differences through the actions of the welfare states (e.g., Silver, 1993). Meanwhile, at least increasing poverty has been demonstrated in other cities (see Sassen, 1994 and for collections of work on several cities Musterd, 1994; Mingione, 1996; O'Loughlin and Friedrichs, 1996; Musterd and Ostendorf, 1998) and sometimes the findings of the polarization thesis have been directly applied to such cities. However, cities other than London, New York, and Tokyo hardly play an equivalent leading role in the global economy to generate the presence of a transnational elite and the typical accompanying division of labor. In such cases, the use of the polarization thesis as an explanation for growing inequalities is somewhat overstretched.

However, a very similar explanation links economic restructuring and thus changes in the division of labor to technological and organizational changes in production also connected in a dialectical way with globalization (Castells, 1989). Flexibility and geographical competition for investment between cities and regions are the key concepts in this view (Harvey, 1985; 1989). Fordism has been replaced by flexible organization of production, and the Fordist accumulation regime adds economies of scope to the typical economies of scale. (Swyngedouw and Kesteloot, 1990). Geographical competition results from (spatial) flexibility and from the increased mobility of capital in the global economy. Thus, every employment basin, city and region has to compete with the others to attract and retain investment. This line of argument supports the social polarization thesis (it is even present in Sassen's work), and helps explain similar symptoms in cities which are not highly ranked in the world hierarchy. This approach gives a good insight in the recent changes in Brussels (Kesteloot, 1995a). However, since Brussels can also be seen as one of the leading second-tier cities in the world hierarchy because of the presence of the EU and NATO headquarters, Sassen's global city concept could also apply with the necessary amendments (Elmhorn, 1998).

In this chapter, a third theoretical element is added, namely the sociospatial structuring of the city which results from the interaction between past layers of socio-spatial organizations and present-day dynamics. The core of this interaction is between present-day social inequality and the historical layers of the city's socio-spatial organization. This historical approach shows that old socio-economic processes' spatial effects are still present today. One could conceptualize it as an urban application of Massey's (1984) geological metaphor based on the insights of the French regulation theory.[1]

In this context, social and spatial polarizations interact. Depending on the welfare state configuration and the socio-spatial structuring of the housing market (both bearing the logic of past societal structures), the new social dynamics can translate into social mix, at least in certain inner city areas (the case of Dutch cities until recent policy changes – see Van Kempen, 1994). In others, these dynamics are reflected in spatial shifts in deprived and upper class areas (the former is again very peculiar to the Dutch case, see Kesteloot and Cortie, 1998, the latter finds a form in gentrification) and in many cases polarization merely reinforces past divisions in the city. The past is trapped and reflected in the built environment. This historical legacy affects social behavior, and of course it varies from place to place, having been strongly influenced by the economic and socio-political factors operating at various times in the past, including the regulatory environment controlled by governments.

As in any city where market exchange is the main economic regulation mechanism, the correspondence of growing social and spatial inequality in Brussels is related to changes in the labor and housing markets. Using the geological metaphor, three historical layers are most relevant: the first one dates from before the economic crisis of the 1970s and relates to the Fordist development of the urban region; the second bears the impact of the crisis itself and the third layer contains the effects of the restructuring processes carried out during the 1980s and 1990s, the post-Fordist elements. Obviously, other elements such as the scale of the areas, the administrative and fiscal territorial organization of the city, demographic pressures, etc., play a role as well, but they are not within the scope of this paper. The chapter starts with an overview of the Fordist urban restructuring in Brussels which laid the basis for the present-day divided structure. The second section shows the effects of the economic crisis in the late 1970s and the early 1980s – a slowing of middle class suburbanization, and the immigrants becoming trapped economically – in chronic unemployment – and spatially – in the inner city Finally we come to the nature of the polarization processes in the 1980s and 1990s which lead to growing inequalities along the division lines created in the 1960s and consolidated during the crisis. The fact that post-Fordism developed within the spatial canvass established by Fordist development demonstrates the precise interaction between these three recent historical layers of socio-spatial organization of the city.

Fordism in Brussels (1945–1973)

Until the 1960s, the spatial differentiation of Brussels showed a broadly dual pattern (Van der Haegen, 1992) based on the interaction between the medieval functions and the physical environment of the city. In the west, the marshy valley housed the poor; in the east the hills and the forest attracted the nobility. But already in the second half of the 19th century, sectoral subdivisions appeared: to the west, the industrial and working class axis follows a NNE-SSW line along the Senne river and the parallel Antwerp-Brussels–Charleroi canal; to the east, in the direction of the fringes of the Zoniën forest lie two prestigious boulevards. The Louizalaan (named after Leopold I's queen) leads to the former abbey of Ter Kameren in the south-east and the Tervurenlaan to Leopold II's Versailles-like castle on the eastern edge of the forest. Segregation was extended by further developments later in the 19th century and in the interwar period. For example, at the end of the 19th century Haussmann-like central boulevards were built that covered the Senne, so that the river gradually became the city's central sewer, and the creation of the *quartier Leopold*, the first upper class district outside the city walls (Papadopoulos, 1996). Between the wars garden city-like social housing estates were laid out outside the city and the first upper class high rise apartments near the center were constructed. Nevertheless, the segregation brought about by this differentiation of residential space on historical grounds was neither deep nor systematic. A general sense of belonging to and sharing a common territory bridged the gap, making Brussels feel like a rather small provincial town.

These sectoral structures and the peripheral social housing estates are still particularly apparent in the present socio-spatial organization of the city. However, their significance has changed considerably (Map 9.1). Firstly, the internationalization of the city, with both guestworkers and affluent foreigners working in the international organizations housed in the city, has strengthened the contrast between the east and the west, between the NNE-SSW working class axis and the prestigious east and south-east lines. Secondly, massive suburbanization has superimposed an even more significant concentric pattern. As the suburbanization front moved out to the periphery, this concentric structure first contrasts the inner ring of municipalities in Brussels (relatively large parts of which were built in the 19th century) with the other municipalities of the present-day Brussels Capital Region and finally contrasts the whole Brussels Capital Region with the rest of the urban region.[?]

Internationalization and the creation of a Fordist urban region

During the Golden Sixties, the economic development of Brussels was characterized by a process of internationalization, involving both low-skilled

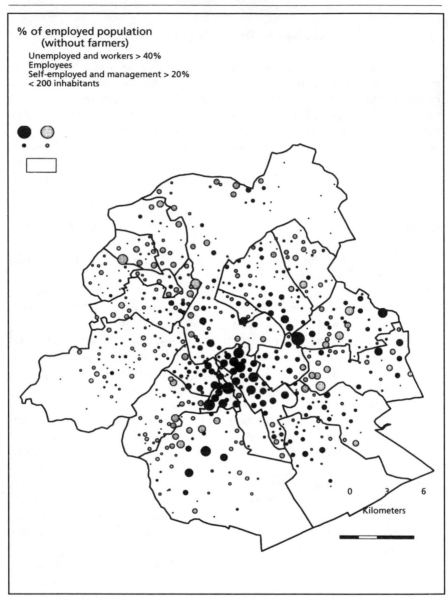

% of employed population
(without farmers)

Unemployed and workers > 40%
Employees
Self-employed and management > 20%
< 200 inhabitants

Map 9.1 The social pattern in the extended Brussels agglomeration, 1991
Source: NIS, 1991

foreign workers from the Mediterranean basin and expatriates from developed countries. The breakthrough of the transnational corporations induced a strong development and centralization of management activities. As a result Brussels' economic growth, both in terms of employment and added value became concentrated in tertiary activities. The city center develops into an international business district. The world fair of 1958 is said to be the start of this development, and indeed it triggered a whole set of urbanistic changes, transforming the city from a fairly provincial capital into a Fordist city. In the same year, the establishment of the NATO headquarters and the provisional hosting of the European Commission fixed the international role of the city and gradually the share of affluent foreigners grew to around eight per cent of the total population of the Brussels Capital Region in 1981. (This figure includes expatriates from neighboring countries who are not all affluent or involved in international relations.) Moreover, 60,000 additional foreigners, most of them wealthy, live in the suburban municipalities outside the Brussels Capital Region. The expansion of the European Community and later the European Union, both in terms of member countries and tasks, largely explains the continuous increase in affluent expatriates. Today, more than 60,000 jobs are derived from the presence of the international institutions in Brussels. While in 1960 only eight per cent of the Brussels population was foreign, the figure jumped to 30 per cent in 1995 and another seven per cent obtained Belgian nationality. Thus Brussels became a cosmopolitan city (see Kesteloot and Van der Haegen, 1997).

During the early 1960s the Brussels population was proud to see the first (modest) skyscrapers emerging and many inhabitants were eager to compare the city with New York. The most vivid sense of modernity was expressed by the "Manhattan plan", a very significant name for a complete transformation of the *Quartier Nord*, a working class area in the 19th-century northern expansion of the city. The plan, launched in 1967, projected a World Trade Center, at the crossroads between North and South and East and West Europe, with more than one hundred skyscrapers, mainly for office and trade, and vertically separated transport networks (from underground metro and trains to helicopters connecting the roofs of the skyscrapers), making it a transport hub connecting the city with the rest of Europe. After the displacement of nearly 12,000 inhabitants and once a few office towers had been built, the building process was halted by the crisis in the mid-1970s (Lievens et al., 1975). The towers had to be let by the local authority in order to avoid the developers' bankruptcy, and for more than ten years a lot of space in the heart of the city was left empty.

Suburbanization as the main cause for socio-spatial division

While these events were symbolic for the structuring of the city in the Fordist age, suburbanization can be seen as the most important feature of the 1960s and the early 1970s and most significant for the present day socio-spatial

Table 9.1 Population change and average taxable income per person compared to the national average 1963–1995

	1963 pop.	1963 income	1975 pop.	1975 income	1985 pop.	1985 income	1995 pop.	1995 income
Brussels Capital region	100	160	101	128	94	106	92	93
District Halle-Vilvoorde	100	105	116	115	121	117	127	120
District Nivelles	100	112	120	119	141	116	159	116
Kingdom	–	100	–	100	–	100	–	100

Population in percentage of 1963 population. Average income in percentage of average income per person of the Kingdom.
Source: NIS

polarization. The Fordist accumulation regime was based upon the distribution of productivity gains over profit and wage increases. Thus growing mass production found a market in growing mass consumption. Houses, cars and consumer durables fueled this growth (Harvey, 1985). Such goods required space, made visible by buying or building a house in the urban fringe, daily commuting by car, and the accumulation of consumer durables at home. Thus suburbanization is the spatial expression of Fordist economic growth in Belgium, just as in the United States (Aglietta, 1976). The changing social class structure also supports the suburbanization process. Rising education levels and the development of tertiary activities pushed a large part of the Belgian population into upward social mobility. The population of Brussels is increasingly middle class and it can draw on a growing income in order to become owner-occupier through individuals building new houses outside the city, in a green environment where land prices are affordable.

Four circumstances explain the relative strength of this process compared with other European countries.

The first is an early entrance of the national economy into Fordist accumulation. As early as 1944, a social pact between employers and trade unions and fostered by the government established a universal social security system and the principle of regular wage raises in accordance with productivity gains. The huge postwar construction activity – particularly self-building and self-promotion – was sustained by rising real wages, security of employment, security of income founded on this social pact, and expansion of the credit system.

The second is a belief in access to home-ownership through self-building. Christian Democrat policies from the end of the 19th century have encouraged this as a means to stress Christian family values rather than the workers' collective interests, and to keep the workers away from the cities and socialism. This idea and the dominance of the Christian Democrats in Belgian politics underpinned the postwar policy of providing grants to families to buy or, particularly, build their own house. (One third of the housing stock built since the war was co-financed by such grants.) In addition there were subvention schemes for the construction of estate infrastructure – which financed part of the collective costs of suburbanization – and cheap mortgages for large households (Goossens, 1983). The consequent building activity resulted in a city widely spatially expanded and very dispersed through the diffusion of car-ownership. In fact the promotion of suburbanization as a key element in a Keynesian economic policy also discharged the State from financing a thorough social housing policy or massive urban renewal schemes.

Thirdly, the absence of any physical planning designed to contain the urban sprawl made cheap construction land available in the periphery of the cities and along the main roads in the countryside.

Finally, in contrast to neighboring countries, there has not been any significant demographic pressure on the housing market after World War II (see, e.g., Kesteloot and Cortie, 1998). Therefore, there was no significant intervention of the state in housing prices or allocation.

Very often, this structure is associated with American cities (Papadopoulos, 1996) where market forces determine the socio-spatial structuring of residential space and result in a similar "doughnut" structure. However, suburbanization in Belgium is different to suburbanization in the United States. It is well known that European cities' historical roots yield a much stronger centrality and sense of urban public space.

In fact, the Belgian state invested huge subventions in access to ownership and in expensive suburban amenities and infrastructure. Moreover, the state thought to solve the problem of poor inner-city housing quality by further encouraging suburbanization which would generate a centrifugal filtering process (Peeters and De Decker, 1997).

The growth of the Belgian middle class and its spatial shift towards the urban fringe had profound influences on the labor and housing markets, which in turn explain the arrival of working class immigrants and their concentration in the inner city. The arrival of the guestworkers from the end of the 1950s – but mainly between the second half of the 1960s and when migration was halted in 1974 – is directly related to the social upward mobility of the Belgians. The immigrants fill up both the socio-economic and the spatial positions left open by the Belgian version of Fordism. Suburbanization involved a profound functional restructuring of urban space. The city had to be reshaped in order to offer the necessary space for offices and for the transport and communication infrastructure demanded by the multinational corporations investing in Belgium. The demand for more office space was also sustained by the growing civil service which managed the burgeoning Belgian welfare state. Urban highways and parking space were needed for the car-borne suburban middle class which continued to work in the inner city. The guestworkers were largely recruited in the construction industry which was heavily involved in the transformation of the urban space, but also in the declining urban light industrial sectors (textile, food, furniture, leather, etc.). In a second phase, they went into public transport, hotels, restaurants and cafes, and low-skilled services.

The term "guestworker" expresses the fact that both the government and the immigrants considered this immigration temporary. Even after immigration halted in 1974, the myth of returning lived on and resulted in the expenses in Belgium being minimized and saving and the remittance of money to the home country maximized. But the low skills and the pressure on the wage levels in the labor-intensive activities in which the guestworkers were involved meant that they never succeeded in their aims of becoming rich and returning to their own countries. Nevertheless, their efforts to do so directed them to the cheapest housing available to them, which were in the

19th-century working class neighborhoods abandoned by the Belgians. The guestworkers thus literally contributed to the making of the Fordist city, while their concentration in the cheapest dwellings in the 19th-century belt illustrated their suffering from the negative effects of this process. One can suspect that they cofinanced suburbanization by giving an income to their landlords which allowed the latter to pay their new suburban dwellings.

The effects of suburbanization are dramatic. While in 1963 the Brussels Capital Region had an average income per person 60 per cent above the national average, it dropped to 28 per cent above the national average in 1975. At the same time, the figures in both surrounding districts[3] rose from 5 and 12 per cent to 15 and 19 per cent respectively (Table 9.1). Thanks to the immigration of guestworkers, the population remains stable until 1975. (The Belgian population has actually been in decline since the early 1960s and Brussels reached its highest population in 1968).

The Economic Crisis and the Locking of a Redundant Working Class in the Inner City (1974–1985)

Suburbanization being based on economic growth, rising incomes and income security, it is no surprise that the process slowed down during the second half of the 1970s and the early 1980s, because in this period economic growth decreased. Some researchers even thought about the end of suburbanization and the emergence of a "back to the city movement" (see Vandermotten and Collard, 1985 for a discussion). At first sight, this could be positive for inner city areas, as crisis limits decay in the inner city. But it also means that the chances for upward mobility on the labor and housing markets is limited for those belonging to the lower income groups, which results in increased competition on these markets. In addition to the deep dual character of the city as a result of suburbanization, this strengthened a second contrast within the city, which is visible through the spatial structure of the housing market.

The trap of the residual rental sector

As a result of suburbanization, the inner city is dominated by a large share of old, private rented dwellings in which the landlords have ceased to invest as the original investment has already been returned several times over. This segment of the housing market is said to be the residual private rental sector (about 30 per cent of the total housing stock), "residual" meaning both that these dwellings are old and relatively cheap and that this is the only sector available for those who cannot afford the other sectors of the housing market (Kesteloot et al., 1997). This first residential belt, which encompasses the city center and the 19th-century working class areas, sharply contrasts with the

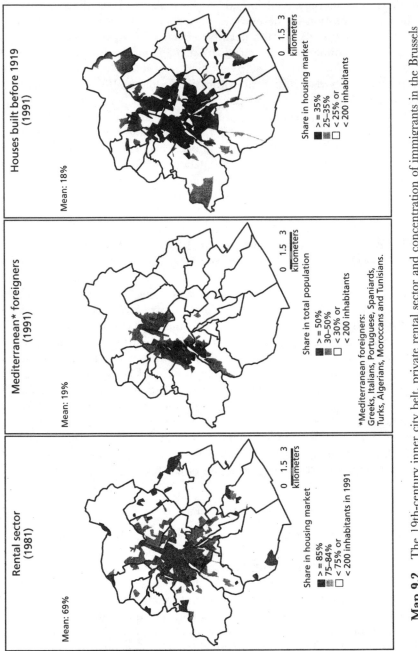

Rental sector
(1981)

Mean: 69%

Share in housing market

> = 85%
75–84%
< 75% or
< 200 inhabitants in 1991

0   1.5   3
kilometers

Mediterranean* foreigners
(1991)

Mean: 19%

Share in total population

> = 50%
30–50%
< 30% or
< 200 inhabitants

0   1.5   3
kilometers

*Mediterranean foreigners:
Greeks, Italians, Portuguese, Spaniards,
Turks, Algerians, Moroccans and Tunisians.

Houses built before 1919
(1991)

Mean: 18%

Share in housing market

> = 35%
25–35%
< 25% or
< 200 inhabitants

0   1.5   3
kilometers

Map 9.2   The 19th-century inner city belt, private rental sector and concentration of immigrants in the Brussels
Capital Region
Source: NIS, 1981–1991

outer belts which offer better quality and more expensive rental dwellings and owner-occupied dwellings. (39 per cent of the Brussels housing stock is owner-occupied and about 20 per cent belongs to the better rental sector; the social housing sector accounts for only eight per cent of the stock).[4] Entrants to the housing market can often only afford cheap rented housing and locate themselves in the 19th-century belt, where they join the remaining original population which could not move to the suburbs. But the dominant group in the inner city is of immigrant origin. Thus, with the exception of only a few areas, one can say that in the Brussels Capital Region, the 19th-century belt, the residual housing sector and the areas with a majority of foreigners from guestworkers origin coincide (Map 9.2).[5]

The economic crisis prevented a gradual deconcentration of these groups out of their original settlement areas for several reasons. The most obvious one is that the economic crisis barred their upward social mobility, which could have been expected (and started in fact for the first wave of immigrants from Italian and Spanish origin). Moreover, the crisis also discouraged many Belgian households from moving to the suburbs because of lower incomes and income security. Some of these households simply delayed building houses in the periphery, but others found it more attractive to buy and renovate cheaper old housing in the city in the neighborhoods popular with immigrants (Kesteloot, 1985). Demographic changes involving an increase in singles and childless couples which more than compensates for the loss of population in terms of number of households has a similar effect on the inner city housing market, reducing the available residual rental stock and preventing access to immigrants. The stagnation of income between 1975 and 1985 and a slowdown of the population increase in the periphery, illustrate these processes (Table 9.1)

The consolidation of ethnic neighborhoods

However the operation of the housing market is not the only cause of the permanence of the ethnic neighborhoods. The share of foreigners of guestworker origin in the local population is rising due to demographic factors: they exhibit a young population structure and high fertility rates. Moreover, despite the immigration being stopped in 1974, new immigrants arrive as a result of family reunification and marriage. Conversely, the Belgian population decreases in these inner city neighborhoods because of the suburbanization (which declined but did not disappear) and because of the old age of those remaining in the inner city. The growing number of immigrants remains confined to those areas (numbering approximately 170,000 in 1995, they reach 18 per cent of the population of the Brussels Capital Region). Such a concentration was required for ethnic infrastructure to develop, and the crisis itself generated a rich infrastructure, which even showed

some overinvestment. Indeed, not only does ethnic entrepreneurship function as a strategy for the individual to escape unemployment, but it also
makes living in ethnic areas cheaper for members of the local community as
products and services are well tuned to the needs of the local population,
tough competition reduces prices, and possibilities to buy on credit are widespread. All this relies on strong social networks within these ethnic communities (Meert et al., 1997). Thus, the consolidation of the ethnic neighborhoods
reveals a spatial strategy to cope with the effects of the crisis, which had
brought even higher unemployment and income insecurity among the immigrants than among the Belgians (Kesteloot, 1995a).

In the same way, the 19th-century inner-city neighborhoods appear as
rich environments for the development of survival strategies, including several forms of informal economy (Kesteloot and Meert, 1999), certainly if
they are compared with poor peripheral post-war estates in north and south
European cities. For most immigrants, leaving the ethnic neighborhoods of
the inner city would entail a loss of spatially concentrated opportunities to
face the difficulties of making a living generated by the economic crisis.
Thus, this could be seen as an enclave rather than a ghetto as far as the
positive effects of concentration are considered (see Chapter 1). Two remarks
are however appropriate here. Firstly, neighborhoods that have concentrations of immigrants and their descendants are always multicultural
neighborhoods in Brussels. Some of them show a dominance of one nationality in the ethnic infrastructure, but the group concerned never reaches
more than 40 to 45 per cent of the total local population. Secondly, the
concentration in these areas is generally not due to choosing local advantages, but must be seen as a result of the interaction between the (generally
disadvantaged) labor market position of the group members and the socio-
spatial structure of the housing market.

Post-Fordism and the Deepening of Polarization (1985 until present)

Since the mid-1980s renewed economic growth has been noticeable. As this
growth does not continue the Fordist regime of the Golden Sixties, but is
based on more flexible production and consumption processes, it coincides
with economic and spatial restructuring. Industrial employment has been in
decline since the 1960s, and those jobs which survive both de-industrialization
and economic crisis are being adapted to new production processes which
demand greater flexibility. This flexibility is not only linked to the organization
of working hours, but also to changing production processes, to differentiating
consumption patterns, to rapidly changing investment strategies, to the multi-
plication and exchange of internal and external company relations, and finally

also to the use of space. Thus, economic and spatial restructuring go hand in hand. However, in Brussels they did not generate dramatic changes in the socio-spatial patterning of the city, but deepened the opposition between the ethnic neighborhoods and the rest of the city, albeit in a complex way.

Polarization on the labor market

Between 1974 and 1995, Brussels lost more than 95,000 (or 59 per cent) of its industrial jobs. The reduction is rather less impressive when one considers manual labor (reduced by 41 per cent). But it is significant that between 1985 and 1995, a period including the latest economic upsurge, the loss of manual jobs continued in Brussels, while their numbers increased in the surrounding districts (Table 9.2). Combined with restructuring to enable flexible production, this change implies the near disappearance of permanent jobs for the low skilled. Moreover, the periphery attracts more new intellectual jobs than the center, which is a second aspect of the shrinking local labor market for the low-skilled inhabitants of the 19th-century belts: there is not only a profound effect of deindustrialization, but also a shift from central to suburban employment, creating an increasing spatial mismatch. Thus, in relative terms, the young people of the Brussels inner city are gradually more severely hit by unemployment. Fortunately, the total number of unemployed young people declined in the last decade because of the better economic circumstances. (However an unknown number of youngsters of guestworker origin do not register as employment seekers and do not appear in the statistics.) However, the share of the young people of the Brussels Capital Region (in fact essentially those from the inner city – see below) in the total youth unemployment of the urban region is increasing (Table 9.2).

If one considers the jobs in terms of qualifications, one expects the famous transition from the "egg structure" of the labor market, typical for the post-war period (narrow basis of low skill, a broad middle field and a narrow top of high-skilled jobs), to the "hourglass structure", with broadening extremes and a shrinking middle field (Marcuse, 1989). This change is mainly found in the service sector and especially in the fast growing sector of producer services, as a result of vertical disintegration and subcontracting. At one end, one finds cleaning, transport, security, catering, and courier services; at the other end marketing, advertising, auditing, lobbying and recruitment services. In Brussels, this evolution is difficult to measure because the classification of economic activity is not adapted to the present changes. Moreover the classification system was changed in 1988 and thus the available evidence is rather patchy. Nevertheless, between 1974 and 1991 producer services were the fastest growing sector (+57 per cent) in the Brussels Capital Region. The category "other services", in which all new producer services are to be found,

Table 9.2 Employment and unemployment in the Brussels urban region 1974–1998

Employment (1000s)

	1974		1985		1995	
	manual	*non-manual*	*manual*	*non-manual*	*manual*	*non-manual*
Brussels Capital Region	207	408	132	416	123	437
District Halle-Vilvoorde	72	54	54	72	60	104
District Nivelles	35	26	24	38	27	54

Changes in employment (%)

	1974–1995		1974–1985		1985–1995	
	manual	*non-manual*	*manual*	*non-manual*	*manual*	*non-manual*
Brussels Capital Region	− 41	7	− 36	2	− 7	5
District Halle-Vilvoorde	− 16	93	− 25	35	12	43
District Nivelles	− 21	106	− 30	48	12	39

Unemployment (1000s)

	1974		1986		1998	
	total	*age<25*	*total*	*age<25*	*total*	*age<25*
Brussels Capital Region	9.3	–	53.4	9.9	57.2	7.8
District Halle-Vilvoorde	3.6	–	15.0	3.4	11.1	1.4
District Nivelles	1.8	–	15.0	3.4	11.1	1.4
Share of BCR	63.5	–	67.1	62.4	70.4	70.3

Source: Social Security Office (RSZ) and Office for Employment (RVA)

tripled over the period in question. In 1991, more than 20,000 jobs in this category were available. Employment change in a selection of activity sectors which can be measured through the 1980s supports the idea of an unbalanced polarization (termed professionalization by Hamnett (1994b)), since

Table 9.3 Employment change in selected sectors, 1980–1990

Top-end sectors	% change	Bottom-end sectors	% change
advertising	132	hotel industry	42
accounting	56	concert, theater and sports	41
legal services	32	road transport (passengers)	31
banking services	26	cleaning industry	16

Source: Social Security Office (RSZ)

the top-end sectors grew more than the bottom-end ones (Table 9.3).

At first sight, even if the bottom-end sectors show less impressive growth, the trends should benefit the low skilled, at least if the employment mismatch can be overcome by sufficient daily mobility. But employment figures reckoned by education level suggest that some low-skilled jobs are taken by relatively well educated people. The number of well educated workers in Brussels increased by 40 per cent between 1988 and 1997. Poorly educated workers (with a primary school education or less) showed a decline of 25 per cent. Both tendencies are at least partly related to the progress of the general education level, but the middle group (with secondary school education) also shows a decline of 12 per cent since 1992, after a growth of 10 per cent in the years of better economic health. (In absolute figures, the middle group — which is also the most important among the 560,000 wage earners of Brussels — experienced an increase of 35,000 jobs between 1985 and 1990 but lost 22,000 jobs between 1990 and 1995.) Therefore one can hardly talk about better job opportunities for the low skilled.

In addition to these quantitative effects, the sectoral changes on the labor market have two negative qualitative consequences for low-skilled people and the relative position of their concentration in the urban socio-spatial division of labor. The first is that they have less chances for upward social mobility through the labor market. Promotion to a better job including a ticket to the lower middle classes is limited by the flexible organization of the market. While the socio-economic profile of the inhabitants of inner cities did not improve during the 1960s and the early 1970s as a consequence of immediate suburbanization of those who entered the middle class, today this stagnation is due to the unavailability of a better job. The second consequence is that Third-World-like low-wage islands are being created in the city, mainly through informal work, sometimes provided by illegal migrants. Within the global economy, specific low-skilled and labor-intensive parts of the economy are relocated to Third World countries and thus the broadening lower segment of the labor market is supplied by people living in these low-wage countries. But some of these activities are not easily relocated, like many service activities where production and consumption are simultaneous or some agro-industrial productions where long distance transport is difficult and can damage the products, or some segments of the garment industry which have to react immediately to changes in local demand. These sectors give rise to the internal urban third world, which is concentrated in some parts of the inner city working class area (Kesteloot and Meert, 1999).

Hence, in deprived areas one can find the bottom-end of the dual labor market. This is characterized by low-paid, irregular, part-time and temporary jobs in difficult labor conditions. These workers undergo the burden of flexibility in a physical and material way. The chances to find jobs which promote social integration for those living in the 19th-century belt continually diminished since the 1960s through suburbanization, later through the economic crisis and finally through the social polarization generated by the recent economic upturn.

Social displacement on the housing market and deepening of socio-spatial polarization

Economic restructuring also brought important negative changes to the housing market. A flexible economy is accompanied by an increased mobility of capital. The more mobile capital, the more economic regions struggle to keep or attract investments. Regional competition for international investment and consequent jobs increases as capital becomes increasingly footless. A lot of recent urban development can be linked to this competition. Cities are restructured to present attractive working and residential conditions, they are endowed with new economic and social infrastructure and try to host decision-making functions and to concentrate consumer power through tourism and cultural events. They build up an image reflecting their position as an attractive center for inward investment in the global economy. In Brussels, nearly all of these investments are located in the eastern half of the inner city, whether it be High Speed Train stations, luxury hotels, office space, shopping centers or upper-market residential renovation projects. The large majority of these investments take advantage of the long-standing superior location factors of this part of the city.

Similar to the adaptation of cities to Fordism (i.e. offices and individual transport, urban motorways, parking) during the 1960s, this new radical change leads to negative consequences for those living in the inner cities, like dispossession and expropriation for those living where the investment takes place, but also to more traffic, noise and pollution, loss of clients for retailers and loss of networks for neighbors, loss of access to amenities and finally rising real estate prices, because this urban restructuring is accompanied by land speculation. As a result, prices on the housing market rise quickly. First visible on the buying market, the rental market too showed price increases of more than 100 per cent between 1988 and 1992 (ASLK, 1997).

This new layer of urban structure has two consequences for the housing market and the location of the poor. First, there is a process of displacement. The pressures on the housing market and more precisely, the residual rental sector – are strongest in the eastern part of the inner city and many immigrants (especially Moroccans) were displaced to the western part of it (De Lannoy and De Corte, 1994; see also Map 9.3).[6] Overcrowding, insufficient social infrastructure and the diffusion of housing price increases often make their new living conditions worse than before.

Second there is the creation of a "secondary owner-occupied sector", as we have called it in Kesteloot et al. (1997). Turks in particular achieved both housing and location security through the purchase of cheap low-quality housing in the neighborhoods under pressure, especially in the north-east part of the inner city. Because they do not rent any more, they are protected against further increases in their housing costs and at the same time they secure their location in a neighborhood with access to ethnic infrastructure, social networks and other assets for developing survival strategies. Thus the number of owner occupiers among the Turkish households increased from 13 to 37 per cent between 1981 and 1991; the respective figures for the Moroccans are 10 and 30 per cent (Kesteloot et al., 1997).

Both processes, displacement and the creation of a secondary owner occupied sector, explain the further consolidation of the ethnic neighborhoods in the inner city, but they introduce a difference within this area between the western part with worsening living conditions and overcrowding and the northern part with a more stable population and a certain amount of social mix (Mistiaen et al., 1995).

The changes on the labor market, added to demographic changes (especially a dramatic increase in one-person households; see Lesthaeghe, 1995), and to the cultural and symbolic use of urban space, would also entail gentrification, certainly if the efforts of the Capital Region and its municipalities to modify the social composition of the resident population are taken into account. Indeed, the Region Development Plan, launched in 1994, aims at bringing 35,000 new inhabitants – most of them affluent single persons – to the Capital Region, (Vandermotten, 1994). However, gentrification remains surprisingly modest compared to the impressive restructuring of the city. The main reason for this probably lies in the modest dimensions of

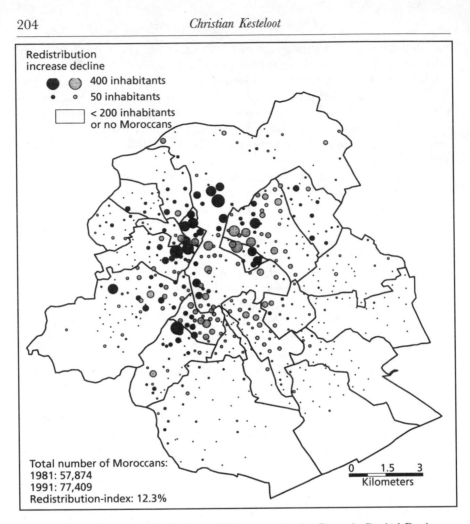

Redistribution
increase decline

● ◐ 400 inhabitants

• ○ 50 inhabitants

☐ < 200 inhabitants
   or no Moroccans

Total number of Moroccans:
1981: 57,874
1991: 77,409
Redistribution-index: 12.3%

0   1.5   3
Kilometers

Map 9.3 Spatial redistribution of Moroccans in the Brussels Capital Region,
1981–1991
Source: NIS, 1981–1991

the urban region, and the relatively good accessibility of the center from the
suburban fringe. In other words, Brussels appears as a small scale global city,
and therefore the trade off between central and peripheral locations is less
relevant than in large cities.

Nevertheless, there is a gentle increase of immigration into the Brussels
Capital Region from the urban periphery since the 1990s (but at the same
time suburbanization also resumed), and small scale gentrification is reported
to be right in the center of the city (Van Criekingen, 1996). In addition, the

expansion of the European Union generated spatial pressures in Brussels, mainly in the eastern edge of the 19th-century belt, matching the other effects of urban competition. The announcement of the European Single Market for 1992 triggered off a wave of land speculation and office building that resulted in doubling housing costs in the whole city. However, the pressure on housing was highest in the east because houses were pulled down and replaced by office space and because some of the new EU-workers chose an urban residence near their place of work.

Among affluent foreigners, most Dutch, Americans, or British comprise families with children and live outside the Brussels Capital Region (Kesteloot and Van der Haegen, 1997). The next most suburbanized groups are made up of Germans, Danish and Irish. These last two groups are comparatively small, but have experienced strong growth in the last decade. Many of these new arrivals tend to live within the city as they are single or couples without children, as do similar households in the former national groups. Newcomers working in the international sector of the city and the second-generation households of the first affluent expatriates in Brussels also seem to prefer the city to a suburban lifestyle (Kesteloot et al., 1998). Since they do not really invade the 19th-century working class areas, but the better off 19th- and early 20th-century areas in the eastern inner city, it is difficult to consider this as gentrification (Map 9.4). This trend gives rise to something like a modest Anglo-Saxon area in the city, where an estimate of up to 10,000 new foreign inhabitants settled between 1991 and 1997. Significantly, the Belgians are not participating to this movement. One can show a rise of young Belgian newcomers in some areas, but this does not compensate for the massive suburbanization. Their preference for suburban living is related to historical elements such as the Catholic policy of literally keeping the working class under the village church tower, and to the vigorous post-war state intervention in favor of access to home ownership, and urban sprawl as key elements of Fordist economic growth.

More than in the 1960s, the Brussels municipalities and the Brussels Capital Region are interested parties in these new developments. This is not only because local authorities are an inevitable partner in urban development, whether it is to make the city an attractive investment location, or to find new initiatives to promote the city. But as the Brussels population decreases and the largest part of the remaining population becomes impoverished, it is essential for their population and/or income to increase in order to keep their financial situation to the required standard. Indeed, in the Belgian public financial system, the income of the local authorities heavily depends on the number of inhabitants and their incomes. Thus the 19 municipalities and the region are tempted to alter the population mix by displacing low-income categories by higher income groups and see gentrification as a very positive process. Moreover, they do not have to fear much opposition from

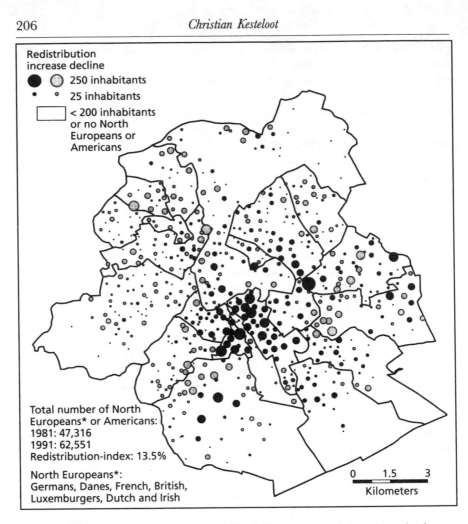

Redistribution
increase decline
● ◐ 250 inhabitants
• ○ 25 inhabitants
☐ < 200 inhabitants
or no North
Europeans or
Americans

Total number of North
Europeans* or Americans:
1981: 47,316
1991: 62,551
Redistribution-index: 13.5%

North Europeans*:
Germans, Danes, French, British,
Luxemburgers, Dutch and Irish

0   1.5   3
Kilometers

Map 9.4   Spatial redistribution of North Europeans and Americans in the
extended Brussels agglomeration, 1981–1997
Source: NIS, 1981–1997

the victims of these processes, since foreigners do not have political rights.
(They will be granted to the EU-foreigners in 2000, following the stipulations
of the Maastricht agreements, but Turks and Moroccans will probably have
to wait until 2006.)

Thus, most urban policy measures boil down to a careful scanning of the
social map of the city in order to select areas or housing blocks which could
become subject to one of three strategies dictated by the increasingly difficult
financial situation of the city and its municipalities: increasing the population, increasing the income or replacing the poorer population by richer

people. Thus renewal projects are mostly located in areas which are still attractive for middle class people and usually include the creation of middle class housing or at least the provision of one- or two-bedroom dwellings not available to large immigrant families. There are no mechanisms to control a housing price increase after renewal. Even in known cases of socially inspired urban renewal, where all actors concerned agree that the maximum effort was made to keep existing inhabitants in the area, one notices fewer poorer families and a careful move to a financially and politically more interesting mix (see, e.g., Vanden Eende and Martens, 1994).

The socio-economic meaning of this dual structure of the city, is remarkably illustrated by socio-spatial divisions among Brussels' youngsters. Children and young people are over-represented on the one hand in the ethnic areas of the inner city and on the other hand in the peripheral estates of the urban region (Map 9.5). In the inner city, the majority of these youngsters are of foreign origin, whereas Belgian youth grows up in suburbia.[7] Chances for personal development are not comparable, not only because of different living conditions, but also because of different amenities, youth infrastructure, initiatives and activities for youngsters. In the inner city, the environment still reflects the living conditions from the 19th century when young people worked from the age of 12 or 14 for 14 hours a day. In contrast, the periphery was built up and organized in the Golden Sixties, when leisure time became an element of mass consumption and local authorities sustained suburbanization and economic growth through important investments in collective consumption. Gradually the inner city, and more precisely the western crescent-like poorest area in it, are becoming an area of despair. The normal paths of social promotion become unreachable for the youngsters living in these areas. Their parents did not make it and their own chances on the labor market are limited and jammed. It is no surprise that this leads to the creation of ways out, such as (sub)cultures, the underworld and informal or criminal activities (Kesteloot, 1995b). However, differences in terms of aspirations, behavior and criminality do not seem to be the main differentiating elements between both zones in Brussels. Rather, strong segregation between schools, brought about by the increase in the school leaving age from 14 to 18 years old in 1983 appears of major significance to explain the dual structure of socialization of Brussels' youngsters (Mistiaen and Kesteloot, 1998).

Conclusions

In the late 1980s and the 1990s Brussels became a divided city where processes on the labor market and on the housing market reinforce each other. Since the city is clearly a second-tier world city, the social polarization

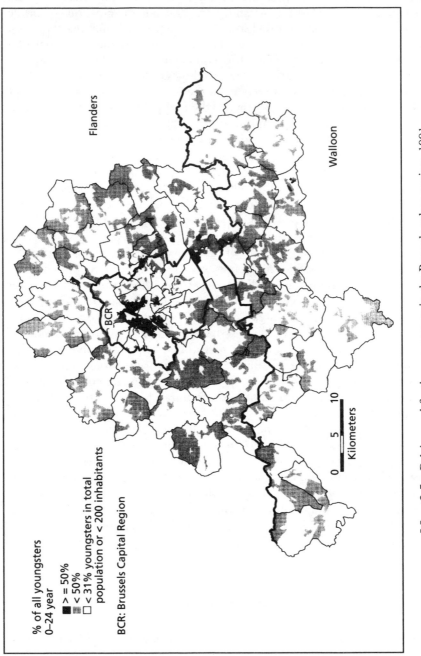

% of all youngsters
0–24 year

■ > = 50%
▦ < 50%
□ < 31% youngsters in total
population or < 200 inhabitants

BCR: Brussels Capital Region

Flanders

Walloon

BCR

0   5   10
Kilometers

Map 9.5   Belgian and foreign youngsters in the Brussels urban region, 1991
Source: NIS, 1991

mechanisms related to the city's function in the world economy are at work. But at the same time, these new divisions have been forced into the dual socio-spatial canvass of the city created by suburbanization in the 1960s. During the second half of the 1970s and the early 1980s, the economic crisis reinforced this dual structure by locking the redundant unskilled immigrants in the 19th-century working class neighborhoods. Gradually these immigrants resisted and developed survival strategies in their neighborhoods, apparently turning ghettos into enclaves. But ghettos in the American sense, (see Chapter 1 of this book) never existed in Brussels. This is because all areas with concentrations of ethnic groups were characterized by a social mix.

Politically, the salient problem is that Brussels, like the other large cities in Belgium, continues to lose population – particularly affluent inhabitants – despite the temporarily slowing of the suburbanization process during the 1970s crisis, and the weak signs of gentrification during the post-Fordist revival. The remaining population increasingly becomes poorer in relative terms. In the long run, this undermines the financial basis and the capacity to fight polarization in the city. But, because of past layers of socio-spatial organization of the city, the main division line runs through the territory of most of the first ring municipalities around the city of Brussels. These local authorities have both an older deprived area belonging to the inner city and a better off part, sometimes reaching as far as the outer limits of the Capital Region. The local authorities remain absent in the poor inner parts of their territory and tend to neglect public investment, except for the attraction of middle class people. In reaction, the remaining Belgian population tends to vote for extreme right parties (Kesteloot and De Decker, 1992).

Thus, post-Fordist Brussels appears to be in a Catch-22 situation. In order to have more financial means to fight dualization, it has to bring middle class households to the city. But this same policy will have adverse effects on the poor (social displacement and over-concentration in the poorest neighborhoods), reinforce socio-spatial polarization, and will require even more financial means (and space). This negative cycle can only be broken by interregional solidarity, which can easily be justified by the fact that suburbanization creates three types of negative financial redistribution for the Brussels Capital Region and its municipalities. Indeed selective out-migration means a relative rise in poverty in the center and creates more needs; the same process creates less income for the Region and for its 19 municipalities since a large part depends on local taxes on their inhabitants' personal income and on land income; the suburban population use collective amenities in the center for which it does not pay. Thus the post-Fordist city appears socially unstable – in regulation school terms, one would say being without a firm mode of regulation – as long as the choice has not been made between more solidarity within the urban community or a more repressive city with increasing territorial control on a growing number of people with vanishing economic and social prospects. And until now, history has shown that repression is not a long term means of regulation.

Notes

1 For the French regulation theory, see Aglietta (1976) and Boyer (1986). The urban application in Belgium is developed in Kesteloot (1990; see also Kesteloot et al., 1997).

2 The geographically defined Brussels urban region comprises 64 municipalities, counting nearly 1.7 million inhabitants. The 19 central municipalities form the Brussels Capital Region, with 950,000 inhabitants is one of the three official regions of the kingdom. In this text, the term Brussels refers to the Brussels Capital Region. The 64 municipalities are referred to with the term urban region.

3 42 of the 45 peripheral municipalities of the urban region (outside the Brussels Capital Region) are situated in the districts of Halle-Vilvoorde and Nivelles, respectively in the Flemish and the Walloon region. The northern half of the Brussels urban region corresponds nearly perfectly to the Halle-Vilvoorde district. The northern and western parts of the Nivelles district, which are the most densely populated, correspond to the southern part of the Brussels urban region. Figures for both districts give a good approximation of the suburban belt of the urban region (see Figure 9.5). More accurate figures, concerning exactly the Brussels urban region are complex to compute because of municipal amalgamation in 1976.

4 A few estates were built in the inner city, especially after 1953 when a program against hovels was launched. But most of the social housing estates are scattered in the periphery, as these were built on cheap land at the edge or even outside the city.

5 The most relevant exceptions concern some areas in the inner cities where the residual rental sector was partly replaced by immigrant owner occupation (this is why the 1981 rather than the 1991 figures are shown – see further) and the peripheral social housing estates which are visible on the rental sector map. While the 19th-century belt is concentric, the Mediterranean immigrants only fill the northern and the western part of it, as a result of the divide between the lower west and the higher east mentioned earlier.

6 The map shows the changes until 1991, whereas figures for 1997 are available. However, changes in the law on the Belgian nationality resulted in approximately 15,000 young foreigners becoming Belgian, giving a somewhat blurred image of the socio-spatial structure under discussion.

7 The suburbanization of affluent foreign households with children explains the dominance of foreign youngsters in some south-east neighborhoods of the urban region.

10

The Imprint of the Post-Fordist Transition on Australian Cities

Blair Badcock

During the last 25 years or so Australian cities have been exposed to forces of economic and political restructuring that are beginning to make for noticeable differences in the established spatial order. In the Australian case, above all else, it is a shifting geography of income and wealth in the cities that contains the seeds of the "new spatial order." This is not to argue for a dramatic divergence from, let alone a complete replacement of the existing Fordist urban structure; but, rather, to acknowledge the gradual ascendance of post-Fordist processes and the creation of recognizably new forms of space imbricated within the urban fabric inherited from a Fordist past. The spatial hints at things to come during this time of transition for Australian cities add up to a growing centralization of wealth combined with the selective dispersion of poverty to structurally vulnerable suburbs. It is the formation of a "cone of wealth," then, at the heart of the cities like Sydney, Melbourne, and Adelaide, and now Brisbane and Perth as well, that most distinguishes urban restructuring in Australia from the experience of most of the other cities discussed in this volume.

One can immediately see that this presents quite a different picture to the doughnut stereotype that has come to characterize North American cities following two decades of "white flight" (US Department of Housing and Urban Development, 1995). While there is nothing to match edge city phenomena in the US (Garreau, 1991), revitalization is transforming the built form and class topography at the heart of Australian cities perhaps more thoroughly than anywhere else. One of the tasks of this discussion is to suggest what processes are producing this divergence under Australian conditions.

The general propositions set out in the introduction to this book point to important shifts in the social organization of capitalism which are beginning to manifest themselves in the social and physical landscapes of some cities (see also Lash and Urry, 1994, pp. 193–222), and conceivably prefigure an emergent post-Fordist spatial order. This rests on the premise that the current restructuring entails a transition from a Fordist mode of economic organization towards a post-Fordist mode characterized by "flexible accumulation" (Piore and Sabel, 1984; Harvey, 1989). However, whilst "post-Fordism" is a convenient way of characterizing the transformations currently taking place with capitalism, it should be noted that the construct is by no means unproblematic (Lovering, 1990; Sayer, 1989).

From the standpoint of political economy, the key to making some interim sense of urban transformation lies not only with the way in which the processes of globalization, economic restructuring and the state are comprehended (Probert, 1990), but in also recognizing what it is that seems to be distinctive about the experience of cities due to varying local conditions. In their account of urban restructuring in global cities, Dieleman and Hamnett (1994, p. 359) give particular stress to national and local differences in the nature and intensity of welfare state intervention, income distribution, the regulatory regime, and planning policy (see also Chapter 1 of this book).

The importance of discerning spatial divergence from context to context is demonstrated by the mixed reception given to the "global city" hypothesis (Sassen, 1991). Sassen's hypothesis has stimulated much critical comment bearing upon the vital differences that exist between genuinely global cities like New York and Los Angeles on the one hand, with their huge immigrant populations, and London or Tokyo on the other (Hamnett, 1996). Furthermore, Saskia Sassen (1991) appears to build her case for polarized global cities on the pronounced juxtaposition of poverty and wealth in neighborhoods at the heart of big conurbations like New York and London. So when she uses the term spatial polarization, it does not convey the same sense of metropolitan-wide inequalities that Larry Bourne detects in his work for Canadian cities (Bourne, 1996), or that Dieleman and Hamnett (1994) have in mind for the Dutch conurbation.

Examination of newly forming patterns of space within cities can help to sharpen our awareness of some of the broader structural and institutional changes taking place within society. Perhaps the most profound shift in western economies during the 1980s and 1990s has been the reassertion of market processes over state management. Recurrent economic crisis – when OPEC lifted energy prices in 1974 and 1979, and with recession in 1981–82 and 1992–94 – accentuated the growing imbalance between domestic productivity in many OECD countries and their capacity to fund welfare. With the onset of unprecedented stagflation in the 1970s, the legitimacy of Keynesian demand management was undermined for the first time since the 1940s, and governments turned to monetarist gurus like Friedman and the Austrian School for economic advice.

What is particularly significant about the response of governments to this economic instability is the variety of strategies that have been adopted. In some cases a radical break has been made with the prevailing relations between markets, state institutions, class arrangements, and ideological legitimacy. Britain and New Zealand have probably gone the furthest in articulating an ideology of legitimization and dismantling highly developed welfare state systems together with their nationalized industries (Gilmour, 1992; Kelsey, 1995). As a dominantly private enterprise economy, the United States has a less extensive welfare system to carve up and fewer publicly owned utilities to privatize. Even the social democracies of Western Europe, whilst leaving social programs essentially intact, have begun to selectively trim outlays and engineer a more competitive environment for public enterprise.

Ultimately, the point of trying to present a forward projection of where the spatial re-ordering of Australian cities might eventually lead to if economic and social trends are allowed to continue, is to confront the Commonwealth and States[1] with the grossly regressive and socially divisive consequences of their present policy directions. From an Australian perspective, therefore, it is vital to ask in a comparative volume such as this one, "Which societies, with which particular policies and spatial arrangements, are coping best with the challenges of globalization and post-Fordist restructuring and what can be learned from them?"

It is quite apparent that by now, in an era of globalization and deregulation, the income gap has widened appreciably in those OECD countries with less fettered market economies; and none more so than those that have crippled the unions, cut back income support, moved to narrower targeting of social provision, and relaxed business regulation (Kuttner, 1996, p. 16).

Structural Adjustment in Australia

How does Australia compare, then, and how is this shift in the balance struck by the state between markets and government programs implicated in any emerging spatial rearrangement to the existing structure of our cities?

Firstly, Australia like other nation states has been drawn into the "globalization" process in pursuit of enhanced competitive advantage (Fagan and Webber, 1994). Globalization refers to the simultaneous integration of trade, investment, and financial flows into a single international economic system (Stilwell, 1996). This involves a corresponding shift in economic power from nation states to the corporate giants that are increasingly determining global trade patterns and capital and information flows. Throughout the 1980s and 1990s, the Commonwealth and the States under both Labor and the conservative parties have been instrumental in forcing the pace of structural adjustment within the economy, often at enormous social cost. But the burden of structural adjustment has fallen very unevenly both sectorally and regionally in the countryside and the cities (Australian Urban and Regional Development Review, 1994).

According to the prevailing neo-liberal dogma embraced by politicians, bureaucrats, and media commentators alike in the 1980s, the federal government was left with no choice in the face of globalization other than to restructure the Australian economy. In Australia this recourse to the logic of the market as an ideological justification for deregulation and micro-economic reform came to be called "economic rationalism" (Pusey, 1991).

Globalization and state-managed structural adjustment have unsettled an older, prevailing Fordist social order, and are now unleashing pressures for change that are recognizably post-Fordist in character. These are the transformations that are being registered in the social and physical space of Australian cities. In the next section I endeavor to sketch out the main features of the Fordist social order at its high point towards the end of the 1970s and its legacy within the fabric of Australian cities. Then the remainder of the chapter is given over to the spatial imprint of recent economic and political restructuring upon Australian cities.

This is to argue, therefore, that the early 1980s represents a watershed so far as Australia is concerned. It marks the beginning of a conjunction between globalizing forces within the international economy, and an institutional shift to a greater market orientation domestically (Probert, 1990; Stilwell, 1996). If anything, the liberalization of markets and the reduction of state functions appear likely to be taken further in the late 1990s now that conservative governments have been installed federally, and in all the states but one (New South Wales). The Commonwealth's Department of Employment, Education, Training and Youth Affairs (DEETYA) is about to transform the delivery of labor market programs and welfare services during 1997–98: "This bold employment experiment is a first within the OECD and international eyes will be on the application of full-blown competition theory to social policy" (Grattan, 1996, p. 1).

Fordist Urban Landscapes from the Australia of the 1950s and 1960s

In 1971 Donald Horne wrote a book trying to capture the essence of Australian popular culture during the prosperous postwar decades which he called *The Lucky Country* (Horne, 1971). In what sense were Australians generally lucky during those years, and how was that reflected in class shares of space and the layout of cities?

By the end of World War II there was a growing realization that Australia needed to reduce its reliance on overseas earnings from primary products by fostering import substitution. The traditional dependence of the six original colonies on resource exploitation and trade meant that the centers of the state capitals functioned as a major break-of-bulk point for outgoing and incoming goods and capital. At the beginning of the 1950s the city centers still concentrated the rail and port functions, retailing and commerce, and key processing industries. And while the 19th-century terrace stock in the inner suburbs housed the bulk of the urban labor force it was becoming progressively rundown and blighted.

The seeds of the social divide that had become so sharply drawn in Australian cities by the end of the 1970s were being sown even in the middle of the 19th century (Badcock, 1984). The docklands and freight marshalling yards, together with industries reliant on water and coal, drew stevedores, laborers, packers, and machinists to one side of the city (South Sydney, Botany and Marrickville in Sydney; South Melbourne, Port Melbourne, and Footscray in Melbourne; Hindmarsh, Thebarton, and Port Adelaide in Adelaide; New Farm and East Brisbane in Brisbane; East Perth in Perth). Workers in commerce and government, or pastoralists with townhouses sought out foothill, or now-leafier suburbs on the opposite side of the city center (around the Sydney Harbor foreshore; Kew and Hawthorn on the terraces of the Yarra River above working class Richmond in Melbourne; Walkerville and Burnside in Adelaide; St. Lucia in Brisbane; Dalkeith in Perth).

After World War II, this social and spatial polarization was extended metropolitan-wide in cities like Sydney, Melbourne and Adelaide as governmental industry, immigration, and housing policies combined to mass-produce the suburbs that now constitute the characteristically modern Fordist landscape (Greig, 1995).

In order to foster import substitution and expand domestic consumption after the War, the Australian government erected tariff barriers against incoming goods and recruited factory workers and their families from Britain and Europe. For their part, the states openly competed for new investment by trying to outdo each other with industrial assistance packages. As a consequence, new manufacturing estates were established in the 1950s and 1960s in what are now middle-distance suburbs like Auburn and Bankstown in Sydney; Broadmeadows, Sunshine, Oakleigh and Dandenong in Melbourne; Elizabeth, Woodville, Tonsley Park, and Lonsdale in Adelaide.

The Great Depression and the diversion of resources during World War II left Australia with a housing shortfall of some 350,000 dwellings in 1948 (Greig, 1995). There were the returned servicemen (or their widows) to be housed, and there was a lot of sub-standard housing in the inner suburbs with arrears of maintenance. The first Commonwealth–States Housing Agreement (CSHA) was signed in 1945 under a Labor Government. It made funds available to the states to help alleviate the housing backlog and provide low-cost accommodation for the "deserving poor." In the 1960s the emphasis shifted to housing the immigrant workforce from Britain and Europe (Marsden, 1986). By 1966 public rental stock had increased to 5.2 percent of occupied dwellings and nationally it has remained between five and six percent ever since.

Thus for the first three decades after the War public housing was largely for workers with steady jobs and their families, some of whom eventually purchased their homes from the state Housing Commissions. According to Jones (1972), at the 1966 Census over three quarters of urban public tenants were married, two-thirds were Australian born, and four-fifths were in paid employment, typically in the manufacturing, transport, or construction sectors. For many households in the 1960s, public housing functioned as a spring board rather than as a tenure of last resort.

With the exception of the high-rise flats built by the Victorian Housing Commission on slum clearance sites in inner Melbourne, the vast majority of this public rental stock is located on suburban estates close to industrial estates. What is striking about these postwar public housing estates, along with the even more extensive tracts of project housing built by property developers, is the extent to which the Housing Commissions and their sub-contractors adopted Fordist production methods (Greig, 1995). Perhaps more than anything else this is the source of the aesthetic and spiritual monotony that anti-urbanists like Robin Boyd (1968) in *The Australian Ugliness* claim was the defining trait of Australian suburbia in the 1960s.

While some of the Australian-born working class families living in deteriorating inner suburban neighborhoods were rehoused by the Housing Commissions in the 1950s, others bought a block of land in the suburbs and began building their own homes. Greig (1995) estimates that 40 percent of all dwellings were constructed by owner–builders (i.e. DIY's – "do-it-yourselfers") in the 1950s – partly because costs ran ahead of earnings, and partly due to the scarcity of building materials and tradesmen.

The cheap rental stock vacated in the heart of the city was occupied in turn during the 1950s and 1960s by the new immigrants, especially Southern Europeans from Italy, Greece, Yugoslavia, Macedonia, and Malta. As "New Australians," they took the jobs in nearby clothing mills and fabricating workshops that "Australians" were no longer prepared to do. In times of full employment they eventually managed to save enough to buy their terrace cottages from the landlord (sub-standard dwellings were subject to rent control during and after World War II, so landlords were glad to sell). Thus it was here, in the inner city, that migrants from Southern Europe initially put down their roots, built their social networks and churches, and opened business and clubs.

Significantly, because many migrant homebuyers were artisans and worked together to make these cottages habitable, they helped arrest the further deterioration of these historic suburbs near the heart of Australian cities, and in a sense primed them for gentrification (Badcock and Urlich-Cloher, 1981). From the early 1970s onwards, therefore, increasing numbers of South European households took the opportunity to capitalize in an inflating inner city housing market by selling their terrace cottages to "new" middle class buyers working in the CBD (Kendig, 1979).

Burnley (1996) traces the outward spread of second-generation, and now third-generation, Italians, Greeks and Yugoslavs to secondary and tertiary settlement areas in suburban Sydney. Not only did the move to the suburbs enable these families to plow their capital gains back into newer and more spacious bungalows, but job prospects for blue-collar workers were much better than in the inner city where manufacturing was in decline. For these reasons, although gentrification displaced some migrant households in inner Sydney and Melbourne (Centre for Urban Research and Action, 1977), it was never on the scale reported for many US cities (LeGates and Hartman, 1986). In fact, by 1986 about 85 percent of all Southern European born households either owned (62.5 percent), or were buying (22.6 percent) their own home in Australia (Troy, 1991, p. 7).

By contrast, throughout the 1960s the more highly skilled British, Dutch and German-born migrants qualified for government-assisted passages or were sponsored by employers, and quickly moved through "on arrival" hostels in the suburbs to nearby housing and jobs. Remarkably, with rates much closer to the national average of about 71 percent in 1986, their home-ownership levels fell well short of Southern European households (Troy, 1991, p. 7).

During the 1960s and 1970s suburbanization processes decanted the Australian-born working and lower-middle classes from the inner suburbs mostly to one side of the central city, and upper-middle class commuters to middle-ring suburbs on the other. In Sydney, Melbourne and Adelaide blue-collar suburbs dominated on the western side of the city, while the eastern suburbs concentrated private schools, city parks, and privilege in mostly middle-distance suburbs (Badcock, 1984). Quite commonly in the Australian case, these white-collar dormitory suburbs feeding commuters to office jobs in the downtown core were progressively outflanked by the spread of the public housing estates and the project home builders' subdivisions beyond them (Johnston, 1973).

Hence the disposition of postwar manufacturing and nearby public housing estates in the suburbs, and office jobs in business and government in the central city helped to cement the 19th-century split between blue-collar workers on one side of the Fordist city, with white-collar workers on the other. But as well as this socio-spatial cleavage, with a fully employed economy and Commonwealth housing subsidies to assist lower-income home buyers, the "Australian dream" of a home on a "quarter acre block" in the suburbs was within reach of many working class families.

This, together with the extensive provision of public rental stock on the fringe where the Housing Commissions held reserves of cheap land, accounts for the presence of working class and lower-middle class suburbs in the outer zone of Australian cities. Indeed, with levels of home ownership exceeding Australian-born households, Australia was a "lucky country" in the 1960s and 1970s for many postwar migrants. And partly because of the occupational composition of these outer zone labor catchments, as we will shortly see, there has been nothing like the same edge city development during the 1980s as North American cities have experienced (Knox, 1993).

The Transition to a Post-Fordist Spatial Order in Australian Cities

In Australia, the last two decades have been dominated by a series of Labor Governments federally, precisely because they successfully pursued uncharacteristically conservative policies to capture and then hold the "middle ground" in Australian politics. Whilst in power Labor sought to *lubricate* globalization processes by rapidly opening up and exposing both the manufacturing and financial sectors to internationally competitive forces. Throughout the 1980s Australian firms were urged by Labor ministers to lift productivity and the export of elaborately transformed manufactures (ETMs), even at the expense of reducing workers' real wages. In addition, this engagement with globalizing processes has been accompanied by *internal* pressures for change upon the cities; that is, over and above internationally-generated processes of urban restructuring.

In the mid-1980s Labor introduced a schedule for the staged elimination of most tariff protection and effectively abandoned any semblance of industry policy. This was justified on the grounds that a government has no part to play in picking "winners" and "losers" in the manufacturing sector. Tens of thousands of private- and public-sector jobs have been shed in pursuit of productivity and efficiency gains. For example, between 1981–91 employment contracted the most in the manufacturing sector (down 16.2 percent), where the majority of jobs were during the Fordist era. Next was the "electricity, gas, and water" sector (down 27.1 percent), which is dominated by public utilities (see Table 9.1 in Badcock, 1995a, p. 201). Victoria led the other states in public service retrenchments in the early 1990s (50,000 of the 220,000 positions were shed). And now the new conservative government in Canberra is proposing a ten percent cut in the Commonwealth Public Service, representing about 30,000 jobs, as part of a strategy to bring the budget into surplus by 1998.

For Harvey (1989) it is the rise of part-time and casual work that best signifies the demise of Fordism and the move by employers to organizational flexibility in the workplace. Of the 1.4 m new jobs created in Australia between 1980 and 1993, 60 percent were part-time, and 75 percent of these jobs were filled by women (Department of Social Security, 1993). In August 1995, median weekly earnings in part-time employment were a mere $217 for women, and even less for men at $164 (Australian Bureau of Statistics, 1995, p.70). As well as these part-time jobs in the formal economy, flexibility has also led to "out-work" and driven down wages in surviving "underground" segments of the clothing industry where Vietnamese fabric cutters and garment makers now have a monopoly.

Flexible practices also permit more of Reich's (1991) "symbolic analysts" to work from home, or set up small offices nearer to home in attractive locations. As the knowledge industries capitalize on the ease of information transfer, this is contributing to a noticeable "thickening-up" of the managerial and professional heartland of Sydney's North Shore and Melbourne's inner eastern suburbs (Newton, 1995).

Flexibility in the workplace is tantamount to "casualization," and is now tending to exacerbate the overall income inequality between households since many more of the women returning to part-time work also have a partner in a job. Two incomes improve tenure choice and location in the housing market so it is not surprising that solo mothers and single women working part-time – that is about 7.2 percent and 4 percent of female households members in Australia (Australian Bureau of Statistics, 1995) – or those dependent upon a pension, comprise the fastest growing group of public tenants. With the state housing authorities only housing about 5.5 percent of Australian households, this effectively confines them to the tenure of "last resort"; and all too often to some of the poorest and outermost suburbs in Australian cities (Cass, 1991).

Given the previous history of trade protection, regulated financial markets, and centralized wage fixing, the accelerated pace of structural readjustment has proven especially traumatic for specific sectors of the Australian economy, and those cities or urban sub-regions narrowly dependent upon them. The brunt of deindustrialization has been borne by steel and/or coal towns like Wollongong (Schultz, 1985), Whyalla (Aungles and Szelenyi, 1979), and now Newcastle, together with postwar industrial suburbs in the western regions of Sydney (Powell, 1993), Melbourne (Winter and Bryson, 1996), and northern Adelaide (Peel, 1995). And within these regions it is the public housing estates that were built for the factory workforce in the 1960s that have been most severely affected by the loss of blue-collar work (Badcock, 1994). Gregory and Hunter (1995b) estimate that in urban areas, employment levels amongst male and female workers living on these public housing estates fell by 45 percent and 35 percent between 1976 and 1991 (Table 10.1).

Table 10.1 Employment and income change between 1976 and 1991 in public housing neighborhoods and other neighborhoods in the bottom 10 percent of SES rankings

	Neighborhoods Public Housing (%)	Neighborhoods No Public Housing (%)
Real Income		
Male	− 29	− 13
Female	− 2	17
Personal	− 19	2
Household	− 34	− 12
Employment		
Male	− 45	− 25
Female	− 35	− 7
Total	− 41	− 18

Source: Gregory and Hunter (1995b, p. 20)

Notwithstanding a series of Accords struck between Labor and the unions to provide workers with social wage off-sets in lieu of lost earnings, these public housing estates have become "poverty traps" in the last decade due to the tighter targeting of housing assistance. For example, the proportion of public tenants that qualify for a rent rebate because of the meagerness of their incomes has climbed from 62 percent in 1984-85 to 86 percent in 1993–94 (Department of Housing and Regional Development, 1995a). The noticeable concentration of poverty on suburban public housing estates, and in central Melbourne's high rise flats, has recently raised the specter in Australia of a "ghetto underclass" forming along American lines (Gregory and Hunter, 1995a). However, while superficial comparisons can be drawn at the level of unemployment and poverty rates, as yet there is nothing to match the degree of spatial concentration or entrapment experienced by blacks in *"extreme poverty"* neighborhoods in some US cities (US Department of Housing and Urban Development, 1995).

It is not uncommon for these public housing estates, or tracts of low-rent housing surrounding Commonwealth resettlement hostels, to also contain a significant proportion of recent migrants, many of whom arrived in Australia as "boat people" and political refugees. Indeed, Forster (1995, p. 106) regards the development in some middle and outer suburbs of large concentrations of recent immigrants from South East Asia, the Middle East, and Latin

America as "the most striking feature of the ethnic geography of Australian cities in recent years."

Burnley (1996) shows how selectively economic restructuring has impacted upon these recent migrants in Sydney's labor and housing markets. In 1991, unemployment rates ranged between 40–50 percent amongst Moslems (from the Middle East), and Vietnamese, men and women seeking work (Burnley, 1996). Without jobs they lack the same housing prospects of earlier waves of immigrants. One response has been to gravitate back to the pockets of low-rent housing around the on-arrival centers in outer Sydney (Fairfield), outer Melbourne (Sunshine, Springvale), and north-west Adelaide (Enfield, Woodville).

The Southeast-Asian community living in Fairfield City, in Sydney's outer west, now numbers 35,000 overseas-born, not to mention second-generation dependents. Prior to the large and recently settled Vietnamese population, earlier migrants from Italy, Malta, Lebanon, and the former Yugoslavia also settled in Fairfield City. All told, at the 1991 Census nearly one-half of Fairfield City's total population of 175,000 was born overseas in non-English-speaking countries (Forster, 1995, p. 107). By contrast, recent Chinese business migrants from Hong Kong, Malaysia and Singapore have tended to disperse and settle on Sydney's prosperous North Shore close to business contacts and good private schools (Burnley, 1996).

With persistent, long-term unemployment since the early 1980s, the presence of rapidly expanding ethnic minorities has provoked some localized hostility, particularly amongst those jobless competing in the same segments of the labor market. Predictably, one of the first actions of the incoming conservative government has been to cut back the migrant intake in 1996–97 by 10.8 percent, especially the quota on "family reunion" (down from 58,200 to 44,700).

This is to argue, then, that the fall-out from structural decline in the Australian economy has impacted quite selectively upon those middle and outer suburbs within Australian cities that formerly contained both the vulnerable manufacturing jobs, and the public housing estates that used to house factory workers and their families. But now these suburbs are housing more and more of the non-working poor. Increasingly, as stricter eligibility criteria are applied by the Department of Social Security (Whiteford, 1995), these households comprise: elderly pensioners living alone; single parent families headed mainly by women; recent immigrants; family members with disabilities.

There is mounting evidence to indicate that one facet of post-Fordism under Australian conditions involves falling household incomes across many middle and outer suburbs combined with a localization of poverty on public housing estates (Badcock, 1994; Burbidge and Winter, 1996; Gregory and Hunter, 1995b; MacDonald, 1995; Raskall, 1995). Otherwise, significant numbers of poorer, aged pensioners and jobless are abandoning high-cost

Table 10.2 Employment change by industry group, Australia, 1971–91

Industry group*	Employment 1971	Employment 1991	Change 1971–91	Percentage distribution % 1971	% 1991	% Change 1971–91	Employment Change (%) 1971–91
Extractive	462,430	407,170	− 55,260	9.2	6.2	− 3.6	− 11.9
Transformative	1,719,099	1,446,379	− 272,720	34.2	22.0	− 17.5	− 15.9
Distributive	1,363,286	1,776,856	413,570	27.1	27.0	26.6	30.3
Producer services	363,418	788,283	424,865	7.2	12.0	27.3	116.9
Consumer services	847,801	1,663,671	815,870	16.9	25.3	52.5	96.2
Personal services	267,511	496,172	228,661	5.3	7.5	14.7	85.5
Total**	5,023,545	6,578,531	1,554,986	100.0	100.0	100.0	31.0

* 'Extractive' comprises agricultural and mining; 'transformative' comprises manufacturing, utilities and construction; 'distributive' comprises trade, transport and communications; 'producer services' comprises the finance and business services sector; 'consumer services' comprises public administration and community services; 'personal services' comprises recreation and personal services.
** Excludes industry not stated/not classifiable.

Source: Prepared by Bell (1995) from ABS 1971 and 1991 Census (unpublished data)

locations like Sydney and Melbourne to move to country areas or regional towns where housing and services are more affordable.

The other key spatial dimension of the post-Fordist transition taking place within Australian cities has its basis in the changing division of labor that has accompanied the growth of producer services and knowledge industries. Table 10.2 from Bell (1995) indicates that between 1971–91 the size of the sector measured by job numbers more than doubled. The flourishing service economy has given rise to the formation of a "new middle class" (Butler and Hamnett, 1994) and the consequential gentrification of the inner suburbs by some of its constituent workers over the last two decades. Table 10.3 confirms that highly paid households (including young professional women) rose dramatically in the inner suburbs between 1981 and 1991, along with the number of residents with degrees.

Impressive levels of housing reinvestment have been sustained in the inner areas of Australian cities for over 25 years now (Badcock, 1995b), and it is this that holds the key to the centralization of wealth evidenced in the recent study by Raskall (1995). When he traces the shift of suburbs by rank-order between 1978–79 and 1992–93, Raskall is struck by ". . . the consistent pattern of dramatic decile rises of incomes in postcodes covering the central business district and immediately surrounding suburbs in each city. . . . In contrast to many other nations, in Australian cities the rich are reclaiming the centers" (Raskall, 1995, p. 56).

There is no doubt that the growth of the services sector in the 1980s also drew impetus from actions taken by the Commonwealth government in the context of globalization. In the mid-1980s the Commonwealth deregulated the financial market and floated exchange rates. This gave overseas banks access to the domestic market on the same terms as local banks, and established an international trading floor in Sydney. But in the wake of financial deregulation, credit expanded voluminously and flowed into speculative investment in downtown property markets. This was partly spurred by the equally spectacular growth in those sectors of the economy grouping producer and consumer services (Table 10.2).

At the same time as the cities were being integrated into international and regional networks, the Commonwealth and the States began a concerted effort to revitalize the city centers. This gained real momentum under Labor in the first half of the 1990s, when the Better Cities program came to full realization (Department of Housing and Regional Development, 1995b). Better Cities detailed the strategic investment in infrastructure necessary to enable cities like Sydney, with its pretensions to global city status, to capture a greater share of information flows and financial transactions occurring in the Pacific region.

Moreover, by underwriting state government projects and levering private sector investment, Better Cities funding has further advanced the revitalization of the urban cores of Australian cities thereby heightening the appeal of inner city living for the "new middle class." But as this new investment is capitalized into appreciating property values, the Better Cities area improvement strategies, at least for the central city, inevitably compromise social justice objectives which seek to reserve some low income housing shares within the urban core (National Capital Planning Authority, 1993).

Around Sydney's Darling Harbor and on the Ultimo-Pyrmont Peninsula, on Brisbane's Southbank, on the southern bank of the Yarra in central Melbourne, and in East Perth, disused tracts of industrial, dockside, and surplus government land have been recycled to recreate the kinds of consumption spaces that now bear the familiar signature of urban revitalization in old waterfront areas around the world. Not only are these post-Fordist spaces intended to boost tourism and provide stadiums, festival venues, casinos, theaters, and galleries for mass entertainment and leisure, but they also provide places where inner city dwellers meet and relax as well.

Table 10.3 The 'New Middle Class' presence in the inner zones of Sydney and Melbourne

| | | Zones | |
	Inner %	Middle %	Outer %
Persons 15+ years with a degree			
Sydney			
1981	9.2	5.9	3.8
1991	18.9	11.6	7.6
Melbourne			
1981	9.8	6.9	2.9
1991	20.6	14.2	6.0
Persons 25–54 year old with incomes >$30,000			
Sydney			
Men	45.4	43.0	44.9
Women	29.2	18.3	13.0
Melbourne			
Men	38.2	44.9	37.5
Women	26.5	18.7	9.4

Source: Prepared by MacDonald (1995) from ABS 1981 and 1991 Censuses (unpublished data)

In Australia the resettlement of the inner city and suburbs by the "new middle class" has proceeded well beyond the preservation of historic urban precincts and the conversion of old tramway shopping strips for the "cafe set." Now, as gentrification begins to penetrate quite improbable and previously unwelcoming industrial "backwaters" around the inner city (Moodie, 1995), a luxury apartment and downtown condominium submarket is beginning to emerge for the first time in cities other than Sydney (Badcock, 1995b). This is perhaps the clearest indication of the growing willingness of some wealthier Australians to live and invest in inner city housing.

The Absence of Edge City Development

If post-Fordist processes are indeed leading to poorer suburbs combined with a centralization of wealth in Australian cities, this is in direct contradistinction to the North American situation where edge city development is such a prominent part of urban restructuring (Garreau, 1991; Knox, 1993). That is not to say there is no equivalent to master planned communities for the pampered upper-middle class at the edges of Australian cities. Such suburbs can be found in recent corridor extensions in all of the state capitals, or in south eastern Queensland where investment in retirement, leisure and tourist activities is producing pure consumption landscapes. However, although quintessentially post-Fordist and consumption-based, these new spaces are not as yet extensive enough geographically to spatially make over the prevailing social mosaic or urban landscape in Australia.

Whilst there is some fledgling office and science park development at North Ryde in Sydney that definitely bears post-modern influences in its architecture and landscaping, it is situated adjacent to Sydney's "only real ring road" midway between the CBD and the edge of the built-up area (Freestone, 1996, p. 19). Not only do Australian cities lack the outer ring of beltways, but it is questionable whether the economy is large enough to support the hi-tech research and development that is responsible for so much of the investment and job creation at the edge of US cities.

Of equal importance in explaining the absence of edge city development is the much stronger tradition of strategic planning and intervention within the urban sphere in Australia. Although planning processes are under siege in some states, there is nothing comparable to the free market ethos that gave rein to edge city development *by stealth* in cities like Houston, Dallas, Denver, or LA's Orange County during the 1980s (Garreau, 1991). Although strategic planning seldom achieves optimal outcomes and instances of market failure in the cities are commonplace (McLoughlin, 1992), urban land release and the staging of corridor development continues to be firmly managed by government planning agencies in each state.

Post-Fordism and Ongoing Spatial Transformation

In comparing the impact of globalization upon Australian and US cities, Marcuse (1996) suggests that political developments rather than economic forces will ultimately determine whether or not urban patterns in the two societies retain their present distinctiveness, or begin to converge in response to post-Fordist processes. He suggests that under circumstances where state intervention once sheltered the poor in Australian cities, the shrinkage of the welfare state may now give rise to a new form of urban poverty along the same lines as witnessed in the United States (Marcuse, 1996). However, while recent political action to free-up labor and housing markets in Australia could reproduce some of the trends observed in the United States, and will no doubt encourage the tendency to spatial polarization, different initial conditions in the two societies render convergence most unlikely.

The enforced liberalization of trade and banking in the mid-1980s contributed to the overheating of the Australian economy and alarming current account deficits. The Hawke Labor government belatedly responded by progressively tightening monetary policy – commercial interest rates peaked at 19 percent in 1989 – which drove the economy deeply into recession in 1991–93 and led to large scale retrenchment. It is now acknowledged that a more restrained approach to tariffs and industrial policy, and the deregulation of financial markets, would have visited less trauma upon working class communities in the cities (Badcock, 1994). Ironically, these industrial suburbs have traditionally formed the Labor heartland of "true believers"; but these were the voters that abandoned their party with such bitterness in federal and state polls through the mid-1990s.

Now, a conservative Commonwealth government, formed by a coalition of the Liberal and Country parties, is intent on pushing flexibility in the labor market to the political limit. Indeed, the force of the reforms to the industrial relations system envisaged by the Commonwealth would replace centralized wage fixing and compulsory arbitration with enterprise bargaining in the workplace. The intention is to allow employers to negotiate wage levels and conditions with individual workers. With the Howard government resigned to unemployment levels above 8 percent until the end of the decade, this is bound to force wages down; and if the recent experience of US labor markets is anything to go by, could lead to the emergence of working poor in Australia.

In addition, micro-economic reforms are being introduced in the 1990s to all three tiers of government which are essentially regressive and must add to the impoverishment produced by the labor process. Principles of fiscal equalization in distribution are being undermined by fiscal self-sufficiency at the regional and local levels which also takes us a step closer to the United

States. These are the processes, then, that have sharpened the disparities between rich and poor suburbs in Australia in the 1990s, and are now altering the Fordist residential mosaic.

The crucial difference between US and Australian cities, though, relates to how these polarizing tendencies are working to spatially redistribute wealth and poverty. In Australia, on the one hand, gentrification and state-managed revitalization underlie the middle-class re-capture of central space; on the other, the occupational mix of labor catchments in the outer zone militates against genuine edge city development on any scale (that is not to overlook the growth of some "back office" employment).

Finally, whilst one or two Australian commentators have recently suggested that conditions now exist that led to the formation of a marginalized urban underclass in the United States (Hunter, 1995), or that gated communities and "fortress city" phenomena are catching on (White, 1996), this really does overstate the case for convergence on both counts. As Stilwell (1996, p. 11) points out: "Australian cities have not had the intensity of urban social conflicts for which many US cities are renowned: there is no comparable equivalent to racially-segregated urban ghettoes, while the crime problem, although of persistent concern, is relatively modest." With one or two notable exceptions like Sanctuary Cove on the Sunshine Coast, there are very few "no-go" zones or areas of statutory exclusion to be found in Australian cities. Whatever other form it might take, the new spatial order within Australian cities embodies neither the extremes of wealth and poverty, nor the degree of compartmentalization that has been consistently documented for cities in the United States (US Department of Housing and Urban Development, 1995).

Note

1   Australia has a federal system of governance which bestows the key powers upon the Commonwealth, including control over the main sources of revenue (company and personal taxation) and redistribution via the states (New South Wales, Victoria, Queensland, Western Australia, South Australia and Tasmania) and Territories (the Australian capital, i.e. Canberra, and the Northern Territory). This inherently unequal division of powers is a constant source of tension in Australian political life.

11

The Globalization of Frankfurt am Main: Core, Periphery and Social Conflict

Roger Keil and Klaus Ronneberger

By the late 1990s, Frankfurt, the glamour capital of the West German growth model of the 1980s, has lost its luster. Bank towers, a mega-airport, a vast fairground and a high cost of living are signs that Frankfurt has succeeded in climbing into the top class of European financial centers; yet poverty, marginalization of social groups, an indebted local state, socio-spatial segregation and the explosion of the traditional relationship of center and periphery show that the formation of a world city had a price.[1] Frankfurt has become one of the places where the contradictions and fissures of the global economy are concentrated.

In this chapter, we examine the ways in which globally induced socio-spatial restructuring has occurred both in the core and in the periphery of Frankfurt, and how social conflict influenced this process: while we recognize the dynamics and power of globalization and restructuring, we will show how local politics and social conflicts shape the transformation we describe. We also argue that in this process the very social (class, ethnicity and gender) and spatial (neighborhood, city, region, countryside) categories with which we commonly understand the urban region are changed as well in the process.

Globalization is now well understood as a central dynamic of the world economy. We do, however, insist that globalization should not be fetishized and reified as a steamroller that rolls over "local places." Rather, we believe that it has to be seen as a distinctive set of social practices that are conflictive and contradictory and subject to social and political struggles. Globalization as a concept has ideological and analytical dimensions. In the first sense, it has become a powerful weapon in the arsenal of the New World Order; in the second sense, it is mostly applied by critical theorists who treat the discourse on globalization as a multitude of processes like migration, capital movement, class formation and cultural change, which gain shape above and seemingly outside of national, regional or urban form and are funneled into these lower levels through a magical black box.

In distancing ourselves from much of the common academic discourse at that point, we have argued instead that globalization is not a removed process with a natural propensity to trickle down from the sky of the global economy but a combination of articulated material processes – such as urbanization (Kipfer and Keil, 1995, p. 61). While globalization happens in all kinds of geographical locales, it gains particular significance in those urban centers that have, for more than a decade, captured the imagination of scholars, activists and politicians: *world or global cities* (Friedmann, 1995; Sassen, 1994; Keil, 1993; Knox and Taylor, 1995).

Restructuring and Globalization: Frankfurt Goes Global

Frankfurt–Rhein–Main has traditionally been one of the economic power-houses of the German economy. It encompasses an area reaching roughly from Mainz–Wiesbaden in the west to Hanau in the east, Gießen in the north and Darmstadt in the south. This area of about 5,000 sq. km. houses about 3.1 m people and has 1.6 m jobs. Frankfurt itself is something like the central city of this otherwise polycentric region. On just 250 sq. km. (five percent of the region) it has 660,000 people and more than 560,000 jobs (more than one third of the region) (Ronneberger, 1994). It is the intricate and interwoven historical geography of this region which has created the strengths on which the current economic success of Frankfurt–Rhein–Main is built (Lieser and Keil, 1988).

In general terms, Frankfurt has maintained a thriving business downtown core surrounded by highly diverse inner city residential areas that span from wealthy (Westend), to socially and culturally heterogeneous (Nordend, Bockenheim) to poor and mostly working class and immigrant (Gallus, Gutleut, Ostend) along the Main River. This residential ring is interspersed with smaller business and commercial areas and office parks and is surrounded by a green belt which covers about 30 percent of the city of Frankfurt's territory (Husung and Lieser, 1996). In the urban periphery we find a mix of 1960s and 1970s high-rise social housing and new and traditional single family housing, as well as industrial and office parks adjacent to agricultural production. The outer periphery of Frankfurt, in the Taunus hills and in the Southeast (Rodgau) has developed into Frankfurt's "blubber belt" (*Speckgürtel*) of wealthy suburban communities which are mostly residential but also house some of the most visible growth sectors of the region's new economy: software production and producer services.

Frankfurt's world city formation really began in the late 1960s.[2] Local subsidiaries of internationally important growth sectors and new middle-class residential populations started to evict existing economic and residential uses in the city center.[3] There is no exact turning point at which Frankfurt can be called a global rather than a national urban center. Yet the combination of the political regime of Walter Wallmann after 1977 and changing global conditions of capital accumulation in the 1980s repositioned Frankfurt in the global interurban competition (Keil and Lieser, 1992).

During the 1980s, Frankfurt was transformed from a national economic core into a classical world city, a hub of the transnationally organized world economy. This has been expressed functionally and symbolically by the continuing growth of the downtown skyline of office towers, home to the headquarters functions of German and international financial capital. Clustered around and catering to the needs of the financial sector, one finds the globalized superstructure of the fairgrounds, the airport and a diversified sector of business services ranging from insurance companies to advertising and software development.

Frankfurt has, until recently, been a strong manufacturing location, with 130,000 jobs in the secondary sector as late as 1987. In the 1990s, under global competition and with the opening of the Eastern European labor market, Frankfurt's industrial base has shown signs of decline which has had tremendous impact on the spatial structure of the city (see next section). Only roughly 80,000 jobs remained in manufacturing in 1994. The spatial aspects of this decline of the manufacturing base have been numerous.

Rising real estate prices in the core and increased efforts of companies to achieve a more efficient management of facilities and production spaces has led to an accelerated dislocation of manufacturing industries from the city. While the city of Frankfurt is suffering huge losses of blue-collar jobs in this process, some of the surrounding cities have double digit growth rates in manufacturing (Ronneberger, 1994) (Map 11.1). With an aggressively expanding services sector and a never ending squeeze on the housing market, industrial sites in the core have often been recycled rapidly into the new socio-spatial pattern of the global city as upscale housing sites or office parks.

Spatial Dimensions of Frankfurt's Restructuring

Notwithstanding the decline of manufacturing, the narrative of restructuring and globalization in Frankfurt is mostly one of growth and expansion, both in discursive construction and in material terms. We can roughly differentiate two growth dynamics: the continuing vertical and horizontal expansion

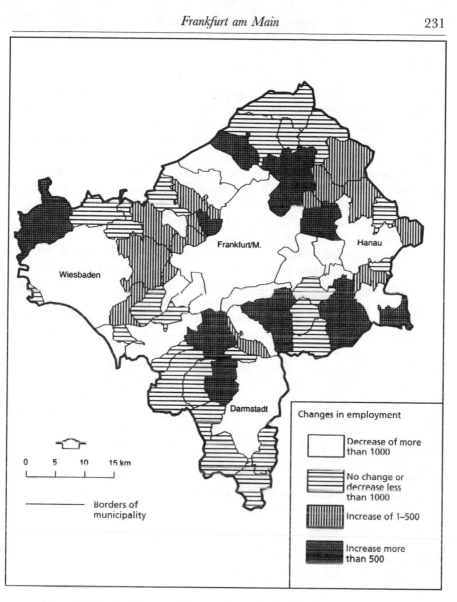

Map 11.1   Employment in manufacturing in the Rhein–Main Area;
changes 1970–1987

of the core and a new type of self-sustained peripheral expansion. Let us look
at these in turn.

The core

At first glance, growth in Frankfurt appears as a derivative of the centralized global city functions, with the financial industry as their flagship. In the beginning of the 1990s, the core city of Frankfurt had about eight m sq.m. of office space. During this decade, about 4.2 m sq.m. more were added or are in some stage of realization (planning, construction).

In physical terms this enormous expansion of downtown office space can be illustrated by the fact that in this period 10 new major office towers for the central city were under construction or in the planning stage. The strength of the CBD economy can be gathered from the peculiarity that the city has the highest jobs per capita ratio of any German city. It needs to be pointed out, though, that the growth in office space far exceeds the growth of jobs: there has been a constant increase in the space used by individual workers while rationalization and trimming of the workforce occurred due to the introduction of computers and information technology.

The spatial and institutional spread of the office economy, primarily from the banking district around the Neue Mainzer Straße into the western areas of the city, first took place along the corridors laid down by the late 1960s *Fingerplan* and later along the axes proposed by Albert Speer Jr.'s general plan of 1983 commissioned by the former conservative local government. The vertical downtown was thus complemented by a star of horizontal areas like the Mainzer Landstraße, and the Theodor-Heuss-Allee, with the *Museumsufer* along the Main River serving as the built environment of culture and spectacle in an era of neo-conservative hegemony and postmodern redevelopment. This restructuring had a significant effect on both the larger structure of the city in terms of traffic flows, the logic of inter-neighborhood links and the micro-structure of communities whose housing stock and local economies came under severe pressure from office space development. The neighborhoods forming the western ring around the CBD were particularly hard hit by gentrification (Westend, Bockenheim) and tertiarization (Gallus, Gutleut, Bahnhofsviertel), with the familiar consequences of rising rents, loss of housing space, intrusion of offices into residential areas and the closing of manufacturing plants.[4]

There are two main thrusts of peripheralization of the core. First, there are all kinds of social and spatial displacement both of people and of industries. Traditional manufacturing (such as metalworking) and craft industries (such as the fur industry) are evicted from the CBD, and the city center is rounded off by new office and industrial parks functioning as flexible supply centers. Economically, lower skilled and unskilled manufacturing jobs – a traditional stronghold of immigrant labor – disappear (Bartelheimer, 1997). At the same time, the expansion of the world city economy creates both a need for and a reserve army of unskilled labor, particularly in the service sector. A structural shift has polarized the local labor market into a high-skill segment on one hand and a low-skill, precarious employment segment on the other. Both are highly internationalized. The presence in Frankfurt of the bottom segment of the labor market is particularly noteworthy. While guestworkers have fed the internationalized segment of the labor market since the early 1960s, the new, precarious economy has changed considerably, so that guestworkers can no longer find work in construction and manufacturing and are now restricted to low-end jobs in the service economy.

Part-time employment increased by 83 percent between 1970 and 1987. The segment of the labor market which includes janitorial services and garbage collection, for example, grew by 10,000 jobs during the same period, an increase of 95 percent (Freyberg, 1996, p. 87). In addition, shadow economies are blossoming in a variety of industries from construction to street vending. The high number of political refugees who are legally not allowed to work but who feed informal labor markets add to this phenomenon. In this case spatial peripheralization coincides with marginalization. The discourses of urbanity and centralization – both on the Left and on the Right – have largely ignored these socio-spatial effects.[5]

Secondly, overspill effects of the core economy have created back-office and housing needs which have been increasingly filled in peripheral areas outside the municipality of Frankfurt. About 120,000 housing units were built in the Frankfurt region between 1980 and 1987, most of which were in the rural and semi-rural villages and towns in the periphery (Wentz, 1991, p. 13). "Office Cities" like Niederrad and Eschborn act as "flood control" devices for the booming inner city economy, sites of back-offices and routine functions of banks and other businesses located in the core. In the wake of such tremendous pressure from the center, suburban jurisdictions, especially those along the Taunus, face two general options: either to give up virtually all individual paths of development by positioning themselves solely in relationship to the demands generated by the CBD (Rahms, 1991); or to pursue a strategy of selective locational competitiveness, attempting to draw inner-city businesses or new companies to peripheral locations. Some of the most active new development areas have been successful in raising their political clout in the region in the process.

The periphery

In recent years, significant parts of the regional world city economy have been established in the peripheries of Frankfurt–Rhein–Main (Maps 11.2, 11.3). An increasingly self-sustaining horizontal growth in a para-urban zone beyond a 10 km radius and inside a 100 km radius around the center is linked to the advent of the global city in the countryside, i.e. the establishment of economic functions linked to the global economy in the urban periphery *without* mediation through the core. The periphery is becoming the prime location for important sectors of the post-Fordist economy (like software production, logistics etc.).[6] The concentration of office towers in the CBD often eclipses the tendency of the "real" economic center of Frankfurt to shift away from the CBD into the forest on the fringe of the city: Frankfurt airport, the largest in Europe after London Heathrow, has developed into the crucial center for processing the global flows of people, goods, and information. The largest employer in the region with over 52,000 jobs in 400 companies, the airport places aggressive demands on space in the area (Ronneberger, 1994, p. 183). An important additional feature of this growth is the construction of a new railway station tying the airport into the European high speed rail network.

Meanwhile, "dirty" and less place-dependent functions have been displaced from the actual airport area. This development mirrors a tendency visible in Frankfurt–Rhein–Main in general: manufacturing, waste management, supply industries like the slaughterhouse and the produce wholesale market are being shifted from the core to the periphery. This practice still coincides largely with a center-oriented real estate market. Yet, with the growing significance of the airport (and possibly other sub-centers), these markets become more nodal. Locational logics and logistics are now increasingly made to fit the needs of the airport rather than the inner-city economy alone. While the airport–CBD axis remains the single most important spatial connection in Frankfurt–Rhein–Main, airport-related activities are being diffused into the region.

Frankfurt–Rhein–Main's spatial structure tends to form "insular configurations." In contrast to earlier spatial expressions of divisions of labor, these new islands are ". . . 'specific', yet internally highly complex, multifunctional and integrated" (Brake, 1991, p. 101). The airport is just one, albeit the biggest of such insular spaces in Frankfurt–Rhein–Main. Others like the City West or Kaiserlei have similar potential for development. Brake notes a "regional ring" of office locations some of which ". . . are quite large although they have emerged in fairly small communities." This regional ring of small and semi-autonomous municipalities has become a significant area of foreign investment (Brake, 1991, pp. 32ff.). We can interpret this as a peripheralization of internationalization. It spreads internationalization, if unevenly, across the entire region and increases the overall impact of transnational actors on individual communities. Also, the commercial and industrial parks which form a rim around Frankfurt provide accommodation consultancy services, and marketing outlets for domestic and foreign computer and electronics firm. Housing construction both in the core and in the periphery has, in the meantime, hardly been able to keep up with the continuing office boom, putting considerable stress on the regional socio-economic situation.

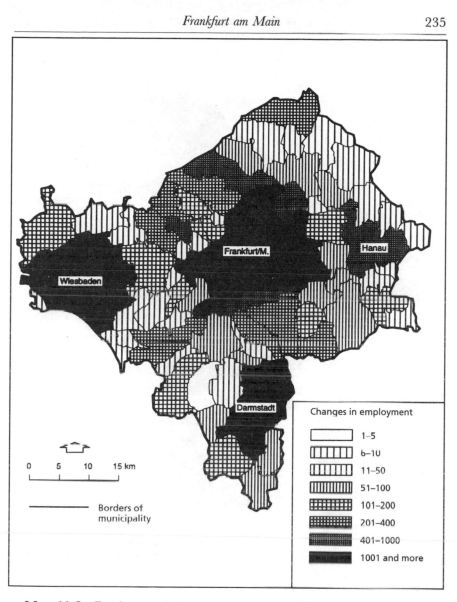

Map 11.2 Employment in business services in the Rhein–Main Area, 1970

The spatial form of the periphery is produced by a contradictory dynamic. The periphery has not just been colonized by the core but appears as the product of exchange processes both of core and periphery and of various subcenters on the fringe. Waves of housing construction conquered the green periphery. From the garden cities of the 1920s to the satellite towns of the

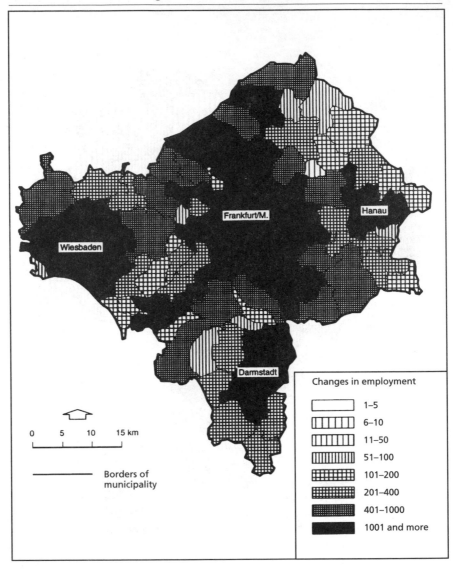

Map 11.3 Employment in business services in the Rhein–Main Area, 1987

1960s, generations of urban planners in Frankfurt attempted to solve urban problems by expanding the city towards the periphery. The peripheral housing estates, although often built for established middle-class families, sometimes became a "dump" for impoverished or marginalized citizens as well as new immigrants. This process was often fueled by political or administrative decisions such as the housing office's clustering of applicants by nationality or ethnicity.

However, it is not just the center of the city which tries to rid itself of social problems by shifting them to the edge. Autonomous municipalities in the agglomeration also practice peripheralization. In recent decades almost all municipalities in the region have reproduced the urban form associated with the Fordist–Keynesian era in Germany: industrialization of the suburbs, peripheralization of commercial activities (e.g. malls), and a mix of single family home, town house and high-rise residential developments at the fringes of each small community.

To sum up, one can speak of oscillating growth dynamics between the urban core and the urban periphery. Growth in the CBD triggers expansion in the periphery; in turn, the newly emerging polynuclear nodes along the Taunus hills, in the Rodgau and along the A5 autobahn corridor engender higher density in the central city. Frankfurt, in this view, is not just a hub of international capital movement but also the central place of an economically diversified European growth region with its own demands on the citadel.

We would argue, though, that Frankfurt–Rhein–Main, while showing signs of "Americanization" both in its vertical growth and horizontal sprawl, re-mains a very European region. Frankfurt's spatial deconstruction in the cur-rent period does not reach the dimensions of Los Angeles and other North American cities. The region is not just a new industrial district of sorts held together by a globalized, flexible *economy*, but is *culturally, politically*, and *socio-spatially* meaningful. World city formation in Frankfurt has shifted from a central to a regional focus. During the 1980s, conservative urban govern-ments encouraged centralized urban development based on the "citadelization" of the core of Frankfurt and neglected both individual communities in the city proper and the surrounding region. Since the 1990s, some attention has been redirected towards the neighborhoods on the one hand (e.g. by way of strengthening local advisory boards called *Ortsbeiräte*), and towards the region on the other hand. The latter in particular has increasingly become an important point of reference of policy makers and planners.

The shift from the center to the region implies a new hegemony of metropolitanization over the region. Whereas local actors in the periphery fought the world city's encroachment on their semi-rural neighborhoods, the metropolitanization of the *Umland* proceeded apace because of the attention now given to formerly peripheral areas in the evolving multicentered, nodal, flexible, and globalized urban region.[7] This metropolitan regionalization has been taking a powerful hold, even though many inhabitants see themselves as "local", non-urban people. The existing dichotomy has been reinforced by recent developments (Körner and Ronneberger, 1994).

Power and Spatiality

We are starting to find in the periphery a socio-spatial structure as complex as (or even more complex than) in the inner city. This means that our traditional understanding of urban life and urban civil society is insufficient. The difference of core and periphery implies a competition between different factions of urban elites fighting over territorial control of the city or its important parts, in order to put their specific stamp on the structured coherence of this particular urban region. The first line of power is redrawn horizontally mostly within the urban elite and the middle classes. During Wallmann's regime in 1980s' Frankfurt, neo-urban (progressive and conservative) elites defined urban phenomena from the point of view of the core and continued to regard the periphery as a compensatory space (recreation, elite housing) and a container of problems (social housing megaprojects). By reclaiming the urban in its cosmopolitan world city incarnation as a positive force, these strata served as translators of global dynamics into local space (Keil and Lieser, 1992). To the neo-urban camp, urban oriented middle classes, who are still the most influential, popular faction of the political class in Frankfurt, the city they recognize and use has changed into a set of highly selected partial spaces wherein the periphery has a minor role. The model behind the resurgence of "urbanity" remains the 19th-century modern (European) metropolis.

In the periphery, and mostly with the newly arrived former urbanites whom we will call neo-rurals, concepts of "urban villages" have taken hold which borrow from images reaching back to a pre-industrial urban form. The world view of the neo-rurals is marked by a peculiar contradiction. A large part of the peripheral population is fairly dependent on the economic power of the metropolis for their professional success and income, and many of them have been contributors to the urbanization of the periphery. Yet it is particularly in the suburban areas, where the social and ecological consequences of the "growth machine" are starting to be felt, that various forms of "slow growth" and "no growth" movements spring up. The suburban actors, often economically strong and politically astute individuals and groups with professional backgrounds and histories of activism, distance themselves from urban ills by urging for them to be concentrated in the inner city or by advocating the concentration of problem areas outside their neighborhood elsewhere in the region. While they downplay the fact that they consume the cultural and commercial amenities of the central city, they would not want to miss the growing skyline as the symbolic representation of the power of the region and an aesthetic backdrop to their semi-rural lifestyles.

At the same time, a growing rupture along class lines is showing in the city's structured coherence. The formation of a world city economy was linked to a new type of polarization in urban society, highlighted by the rampant demographic internationalization of Frankfurt. "Citadel" functions produced low-wage, precarious labor markets and marginalized living conditions. While not as drastic as in cities like Los Angeles, the social structure of Frankfurt has changed from largely middle class and petty bourgeois Fordist equality with pockets of subculture and poverty to an increasingly polarized yet segmented inequality both in the socio-economic and spatial sense. In post-Fordist Frankfurt, the petty bourgeois and salaried middle classes are coming under pressure from two sides: firstly from the upper class elites who – by an array of cultural politics, gentrification and commercialization of former housing areas – have taken back the city; and secondly from the lower classes who have returned to the street life which had been believed to be sanitized in the wake of the postmodern restructuring of the 1980s.[8]

The *spatial* consequences of this dynamic are multiple and often contradictory. Peter Marcuse (1989) with his concept of the "quartered city" has attempted to find a typology which would capture the complexity of American urban space. He uses the categories luxury city, gentrified city, suburbia, tenement city and the abandoned city. These socio-spatial units (and possibly others) are now spatially redistributed in the city, their borders are redrawn and their social and physical environments are being restructured. Generally, we can observe similar dynamics in Frankfurt. On the one hand, unprecedented segmentation segregates the poor and the rich who are kept apart in social housing towers and condominium complexes respectively. On the other hand, the middle classes, who in previous eras of urbanization had been hoping to realize an autonomous privatized lifestyle, are now experiencing a close and inescapable proximity to metropolitan problems.

For our analysis, it is important to point out the mixture of fragmented (as opposed to large scale) segmentation and overall diffusion of residential and other uses of the city's public spaces as a specific spatialization of restructuring in Frankfurt. This "proximity"-model has immediate consequences for the political and social discourse on urbanity in Frankfurt. In the commercialized postmodern core of Frankfurt where homeless people and substance abusers are part and parcel of the daily shopping experience, as well as in the peripheral social housing areas where middle-class families now share buildings with welfare recipients, the middle classes find themselves confronted with the imponderable matters of urban life which they had considered to have reduced to a domestic scale in suburbia.[9]

The mode of regulation of the functional separation of lifestyles in the Fordist city begins to dissolve. Ideologically, the discourse of equality expressed in the feeble Fordist compromise (*nivellierte Mittelstandsgesellschaft*) has been replaced by a "renaturalization" of social and cultural difference, meaning that socially produced inequalities and injustices are redefined as necessary human conditions. In addition, this new inequality is concealed by the neo-urban middle class who had masterminded the discourse on urban life calling for a center-oriented, urban future for Frankfurt in the 1980s (Ronneberger, 1990). Poverty and conspicuous wealth had become accepted signs of the time during this period. The acceptance of difference, largely supplied with concepts of a pluralist discourse, has reached its limits in an increasingly racist reality.

In contrast to the American model, though, Frankfurt has not experienced clear, large-scale spatial segregation by "race", ethnicity, and social class.[10] While there are pockets of concentration of poor people, immigrants, etc. as well as rich enclaves throughout the city, the Frankfurt model of socio-spatial distribution remains one of segmented diffusion rather than segregation. Neither in negative terms (like forced exclusion) nor in positive terms (like in ethnic neighborhoods resembling North American Chinatowns) has the spatialization of residential populations reached the dimensions of segregation common in United States cities. In fact, the very concept of a "ghetto" has been warned against consistently by most politicians and civic leaders even when some have been suggesting that self-chosen clustering of ethnic populations – called congregation by some – might be a beneficial model of urban structuring in the future. Assimilation is the expected form of integration of foreigners into German society, which does not leave much breathing space for different cultural communities in German cities.[11] This public policy discussion is contextualized in Germany's general immigration policy debate. In contrast to other countries, in the case of the Federal Republic the so-called *Gastarbeiter*-system was introduced as a preventive measure against the status of an immigration country. The national state in Germany operates as an instrument of exclusion and marginalization. This is true for both the *jus sanguinis*-based German citizenship and the German population policies: from administrative measures regulating *Ausländerrückführung* (repatriation of foreigners), to discriminatory regulations governing the status of foreigners in Germany, to retrenchment in the treatment of asylum seekers.

Lastly, the vertical ruptures in Frankfurt's new landscape of power also point to *globalization* as a central issue. Demographic globalization can be seen at both ends of the regional labor market: in the highly paid jobs of the finance industry and related business services and in the low wage sectors, some of which are being created by the office boom downtown and in the peripheral centers. With a registered immigrant population of 190,000 and an additional estimated 12,000 to 30,000 non-documented immigrants, Frankfurt's landscape of power has been thoroughly globalized. The immigrant populations' national and ethnic make-up is changing rapidly from a largely Mediterranean guestworker-population to refugees and migrants from Eastern Europe and the Third World on the one hand and an international professional, clerical and managerial class on the other hand.

Poor immigrants still tend to live in or near the central city, in the working class neighborhoods along the Main river, where their share of the total population reaches up to 70 percent. But as they are driven out of these neighborhoods by gentrification and conversion of affordable housing, they can be found increasingly in the peripheral social housing projects built since World War II. It is actually in these peripheral districts where the increase in foreigners was most pronounced since 1970. The "blubber belt" is experiencing increasing social polarization. Poverty rates have risen rapidly during recent years. In 1980, the core cities of the Frankfurt–Rhein–Main (in the jurisdiction of Hesse) had three times as many welfare recipients than the suburban counties (*Kreise*); in 1994, this relationship was rather two to one (Bartelheimer, 1997, p. 111). Immigration and poverty are now growing faster in the rural and suburban counties than in the cores of the cities. In Frankfurt (45.3 percent), Offenbach (41.4 percent) and Darmstadt (36.7 percent), the share of foreigners in the population rose markedly less quickly than in the rural and suburban counties between 1987 and 1993: Limburg–Weilburg 109.7 percent; the Rheingau–Taunus Kreis 102.9 percent. "In the six counties adjacent to Frankfurt, migration developed at an average pace, while it increased more pronouncedly in the Taunus hills and in the Wetterau in the north and in the Main–Kinzig region in the East. These three counties had – with a share of less than 10 percent non-Germans in 1987 – the lowest percentage of immigrant settlement. Outside the immediate surroundings of Frankfurt, migration grew above average" (Bartelheimer, 1995, p. 40). This marginalizing peripheralization in fact means that the new city becomes the urban form of multinational society. The crisis of the outer city, from this perspective, appears as the crisis of the Third World come home. Frankfurt has become a significant hub of a new Europe of cities which also has become a Europe of urban peripheries.

Socio-spatial restructuring in Frankfurt reshuffled traditional categories of social identity and division in that city. Change was qualitative as much as it was quantitative. Frankfurt did, for example, not just add more "foreigners" to its population (from 78,857 in 1970 to 190,000 in 1995; or from 11.7 percent to 28 percent). The composition of this population changed simultaneously and the nature of migration shifted. In fact, while in the early 1970s discourse on foreign populations in Frankfurt was one of guestworkers and foreigners, the current discourse emphasizes immigration and multiculturality. We posit that this shift has dramatically altered the way in which we need to think about Frankfurt as a demographically internationalized city and the way in which socio-spatial relations in that city are defined. The lines of racism, as a visible reaction of native German residents of Frankfurt, have been redrawn as well. "Xenophobia", a term which denotes fear of strangers, is no longer a useful term to describe social relations between Germans and long-term residents of Frankfurt. Foreigners have become immigrants. Strangers have become neighbors.

Furthermore, socio-spatial segmentation is neither a natural process of succession and displacement nor result of such a process. Notions of market-driven segmentation can also not account entirely for social and spatial clustering. Rather, it has to be viewed as a political event and as the outcome of political and social struggles and decisions which occur at the level of the local state. It is to these political aspects that we now turn.

Social Struggles and Spatial Change: Core and Periphery in Turmoil

"My route (on bicycle) leads me past the university and down the Bockenheimer Landstraße. Here, in the early 1970s, we fought to stop the destruction of the lovely patrician homes – and lost. In their place stand postmodern office complexes, the symbols of Frankfurt's position as the financial center of Germany and Europe. My nostalgia for the noble old houses – which in our youthful zeal we occupied but whose leveling we failed to halt – is tempered with the pleasure at the sight of Frankfurt's new skyline. (But please don't tell anyone: my friends here would be shocked!)" Cohn-Bendit (1996, pp. 17–18).[12]

If globalization leads to a newly partitioned city, it does so only through the filter of localized political processes. The structural changes in the Frankfurt region over the past decade have been influenced, resisted, produced and furthered by various social and political activities of local agents. The emergence of a new urban form as described above is, in fact, connected to a distinctively novel sphere of social and political agency. During the past forty years, growth periods in Frankfurt have always been linked to forms of local resistance against the disadvantages of such growth for the resident population. Urban social conflicts usually erupted where the new phase of expansion manifested itself most visibly. At the end of the 1960s, when the CBD began to spread into the residential areas closest to the inner city, a culture of resistance developed in the largely middle class *Westend*. It resulted in a violent housing struggle (*Häuserkampf*) and a preservation ordinance (*Erhaltungssatzung*). In the early 1980s, when the expansion of the Frankfurt airport was pursued as the most obvious sign of Frankfurt's world city ambitions, the region saw its most severe social disturbances and struggles of post World War II history (Keil and Lieser, 1992).

The displacement of residential population from the inner-city neighborhoods and the conversion of apartments into office space were the main issues of urban discourse in the 1970s. The governing Social Democratic Party was intent on controlling emerging conflicts. This implied a more repressive stance of the local state. At the same time, however, more comprehensive and democratic planning processes were instituted. Increasing political repression against the radical squatters alongside more open and participatory planning processes made urban politics in Frankfurt during that era a contradictory affair. It eventually led to an irresolvable crisis of legitimacy for the Social Democratic government, a weakening of its powers *vis-à-vis* both the right-wing opposition and popular resistance. This phase of heavy social struggles ended with the end of a phase of radical opposition against the expansion of Fordist mono-structures and the dissolution of local Social Democratic hegemony by 1977.

During the 1980s, a host of inner city groups were continuing the struggle against the destruction of housing and community space by the expansion of the office economy. In both rhetoric and action, these groups were rehashing the anti-speculation-politics of the 1970s housing movement. Often based in the remnants of the 1970s left-wing radical milieu of communes and collectives, this traditional movement of resistance to the global city gained political support in the 1980s mostly from two groups. Both the fundamentalist wing of the local Green Party and working class activists from the trade union movement, from the far left of the SPD and from the German Communist Party (DKP) operated as the cadres of neighborhood-based struggles. In the case of the Campanile office tower project across the street from the central train station, a combination of political activism, legal rulings and a slump in the real estate market led to a surprise success of neighborhood political activism in keeping a major symbol of global economic forces out of the community. This project would have threatened the integrity of this neighborhood with a majority immigrant population. At the same time, however, in other parts of the city, this type of neighborhood-based defensive activism against gentrification and conversion of housing into office space, based on left wing ideologies and working-class neighborhood cultures, became increasingly irrelevant politically and was eclipsed by other forms of social protest. Throughout the end of the 1980s and into the 1990s, squatting as a form of defensive appropriation of urban living space and as a politics of resistance to gentrification became less relevant in the political discourse as a whole and even more isolated in the neighborhood than it had been in earlier years.

Throughout the 1970s and into the 1980s, opposition to growth was fueled by left-wing analyses of the urban process and integration of the urban struggle into the general context of anti-capitalist politics in the city as well as by petty bourgeois groups in defense of inner-city residential areas. In contrast to the eclectic 1970s combination of revolutionary rhetoric on the one hand and steadfast defense of property values and living space on the other hand, resistance to growth has now become a populist endeavor which does not lend itself to simple ideological classification. The cultural hegemony of modernity has given way to a contradictory and fragmented reality. Correspondingly, social agents in local movements are critical both of traditional forms of habitus and of specific consequences of modernization. Actors now often combined conservative, anti-modern ideology with an acceptance of technological or economic modernization without much effort. Local resistance to growth has, therefore, become increasingly hard to classify in terms of its material or ideological background.

Materially, social and political agents are faced with a new political space created by peripheral urbanization. In Frankfurt, this new emphasis on peripheral spaces as the real centers of growth turns areas which had until recently been agricultural and rural into complex modules of world city formation. Spaces in the geographical periphery of the city become crystals of current urbanization where contradictory growth dynamics occur in a variety of forms: Zones of affluence mix with marginalized housing areas; industrial development happens adjacent to a green belt-area; new housing construction both creates the need for and competes spatially with new infrastructure such as transportation corridors. This new thrust of urbanization was in turn met with protest and political resistance where it had or threatened to have its major effects. After the "discourse of the metropolis" had been pre-eminent throughout most of the 1980s, the impact of world city expansion now began to be noticed far beyond the citadel of the financial core, in the ex-urban spaces of the agglomeration. What growth meant was put up for discussion by new social groups who had mostly not been considered politically relevant during previous periods of expansion: long-time village dwellers, farmers, suburbanites. This complicated the very meaning of growth in public discourse. Class remains the most important qualifier in articulating residents' relationship to growth – both business and residential. The experience of social class (here understood in terms of income and property ownership) is embedded in a set of cultural conditions. Spatiality, ethnicity, gender, urban versus rural identity are some of these conditions. They influence the way in which social collectives and individuals attach themselves to questions of expansion in place-specific and peculiar ways that can only be understood through detailed empirical analysis. While such attachments and articulations follow certain general rules – like those elaborated upon by the political economy literature in the United States (Logan and Molotch, 1987) – they often take on unpredictable and often surprising forms.

In the western suburb of Sossenheim, for example, the encroachment of expansion triggered and shaped by world city growth (economic and demographic) has led to a unique constellation of social and political struggles articulated in complex ways with novel and traditional social identities. For a long time, German residents of housing estates have felt threatened by both immigration and the expansion of the metropolitan character of their neighborhood. They tend to perceive most changes as encroachments on the world they live in and their local identities. These identities have a core of class positions but are strongly influenced by the location of social groups on other socio-political faultlines: old versus new, native versus immigrant, periphery versus city, property owner versus tenant etc. (Körner and Ronneberger, 1994).

In the north of Frankfurt, the single most important peripheral conflict erupted when the red–green coalition municipal government decided to move the city's slaughterhouse from the banks of the Main River to a suburban location in the northern district of Nieder-Eschbach. The old site at the river was to be used for a major housing project which was part of the city authorities' ambitious plan to use the axis of the river as one of the focal points of Frankfurt's urban space.[13] In addition to angry protests against the slaughterhouse project, the city authorities also met with fierce resistance by mostly conservative citizens over major housing projects on the urban periphery.

The configuration of protest in the north of Frankfurt was characterized by a populist particularism which links the desire for local identity and the disdain for centralized urban planning on the one hand with aggressively protectionist status politics and the exclusion of marginal segments of society on the other hand. This political brew has led to a brand of populist regionalism created a challenge both to traditional left wing movement politics and to the established conservative mainstream in city politics. In any case, the events in north Frankfurt represent a clear departure from the notion that urban social movements in Frankfurt were hegemonized by the left wing or green milieu alone (Roth, 1991). Rather, as was expressed by the near total eclipse of Green Party politicians in the uprising of the north, the new populist milieu, while having connections to earlier periods of struggles, social institutions like trade unions or environmental groups and established parties, has developed an original and fairly independent stance (which is not to say that their ideas were new and without influence from outside developments). Far from being the lunatic fringe of Frankfurt's suburban political space or "uppity garden elves" as they were viewed by many of the traditional neo-urbanist political class in the center of Frankfurt, the new social agents are politically savvy, professionally educated middle-class activists whose populist agenda has anchored them deeply in the social space of the periphery.

Conclusion

The new spatial model has been sketched above with only the most important new lines of vertical and horizontal power shifts, but it clearly puts new demands on the regional mode of regulation which remains stuck in the logic of core–periphery. This is true both for conflicts pertaining to issues of spatial restructuring inside the municipality of Frankfurt and for intraregional affairs involving a number of local states. Politicians have hesitated to realize that Frankfurt by no means is autonomous but "the center, the inner city" of the Rhein–Main–Region. But in the mid 1990s, the global restructuring of Frankfurt–Rhein–Main is articulated mostly in a discourse of regionalization. This discourse mirrors the aspects of the current urban crisis: the metropolitanization of the region, "fattening" of the urban periphery and social peripheralization of the core. Metropolitanization means the dissolution of the city into the region.[14] The regionalist discourse builds on but increasingly replaces the discourse of urbanity which during the 1980s had focused on the development of the core. Regionalizing the urban crisis also means that conflicts are now spread all over the territory of Frankfurt and its environs. In contrast to previous images of core and periphery, the region is now increasingly being viewed as a complex urban landscape from which a new consciousness, a new politics, a new economic regime of accumulation as well as a new regional mode of regulation emerge.

The new geography of industrial and commercial development engenders a new structure of urban conflict. Generally, the importance of struggles over urban space has increased. Both core and periphery are in turmoil. Lines of social and spatial distinction and separation are redrawn in these conflicts. The very meaning of social status, territorial community, and urbanity is redefined as new spatial practices and representations evolve. Political and social practices of exclusion, especially racism, redraw the lines of racialization and prejudice and lead to new forms of discrimination (Grimm and Ronneberger, 1995). Policies and reformist concepts like multiculturalism gain currency and redefine identities of social groups. In the city center, socially marginalized people, remaining liberal middle class groups, and residual forces from older urban social movements wage a defensive battle against the takeover of the built environment by global capital, mostly symbolized by more office towers. On the edge of the city, farmers and suburbanites have embarked on a campaign against the threat to their livelihoods, privileges and lifestyles posed by what they call "urbanization." Perhaps the election of conservative Petra Roth, a political representative of the northern periphery, as mayor of Frankfurt in the summer of 1995 was an indication of the emerging power of the "blubber belt" even in the city itself.

While the causes of urban growth in Frankfurt appear expressed in rather abstract terms at first sight (globalization, restructuring), it has become clear that the real globalized flows of capital and people moving into and out of the city are very concretely guided, fought over and facilitated by local actors. Local actors rarely initiate growth and decline but they do have to deal with the consequences of each new period of creative destruction. For the time being, competing centralized neo-urban notions and peripheral neo-rural notions of regionalism are engaged in a struggle of middle-class hegemony in an entirely globalized urban region. Competing concepts of regional hegemony include politically articulated ideas and practices of exclusion, segregation and separation. Frankfurt's immigrant communities have started to express their identities and demands on the political world of the global city in their own terms and with the help of policy reforms at the municipal level. Our analysis of Frankfurt shows that spatial restructuring cannot be understood as a purely statistical event in which social categories (class, ethnicity, gender) or spatial categories (neighborhood, city, region, countryside) remain unchanged. Social and spatial restructuring rather must be seen as a complex process resulting from and producing social struggles and the articulation and disarticulation of different spatial images of local and global agents in the urban. As yet, no clearly delineated regional mode of regulation has emerged. In the absence of a viable progressive alternative both to unrestricted access of global capital to every nook and cranny of the region and to restrictive conservative–populist tendencies, the search for a new regionalism based on communitarian democracy and negotiated spatial compromise (Lipietz, 1992) remains a main task.

Notes

1 On world city formation see Friedmann (1986) and Keil (1993, pp. 21–27).
2 We have documented and interpreted the rise of Frankfurt as a world city or global city widely elsewhere and can, unfortunately, not repeat it here without exceeding the purpose of this chapter which is more narrow in scope. Please see the following publications for more detailed reference: Lieser and Keil (1988); Keil and Lieser (1992); Keil and Ronneberger (1994); Ronneberger (1994); Ronneberger and Keil (1993; 1995).
3 On global city formation as a narrative of eviction see Sassen (1994).
4 These tendencies can be studied in Freyberg (1996) and Bartelheimer (1997).
5 We have discussed these discourses extensively in Ronneberger and Keil (1995).
6 We are aware of the recent discussions around the regulation school's major categories, particularly in the British context (for an excellent summary see a special issue of Economy and Society, Volume 24 (3) (August 1995)). While we share the concern of many participants in these discussions to move away from a static Fordism/post-Fordism distinction in the direction of seeing regulation as a process (rather than a fixed mode), we would like to stick with the periodization for a variety of reasons. When we say "post-Fordism", we do not mean to imply that a clearly defined new regime of accumulation/mode of regulation has materialized after the crisis of Fordism but that we are clearly not in Fordism anymore. "Post" here stands simply for "after"; the local or regional mode of regulation we describe here for Frankfurt is fleeting and unstable, as will become clear.
7 We have documented these struggles in detail in Keil and Ronneberger (1994) and Ronneberger and Keil (1995).

8   It is necessary to point out that – in contrast to most American cities yet similar
     to many European and Canadian cities – significant parts of Frankfurt's middle
     classes embraced urban living and central residential locations as positive values
     around which they organized their spatial and cultural politics.

9   The uncomfortable proximity of various "user groups" in the inner city is con-
     stantly subject to attempts by the provincial government to regulate and order
     their relationships. The public space of the inner city is increasingly cleared of
     unwanted users and inhabitants: the poor, the immigrants. Subcultures are
     being displaced from there through a combination of economic and police
     pressures.

10   There is only now a nascent discussion on long term poverty and the concept of
     an "(urban) underclass" in Germany. Bremer and Gestring (1997) end their
     recent overview discussion of new forms of exclusion in German cities in the
     following way: "The term *underclass* denotes a new quality of a social split, the
     emergence of a stratum of people who are continuously excluded from the labor
     market, live in poverty and are dependent on transfer payments by the state."
     They continue to observe that while German poverty research has maintained
     that poverty is mostly a temporary event, we can now say with some certainty
     that " . . . a segment of the poor suffers long term exclusion even in the Federal
     Republic [of Germany]. We have shown that certain groups of foreign residen-
     tial populations are threatened to a high degree by exclusion" (1997, p. 73). The
     authors conclude that both early post-war guestworkers (*Gastarbeiter*) and current
     asylum seekers have been relegated to underclass status over the past decades.
     However, it is important, while recognizing the systematic discrimination against
     Germany's migrants, to use the contentious term "underclass" with care, in
     order not to conceptionally collapse the US situation with the German one and
     in order to avoid the conceptual problems of the term itself.

11   For a discussion of local immigration policy of the *Amt für multikulturelle Angelegenheiten*
     in Frankfurt after 1989 see Friedmann and Lehrer (1997). The AMKA can be
     understood as a locally specific response to a nationally restrictive immigration
     policy in Germany.

12   Dany Cohn-Bendit, a leader of the French student rebellion in Paris 1968, has
     been Frankfurt's municipal councillor for multicultural affairs and has been a
     member of the European Parliament for both the German and French Green
     Parties.

13   In the end, the new slaughterhouse was never built. For a while the old facility
     was maintained and, in the future, meat for the Frankfurt markets will be
     supplied by other slaughterhouses in the region. For a more detailed analysis of
     the red–green government's relationship with urban civil society in Frankfurt
     see Ronneberger and Keil (1993).

14   Further on regionalization see Prigge and Ronneberger (1995).

12

Conclusion: A Changed Spatial Order

Peter Marcuse and Ronald van Kempen

In this concluding essay, we begin by describing the changes that we have found in the spatial order of cities, both from the pieces in this volume and from our own other work and analyses.[1] They fall into three areas:

- strengthened structural spatial divisions with increased inequality among them and increasing walling between each;
- specific new (in prevalence and depth) spatial formations within these structural divisions; and
- a set of "soft" locations in which change is taking place.

We then explore some frequently used terms in the globalization discussion, and challenge some generalizations about them:

- American exceptionalism
- globalization
- global cities
- globalizing cities

Thinking back over our collective work, we then express some cautions about the state of our knowledge and some limitations of a too rigid approach to comparative studies, pushing generalizations in the face of multiple contingencies. Specifically, we are concerned with:

- the limitations of spatial analysis of societal change
- the necessity of seeing the different dimensions of the layered city; and
- the multiple contingencies in the comparative analysis.

We conclude by presenting our present view of the answer to the question: "is there a new spatial order of cities," with a final comment on the policy implications of our analysis.

The Changed Spatial Pattern

Strengthened structural spatial divisions

The concept of divisions underlies a great deal of recent discussions of urban development. We referred in the Introduction to the literature on divided cities, dual cities, quartered cities, fragmented cities. While they differ in their descriptions of the number of parts into which the city is divided and the nature of those parts, the contributions in this book support (although with significant variations) the conclusion that division is increasing, and that there is something at least worth serious concern in the extent of that increase. Hence our conclusion that the nature and extent of divisions are one clear indicator, at the most basic level, of what is happening to cities under the influence of globalization.

Cities have always shown functional, cultural and status divisions, but the differentiation between areas has grown and lines between the areas have hardened, sometimes literally in the form of walls that function to protect the rich from the poor. What is more: the relation between these stronger spatial differentiation is a double one. On the one hand, walls, literal or symbolic, prevent people from seeing, meeting and hearing each other; at the extremes, they insulate and they exclude. Contact across the walls is minimal, and if it takes places, business-like and commodified.

On the other hand, within the walls life can be lived in its totality: places of residence, of work, of recreation, of socialization, are increasingly available within the walls themselves, whether it be the citadel, the edge city, or the excluded ghetto. The quarters of the city become *totalized*. Everyday life can be reasonably conducted within the quarter itself, and the necessity – and the opportunity – for external contact is steadily diminished.

The divisions of space are not only the product of divisions in society; they help to create those divisions. Those within the walls of the upper quarters decide for the others what will happen in the spheres of economic activity, government, and to an increasing extent cultural and social life. Partially out of self-interest and partially simply because they do not see, meet and hear the others, decisions painful to others are easily made. Goldsmith has indicated this process very well in his chapter: following Sennett (1970) he states that where those in power have to rely on television and other media for knowledge of those below, we might end up in a situation in which opinions are only formed by stereotypes and decisions are made on the basis of uninformed preconceptions.

Structural economic and political change produces both extreme wealth and extreme poverty, concentrated power and concentrated powerlessness, ghettoization and citadelization, and not by accident: the decrease at the one end is in large part the result of the increase at the other. The distribution of power, and to an important extent of wealth, inevitably has winners and losers. And changes at both ends have major impacts on the life-worlds of those in between, the various segments of the "middle class." Isolation from the unlike and homogenization with the like, essentially two faces of the same development, physically as well as culturally, become prevalent in all quarters.

So the changing spatial order of cities exhibits two characteristics: divisions between quarters, with each quarter more and more cut off from its surroundings, and a totalizing trend, in which each quarter more and more internalizes within its boundaries all of the necessities of life. But each characteristic represents trends manifest well before the period of globalization, and is represented in cities in various relationships to globalization. Whether the scale of change, clearly accelerated if not caused by globalization, is sufficient to call the result a new spatial order is a judgment call. Our conclusion is that it is not.

Nor is the definition of the structural components of the city radically different from what it had been in earlier periods, over the last hundred if not two hundred years. It is not a two-part division, with partitions, walls, between those two only. In sophisticated discussions, such as those around the "two-thirds society" in Germany, the two-part division has a direct political import: it is between those doing well and those doing poorly, those benefiting and those paying, the winners and the losers. It has real value in pointing out that there are indeed losers as well as winners in the process of economic advance, of challenging the notions of unitary societies (or unitary cities) in which all sink or all swim together. But it also has real dangers, not only in the suggestion that the majority is doing well, and thus change is unlikely, but also in eliding the substantial differences among those who are indeed doing well at any given time, but in quite different fashion, with different vulnerabilities, different disadvantages, different roles, and perhaps different interests in change. It further underplays the differences among those who are not doing well, differences often (particularly when accompanied by "racial" or ethnic differences) dividing the lower one-third not only from the upper two-thirds but also from each other.

The more complex divisions suggested in earlier work (Marcuse, 1989), based on the quartered city analysis, holds up in general based on the presentations in this book, but only in general. It is sharpest at the extremes, with the partitions between the excluded ghetto and the rest of the city and between the luxury city and the rest of the city. Ask any resident where the most impoverished ethnic or "racial" minority live in any globalizing city (we take up the definition of "globalizing" below), and they will tell you; likewise, they will tell you where the very rich and very powerful live and work. But the likelihood of human contact with others outside the excluded ghetto or the luxury city by their residents, across the lines separating them spatially, is small – contact other than in a temporally limited and purely functional way, e.g. as servants to the rich or beggars seeking charity.

Social contact across class lines has always been limited, of course; what is different today is the sharpness of the spatial boundaries inhibiting such contact, the extent of the concentration by class within those boundaries. For the luxury city, the boundaries, sometimes collective as in gated communities or citadels, sometimes in separate free-standing high-rise buildings, are physical: entrance is barred to those having no business there. For the excluded ghetto, its boundaries are known and maintained, for outsiders by the perception of danger, for insiders by the multiple forms of discrimination encountered on the outside and the triage practiced on the inside.

Other quarters, however, while showing increased clustering and more perceptible boundaries, are still more fluid in their composition, their boundaries more permeable and more elastic. Thus technical experts and professionals, although not in decision-making roles, may be spatially close to those who do make decisions, certainly by day, to some extent by night (hence the reference to the "layered city," below). Suburban middle-class areas house better-earning factory or construction workers as well as small-business people and many professionals. The market segregates by price, as it always did, and while the lines of separation may be clearer, with no need for crude redlining to enforce them, the underlying pattern of differentiation is the same.

The resulting pattern, in structural terms, is not so different from what it was in earlier periods. Change lies rather (in addition to changes in the lines between them, discussed above) within the components of that structure.

New socio-spatial formations within the divisions

Rather than structural change in the basis of divisions, what has become clear to us as we have worked on this book is that there are formations within each of these quarters of the city that are indeed new – new, not in the sense of without precedent, but new in that their prevalence, their prominence, their magnitude, put together justify calling them new. There are three ways of looking at the impact of macro-societal factors on the internal spatial structure of cities. One is at the structural level: on a macro basis, to try to generalize from macro forces, and formulate a set of broad spatial patterns that will be more or less congruent to broad societal patterns. The literature using such concepts as dual city, divided city, fragmented city, is in this vein; the quartered city formulation we used in the Introduction is an explicit effort in this direction (see, e.g., Marcuse, 1989; Mollenkopf and Castells, 1991, last chapter). A second way is to begin at the opposite end, the level of places: it is the most concrete, and would look at the particular types of space most likely to be affected by macro forces and generalize from there: to look at waterfronts, for instance, or old industrial sites. Several of the contributors to this book give persuasive evidence of what can and cannot be learned from such changed an approach, and we use it in the discussion of "soft" locations below. In this Conclusion, however, we attempt an intermediate approach, at what might be called the level of socio-spatial formations.[2] We find at least seven such changed formations defined by spatial and social characteristics: citadels, gentrified neighborhoods, exclusionary enclaves, urban regions, edge cities, ethnic enclaves and excluded "racial" ghettos. These formations and their relationship to the more general structural spatial developments are strongly related to the processes of globalization, and we believe merit much further attention.

Citadels, in the form of hi-tech, generally hi-rise megaprojects, are becoming prevalent throughout the world, from London to Shanghai, Los Angeles to Kuala Lumpur, Detroit to São Paulo, Paris to Bandung. Of the cities discussed in this book, Frankfurt, New York City, Sydney, Singapore and Brussels contain classic examples, as does Tokyo, where citadels of government and of business share the skyline; Calcutta is on the way; Rio de Janeiro would like to be. The architectural style remains modern; it was dubbed the international style already in 1932, but has really earned that name now. Postmodern treatment of the edges (or more literally the tops) of such edifices do nothing to alter the modern technical rationality of their construction. Fashions in styles may vary, but the representation of power, of wealth, of luxury, is inherent, as is the isolation, the separation, the distancing from the older urban surroundings. The grid of lower Manhattan may be carried into the street pattern of Battery Park City and visible to an interested observer in a helicopter, but the separation of the World Trade Center/Battery Park City complex from the rest of the city visually, and in terms of secure entrance, is obvious to all.

The use of the citadels is not however confined to those living in the luxury city; professionals, technicians, managers, administrators to carry out the functions assigned to them are indispensable. And, layered in time, the janitors, parking garage attendants, security guards needed for the effective operation of the citadel must be allowed in. Residentially, a few may walk to work there from the gentrified city, the city of the gentry, if it has a foothold nearby; some may fly in by helicopter to land on the roof landing pads that characterize, for instance, almost every office building in Bernini, in São Paulo; but most will commute in by some form of limited transportation access, likely to be expensive but publicly subsidized, and likely to permit access even from a distance without treading on the ground of the rest of the more mundane city.

Gentrified neighborhoods are well known to the literature, and their essential characteristics were described in our Introduction. Functionally, globalization has produced a class of professionals, managers, technicians, that may well be analogized to the gentry of earlier days in feudal systems. As they increase in numbers, so do they increase in importance and in income, and the residential locations they choose become ever more clearly identified and separated. The gentrified city is often located in the inner parts of the older cities, or in neighborhoods adjacent to this part. The attractiveness of areas close to the inner cities, the places where "urban" activity is centered, is particularly attractive to the gentry; and because these are often areas formerly occupied by the working class, the link between gentrification and displacement is close (Marcuse, 1985).

The relationship between gentrified areas and citadels requires further detailed investigation. There is probably, in each urban area, a separation between those truly in control, and those who work for them, even at high levels within organizational structures. The separation is probably visible in the size and location of second homes, but very likely of first homes also. The top of the hierarchy is not likely to be involved in the process of gentrification, although, after a neighborhood has been converted, units within it may serve them as *pieds-à-terre*. More likely, they will find more convenient accommodation, whether within the citadels themselves or in the older fashionable upper-class neighborhoods of the city.

Exclusionary enclaves are not new in the world, but their spread has been phenomenal in the last several decades. The walled communities of the rich, gated communities more closed from the rest of society than ever before, are now to be found, not only in the United States, but also in Johannesburg, Rio de Janeiro and many cities all over the world. Such luxury sites are still not very usual in European countries, but are becoming more and more important there also. We would expect to see a substantial expansion of these kinds of enclaves, housing many of those most directly benefiting from processes of globalization, business people, managers, leading artists and politicians, who have homes in many places of the world and are quite able to live isolated from their immediate surroundings. The residents live in walled communities, not spatially dependent on any particular geographical location in relation to the rest of the city. They rather create and control their own environment at the micro level.

Walling and gating by themselves are not sufficient to define a socio-spatial pattern, for the fact (or the symbol) of gating has spread to virtually all sectors of society; today one finds public housing projects in the United

States, middle class suburbs, upper-middle class enclaves, retirement communities, with walls of various sorts around them, or with the equivalent measures designed to provide physical protection against social dangers (Blakely and Snyder, 1995; Marcuse, 1997a). It is the extent of this development, with a specific focus on its appearance for communities of those made prosperous by the processes of economic change, to which we wish to call attention here.

Exclusionary enclaves have been formed, not only by the gentry, but also around some areas of the rich, and are wished for, and often obtained, by residents of the suburban city, and even on occasion by those in the working class. Passing a certain stage in life, retirement communities may house (although separately) people with varying economic resources and earlier positions. Gentrified areas, almost by definition, cannot erect walls to define their boundaries, since they are encroachments on and reuses of areas previously occupied by poorer residents. Here the exclusion and control are accomplished by social, rather than physical, means (although individual buildings will have their own security systems, bars on windows, fences and gates at entry): the police presence will be enhanced, and private security guards will patrol.

Regionalization both of residences and workplaces is the general phenomenon of which edge cities are a major component. As Keil and Ronneberger describe it most specifically, it goes well beyond the metropolitanization and sprawl that have long been known. It includes not only edge city development but also closer relationships between long-time independent cities to form economically integrated regions. In this book, the "insular configurations" described around Frankfurt, Waley's description of the developments around Tokyo, and Chakravorty's of "new town" development around Calcutta, reveal the regional nature of development "at the edge."

Edge cities are a component of these new regions that may be seen as a totalized form of the suburban city that is significantly new. The definition of course cannot be that used by Garreau (1991), for he considers only those that in fact have only recently been built, rather than all those that carry the function of edge cities, and attributes their existence to simple consumer preferences, while in fact they are the results of much more complex processes in which consumer preferences initially play a very minor role. Our reference here is to clusters of residence, business, commerce, and recreation, on an urban scale, removed from major central cities but related to them, whose independence in daily life from those central cities is in large part their reason for being. Keil and Ronneberger's discussion of Frankfurt in this volume highlights the regional view which must be taken to understand properly the economic as well as social role of such edge cities. As opposed to metropolitan development, or megacity growth, the point here is insulation, the down-playing of dependence, coupled with the development of activities that emulate and in fact bring to the suburban location the same international business firms, the same professional consulting activities, the same cultural amenities, the same concerts and museums and theaters, the same religious institutions, that the central city has, if on a smaller scale.

Ethnic enclaves (to be distinguished both from exclusionary enclaves and from excluded ghettos) are perhaps the purest form, the functional equivalent, of the working class quarters of the traditional industrial cities of the 19th century. The pattern is the same everywhere (and only stringent government regulation prevents its reproduction in Singapore): new arrivals in the cities are used for lower-paid work, exploited more than their longer fellow-residents might tolerate, and residentially stay together for mutual support in difficult conditions. In time, such areas may lose their economic function because the pressures that prompted their residents to maintain them have abated, though residents of similar cultural or ethnic or religious background may still stay near each other, as Logan shows for New York City. The clustering such data shows may be seen as moving from the economic to cultural as its binding force. Singapore provides another example: as Van Grunsven describes it, the reclustering of Malays in social housing despite strenuous governmental efforts to produce integration shows the strength of cultural ties (as well, perhaps, as the lack of real economic and political integration).

The *excluded ghetto*, as defined in our Introduction, seems to be, thus far, primarily a phenomenon of the United States. It takes, in our analysis, a specific combination of "racial", political and economic circumstances to produce such a ghetto: specifically, a combination of 1) a new form of urban poverty, long-lasting and deep and excluded from the expectation of conjunctural change, 2) discrimination against a specific and identifiable (most readily by color) group, discrimination with wide social prevalence and deep historical roots, but against a group with strong formal claims to equality and full citizenship, and 3) the absence of countervailing state action.

The first of these factors, the new form of urban poverty, exists not only in the United States, but has its parallel in almost every major city in the world. In some cases, such as Calcutta or Rio de Janeiro, it is overlaid on a century or more of both abysmal poverty and social exclusion; in others, as in Sydney or Frankfurt, it is a new appearance, a matter of growing concern but yet nowhere near the dimensions of the first group. In New York City, it is well documented (e.g., Fainstein et al., 1992); in Tokyo, Waley suggests here, official denial of the existence of concentrated poverty is probably contrary to fact. But the tendency to impoverishment and exclusion is detectable in all globalizing cities, and its sources have been extensively elucidated in the literature. The second characteristic, discrimination against an easily targeted group, is also increasingly visible in many places, and a source of concern in most. By and large that discrimination is against non-citizens, however, so that the claims that account for some of the tensions in "race" relations in the United States are absent. Where there is full citizenship and concern about discriminatory treatment, as in West Germany against residents of the former East German state, there is no color line to facilitate discrimination, and the spatial pattern tends to be more regionally based than intra-urban. In other cases, as in the Netherlands, the third factor is critical: affirmative state action to avoid ghetto formation (see Van Kempen and Priemus, 1997).

Thus the pattern of "racial" exclusion and segregation as found in the United States is not at this time replicated elsewhere on any comparable scale. Whether the forces that lead to economic polarization and the social relations attendant on immigration will spread after the pattern of the United States remains a matter not yet determined. On the issue of levels of discrimination, William Goldsmith argues strongly that the very strength of the pattern in the United States influences directly the strength of patterns elsewhere, thus an argument supporting the expectation of increased replication of the United States pattern. But it is also clear that the end result, in spatial as well as social terms, will be dependent to a large degree on the future direction of governmental policies and their implementation in each country.

Soft[3] *locations*

We outlined, in the Introduction, our expectation that there would be a particular set of locations in which the processes of globalization and post-Fordist economic change were likely to have a particular impact. Recapitulating but adding to that list:

- waterfronts
- currently centrally located manufacturing areas
- brownfields (formerly industrial sites)
- central city office and residential locations
- central city amusement locations and tourist sites
- concentrations of social housing
- locations on the fringe of central business districts
- historic structures
- public spaces

Beauregard and Haila have looked at some of these locations: waterfronts, brownfields and centrally located manufacturing areas (hollowed-out manufacturing zones), and suburbs (edge cities). They conclude that in each case there are changes, but that they follow earlier changes and are part of older patterns of change as well as new ones. That point can, of course, be made, *pari passu*, of all of the soft locations mentioned above. But the chapter also concludes that spatial change in the already built environment lags behind broader social and economic changes, and the question now becomes, as time goes on, will the changes grow and/or turn into something "new?" Bearing in mind our earlier comment on the imprecision of the concept "new," we here present some tentative conclusions for the areas mentioned above.

Waterfronts: Building on arguments made by Beauregard/Haila and Chakravorty in this volume, two periods may be separated out in the evolution of the use of waterfronts in the last one hundred years. The first has to do with the role of shipping. In the most industrialized countries, waterfronts are no longer vital shipping or trans-shipping locations. In many cities where they had once played a central role, shipping is rather concentrated in fewer locations where larger scale facilitates, efficient modernization, and inland transportation access is good. Thus New York City, originally located where it is because of its harbor, now finds most of its waterfront obsolete for shipping purposes. That is a phenomenon that has indeed been going on since the 1920s, and certainly since the 1950s.

Sometime thereafter, however, a second phase of change set in. Modern port development changed the old nature of waterfront activity radically, in some cases replacing it with large-scale modern facilities, sometimes in areas distant from old port activities (London, Tokyo), in other cases reducing it in favor of major new port development outside the city (Calcutta, Rio de Janeiro). In the older cities in the industrialized world in which economic restructuring and globalization have reduced or eliminated industrial uses of the waterfront, major efforts developed, struggling against heavy past investment in the built environment, to transform the nature and uses of the waterfront. And closely related, as we see it, to the current process of globalization, and thus defining a new period in the evolution of waterfronts as locations, is the absorption of these previously neglected and under-utilized waterfront areas as adjuncts to the growing dominance of downtown service-oriented activities for the benefit of the new gentry. Waterfronts become amenities making CBDs more attractive. The common cultural essence of these reuses are traced in Beauregard Haila's contribution here. The movement from the first phase to the second phase warrants the characterization of major change, although the process of change is itself hardly new.

Centrally located manufacturing locations: Again, we find a long-term process of change, and "new" developments. The movement of large-scale manufacturing from crowded central locations to the outskirts of cities has long been noted; greenfield sites are both physically and economically more advantageous for large-scale manufacturing, and the transportation and communication disadvantages of outlying sites have steadily been reduced or in fact reversed. The extension of this trend to small manufacturing, however, including to those involved in production directly related to other central city activities (e.g. printing, fashion dress design, repair facilities), is of more recent origin. These are activities conducted more efficiently in close proximity to the center, unlike the earlier out-movers. But they also are being displaced, as the growth of pure service sector activities and their internationally-linked financial returns raises real estate prices to the point where socially incompatible uses are displaced, even if economically integral to the activities displacing them. The current dispute about the rezoning of the area occupied by printing firms in the heart of the business district of New York City is an example.

Brownfield sites: Certainly the movement of manufacturing activities from less to more favorable locations (whether physically or economically judged) is not a new phenomenon. The difference between brownfield locations, generally not in the centers of cities, and those described above is that here the process is not of displacement, as in central locations, but rather simply of abandonment. Partially because of the difficulty of adapting the massive built form of outdated industrial plants to other uses (although cases exist of transformation of warehouses to condominiums, artist's lofts, etc.) and partially because of enduring environmental pollution, such sites often find no re-use: hence "hollowed-out." The scale of such hollowing-out has significantly accelerated in the period of globalization, as is traced above. It is also beginning to affect locations recently developed, where there is no physical problem of obsolescence but simply shifts of international or national investment: thus automotive plants built in São Paulo on what were greenfield sites just thirty years ago now face abandonment. The pace of the process of industrial abandonment seems to be remarkably accelerated today.

Locations of *concentrations of social housing* of have been subject to much study recently (Power, 1997; Vale, 1993; Varady et al., 1998). Some of the issues are large-scale, as in the rehabilitation of the large developments built in the after-war years throughout eastern Europe and in much of the West. Other concerns deal with inner-city high-rise developments, often deteriorating for political as well as physical and social reasons. The problems are not, of course, new, but the process of globalization and its accompanying economic changes and social impacts, in particular polarization of incomes and exclusion, put concentrated locations of social housing at the center of issues of segregation and abandonment or gentrification. The locational aspects of these problems, and their relationship to the overall spatial structure of cities, is however as yet under-researched.

Other soft locations have been dealt with in various contributions in this volume, as well as in many other places. Gentrification is an aspect of change in *locations on the fringe of central business districts*, but such locations are subject to other forms of change besides gentrification: sometimes simply clearance to provide amenity benefits to the center, sometimes changes of uses, from low-level to high-level services (warehousing to offices or residences), or from office to residence or the reverse, or for transportation infrastructure whose location and form have clear dividing effects. In general, the result is a shift in uses from residential to business, meaning generally a net reduction in the residential use of central areas, as Waley for instance points out in Tokyo.

The examples above suggest that an approach focusing on "soft locations" deserves more thorough comparative study than it has hitherto received. The attitudes towards *structures of historic meaning*, for instance, have changed significantly in the last few decades, in ways not unrelated specifically to the pressures of globalization. As national boundaries are more readily and frequently crossed, the threat to local identity mounts; at the same time, the importance of identity, and specifically the linkage of identity to territory (in different ways both on the national, the regional and the local level) grows.

Public spaces have similarly undergone significant change, in form, usage, and control. The general movement is towards private control of what is done in public spaces. Sometimes that private control is exercised through pressure on public authorities, as in the "cleaning up" of Times Square (New York) or "amusement districts" in European cities; sometimes it is done directly privately, as in the use of private security guards by Business Improvement Districts or the managers of gated communities. Sometimes, ironically, the privatization of public space comes about through the offering of semi-public facilities in legally private spaces, e.g. malls, shopping centers. The net result is the same: the amount and openness of space for "public" activities is eroded (Christopherson, 1994). *Tourist locations* are increasingly prominent as the object of both public attention and private investment, producing spatial changes in many cities. Thus a common pattern of change in comparable locations is visible, though it does not rise to the scale of a new structural spatial order, because it largely represents a continuation of pre-existing trends.

The Dangers of Common Generalizations

American exceptionalism

William Goldsmith, one of our contributors, has written (1997): "European cities are the envy of the world. They enjoy prosperity and harmony" (p. 299) and " . . . compared either to cities in America or those of the Third World, they still are well-watered oases in a world of urban drought" (p. 310). Although he might be overstating the positive aspects of European cities, we think that indeed the comparison between American cities – and especially those in the United States – and cities elsewhere reveals striking contrasts, contrasts derived from their location in different states, with different ideologies, different economies, different histories, different physical settings. Extreme situations like the new urban ghetto and the exclusionary enclave are, however, not something weird and typical only of urban areas on one side of the north Atlantic. Dangers that such areas will become typical for other cities are evident, and the tendencies in that direction are revealed in the contributions in this book.

But is the exclusionary ghetto at this time typical of the United States only? For the moment we would say yes, because only in the United States can we find the awkward combination of economic developments that lead to structural unemployment with racism, and with a private market ideology which in combination legitimate the exclusion of the poor and the concomitant restricted influence of the state. These are the factors that lead to ghetto formation. According to Badcock (this volume) and Stilwell (1996), Australian cities do not have ghettos. According to Dutch researchers, the same holds for the Netherlands (e.g. Van Kempen 1997).

If we accept that the excluded ghetto is now a typical US phenomenon, the next question would be if we expect the excluded ghetto to emerge in other countries and on other continents in due time. Tendencies certainly point in this direction. The retreat of the welfare state in Western European countries, in combination with bad economic perspectives, especially for those who have the wrong education, and more specifically for those who belong to specific ethnic or racial groups – the former guestworkers in Western Europe are a case in point must be seen as a dangerous combination of factors and developments (Van Kempen and Van Weesep, 1998). The situation in Third World countries, on the other hand, presents a substantially different pattern from that of those in the first World; Sanjoy Chakravorty makes the point explicitly, and we return to it below in the discussion of contingencies.

Thus the trends to be found in the United States are not strikingly different from the trends in other developed countries discussed in this book, although the patterns resulting from them may have developed further. The United States manifests many of these trends – and in particular the development of the excluded ghetto – in extreme form. The reason for the differences are not so hard to find: size and wealth, permitting a tolerance for a degree of social tension by providing a way out and a general lifting of boats (from the movement west to the exploitation of vast natural resources to triumph in the last world war); a historical tradition of little government, with a free private market ideology; and racism, which legitimates the exclusion of a major group of citizens. Thus, the contingencies that differentiate developments in the United States from those in other countries are variations in the same contingencies that differentiates each country from the others.

Globalization, global cities, globalizing cities

Globalization is a controversial concept, whose very definition is unclear. We have specified our use of the term in the Introduction. While there is little doubt that the process of globalization is a real one, it is still unclear how far the effects of globalization reach in particular cities. What has become clear from the present book is that what is changing is related to the processes of globalization, but not only globalization, and often indirectly more than directly. If globalization is understood with the contents we have outlined in the Introduction, then it is only one of a number of contingencies in explaining the formation of changes in the spatial order: we begin to enumerate the others we find central below.

Further, globalization is an extension of an internationalization of economic activity that has been going on since history began, marked by a radically increased mobility of capital and international integration of production and control, facilitated by advances in communications and transportation technology. The decline of the provision of welfare by the state, most explicitly symbolized by Thatcher in the United Kingdom and Reagan in the United States, is a shift in what the state does, not a decline in its overall role. The state remains even more involved in facilitating business activity than before (Panitch, 1998), but with less redistributive intent than in the immediate postwar period. Labor organizations are weaker, and capital stronger, both as a result and as a cause of these tendencies; union membership has declined dramatically since the immediate postwar period. Thus the ability of working class forces and their allies to move, or keep, the state in a welfare orientation, and to resist the negative impacts of globalization on working conditions and employment, is severely diminished.

Thus globalization, important as it is, is only one of the forces determining the spatial pattern of cities, and a force not coming into play for the first time in the recent period. It must be seen as the extension of forces already present over a much longer period of time.

Global cities is a term that has become accepted as a way to describe cities at the apex of a postulated global hierarchy of cities, determined primarily by their role as locations of the control functions of multinational finance. Aspects of two of the cities universally included among the "global," Tokyo and New York, are commented on in chapters in this volume. They are very different from each other in their spatial configurations. While they have trends in common, they have major differences, and do not lend themselves to the construction of some "generally applicable model of the 'global city'" (Harloe and Fainstein, 1992, p. 246), abstracted from historical context and other contingencies. And they each have trends in common with, and major differences from, cities lower in the international hierarchy of cities, as the other contributors in this volume show. Keil and Ronneberger would propose Frankfurt as a global city, but stress that it is the region as a whole that should thus considered. Logan raises doubts as to whether economic change is so different in New York from that in "non-global" cities. Waley, in the other "global city" discussed in this volume, argues that the "new" spatial patterns there are as much an accentuation of pre-existing trends as a product of a new globalization. For purposes of examining changes in spatial form, the "global cities" focus is something of a red herring.

Globalizing cities is thus the term we are using, to reflect two different points: that (almost)[4] all cities are touched by the process of globalization and that involvement in that process is not a matter of being either at the top or the bottom of it, but rather of the nature and extent of influence of the process. We do *not*, by using the term, suggest that the nature of that involvement is uniform, and certainly not that all cities are converging on a single model of "globalized" city. And in fact it may be appropriate to speak of "deglobalizing cities," at least relatively: Rio de Janeiro, as Telles and Ribiero describe it, may be such a one.

The Limitations of a Purely Spatial Focus

Even though the metaphor of the divided city, or the quartered city with walls between the quarters, highlights key changes, in scale if not in nature, of the spatial order of cities, it does not adequately capture the life-world experience of the residents and users of these separate quarters. Spatial change is both a consequence and a cause of changes in the lives of urban residents, but those changes cannot be adequately captured through examination only of spatial patterns. This is so for a number of reasons.

The first is that individuals experience the city both as part of their life-worlds and as part of their integration into its economic world. The residents and the business users of the city are not necessarily the same people, and even when they are, they experience the city in quite different capacities. A striking example of the differences can be seen in some of the political conflicts in New York City in recent years. Here individuals who are in the real estate business and act as developers of property in Manhattan strongly support the loosening of zoning restrictions, the building to high densities and the gentrification of neighborhoods. But at the same time, as residents of the city, they oppose building in the immediate vicinity of their homes, oppose higher appraisals of their residences that would increase their taxes, fight development proposals that would harm their personal lives outside of work. They use the city in one way, experience it as residents in another.

Secondly, the metaphor of the walled and quartered city implies, incorrectly, that individuals are confined within their quarters for all of their activities and at all times. But, precisely because the residential and the economic quarters of the city are not congruent, there is passage from one to the other by most people and generally every day. The conception of the ideal city (in the past often espoused by planners) as one where one lives and works in the same place – minimizing the travel time to work is the standard formulation – hardly has substance today. Commuting is taken for granted; making it short and comfortable is the goal, not eliminating it. Only in odd and questionable circumstances is the approach to provide employment where a person lives.

Again, the United States, and specifically New York City, gives us two examples: the Empowerment Zone plans, in which poor African Americans are to be supplied with jobs within the zones where they already live, and the so-called "edge cities," in which a deliberate attempt is made to provide work space, overwhelmingly offices, in suburban communities also being developed for housing. "Race," in the United States context, plays a major role in both conceptions: in the one case, to keep blacks in the ghettos, in the other, to prevent middle-class whites from having to have contact with them. Otherwise, even where communities are existing or developed with both economic and residential opportunities, the two are kept spatially separate. Working at home remains the exception rather than the rule, and working in the same district as where one lives is not always possible, because the jobs available may not coincide with the education or the skills of those who live in that neighborhood, for economic or political reasons or for reasons of racial separation. The point to be taken here is that a given individual occupies different spaces for different activities. Every metaphor of the city, be it the divided, the dual, the fragmented, quartered or the divided city must reflect these dynamics.

This brings us to the third reason the static metaphor of walling and quartering is inadequate: the time dimension. Not only do people occupy their homes and go to work in different places, they also do so at different times each day. In the rich white suburbs of Johannesburg the white home owners go to work in the morning, and the black servants come in as they leave; the residential area changes from white to black at eight in the morning. In the downtown skyscrapers in the Central Business Districts of many cities all over the world, the lawyers leave their offices at five or six in the evening; the cleaning crews, earning one-fiftieth of what the lawyers make, come in after they go, and are gone when the lawyers return the next morning. The same space is occupied by very different people at the different times. In the recent rediscovery of the importance of space, the time nexus is often overlooked.

So the image of the divided city must take into account the different spatial structure of residential as against economic activities; must take into account the movement of individuals between one and the other quarter; must reflect the temporal aspect, in which different spaces are occupied by different persons as different times for different purposes; and must reflect the nature of the differences across the lines of division.

The Layered City

These limitations on simple spatial analysis of divisions in a quartered city bring us to another issue. It is misleading to speak of "*the* city" as if it were a whole, organic, entity. The organic metaphor for the city stems from the Chicago school in the 1920s, which envisaged cities as growing and/or declining organically, with a life cycle that could be described as that of any organism could be. But this conception is simply wrong. "The city" is not an actor; it is a place occupied and used by many actors. A city does not prosper or decline, particular groups in it do, and generally in very different fashion. What is a crisis for one group may be prosperity for the other. Development may mean profits for one, displacement for the other. A corporate headquarters moving out of town may be a disaster for its local employees, but bring a surge in the price of its stock for its owners. Gentrification is a move up for some, a burden for others. A "city" is not global; some of those doing business in it are, but others very like them will do business very similar to that in other "non-global" cities. Those doing business on a global scale will have a similar impact on the spaces of the cities in which they do business, wherever they are. That impact may be concentrated in some cities, but that is because of what those actors do in them, not because that "city" has done something.

If cities were ever unitary entities, as both common usage, which sees cities as "actors," and many sociologists considered them to be, that characterization does not hold today. Each city is multiple cities, layered over and under each other, separated by both space and time, constituting the living and working environment of different classes and different groups, interacting with each other in a set of dominations and dependencies that reflect increasing distance and inequality. David Harvey (1994, p. 381) appropriately speaks of the dangers of "reinforcing reifications . . . it is invidious to regard places . . . cities . . . as 'things in themselves.'" He is speaking of the impact of global processes in particular, but the point applies to internal processes and divisions as well.

We suggest the metaphor of a *layered city* as one that begins to capture these complex dimensions of division.[5] One separation would be into different layers reflecting separations in life-worlds. This conception gives us the possibility to see that black and white professionals live at different locations, but that a map of their workplaces will show much less difference; it operates at a different layer. One layer represents residential space; a second layer represents workplace. On a third layer, one could visualize transportation patterns, with usage at each hour of the day. A different layer may show where children go to school; another, where the recreational facilities or the commercial facilities used by each group are located. Each layer shows the entire space of the city, but no one layer shows the complete city. Some layers reflect differences in usage, others differences in time, others differences in the components of the built environment. Each one reflects a divided city.

The concept of layering and the introduction of the element of time into the analysis of spatial patterns highlights the importance of a fact that has impressed us more and more forcefully as we have reviewed the contributions to this book: that the trends here described cannot be understood without placing them in the context of earlier developments (see also Kesteloot's chapter in this volume). Specifically, what is new is often a continuation, in more extreme form, of conflicts and divisions that have existed since the beginning of the capitalist transformation of cities, and to some extent since the beginnings of the formation of cities themselves. In physical terms, then, the spatial order of cities today reveals a layering of different cities, an overlapping in space and in time. What is changing in the present period may be the extent to which the layers are unconnected socially, economically, and politically from each other.

The Multiple Contingencies of Comparative Analysis

The trends revealed in the contributions to this volume are much more contingent than we had expected. The new and/or globalizing trends vary substantially in their impact on different cities. Specifically, the extent and forms of impact hinges on an ascertainable and limited number of contingencies. We list here the major contingencies affecting the way in which the general trends we have outlined become manifest. The list contains nothing surprising. We discuss each item briefly, simply to indicate the nature of the influences involved and to suggest a possible framework for systematic study in the future.

Variations in patterns are to be expected as consequence of:

- The contingency of geography (the pre-existing natural and built environment of the city)
- The contingency of history
- The contingency of economics (level of economic development)
- The contingency of globalization (position in the processes of globalization)
- The contingency of race (its history of racial and ethnic relations)
- The contingency of inequality (polarization both in numbers and in shares of wealth)
- The contingency of politics (the distribution of political power in its decision-making structure)

We take it for granted that *geography*, the physical pattern of development of a city, will be heavily influenced by its physical setting. Manhattan would not have skyscrapers were it not situated on bedrock, Amsterdam's central business district was irrevocably tied to the canals running through it, Johannesburg's development was dependent on the extent and location of gold-bearing strata, for many cities their relation to their harbor is crucial, and so forth. Such factors are largely background for our purposes, although the extent to which "natural" factors were or are rigid constraints should not be exaggerated. The same is true, if to a lesser extent, to the influence of the *existing built environment*: the existing location of major buildings, of residential settlements, of transportation infrastructure, of utilities, will constrain the impact of forces of change and be subject to policy input only at the margins. Going into these constraints in detail goes beyond the scope of this volume, although it is ultimately essential for a detailed understanding of developments in any particular city. We take them to establish the canvas on which new shapes may be painted, the physical bounds within which social and economic changes must take place.

The contingency of history. History is of course an all-encompassing term that can embrace the examination of everything that has developed in the past. In this sense it is really the major determinant of physical form and spatial pattern. But we mean it more narrowly here, to call attention to the rootedness of political, social, economic, and ideological events in their own past development and interrelatedness, very much in the spirit of John Friedmann's caution:

"If we neglect the . . . rootedness [of world cities] in a politically organized 'life space', with its own history, institutions, culture, and politics (the difference between Paris and London, for example) – much of what we observe will remain unintelligible." (Friedman in Knox and Taylor, 1995, p. 34).

The comment applies not only to world cities, and not only to their life spaces. The much longer history of European cities compared to North American ones, their background in a feudal system absent in the United States, the non-capitalist history of eastern European cities, the impact of colonialism both on imperial and colonized countries, the variations in local autonomy, are all critical in understanding the differences in development of the cities discussed in this volume. Sanjoy Chakravorty stresses this point eloquently in his discussion of Calcutta. A few studies have disaggregated these historical factors to examine their separate impact on city development and they reveal the importance of looking at political/institutional/cultural factors as a whole, rather than focusing on, say, the level of centralization as a separate factor.

The *type of development* can be decisive in shaping change. Type, not stage, of development, for it is not at all clear that development proceeds in a linear fashion, or that less developed countries must follow the patterns established by their more developed cousins. Not only are alternate paths of development conceivable, but the very definition of development may vary. Certainly the extent of the resource available in the society as a whole has an impact on the shape of that society: that the poor are pushed to the outskirts of cities in many Third World countries, for instance, while similar locations are desirable for the middle class in others, has something to do with the ability to provide infrastructure over large territories in the one and the scarcity of resources for the purpose in the other. The level of urbanization itself, including for instance the importance of rural-to-urban migration, will similarly affect how other trends play themselves out.

Related to the level of economic development, often paralleling the degree of urbanization, the presence or absence of often rural-based traditions of family and kinship are significant contingencies affecting the way in which production is organized and consumption takes place. Development is not only an economic concept, but as well a cultural, social, and institutional one.

Just as speaking of the level of development should not imply a single linear range of possibilities, so *position in the process of globalization* should not imply that cities can be measured on a linear scale of "more" or "less" globalized. Not only does globalization take many forms (from extent of informationalization to importance of international trade to level and form of technological development), but the proportional role of any of these forms in the life of a city can vary. Thus some cities may have highly advanced and tightly concentrated isles of communications sophistication in a surrounding that is essentially independent of it, perhaps still agriculturally based, while another may have residents most of whose incomes are derived from working for low-wage international companies, thus tightly integrated into global production, but very little affected by hi-tech communication. On the other hand, there may be cities in countries largely outside the circle of any of these aspects of globalization, as is often said about many African cities. Whether a city is a "globalizing city," therefore, cannot be answered by any simple measure on a linear scale of "more" or "less" globalized, ignoring the way in which it is integrated into globalization processes.

Third World cities differ both in their position in the process of globalization and in their type of development from First World cities. Where relative deindustrialization is the pattern in the typical First World city, this is in large part because industrial production has been moved to the Third World. New York City may experience deindustrialization, but Calcutta is industrializing. The processes involved may, however, fundamentally be similar: Rio de Janeiro makes an interesting comparison with Detroit, for instance, in losing industry (after a period of rapid industrial growth) and seeking but not finding services to take its place.

"Race" plays a very large role in some countries, an insignificant one in

others. The category itself, of course, is not a scientific one; it can only be defined in social terms, and then only in terms of social relationships between groups. To say that a country is "racially homogeneous" is simply to say that its residents do not separate themselves from each other by a category they denominate "race", to say that it is "racially mixed" is simply to say that lines of division have been socially shaped and called "race." In this sense "race" is a dominant factor in examining the distribution of residence in the United States, paralleled only, perhaps, by South Africa. While "racial" divisions play some role elsewhere, nowhere else do they approach the order of magnitude they have in these two countries. Two distinctions are important here: between cultural differences and racial differences, and between racially defined groups and immigrants.

The literature on post-colonialism has raised some critical questions about the relationship between imperialism/colonialism, nationalism, and "race", and the relation of each to cultural differences. Thus, Etienne Balibar writes of what he calls the "new racism:"

"The new racism is a racism of the era of decolonization, of the reversal of population movements between the old colonies and the old metropolises, and the division of humanity within a single political space. It is a racism, whose dominant theme is not biological heredity but the insurmountability of cultural differences . . . differential racism " (Balibar, 1991, p. 186; see also: Balibar and Wallerstein, 1991).

Balibar is speaking of the linkage between racism, cultural differentiation, and colonialism. These ingredients are found in different mixes; it seems to us important to separate out those cultural differences which are non-hierarchical in nature, for whose spatial reflection we have used the term "enclaves", from those that are hierarchical, and generally associated with "race" and often with colonialism, which we label "ghettos" (Marcuse, 1997b).

"Immigrants" is too broad a category to be satisfactory for our purposes, as Logan points out. Immigrants living in the American Colony in Jerusalem, the employees of multinationals abroad, the English in Canton in the first third of the century, all formed imperial citadels in the cities in which they lived. Working class immigrants in the United States, guestworkers in Western Europe after the war, rural-to-urban migrants in many Third World countries, formed enclaves for their mutual support and advancement. Dark-skinned immigrants in some of these countries were isolated, in the United States largely treated as on the other side of a racial boundary, and ghettoized (Häußerman et al., 1995). Some population groups are treated as immigrants, which establish residential patterns (as Logan shows) well into the second and third generation; others, although legally not "immigrants" at all – as Russian newcomers of German origin in Germany today, who are automatically citizens – are treated in the housing market much like Turkish,

Italian, or Greek immigrants. The same is true of Indonesians in Amsterdam. The contingency of migration, the mobility of populations, plays itself out in very different ways in the spatial patterns of cities. Visible differentiation and cultural differentiation clearly play a significant role.

Levels of *inequality* differ widely among countries; Waley places Japan among those with the least inequality, the United States is among those with the highest. The level of inequality is itself a function of other contingencies we have discussed above – as indeed each contingency is related to the others. However, having been produced, it then exercises an independent influence on the divisions of cities (in the same way that the built environment does, also a result of other contingencies but then exercising an influence of its own).

One of the most significant general outcomes of differential economic and political developments is the overall level of social inequality and social polarization within countries and cities.[6] It is possible that the degree of polarization and inequality (for a sensible discussion of the distinction between the two, see Hamnett and Cross, 1998), on the one hand, and the extent of spatial separation on the other hand, would be roughly parallel, but it would be a mistake to see this relation as an automatic one.

The final contingency to be mentioned is that of the balance of *political power*, which of course is a primary determinant of the national policy issues just mentioned. For the briefest of summaries: in most nations of the world in the immediate postwar period, a relatively stable, essentially social-democratic regime dominated policy-making, which was in most cases relatively able to provide an improvement in living conditions for the large majority and an adequate level of profits for the business community. With the election of Margaret Thatcher in Britain, Ronald Reagan in the United States, and Helmut Kohl in Germany, a political turn to the right accompanied the increase in the level of those activities summarized under the caption of globalization. The shift to the right paralleled the shift of the balance of power in the economic sphere from labor to capital. Periodic protests throughout the period, particularly if they rose to the level of civil unrest, as in the mid-1960s, produced different constellations of power, but generally only briefly.[7] These shifts have obvious consequences in national policy, which in turn has consequences on spatial structure (Levine, 1995, pp. 106/7; Logan and Swanstrom, 1990). Asking what those consequences are, or can be, leads us, after a brief summary, directly to our final point: the policy implications of our analysis.

Summary

"Is there a new spatial order in cities" is the question around which this book has been centered. Our answer is: "No". But there is change, important and visible change, with very significant impacts on the lives of our cities' people. Those changes may be summarized as an increase in the strength of divisions in the city and the inequality among them. Their specific spatial manifestations include:

- strengthened structural spatial divisions among the quarters of the city, with increased inequality and sharper lines of division among them;
- wealthy quarters, housing those directly benefiting from increased globalization, and the quarters of the professionals, managers, and technicians that serve them, growing in size and in the defensiveness of the walls erected against others;
- quarters of those excluded from the globalizing economy, with their residents more and more isolated and walled in;
- increasing walling among the quarters, from defensive citadels to gated upper and middle income communities to confined and barricaded poor neighborhoods;
- increased totalization of life within each quarter, combining residential, work, commercial, and recreational uses separately for the occupants of each;
- the increase in prevalence and depth of specific new spatial formations within these structural divisions;
- more prominent and more extensive citadels at the top, disproportionately serving a global elite;
- edge cities, an extension and expansion of the suburbanization of residence and work for the middle class and some of the professional–managerial class;
- continuing formation of immigrant enclaves of lower-paid workers both within and outside the global economy, with a continuing and often increasing emphasis on ethnic solidarity within them;
- a more integrated and much larger regionalization of economic activity, with new outer centers of activity increasing in importance;
- ghettoization of the excluded, developed in the United States, but a visible tendency in many other countries;
- a set of "soft" locations particularly vulnerable to change, which may also serve as markers of the direction and intensity of influence of globalization trends.

There is, then, no standard pattern, no "*The* Globalized City," no single new spatial order within cities all over the world. The patterns produced by the processes summarized as "globalization" are quite varied, and some are described in detail in the book. But there is a set of common trends that, taken together, form a pattern, standing in some orderly relationship to each other. Looking back at the alternate theories of the consequences of globalization, interdependent polarization vs exclusion, in effect both are correct: the rich get richer (and form citadels and exclusionary enclaves) and the poor get poorer; most are needed (often forming immigrant enclaves), but some poor are left out (and confined to excluded ghettos).

The trends we have outlined have substantial negative consequences in terms of social justice and democracy: inequality, divisions, poverty, lack of democratic public control. Zygmunt Bauman's (1998) little book gives an excellent generalized discussion of them; the detailed accounts are legion. The rhetoric of globalization and the exaggeration of its influence can be a contributing factor legitimating those negative consequences, and making resistance to them seem futile – the TINA syndrome, "There Is No Alternative." We believe that conclusion is false. As Beauregard and Haila say, "actors . . . who control the built environment are not simply puppets dancing to the tune of socio-economic and political logics . . . " We believe their actions can, and should be, controlled, for the general public benefit. We thus turn, briefly, to examine some of the policy implications of our conclusions.

Implications for Public Policy

Reflection on the importance of governmental action in determining the extent and nature of changes in the spatial order of cities leads us to the single most important conclusion of our study: that the pattern of development of cities today is subject to control, *is not* the result of uncontrollable forces, *is not* the result of iron economic laws whose effects states are powerless to influence. On the contrary, in case after case we have found agency to have a major impact on structure: the actions of the state, of nation states, determined by the balance of power between/among contending forces in the economic and political sphere, is a major determinant of a city's spatial pattern, heavily influenced though it may be by the contingencies we have mentioned. A growing body of literature support the conclusion as to the key role of the state in shaping the outcomes of processes of globalization (Panitch, 1998; Longworth, 1998; Hirst and Thompson, 1996; Piven, 1995; Sassen, 1996). The changed spatial order is thus determined in large part by the outcomes of conflicts among real men and women and the organizations through which they act, aligned along fissures of class, race, gender, and ideology.

Given these concerns, what policy implications follow?

First, policies oriented only to spatial patterns in a city will not work, at least if the goal is to influence the trends on which we have focused: the divisions of the city, ghettoization, exclusionary suburbanization, citadel formation. One of us is an urban planner, the other a geographer, but the traditional spatially-oriented tools of these professions, focused on land use and geographical patterns, are not adequate to deal even with spatial divisions. That is because spatial patterns are brought about by processes that are not themselves simply spatial. Globalization of course takes place in space, inherently so, but it is produced by developments in the production of goods and services, their control, the technology they use, the shifting economic and political relations among owners, workers and users. Power relations are manifested in space, and can be strengthened by spatial patterns, but the major bases for the distribution of power have today only secondarily to do with its spatial location; the power of a multinational can be exercised wherever it is located. The actual and potential power of the state over the uses of space within its borders is great; whether and in what direction that power is used is not determined by the existing distribution of space, but rather by the existing distribution of decision-making power in and over the state. The same is true of the other key factors that we have found to influence spatial patterns: racism, for instance, while both strengthened by and promoting patterns of segregation within cities, does not have its origins in such patterns. The measures required go beyond the bounds of this book; they include such matters as welfare state policies generally; internationally-agreed-upon social standards such as were attempted to be introduced in the Maastricht and NAFTA treaties; environmental regulation; national and international improvements in labor standards, and in the rights to organize by labor; increases in informed democratic decision-making; readjustment of the balance between private property rights and public policy decisions; and so on. Policies designed to influence spatial patterns cannot be confined to spatial policies.

Nevertheless, and this is the second implication, state spatial policies can have a dramatic effect on the divisions of the city. This can work positively (for example in the Netherlands, where the enormous number of attractive dwellings in the social rented sector has prevented large-scale segregation) or negatively (for example in the United States, where the concentration of public housing in ghetto areas has served to reinforce the exclusionary ghettos described earlier in this chapter). The allocation of social housing, as Van Grunsven describes in Singapore, and land use policies, as Keil and Ronneberger describe for Frankfurt, have dramatic effects on spatial structure, and can be used to reduce the divisions created by globalization. Examples could be multiplied: they range from the socially-oriented handling of competition among cities (or national-level legislation limiting it) to the ways tourism is promoted, to sensitive territorially-based development programs, to finding the right balance between privatization and public enterprise, to educational and training programs, to regulation of the private rental housing market, to socially-oriented zoning and land use regulations.

On a few issues, a third implication of the analysis here, spatial policies need to come to grips with contradictions as yet insufficiently thought through.

Key among these are attitudes towards enclaves and attendant goals for integration. Ethnic enclaves have strong positive attributes, as well as social dangers: they promote solidarity and supportive networking, but separate and inhibit interaction with others. Both land use and economic development policies can encourage or hinder their solidification; the balanced approach to these conflicting aspects has yet to be found. The theoretical goal of openness and diversity conflicts with freedom of choice and social solidarity (as well as with racism and prejudiced exclusion); a democratically sound and practically feasible balance needs to be found. In principle, there is no reason why public policy should interfere with enclave formation, so long as it is truly voluntary, that is, that anyone resident in an enclave has the realistic possibility of moving out. We would thus conclude that the policy in Singapore (see Van Grunsven in this volume), which is directly aimed at weakening the solidarity that co-residence in an enclave promotes, is wrong.[8] It was a policy very similar to that of the south in the United States in the days of slavery, when "the basic housing custom was to keep the Negroes divided; to require that slaves live with their masters or their agents; to spread the blacks throughout the town; to prevent concentration of colored people free from the control of whites" (Wade, 1964 in Bracey et al., 1971, pp. 11–12). In a sense, the policy of precluding free enclave formation might be considered *negative ghettoization*, similarly, forcing people to live where they do not wish, in this case away from those with whom they would like to be near. Yet the dangers of real ghetto formation must also be of concern.

*   *   *

We conclude, perhaps surprisingly, on an optimistic note. The specter of an overwhelming tidal wave of globalization, sweeping across continents, engulfing all cities, producing a consistent pattern of polarization, exploitation and exclusion around the world, is unfounded – perhaps not unfounded as a fear, but unduly pessimistic as a reality. For the citizens (and residents, for rights of citizenship remain subject to contestation too) of cities around the world have influenced their development in many active ways, and produced results, through political measures, through the instrumentality of the state and through resistance in civil society, that show globalization to be far from an unstoppable and unidirectional force. In comparing developments in the cities in this volume the impact of what people have done in confronting global economic forces is everywhere visible. The literature on globalization is beginning to focus more on the possibilities of control of the processes and their consequence, beginning less to accept those consequences as inevitable or be content simply to describe them as fait accompli.[9] We believe that, too, reflects something new in the spatial ordering of cities, and something which gives hope that the forces that we lump together under the heading "globalization" may be turned to the improvement and (re-?)unifi-cation of our cities, and away from the quartering and layering that is so evident in so many of them today.

Notes

1 We have avoided encumbering this chapter with citations except in a very few instances, since it relies on other chapters in this book itself and on our own previously published work, which is referenced in the List of References at the end.

2 "Social area" might not be a bad term for the level to which we have reference, but that term has already acquired a technical connotation as used in social area analysis, an approach we do not find adequate for our purposes, since it is an entirely statistical, untheorized presentation of only portions of important proc-esses that are not only social (and perhaps only superficially social), but more deeply economic and political.

3 We use the term "soft" by analogy to its use in zoning practice, where a "soft" site is spoken of as one not developed to the limits its legal zoning permits, i.e. one viewed as ripe for change and new development.

4 The question of whether some cities are in fact barely touched by the processes of globalization is one we have been unable to pursue within the scope of this book, but there is a substantial argument that portions of Africa and portions of Asia are essentially outside the process of globalization beyond the point of their role in international commerce one hundred years ago (Amin, 1994).

5 The image of the layered city was first suggested in Marcuse (1999a) and is developed further in Marcuse (1999b).

6 We should of course realize that social inequality and social polarization is not fully determined by economic developments. The way the state is involved in, for example, supporting those without employment, is a powerful determinant of both kinds of inequality (see, e.g. Burgers, 1996).

7 "If the tension and anger increases sufficiently to cause civil unrest or territorial revolts, the pace to a liberalized global economy will be slowed, but only in rare cases will it be reversed. Enough of the economic surplus could be directed to strategic side payments to pacify significant areas of severe economic pain," is a cold-blooded formulation, by Gary Gappert (1997, p. 297).

8 Our judgment is influenced by the likely relation between the policy in Singa-pore and its non-democratic political history, but we are not in a position adequately to assess this complex relationship.

9 Among the growing body of work, see particularly that of Sassen, the Institute for Policy Studies, the World Bank Monitoring Project, and much of the discus-sion around the consummation of the European Union, the passage of NAFTA, the resistance to the Multinational Agreement on Investments, and the activities of the World Trade Organization.

List of References

Abeyasekere, S. 1987: *Jakarta: A History*, Singapore: Oxford University Press.

Aglietta, M. 1976: *Régulations et Crises Du Capitalisme: l'Expérience des Etats-Unis*, Paris: Calmann-Lévy.

Ahluwalia, I. J. 1985: *Industrial Growth in India*, New Delhi: Oxford University Press.

Aita Kaoruko 1995: A 'futuristic city' drowns in red ink. *Japan Times*, 12 September 1995, 3.

Alba, R.D. and Logan, J.R. 1992: Analyzing locational attainments: constructing individual-level regression models using aggregate data. *Sociological Methods and Research*, 20, 367–97.

Alba, R.D., Logan, J.R. and Crowder, K. 1997: White neighborhoods and assimilation: the Greater New York Region, 1980–1990. *Social Forces*, 75, 883–909.

ASLK (Algemene Spaar- en Lijfrentekas) 1997, *Waarden van de Onroerende Goederen*, Brussels: ASLK

Allen-Mills, T. 1998: Disco survivors accuse neo-Nazis. *Sunday Times*, 1 November 1998.

Amin, A. (ed.) 1994: *Post-Fordism: A Reader*, London: Basil Blackwell.

Amsden, A.H. 1993: Asia's Industrial Revolution: "Late Industrialization" on the Rim. *Dissent*, 40, 324–32.

Amsden, A.H. 1997: Editorial: bringing production back. *World Development*, 25 (4), 469–80.

Amsden, A.H., Kochanowicz, J. and Taylor, L. 1994: *The Market Meets its Match: Restructuring the Economies of Eastern Europe*, Cambridge (MA): Harvard University Press.

Anderson, G.A. 1996: *National Differences in Social Welfare Policies*. Paper presented at the Conference of the Status of Women, Copenhagen.

Angotti, T. 1993: *Metropolis 2000*, London: Routledge.

Ashihara Yoshinobu 1986: *Kakureta chitsujo*, Tokyo: Chûô Kôronsha (translated as *The Hidden Order: Tokyo through the Twentieth Century*, Tokyo: Kodansha International, 1989).

Atkinson, A.B., Rainwater, L. and Smeeding, T.M. 1995: *Income Distribution in OECD Countries: Evidence from the Luxembourg Income Study*, Paris: OECD.

Aungles, S. and Szelenyi, I. 1979: Structural conflicts between the state, local government and monopoly capital – the case of Whyalla in South Australia. *Australian and New Zealand Journal of Sociology*, 15, 24–35.

Australian Bureau of Statistics 1995: *Labour Force in Australia*, December 1995, Canberra: Australian Government Publishing Service.

Australian Urban and Regional Development Review 1994: *Australian Cities and Regions: A National Approach*, Canberra: Department of Housing and Regional Development.

Baar, K.K. 1981: Property tax assessment discrimination against low-income neighborhoods. *The Urban Lawyer*, 13 (3), 333ff.

Badcock, B.A. 1984: *Unfairly Structured Cities*, Oxford: Basil Blackwell.

Badcock, B.A. 1994: "Stressed out" communities: "out-of-sight, out-of-mind"? *Urban Policy and Research*, 12, 191–7.

Badcock, B.A. 1995a: Towards more equitable cities: a receding prospect? In P. Troy (ed.), *Australian Cities. Issues, Strategies and Policies for Urban Australia in the 1990s*, Melbourne: Cambridge University Press, 196–219.

Badcock, B.A. 1995b: Building upon the foundations of gentrification: inner-city housing development in Australia in the 1990s. *Urban Geography*, 16, 70–90.

Badcock, B.A. and Urlich-Cloher, D.U. 1981: Neighbourhood change in Inner Adelaide, 1966–76. *Urban Studies*, 18, 41–55.

Bairoch, P. 1988: *Cities and Economic Development: From the Dawn of History to the Present*, Chicago: University of Chicago Press.

Bairoch, P. 1991: The city and technological innovation. In P. Higonnet, D.S. Landes and H. Rosovsky (eds), *Favorites of Fortune: Technology, Growth, and Economic Development since the Industrial Revolution*, Cambridge (MA). Harvard University Press.

Balibar, E. 1991: Es gibt keinen Staat in Europa: racism and politics in Europe today. *New Left Review*, 186.

Balibar, E. and Wallerstein, I. 1991: *Race, Nation and Class: Ambiguous Identities*, London: Verso.

Ball, R. and Pratt, A.C. (eds) 1994: *Industrial Property*, London: Routledge.

Bandyopadhyay, R. 1990: The inheritors: slum and pavement life in Calcutta. In S. Chaudhuri (ed.), *Calcutta: The Living City*, Calcutta: Oxford University Press, 78–87.

Banerjee, A. 1906: A city with two pasts. In J. Racine (ed.), *Calcutta 1981*, New Delhi: Concept Publishing, 89–104.

Barbanel, J. 1989: How despair is engulfing a generation in New York. *New York Times*, April 2.

Bardhan Roy, M. 1994: *Calcutta Slums: Public Policy in Retrospect*, Calcutta: Minerva Publications.

Bartelheimer, P. 1995: *Frankfurter Sozialberichterstattung, Zwischenbericht, September 30*, Frankfurt am Main: Frankfurter Büro für Armutsberichterstattung.

Bartelheimer, P. 1997: *Risiken für Frankfurt als soziale Stadt. Erster Frankfurter Sozialbericht*

1995/6, Frankfurt am Main: Frankfurter Büro für Armutsberichterstattung.

Bastide, R. and Van den Berghe, P. 1957: Stereotypes, norms and interracial behavior in São Paulo, Brazil. *American Sociological Review,* 22, 689–94.

Bauman, Z. 1998: *Globalization: The Human Consequences,* New York: Columbia University Press.

Beauregard, R.A. 1989: Urban restructuring in comparative perspective. In R.A. Beauregard (ed.), *Atop the Urban Hierarchy,* Totowa, NJ: Rowman & Littlefield, 239–74.

Beauregard, R.A. 1994: Capital switching and the built environment: United States, 1970–1989. *Environment and Planning A,* 26, 715–32.

Beauregard, R.A. 1995: Edge cities: peripheralizing the center. *Urban Geography,* 16 (8), 708–21.

Beauregard, R.A. 1998: Edge cities: die peripherisierung des Zentrums. In W. Prigge (ed.), *Peripherie Ist Uberall,* Frankfurt: Campus Verlag, 52–61.

Beauregard, R.A. and Deitrick, S. 1995: From front-runner to also-ran: the transformation of a once-dominant region, Pennsylvania, USA. In P. Cooke (ed.), *The Rise of the Rustbelt,* New York: St Martin's Press, 52–71.

Beauregard, R.A. and Haila, A. 1997: The unavoidable incompleteness of the city. *American Behavioural Scientist,* 41 (3), 327–41.

Bell, M. 1995: *Internal Migration in Australia 1986–91: Overview Report, Bureau of Immigration, Multicultural and Population Research,* Canberra: Australian Government Publishing Service.

Bell, W. 1968: The city, the suburb and a theory of social choice. In S. Greer (ed.) *The New Urbanization,* New York: St Martins, 132–68.

Bello, W., Cunningham, S. and Rau, B. 1994: *Dark Victory: The United States, Structural Adjustment, and Global Poverty,* London: Pluto; Oakland, CA: Institute for Food and Development; Amsterdam: Transnational Institute.

Beneria, L. and Mendoza, B. 1995: Structural adjustment and social investment funds: the cases of Honduras, Mexico and Nicaragua. *European Journal of Development Research,* June, 53–75.

Bentham, G. 1986: Socio-tenurial polarisation in the United Kingdom, 1953–83: the income evidence. *Urban Studies,* 23, 157–62.

Berque, A. 1993: *Du geste à la cité,* Paris: Gallimard.

Bestor, T. 1989: *Neighborhood Tokyo,* Stanford, CA: Stanford University Press.

Betts, R. 1975: *Multiracialism, Meritocracy and the Malays in Singapore,* Boston: Massachusetts Institute of Technology (PhD thesis).

Bingham, R.D. and Kimble, D. 1995: Industrial composition of edge cities and downtowns. *Economic Development Quarterly,* 9 (3), 259–72.

Blakely, E.J. and Snyder, M.G. 1995: *Fortress America: Gated and Walled Communities in the United States,* Cambridge, MA/Washington D.C.: Lincoln Institute of Land Policy/Brookings Institution Press.

Blanc, M. 1993: Housing segregation and the poor: new trends in French social rented housing. *Housing Studies,* 8, 207–14.

Bluestone, B. and Harrison, B. 1982: *The Deindustrialization of America,* New York: Basic Books.

Bognar, B. 1990: *The New Japanese Architecture,* New York: Rizzoli.

Bolt, G., Burgers, J. and Van Kempen, R. 1998: On the social significance of spatial location; spatial segregation and social inclusion. *Netherlands Journal of Housing and the Built Environment*, 13 (1), 83–95.

Bonelli, R. and Sedlacek, G.L. 1989: Distribuição de renda: evolução no último quarto de século. In Instituto de Planejamento e Economia Aplicada, *Mercado de Trabalho e Distribuição de Renda: Uma Coletânea*, Rio de Janeiro: IPEA/INPES.

Bourdier, M. 1992: Tokyo sur mer, ou le devenir de la zone portuaire de la métropole nippone. *Les Annales de la Recherche Urbaine*, 55, 170–81.

Bourne, L.S. 1996: *Social Inequalities, Polarization and the Redistribution of Income Within Cities: a Canadian Example*. Paper presented to a GISCA Workshop on Urban Indicators, Key Centre for Social Applications of GIS, Adelaide: Adelaide University, April.

Boyd, R. 1968: *The Australian Ugliness*, Ringwood: Penguin Books (2nd edition).

Boyer, R. 1986: *La Théorie de la Régulation; Une Analyse Critique*, Paris: La Découverte.

Bracey, J.H., Jr., Meier, A., and Rudwick, E. 1971: *The Rise of the Ghetto*, Belmont, CA: Wadsworth Publishing Co., p. 11–12.

Brake, K. 1991: *Dienstleistungen und räumliche Entwicklung Frankfurt: Strukturveränderungen in Stadt und Region*, Oldenburg: Universität Oldenburg, Stadt- und Regionalplanung.

Braudel, F. 1985: *Civilization and Capitalism, 15th–18th Century: Volume 2, The Wheels of Commerce*, New York: Harper and Row.

Brecher, J. and Costello, T. 1994: *Global Village or Global Pillage*, Boston: South End Press.

Bremer, P. and Gestring, N. 1997: Urban Underclass – neue Formen der Ausgrenzung in deutschen Städten? *Prokla*, 27 (106), 55–76.

Britton v Town of Chester 525 A.2d 492 (N.H. 1991).

Brunet, J.P. 1979: *Saint Denis, la Ville Rouge*, Paris: Fayard.

Buck, N. and Fainstein, N. 1992: A comparative history: 1880–1973. In S. Fainstein, I. Gordon, and M. Harloe (eds), *Divided Cities: New York and London in the Contemporary World*, Oxford: Blackwell, 29–67.

Budd, L. 1992: An urban narrative and the imperatives of the city. In L. Budd and S. Whimster (eds), *Global Finance and Urban Living*, London: Routledge, 260–81.

Burbidge, A. and Winter, I. 1996: Investigating urban poverty: the impact of state intervention and household change. *Urban Policy and Research*, 14, 97–108.

Burgers, J 1996: No polarisation in Dutch cities? Inequality in a corporatist country. *Urban Studies*, 33, 99–105.

Burgers, J. 1998: In the margin of the welfare state: labour market position and housing conditions of undocumented immigrants in Rotterdam. *Urban Studies*, 35 (10), 1855–68.

Burgers, J. and Engbersen, G. 1996: Globalisation, migration, and undocumented migrants. *New Community*, 22, 619–35.

Burnley, I. 1996: Relocation of overseas-born populations in Sydney. In P.W. Newton and M. Bell (eds), *Population Shift. Mobility and Change in Australia*, Canberra: Australian Government Publishing Service, 83–102.

Butler, T. and Hamnett, C. 1994: Gentrification, class, and gender: some comments on Warde's 'Gentrification as consumption'. *Environment and Planning D*, 12, 477–93.

Camarano, A.A. 1997: *Mudancas na fecundidade nas areas metropolitanas do Brasil, como vai a populacao Brasileira*, Brasilia: IPEA.

Carr, J.H. and Megbolugbe, I.F. 1993: *The Federal Reserve Bank of Boston Study on Mortgage Lending Revisited*, Washington, D.C.: FNMA.

Cass, B. 1991: *The Housing Needs of Women and Children*, Canberra: Australian Government Publishing Service

Castells, M. 1989: *The Informational City*, Oxford: Blackwell.

Castells, M. 1994: European Cities, the Informational Society, and the global economy. *New Left Review*, 204, 18–32.

Celarier, M. 1998: Too many risks, too few rewards. *Euromoney*, 353 ff.

Centre for Urban Research and Action 1977: *The Displaced. A Study of Housing Conflict in Melbourne's Inner City*, Melbourne: CURA.

Chakravorty, S. 1998: *Oh Lucky Region: Structural Reform and the Distribution of Investment in India*, paper presented at the Center for Studies in the Social Sciences, Calcutta, June 1998.

Chakravorty, S. and Gupta, G. 1996: Let a hundred projects bloom: structural reform and urban development in Calcutta. *Third World Planning Review*, 18, 415–31.

Cheng Lim Keak 1995: *Geographical Analysis of the Singapore Population*, Singapore: Department of Statistics.

Chiew Seen Kong 1976: Singapore national identity, an alternative view. *Review of Southeast Asian Studies*, 6, 1–10.

Chiew Seen Kong 1983: Ethnicity and national integration, the evolution of a multi-ethnic society. In P. Chen (ed.), *Singapore, Development Policies and Trends*, Singapore: Oxford University Press, 29–64.

Chiu, S.W.K., Ho, K.C. and Tai-Lok Lui 1997: *City-states in the Global Economy: Industrial Restructuring in Hong Kong and Singapore*, Boulder, Co.: Westview Press.

Christopherson, S.M. 1994: Fortress city, privatized spaces, consumer citizenship. In: A. Amin (ed.), *Post-Fordism: A Reader*, Oxford: Blackwell, 409–27.

Chua Beng Huat 1996: *Private Ownership and Public Housing in Singapore*. Working Paper No. 63, Asia Research Centres on Social, Political and Economic Change, Perth: Murdoch University.

Clark, W.A.V. and Dieleman F.M. 1996: *Households and Housing; Choice and Outcomes in the Housing Market*, New Brunswick NJ: Center for Urban Policy Research.

Clarke, J.H. 1976: *Black–White Alliances: A Historical Perspective*, Chicago: Institute of Positive Education.

Coaldrake, W. 1996: *Architecture and Authority in Japan*, London: Routledge.

Cohen, R. 1997: Liberty, equality, anxiety: a special report. For France, sagging self-image and esprit. *The New Yorker*, 2 November 1997.

Cohn-Bendit, D. 1996: Frankfurt: my homeland babylon. *Enroute*, April, 17–18.

Coldwell Banker 1987: *National Survey of International Investment Ownership of Major Office Buildings in 19 Largest United States Downtown Office Markets*, Boston: Coldwell Banker.

Connell, J. 1993: *Kitanai, kitsui and kiken: The rise of labour migration to Japan*. Sydney: ERRRU.

Corbridge, S. 1991: The poverty of planning or planning for poverty: an eye to economic liberalization in India. *Progress in Human Geography*, 15, 467–76.

Cornia, G.A., Jolly, R. and Stewart, F., (eds) 1987: *Adjustment with a Human Face*, Oxford: Clarendon Press.

Crozier, M., Huntington, S.P. and Watanuki, J. 1975: *The Crisis of Democracy: Report of the Governability of Democracies to the Trilaterial Commission*, New York: New York University Press.

Dahya, B. 1974: The nature of Pakistani ethnicity in industrial cities in Britain. In A. Cohen (ed.), *Urban Ethnicity*, London: Tavistock, 77–118.

Davis, M. 1990: *City of Quartz: Excavating the Future in Los Angeles*, London/New York: Verso.

Davis, M. 1995: Hell factories in the field. *In the Nation*, 260 (7), 229ff.

Day, T. 1992: Capital-labor substitution in the home. *Technology and Culture*, 33, 302–27.

De Lannoy, W. and De Corte, S. 1994: De migraties van Marokkanen en Turken binnen het Brusselse Gewest in de periode 1988–1992. *Acta Geographica Lovaniensia*, 34, 63–69.

De Villanova, R. 1997: Turkish housing conditions in France: from tenant to owner. In A. Ş. Özüekren and R. van Kempen (eds), *Turks in European Cities: Housing and Urban Segregation*, Utrecht: European Research Centre on Migration and Ethnic Relations, 98–121.

Dear, M. 1991: The premature demise of postmodern urbanism. *Cultural Anthropology*, 6 (4), 539–52.

Dear, M. and Flusty, S. 1998: Postmodern urbanism. *Annals of the Association of American Geographers*, 88 (1), 50–72.

Degler, C.N. 1971: *Neither Black nor White; Slavery and Race Relations in Brazil and the United States*, New York: MacMillan.

DeMaziere, C. and Wilson, P.A. (eds), 1995: *Local Economic Development in Europe and the Americas*, London: Mansell.

Denton, N.A. and Massey, D.S. 1989: Racial identity among Caribbean Hispanics: the effect of double minority status on minority segregation. *American Sociological Review*, 54, 790–808.

Department of Housing and Regional Development 1995a: *Community and Nation*, Canberra: Australian Government Publishing Service.

Department of Housing and Regional Development 1995b: *Better Cities. National Status Report*, Canberra: Commonwealth of Australia.

Department of Social Security 1993: *Meeting the Challenge – Labour Market Trends and the Income Support System*, Canberra: Australian Government Publishing Service.

Department of Statistics, Singapore (several years): *Yearbook of Statistics Singapore*, Singapore: National Printers.

Dieleman, F.M. 1994: Social rented housing: valuable asset or unsustainable burden? *Urban Studies*, 31, 447–63.

Dieleman, F.M. and Hamnett, C. 1994: Globalisation, regulation and the urban system: Editors' introduction to the special issue. *Urban Studies*, 31, 357–64.

Diniz, C.C. 1994: Polygonized development in Brazil: Neither decentralization nor continued polarization. *International Journal of Urban and Regional Research*, 18, 293–314.

Do Rosario, L. 1990: The propertied class: Land boom poses threat of increased social disparities. *Far Eastern Economic Review*, 13 September, 23.

Domar, E.D. 1957: *Essays in the Theory of Economic Growth*, Fair Lawn, NJ: Oxford University Press.

Dorfman, A. and Mattelart, A. 1975: *How to Read Donald Duck: Imperialist Ideology in the*

Disney Comic, New York: International General.

Douglass, M. 1988: The transnationalization of urbanization in Japan. *International Journal of Urban and Regional Research,* 12 (3), 425–54.

Douglass, M. 1993: The 'new' Tokyo story: Restructuring space and the struggle for space in a world city. In K. Fujita and R. Hill (eds), *Japanese Cities in the World Economy,* Philadelphia: Temple University Press, 83–119.

Du Bois, W.E.B. 1903/1965: *The Souls of Black Folk* in *Three Negro Classics: Up From Slavery; The Souls of Black Folk; The Autobiography of an Ex-Colored Man,* New York: Avon Books.

Duncan, B. and Lieberson, S. 1970: *Metropolis and Region in Transition,* Beverly Hills, CA: Sage.

Dutt, A. 1993: Cities of South Asia. In S.D. Brunn and J. F. Williams (eds), *Cities of the World: World Regional Urban Development,* New York: Harper Collins, 351–87.

Economist, The, 1987: April 18.

Ellin, N. 1996: *Postmodern Urbanism,* Cambridge, MA: Blackwell.

Elmhorn, C. 1998: Brussels in the European Economic Space: the emergence of a world city? *Tijdschrift van de Belgische Vereniging voor Aardrijkskundige Studies,* 67, pp. 79–102.

Fagan, B. and Webber, M. 1994: *Global Restructuring. The Australian Experience,* Melbourne: Oxford University Press.

Fainstein, S.S. 1994: *The City Builders,* Oxford: Blackwell.

Fainstein, S.S., Gordon, I. and Harloe, M. (eds) 1992: *Divided Cities; New York & London in the Contemporary World,* Oxford: Blackwell.

Farley, R. 1996: Black–white residential segregation: the views of Myrdal in the 1940s and trends of the 1980s. In O. Clayton Jr. (ed.), *American Dilemma Revisited: Race Relations in a Changing World,* New York: Russell Sage Foundation, 45–75.

Farthing, L. 1997: Social impacts associated with anti-drug law 1008. In M.B. Leons and H. Sanabria (eds), *Coca/Cocaine, and the Bolivian Reality,* Albany: State University of New York Press, 253–69.

Federal National Mortgage Association (FNMA), 1989: *Form RE-414W 12/89.*

Fernandes, F. 1955: Relaçoes entre Brancos e Negros em Sao Paulo, Sao Paulo: Editora Anhembi Limitada.

Field, N. 1989: Somehow: The postmodern as atmosphere. In M. Miyoshi and H. Harootunian (eds), *Postmodernism and Japan,* Durham, NC: Duke University Press, 169–89.

Fielding, T. and Mizuno Makiko 1995: *Japan's 'Newcomers': The Causes and Consequences of Recent Immigration to Japan.* Paper for the Annual Conference of the British Association of Japanese Studies, Oxford, April.

Fishman, R. 1987: *Bourgeois Utopias,* New York: Basic Books.

Fitch, R. 1977: Planning New York. In R.E. Alcaly, E. Roger and D. Mermelstein (eds), *The Fiscal Crisis of American Cities,* New York: Vintage Books.

Forrest, R. and Murie, A. 1990: *Residualisation and Council Housing: A Statistical Update,* Bristol: School for Advanced Urban Studies, University of Bristol.

Forster, C. 1995: *Australian Cities. Continuity and Change,* Melbourne: Oxford University Press.

Fourcaut, A. 1986: *Bobigny, Banlieu Rouge,* Paris: Editions Ouvrières.

Fowler, E. 1996: *San'ya Blues: Laboring Life in Contemporary Tokyo,* Ithaca, NY: Cornell

University Press.

Freestone, R. 1996: The making of an Australian technoburb. *Australian Geographical Studies*, 34, 18–31.

Frieden, B.J. and Sagalyn, L.B. 1989: *Downtowns, Inc.*, Cambridge, MA: MIT Press.

Friedmann, J. 1986: The world city hypothesis. *Development and Change*, 17, 69–83.

Friedmann, J. 1995: Where we stand: a decade of world city research. In P.L. Knox and P.J. Taylor (eds), *World Cities in a World System*, Cambridge: Cambridge University Press, 21–47.

Friedmann, J. and Lehrer, U. 1997: Urban policy responses to foreign in-migration: the case of Frankfurt am Main. *Journal of the American Planners Association*, Winter, 61–78.

Friedmann, J. and Wolff, G. 1982: World city formation: an agenda for research and action. *International Journal of Urban and Regional Research*, 4, 309–43.

Fujita Kuniko and Hill, R.C. (eds) 1993: *Japanese Cities in the World Economy*, Philadelphia: Temple University Press.

Gappert, G. 1997: Conclusion and epilogue: the future of cities and their policies in the global economy. In P. Kresl and G. Gappert (eds), *North American Cities and the Global Economy*, Thousand Oaks, CA: Sage, 286–302.

Garreau, J. 1991: *Edge City: Life on the New Frontier*, New York: Doubleday.

Gilmour, I. 1992: *Dancing with Dogma. Britain under Thatcherism*, London: Simon and Schuster.

Glazer, N. 1997: *We Are All Multiculturalists Now*, Cambridge: Harvard University Press.

Glazer, N. and Moynihan, D.P. 1963: *Beyond the Melting Pot*, Cambridge: MIT Press.

Goldberger, P. 1989: Why design can't transform cities. *New York Times*, June 23.

Goldfield, M. 1990: Class, race and politics in the United States. *Research in Political Economy*, 12, 83–117.

Goldsen, R.K. 1978: *The Show and Tell Machine: How Television Works and Works you Over*, New York: Dell Publishing Company.

Goldsmith, W.W. 1974: The ghetto as a resource for Black America. *Journal of the American Institute of Planners*, 40, 17–30. Reprinted in (1995) *Classic Readings in Planning*, Jay Stein editor, New York: McGraw Hill.

Goldsmith, W.W. 1977: The war on development. *Monthly Review* (March) 50–7.

Goldsmith, W.W. 1994: Introduction to the U.S. edition, São Paulo as a world city: industry, misery, and resistance. In: L. Kowarick (ed.), *Social Struggles and the City: The Case of São Paulo*, New York: Monthly Review Press, 13–29.

Goldsmith, W.W. 1997: The metropolis and globalization: the dialectics of racial discrimination, deregulation, and urban form. *American Behavioral Scientist*, 41 (3), 299–310.

Goldsmith, W.W. 1998: Fishing bodies out of the river: can universities help troubled neighborhoods? *Connecticut Law Review*, 30 (4), 1205–46.

Goldsmith, W.W. and Blakely, E.J. 1992: *Separate Societies: Poverty and Inequality in U.S. Cities*, Philadelphia: Temple University Press.

Goossens, L. 1983: Het sociaal huisvestingsbeleid in België sinds 1830. In Koning Boudewijn Stichting (ed.), *Sociaal Woonbeleid*, Brussels: Koning Boudewijn Stichting, 12–31.

Gordon, D. 1978: Capitalist development and the history of the American city. In

W.K. Tabb and L. Sawers (eds), *Marxism and the Metropolis,* New York: Oxford University Press, 25–63.

Goswami, O. 1990: Calcutta's economy 1918–1970: the fall from grace. In: S. Chaudhuri (ed.), *Calcutta: The Living City,* Calcutta: Oxford University Press, 88–96.

Government of India 1995: *Economic Survey: 1994–95,* New Delhi: Ministry of Finance, Economic Division.

Grattan, M., 1996: Unemployment: the big new business opportunity. *Australian Financial Review,* 30 (December), 1/8.

Grava, S. 1991: *Battery Park City: Between Edge and Fabric,* New York: Columbia University, School of Architecture, Planning and Preservation.

Greenberg, S. 1981: Industrial location and ethnic residential patterns in an industrializing city: Philadelphia, 1880. In T. Hershberg (ed.), *Philadelphia: Work, Space, Family and Group Experience in the Nineteenth Century,* New York: Oxford University Press, 204–29.

Greenhouse, S. 1992: Why Paris works. *The New York Times Magazine,* 19 July 1992.

Greer, S. 1962: *The Emerging City; Myth and Reality,* New York: The Free Press.

Gregory, R. and Hunter, B. 1995a: *The Macro-Economy and the Growth of Ghettos and Urban Poverty in Australia,* Centre for Economic Policy Research, Australian National University.

Gregory, R. and Hunter, B. 1995b: Further remarks on increased neighbourhood inequality. *Social Security Journal,* June 1995, 20–28.

Greig, A. 1995: *The Stuff That Dreams Are Made Of: Housing Provision in Australia 1945–1960,* Melbourne: Melbourne University Press.

Grimm, S. and Ronneberger, K. 1995: Städtische Professionelle zwischen Weltstadt und Nationalstaat: Multikulturelle Gesellschaft und Stadtentwicklung. In P. Noller and K. Ronneberger (eds), *Die neue Dienstleistungsstadt; Berufsmilieus in Frankfurt am Main,* Frankfurt/New York: Campus Verlag, 219–48.

Gyourko, J. and Summers, A.A. 1995: Block grants should reward efficient cities. *The Philadelphia Inquirer.* March 3.

Haila, A. 1991: Four types of investment in land and property. *International Journal of Urban and Regional Research,* 15 (3), 343–65.

Haila, A. 1997: The neglected builder of global cities. In O. Källtorp et al. (eds), *Cities in Transformation–Transformation in Cities,* Aldershot: Avebury, 51–64.

Haila, A. 1998: *Real Estate Policy.* Paper presented at The First International Conference on Quality of Life in Cities, National University of Singapore, Singapore, March 4–6.

Hall, P. 1966: *The World Cities,* New York: McGraw-Hill.

Halpern, R. and Morris, J. (eds) 1997: *American Exceptionalism? U.S. Working-Class Formation in an International Context,* New York: St Martin's Press.

Hamnett, C. 1984: Housing the two nations: socio-tenurial polarisation in England and Wales. *Urban Studies,* 21, 389–405.

Hamnett, C. 1994a: Social polarisation in global cities: theory and evidence. *Urban Studies,* 31, 410–24.

Hamnett, C. 1994b: Socio-economic change in London: professionalisation not polarisation. *Built Environment,* 20, 192–203.

Hamnett, C. 1996: Why Sassen is wrong: a response to Burgers. *Urban Studies,* 33,

107–10.

Hamnett, C. 1998: Social polarisation, economic restructuring and welfare state regimes. In S. Musterd and W. Ostendorf (eds), *Urban segregation and the welfare state*, London: Routledge, 15–27.

Hamnett, C. and Cross, D. 1998: Social polarisation and inequality in London: the earnings evidence, 1979–95. *Environment and Planning C*, 16, 659–80.

Hanchett, T.W. 1998: *Sorting out the New South City: Race, Class, and Urban Development in Charlotte, 1875–1975*. Chapel Hill: University of North Carolina Press.

Harloe, M. and Fainstein, S.S. 1992: Conclusion: the divided cities. In S.S. Fainstein, I. Gordon, and M. Harloe (eds), *Divided Cities; New York & London in the Contemporary World*, Oxford: Blackwell, 236–68.

Harrod, R.F. 1948: *Towards a Dynamic Economics*, London: Macmillan.

Harvey, D. 1985: *The Urbanisation of Capital*, Oxford: Blackwell.

Harvey, D. 1987: Flexible accumulation through urbanization: reflections on "Post-Modernism in the American City". *Antipode* 19 (3), 260–86.

Harvey, D. 1989: *The Condition of Post-modernity*, Oxford: Blackwell.

Harvey, D. 1994: Flexible accumulation through urbanization. In: A. Amin (ed.), *Post-Fordism: A Reader*, Oxford: Blackwell, 361–86.

Hassan, R. 1971: Class, ethnicity and occupational structure in Singapore. *Ekistics*, 32, 58–65.

Häußerman, H., Münz, R. and Kapphan, A. 1995: *Migration, Berlin. Zuwanderung, Gesellschaftliche Probleme, Politische Ansatze*, Berlin: Senatsverwaltung für Stadtentwicklung, Umweltschutz und Technologie.

Hayakawa, K. and Hirayama, Y. 1991: The impact of the *minkatsu* policy on Japanese housing and land use. *Environment and Planning D*, 9, 151–64.

Hebbert, M. and Nakai Norihiro 1988: *How Tokyo Grows: Land Development and Planning on the Metropolitan Fringe*, London: STICERD.

Herbert, B. 1999: Mr. Lott's 'Big Mistake'. *New York Times*, New York, NY, A-31.

Hershberg, T., Greenberg, S., Burstein, A., Yancey, W. and Ericksen, E. 1981: A tale of three cities: blacks, immigrants, and opportunity in Philadelphia, 1850–1880, 1930, 1970. In T. Hershberg (ed.), *Philadelphia: Work, Space, Family and Group Experience in the Nineteenth Century*, New York: Oxford University Press, 461–91.

Hill, R.C., and Fujita, K. 1995. Osaka's Tokyo Problem. *International Journal of Urban and Regional Research*, 19 (2), 181–91.

Hines, M.A. 1988: International dimensions of real estate. *The Appraisal Journal*, 56 (4), 492–501.

Hirst, P. and Thompson, G. 1996: *Globalization in Question: The International Economy and the Possibilities of Governance*, Cambridge: Polity Press.

Hodder, B.W. 1953: Racial groupings in Singapore. *Malayan Journal of Tropical Geography*, 1, 25–36.

Holston, J. 1989: *The Modernist City: An Anthropological Critique of Brasilia*. Chicago: University of Chicago Press.

Honma Masahito 1986: *Kan no toshi, min no toshi* (Official city, people's city). Tokyo: Nihon Keizai Hyôronsha.

Horne, D. 1971: *The Lucky Country*, Ringwood: Penguin Books (revised edition).

Horton, J. 1995: *The Politics of Diversity: Immigration, Resistance, and Change in Monterey Park, California*, Philadelphia: Temple University Press.

Housing and Development Board (HDB), Singapore 1960–1994: *Annual Reports*, Singapore: HDB.

Hoyle, B.S., Pinder, D.A. and Husain, M.S. (eds) 1988: *Revitalizing the Waterfront*, London: Belhaven Press.

Humphrey, J.W. 1985: *Geographic Analysis of Singapore's Population*, Singapore: Department of Statistics.

Hunter, B. 1995: Is there an Australian underclass? *Urban Futures*, 18, 14–25.

Husung, S. and Lieser, P. 1996: GreenBelt Frankfurt. In R. Keil, G.R. Wekerle, D.V.J. Bell (eds), *Local Places in the Age of the Global City*, Montreal: Black Rose Books, 211–22.

Ianni, O. and Cardoso, F.H. 1959: *Cor e Mobilidade Social em Florianopolis*, Sao Paulo: Companhia Editora Nacional.

Ishida Yorifusa 1992: *Mikan no Tôkyô keikaku* (Tokyo's uncompleted plans). Tokyo: Chikuma Shobô.

Ishida Yorifusa 1994: *The Results Fell Far Short or Even the Contrary: The Dispersion Policies of Tokyo from the 1860s to the 1990s and in the Future.* Paper for the Seventh Conference of the European Association of Japanese Studies, Copenhagen, 22–26 August.

Jackson, K.T. 1985: *Crabgrass Frontier: The Suburbanization of the United States*, New York: Oxford University Press.

Jacobs, J.M. 1996: *The Edge of Empire*, London: Routledge.

Jakle, J.A. and Wilson, D. 1992: *Derelict Landscapes*, Savage, MD: Rowman & Littlefield.

Jameson, F. 1991: *Postmodernism or the Cultural Logic of Late Capitalism*, Durham, NC: Duke University Press.

Jet Magazine (1997), 91 (17) 23, Chicago, IL: Johnson Publications.

Johnston, R. 1973: *Urban Residential Patterns*, London: Bell.

Jones, J. 1996: The new ghetto aesthetic. In V.T. Berry and C.L. Manning-Miller (eds), *Mediated Messages and African-American Culture: Contemporary Issues*, Thousand Oaks: Sage, 40–51.

Jones, M.A. 1972: *Housing and Poverty in Australia*, Melbourne: Melbourne University Press.

Kantrowitz, N. 1969: Ethnic and racial segregation in the New York Metropolis, 1960. *American Journal of Sociology*, 74, 685–95.

Kasinitz, P. 1992: *Caribbean New York: Black Immigrants and the Politics of Race*, Ithaca: Cornell University Press.

Katznelson, I. 1981: *City Trenches, Urban Politics and the Patterning of Class in the United States*, New York: Pantheon Books.

Keil, R. 1993: *Weltstadt – Stadt der Welt: Internationalisierung und lokale Politik in Los Angeles*, Münster: Westfälisches Dampfboot.

Keil, R. and Lieser, P. 1992: Global city – local politics. *Comparative Urban and Community Research*, 4, 39–69.

Keil, R. and Ronneberger, K. 1994: Going up the country: internationalization and urbanization on Frankfurt's northern fringe. *Environment and Planning D*, 12, 137–66.

Kelsey, J. 1995: *Economic Fundamentalism: the New Zealand Model*, London: Pluto Press.

Kendig, H. 1979: *New Life for Old Suburbs*, Sydney: Allen & Unwin.

Kesteloot, C. 1985: L'évolution du mode d'occupation des logements à Bruxelles,

1970–1981. *Revue Belge de Géographie*, 109 (4), 227–34.

Kesteloot, C. 1990: Economische determinanten van stedelijke structuren. *Ruimtelijke Planning*, 25, 1–42.

Kesteloot, C. 1995a: The creation of socio-spatial marginalisation in Brussels: a tale of flexibility, geographical competition and guestworkers neighbourhoods. In C. Hadjimichalis and D. Sadler (eds), *Europe at the Margins: New Mosaics of Inequality*, Chichester: John Wiley, 69–85.

Kesteloot, C. 1995b: La problématique d'intégration des jeunes urbains: une analyse géographique du cas bruxellois. In: C. Fijnaut et al. (eds), *Changes in Society, Crime and Criminal Justice in Europe, Volume I. Crime and Insecurity in the City*, Antwerpen: Kluwer Rechtswetenschappen België, I.113–29.

Kesteloot, C. and Cortie, C. 1998: Housing Turks and Moroccans in Brussels and Amsterdam: the difference between private and public markets. *Urban Studies*, 35 (10), 1835–53.

Kesteloot, C. and De Decker, P. 1992: Territoria en migraties als geografische factoren van racisme. In E. Deslé and A. Martens (eds), *Gezichten van het Hedendaags Racisme*, Brussels: VUB-Press, 69–108.

Kesteloot, C., De Decker, P. and Manço, A. 1997: Turks and housing in Belgium, with special reference to Brussels, Ghent and Visé. In A.Ş. Özüekren and R. van Kempen (eds), *Turks in European Cities: Housing and Urban Segregation*, Utrecht: European Research Centre on Migration and Ethnic Relations, 67–97.

Kesteloot, C. and Meert, H. 1999: Informal space: the socio-economic functions and spatial location of informal economic activities in Belgian cities. *International Journal for Urban and Regional Research*, 23, pp. 232–251.

Kesteloot, C., Peleman, K. and Van der Haegen, H. 1998: Vreemdelingen in België: de ruimtelijke evolutie in de jaren negentig. *Acta Geographica Lovaniensia*, 37, 273–94.

Kesteloot, C. and Van der Haegen, H. 1997: Foreigners in Brussels 1981–1991: spatial continuity and social change. *Tijdschrift voor Economische en Sociale Geografie*, 88 (2), 105–19.

King, A.D. 1976: *Colonial Urban Development: Culture, Social Power and Environment*, New York: Routledge.

Kipfer, S. and Keil, R. 1995: Urbanisierung und Technologie in der Periode des globalen Kapitalismus. In H. Hitz, R. Keil, U. Lehrer, K. Ronneberger, C. Schmid and R. Wolff (eds), *Capitales Fatales: Urbanisierung und Politik in den Finanzmetropolen Frankfurt und Zürich*, Zürich: Rotpunktverlag, 61–87.

Knight, R.V. 1986: The advanced industrial metropolis: a new type of world. In H.-J. Ewers, J.B. Goddard and H. Matzerath (eds), *The Future of the Metropolis*, Berlin: Walter de Gruyter, 391–436.

Knox, P.L. 1991: The restless urban landscape. *Annals of the Association of American Geographers*, 81 (2), 181–209.

Knox, P. 1993: *The Restless Urban Landscape*, Englewood Cliffs: Prentice-Hall.

Knox, P.L. and Taylor, P.J. (eds) 1995: *World Cities in a World System*, Cambridge: Cambridge University Press.

Kohl, B. 1996: Coca/Cocaine Control Policy in Bolivia. *Colloqui*, 11, 1–7.

Kohl, B. 1999: *Market and Government Reform in Bolivia: Global Trends and Local Responses*, Ithaca, NY, Cornell University (doctoral thesis).

Kohli, A. 1987: *The State and Poverty in India: The Politics of Reform*, Cambridge: Cambridge University Press.

Kokudochô (National Land Agency) 1991: *Shutoken hakusho* (White paper for the national capital region), Tokyo: Japanese government publication.

Kokudochô (National Land Agency) 1996: *Shutoken hakusho* (White paper for the national capital region), Tokyo: Japanese government publication.

Körner, W. and Ronneberger, K. 1994: Last exit Sossenheim? *Bauwelt*, 1/2, 58–63.

Kunzmann, K.R. 1996: Euro-megalopolis or Themepark Europe? Scenarios for European spatial development. *International Planning Studies*, 1, 143–63.

Kuttner, R. 1996: Market-worship widens income gap. *Guardian Weekly*, June 30, 16.

Ladd, B. 1997: *The Ghosts of Berlin: Confronting German History in the Urban Landscape*, Chicago: University of Chicago Press.

Lal, D. 1995: India and China: contrasts in economic liberalization. *World Development*, 23, 1475–94.

Lamphere, L. 1992: *Structuring Diversity: Ethnographic Perspectives on the New Immigration*, Chicago: University of Chicago Press.

Larudee, M. 1993: Trade policy: who wins? Who loses? In G. Epstein, J. Graham and J. Nembhard (eds), *Creating a New World Economy: Forces of Change & Plans for Action*, Philadelphia: Temple University Press, 47–63.

Lash, S. and Urry, J. 1994: *Economies of Signs and Space*, London: Sage.

Laurie, B., Hershberg, T. and Alter, G. 1981: Immigrants and industry: the Philadelphia experience, 1850–1880. In T. Hershberg (ed.), *Post-Fordism: A Reader*, New York: Oxford University Press, 93–119.

LeGates, R.T. and Hartman, C. 1986: The anatomy of displacement in the United States. In N. Smith and P. Williams (eds), *Gentrification of the City*, Boston: Allen & Unwin, 178–203.

Lehrer, U.A. 1994: Images of the periphery: the architecture of FlexSpace in Switzerland. *Environment and Planning D*, 12, 187–205.

Lemann, N. 1996: Kicking in Groups (Alleged Decline of America's Communal Culture). *The Atlantic Monthly*, 277 (4), 22ff.

Lesthaeghe, R. 1995: La deuxième transition démographique dans les pays occidentaux: une interprétation. *Actes de la Chair Quetelet*, Paris: L'Harmattan, 133–80.

Levine, M.V. 1995: Globalization and wage polarization in U.S. and Canadian cities: does public policy make a difference? In P. Kresl and G. Gappert (eds), *North American Cities and the Global Economy*, Thousand Oaks, Ca.: Sage, 89–111.

Levy, F. 1987: *Dollars and Dreams: The Changing American Income Distribution*, New York: Russell Sage Foundation.

Lewis, W.A. 1954: Economic development with unlimited supplies of labor. *Manchester School of Economic and Social Studies*, 22, 139–91.

Li, T. 1989: *Malays in Singapore: Culture, Economy and Ideology*, Singapore: Oxford University Press.

Lieberson, S. 1963: *Ethnic Patterns in American Cities*, New York: The Free Press.

Lieberson, S. 1980: *A Piece of the Pie: Blacks and White Immigrants Since 1880*, Berkeley: University of California Press.

Lieser, P. and Keil, R. 1988: Zitadelle und Getto: Modell Weltstadt. In W. Prigge and H.-P. Schwartz (eds), *Das Neue Frankfurt: Städtebau und Architektur im Modernisierungsprozeß 1925–1988*, Frankfurt: Vervuert, 183–208.

Lievens, J., Martens, A. and Brasseur, N. 1975: *De Grote Stad, Een Geplande Chaos*, Leuven: Davidsfonds.

Lin Kuo Ching and Amina Tyabji 1991: Home ownership policy in Singapore: an assessment. *Housing Studies*, 6 (1), 15–38.

Lindahl, D.P. 1995: *Changes in Commercial Real Estate Finance and the Transformation of Regional Economics*. Paper presented at the meeting of the Association of American Geographers, Chicago, March.

Lipietz, A. 1992: A regulationist approach to the future of urban ecology. *Capitalism, Nature, Socialism*, 3 (3), 101–10.

Lipset, S.M. 1996: *American Exceptionalism: A Double-Edged Sword*, New York: W.W. Norton.

Logan, J. 1993: Cycles and trends in the globalization of real estate. In P.L. Knox (ed.), *The Restless Urban Landscape*, Englewood Cliffs, NJ: Prentice-Hall, 35–54.

Logan, J.R. and Alba, R.D. 1996: *Does Upward Mobility Mean Living in a Better Neighborhood? The Experience of Minorities and Immigrants in the New York Metropolis*. Paper presented at the 1996 W.E.B. DuBois Conference on Conservatism, Affirmative Action, and Other Public Policy Issues, Wright State University, October 17–19.

Logan, J.R., Alba, R.D., Dill, M. and Min Zhou 1999: Ethnic segmentation in the American metropolis: increasing divergence in economic incorporation, 1980–1990. *International Migration Review*, forthcoming.

Logan, J.R., Alba, R.D., McNulty, T. and Fisher, B. 1996: Making a place in the metropolis: locational attainment in cities and suburbs. *Demography*, 33, 443–53.

Logan, J.R. and Molotch, H. 1987: *Urban Fortunes: The Political Economy of Place*, Berkeley: University of California Press.

Logan, J.R., Taylor-Gooby, P. and Reuter, M. 1992: Poverty and income inequality. In S. Fainstein, I. Gordon, and M. Harloe (eds), *Divided Cities: New York & London in the Contemporary World*, Oxford: Blackwell, 129–50.

Logan, J. and Swanstrom, T. 1990: *Beyond City Limits: Urban Policy and Economic Restructuring in Comparative Perspective*, Philadelphia: Temple University Press.

Longworth, R.C. 1998: *Global Squeeze: The Coming Crisis for First-World Nations*, Lincolnwood, Ill.: Contemporary Books.

Lovering, J. 1990: Fordism's unknown successor: a comment on Scott's theory of flexible accumulation and the re-emergence of regional economics. *International Journal of Urban and Regional Research*, 14, 159–74.

Lubiano, W. (ed.) 1997: *The House that Race Built: Black Americans, United States Terrain*, New York: Pantheon.

MacDonald, P. 1995: *Places for Everyone. Social Equity in Australian Cities and Regions*, Canberra: Australian Government Publishing Service.

Machimura Takashi 1992: The urban restructuring process in Tokyo in the 1980s: Transforming Tokyo into a world city. *International Journal of Urban and Regional Research*, 16 (1), 114–28.

Machimura Takashi 1994: "*Sekai toshi*" *Tôkyô no kôzô tenkan: Toshi risutorakucharingu no shakaigaku* (The structural transformation of "world city" Tokyo: A sociology of urban restructuring), Tokyo: Tôkyô Daigaku Shuppankai.

Madanipour, A., Cars, G. and Allen J. (eds) 1998: *Social Exclusion in European Cities – Processes, Experiences and Responses*, London: Jessica Kingsley Publishers.

Mainichi Shinbunsha (ed.) 1986: *Shitamachi: Kokusai shinpojiumu no kiroku* (Shitamachi:

Records of an international symposium), Tokyo: Mainichi Shinbunsha.

Mallick, R. 1993: *Development Policy of a Communist Government: West Bengal since 1977*, Cambridge: Cambridge University Press.

Marable, M. 1991: *The Crisis of Color and Democracy: Essays on Race, Class, and Power*, Monroe, ME: Common Courage Press.

Marcuse, P. 1985: Gentrification, abandonment, and displacement: connections, causes, and policy responses in New York City. *Journal of Urban and Contemporary Law*, 28, 195–240.

Marcuse, P. 1989: Dual city: a muddy metaphor for a quartered city. *International Journal of Urban and Regional Research*, 13 (4), 697–708.

Marcuse, P. 1996: *Is Australia Different? Globalisation and the New Urban Poverty*, Melbourne: Australian Housing and Urban Research Institute.

Marcuse, P. 1997a: The enclave, the citadel, and the ghetto: what has changed in the post-fordist U.S. city. *Urban Affairs Review*, 33 (2), 228–64.

Marcuse, P. 1997b: The ghetto of exclusion and the fortified enclave; new patterns in the United States. *American Behavioral Scientist*, 41 (3), 311–26.

Marcuse, P. 1998: Space over time: the changing position of the black ghetto in the United States. *Netherlands Journal of Housing and the Built Environment*, 13 (1), 7–23.

Marcuse, P. 1999a: The layered city. In P. Madsden (ed.), forthcoming.

Marcuse, P. 1999b: Of time and the fetishization of the built city. In M. Speaks (ed.), *Cities in Transition*, forthcoming.

Marsden, S. 1986: *Business, Charity and Sentiment. The South Australian Housing Trust 1936–1986*, Adelaide: Wakefield Press.

Massey, D. 1984: *Spatial Divisions of Labour: Social Structures and the Geography of Production*, London: Macmillan.

Massey, D.S. 1978: *Residential Segregation of Spanish Americans in United States Urbanized Areas*. Princeton: University of Princeton (thesis)

Massey, D.S. and Bitterman, B. 1985: Explaining the paradox of Puerto Rican segregation. *Social Forces*, 64 (2), 306–31

Massey, D.S. and Denton, N.A. 1993: *American Apartheid: Segregation and the Making of the Underclass*, Cambridge, MA: Harvard University Press.

Mattar, A. 1984: Changes in the social and economic status of the Malays. *People's Action Party 1954–1984, Petir 30th Anniversary Issue*, 112–25.

McGee, T., and Yeung Yue-man 1993: Urban futures for Pacific Asia: Towards the 21st century. In Yeung Yue-man (ed.), *Pacific Asia in the 21st Century*, Hong Kong: Chinese University Press, 47–69.

McIntosh, P. 1988: *White Privilege and Male Privilege: a Personal Account of Coming to See Correspondences Through Work in Women's Studies*. Wellesley: Wellesley College, Center for Research on Women.

McIntosh, P. 1990: White privilege: unpacking the invisible knapsack. *Independent School* (Winter) 31–6.

McKenzie, E. 1994: *Privatopia*, New Haven: Yale University Press.

McLoughlin, B.J. 1992: *Shaping Melbourne's Future?* Melbourne: Cambridge University Press.

McMahon, J. 1990: Foreign investment in U.S. real estate. *Real Estate Issues* (Fall), 35–7.

Meert, H., Mistiaen, P. and Kesteloot, C. 1997: The geography of survival: household strategies in urban settings. *Tijdschrift voor Sociale en Economische Geografie*, 88 (2), 169–81.

Merton, R.K. 1968: *Social Theory and Social Structure*, London: Glencoe.

Meusen, H. and Van Kempen, R. 1995: Towards residual housing? A comparison of Britain and the Netherlands. *Netherlands Journal of Housing and the Built Environment*, 10, 239–58.

Mingione, E. (ed.) 1996: *Urban Poverty and the Underclass*, Oxford: Blackwell.

Ministry of Labor, Research and Statistics Department, Singapore 1995: *Profile of the Labor Force of Singapore 1983–1994*, Singapore: National Printers.

Mistiaen, P. and Kesteloot, C. 1998: Socialisation et marginalisation des jeunes de la zone défavorisée de Bruxelles, un accès différencié à l'école. *Espace–Populations–Sociétés*, 1998 (2), 249–62.

Mistiaen, P., Meert, H. and Kesteloot, C. 1995: Polarisation socio-spatiale et stratégies de survie dans deux quartiers bruxellois, *Espace–Populations–Sociétés*, 1995 (3), 277–90.

Mitra, M. 1990: *Calcutta in the 20th Century: An Urban Disaster*, Calcutta: Asiatic Book Agency.

Moffett, S. 1996: It'll cost you: Can Hashimoto's popularity weather a *juwen* bailout? *Far Eastern Economic Review*, 15 February, 17.

Mollenkopf, J. 1992: *A Phoenix in the Ashes: The Rise and Fall of the Koch Coalition in New York City Politics*, Princeton, NJ: Princeton University Press.

Mollenkopf, J. and Castells, M. (eds) 1991: *Dual City: Restructuring New York*, New York: Russell Sage Foundation.

Moodie, A-M. 1995: Next best proves better as inner-city demand surges. *Weekend Australian*, October 7–8, 5.

Muehring, K. 1998: The fire next time. *Institutional Investor*, 32 (9), pp. 74ff.

Mukherjee, S. 1975: *Under the Shadow of the Metropolis: They are Citizens Too* (report on the survey of 10,000 pavement dwellers in Calcutta), Calcutta: CMDA.

Mukherjee, S. and Racine, J. 1986: The urban poor: an outlook of Calcutta's pavement dwellers. In J. Racine (ed.), *Calcutta 1981*, New Delhi: Concept Publishing, 229–36.

Muller, P.O. 1976: *The Outer City*, Washington, DC: Association of American Geographers.

Munnell, A.H., Browne, L.E., McEneaney, J. and Tootell, G.M.B. 1992. *Mortgage Lending in Boston: Interpreting the HMDA Data*, Boston: Federal Reserve Bank of Boston (Working Paper # 92–7)

Munshi, S.K. 1975: *Calcutta Metropolitan Explosion: Its Nature and Roots*, New Delhi: People's Publishing House.

Munshi, S.K. 1986: The genesis of the Metropolis In: J. Racine (ed.), *Calcutta 1981*, New Delhi: Concept Publishing, 29–50.

Musterd, S. (ed.) 1994: A rising European underclass? *Built Environment*, 20, 184–268.

Musterd, S. and Ostendorf, W. (eds) 1998: *Urban Segregation and the Welfare State: Inequality and Exclusion in Western Cities*, London: Routledge.

Nakabayashi Kazuki 1990: *Tôkyô no chika to toshi kôzô no henka* (Land prices in Tokyo and changes in the urban structure). In Ishida Yorifusa (ed.), *Dai toshi no tochi mondai to seisaku* (Land problems and policies in the metropolis), Tokyo: Nihon Hyôronsha, 46–81.

National Capital Planning Authority 1993: *Affordable Housing in High Value Locations*, Canberra: Australian Government Publishing Service.

National Realty Committee 1989: *America's Real Estate*, Washington, DC: National Realty Committee.

Neary, I. 1997: Burakumin in contemporary Japan. In M. Weiner (ed.), *Japan's Minorities: The Illusion of Homogeneity*, London: Routledge, 50–78.

Neville, R.J.W. 1965: The areal distribution of population in Singapore. *Journal of Tropical Geography*, 20, 16–25.

Neville, R.J.W. 1966: Singapore, ethnic diversity and its implications. *Annals of the Association of American Geographers*, 56, 236–53.

Neville, R.J.W. 1969: The distribution of population in the post-war period. In Ooi Jin Bee and Chiang Hai Ding (eds), *Modern Singapore*, Singapore: University of Singapore Press, 52–68.

Newfield, J. 1976: How the power brokers profit. In R.E. Alcaly and D. Mermelstein (eds), *The Fiscal Crisis of American Cities*, New York: Random House, 296–314.

Newton, P.W. 1995: Changing places? Households, firms and urban hierarchies in the information age. In J. Brotchie, M. Batty, E. Blakely, P. Hall and P. Newton (eds), *Cities in Competition. Productive and Sustainable Cities for the 21st Century*, Melbourne: Longman Australia, 161–90.

Noguchi Yukio 1994: The 'bubble' and economic policies in the 1980s. *Journal of Japanese Studies*, 20 (2), 291–329.

O'Leary, J. and Machimura Takashi 1995: Between state and capital: Third sector organizational development in Tokyo. *Comparative Politics*, 27 (3), 317–37.

O'Loughlin, J. and Friedrichs, J. 1996: *Social Polarization in Post-Industrial Metropolises*, Berlin: Walter de Gruyter & Co.

Ogburn, W.F. 1937: *Social Characteristics of Cities*, Chicago: The International City Managers' Association.

Oizumi E. 1994: Property finance in Japan: Expansion and collapse of the bubble economy. *Environment and Planning A*, 26 (2), 199–214.

Ôtani Sachio (ed.) 1988: *Toshi ni totte tochi to wa nanika* (What is land for a city?). Tokyo: Chikuma Shobô.

Özüekren, A.Ş. and Magnusson, L. 1997: Housing conditions of Turks in Sweden. In A.Ş. Özüekren and R. van Kempen (eds), *Turks in European Cities: Housing and Urban Segregation*, Utrecht: European Research Centre on Migration and Ethnic Relations, 191–222.

Özüekren, A.Ş. and Van Kempen, R. (eds.) 1997: *Turks in European Cities: Housing and Urban Segregation*, Utrecht: European Research Centre on Migration and Ethnic Relations.

Pang Eng Fong 1974: Growth, inequality and race in Singapore. *International Labour Review*, 3, 15–28.

Panitch, L. 1998: The state in a changing world: social-democratizing global capitalism? *Monthly Review*, 50 (5), 11–22.

Papadopoulos, A.G. 1996: *Urban Regimes and Strategies: Building Europe's Central Executive District in Brussels*, Chicago: The University of Chicago Press.

Pasquier, D. 1993: The salt mines: television authors and scriptwriters. *Sociologie du Travail*, 35 (4), 409–30.

Patrick, H. and Rohlen, T. 1987: Small-scale family enterprises. In K. Yamamura and Y. Yasuba (eds), *The Political Economy of Japan, Vol 1: The Domestic Transformation*, Stanford, CA: Stanford University Press, 331–85.

Peach, C. 1981: Conflicting interpretations of segregation. In P. Jackson and S. Smith (eds), *Social Interaction and Ethnic Segregation*, London: Academic Press, 19–33.

Peach, C. 1996: Does Britain have ghettos? *Transactions of the Institute of British Geographers*, 21 (10), 216–35.

Peel, M. 1995: *Good Times, Hard Times: The Past and the Future in Elizabeth*, Melbourne: Melbourne University Press.

Peet, R. 1991: *Global Capitalism*, London: Routledge.

Peeters, L. and De Decker, P. 1997: *Het Woonbeleid in Vlaanderen op een Tweesprong*, Berchem: EPO.

Perry, M., Kong, L. and Yeoh, B. 1997: *Singapore: A Developmental City State*, Chichester: John Wiley & Sons, Ltd.

Philpott, T.L. 1978: *The Slum and the Ghetto: Neighborhood Deterioration and Middle-class Reform, Chicago, 1880–1930*, New York: Oxford University Press.

Piore, M.J. and Sabel, C. 1984: *The Second Industrial Divide*, New York: Basic.

Piven, F.F. 1995: Is it global economics or neo-laissez-faire? *New Left Review*, 213, 107–15.

Pons, P. (ed.) 1984: *Des villes nommées Tokyo*, Paris: Autrement.

Portes, A. and Bach, R.L. 1985: *The Latin Journey: Cuban and Mexican Immigrants in the United States*, Berkeley: University of California Press.

Powell, D. 1993: *Out West: Perceptions of Sydney's Western Suburbs*, Sydney: Allen and Unwin.

Power, A 1997: *Estates on the Edge: The Social Consequences of Mass Housing in Northern Europe*, London: Macmillan.

Pratt, A.C. 1994: Information sources for non-commercial research on industrial property and industrial activity. In R. Ball and A.C. Pratt (eds), *Industrial Property*, London: Routledge, 40–62.

Prefeitura de Rio de Janeiro 1995: *Diagnostico da Cidade do Rio de Janeiro. Conçorcio Mantenedor do Plano Estrategico da Cidade*, Rio de Janeiro: Prefeitura da Cidade do Rio de Janeiro.

Preteceille, E. 1988: *Mutations Urbaines et Politiques Locales, Volume 1*, Paris: Centre de Sociologie Urbaine.

Preteceille, E. 1994a: Cidades globais e segmentação social. In L.C.Q. Ribeiro and O.A. Santos Junior (eds), *Globalização, Fragmentação e Reforma Urbana: o Futuro das Cidades Brasileiras na Crise*, Rio de Janeiro: Civilização Brasileira.

Preteceille, E. 1994b: *Mutations Urbaines et Politiques Locales, Volume 2*, Paris: Centre de Sociologie Urbaine.

Prigge, W. and Ronneberger, K. 1995: Globalisierung und Regionalisierung. Zur Auflösung Frankfurts in die Region. In D. Ipsen (ed.), *Stadt–Regionen*, Frankfurt.

Probert, B. 1990: Globalisation, economic restructuring and the state. In S. Bell and B. Head (eds), *State, Economy and Public Policy in Australia*, Melbourne: Oxford University Press, 98–118.

Pucher, J. 1995a Urban passenger transport in the United States and Europe: a comparative analysis of public policies, part 1: travel behaviour, urban development and automobile use. *Transport Reviews*, 15 (2), 99–177.

Pucher, J. 1995b Urban passenger transport in the United States and Europe: a comparative analysis of public policies, part 2: public transport, overall comparisons and recommendations. *Transport Reviews*, 15 (3), 211–27.

Pucher, J. and Lefèvre, C. 1996: *The Urban Transport Crisis in Europe and North America*, London: Macmillan Press.

Pugh, C. 1989: The World Bank and urban shelter in Calcutta, *Cities*, 6, 103–18.

Pusey, M. 1991: *Economic Rationalism in Canberra. A Nation Building State Changes its Mind*, Melbourne: Cambridge University Press.

Putnam, R.D. 1995: Bowling alone: America's declining social capital. *Journal of Democracy*, 6 (1), 65–78.

Putnam, R.D., Leonardi, R. and Nanetti, R.Y. 1993: *Making Democracy Work. Civic Traditions in Modern Italy*, Princeton: Princeton University Press.

Quadagno, J. 1998: Social security policy and the entitlement debate: the new American exceptionalism. In Y.H. Lo, and M. Schwartz (eds), *Social Policy and the Conservative Agenda*, Malden: Blackwell.

Rahms, H. 1991: Im Bann der Metropole. Eine Kleinstadt im Taunus. *Frankfurter Allgemeine Zeitung*, 14 September.

Raskall, P. 1995: *Who Gets What Where? Spatial Inequality Between and Within Australian Cities*. Paper for the Commonwealth Department of Housing and Regional Development Seminar on Spatial Inequality, Canberra, 20 October, 1995.

Reich, R. 1991: *The Work of Nations*, New York: Random House.

Relph, E. 1987: *The Modern Urban Landscape*, Baltimore: Johns Hopkins University Press.

Ribeiro, L.C. 1993: *Restructuring in Large Brazilian Cities: The Center/Periphery Model in Question*. Paper presented at the meeting of the Urban Sociology section of the International Sociology Association, Los Angeles, 1993.

Ribeiro, L.C.Q. and Cardoso, A. 1996: *A. Dualização e Reestruturação : o Caso do Rio de Janeiro, Rio de Janeiro* : Observatório de Políticas Urbanas e Gestão Municipal.

Rimmer, P. 1986: Japan's world cities: Tokyo, Osaka, Nagoya or Tokaido Megalopolis? *Development and Change*, 17 (1), 121–57.

Robins, K. 1991: Prisoners of the city: whatever should a postmodern city be? *New Formations*, 15, 1–22.

Robinson, R. and O'Sullivan, T. 1983: Housing tenure polarisation: some empirical evidence. *Housing Review*, 32, 116–17.

Rodan, G. 1989: *The Political Economy of Singapore's Industrialization: National State and International Capital*, London: Macmillan.

Rolnik, R. 1989: Territórios negros nas cidades Brasileiras. *Estudos Afro Asiáticos*, 17, 29–41.

Ronneberger, K. 1990: Metropolitane Urbanität, Der Pflasterstrand als Medium einer in die städtische Elite aufsteigenden Subkultur. In H. Schilling (ed.), *Urbane Zeiten, Lebensstilentwürfe und Kulturwandel in einer Stadtregion*, Frankfurt: Institut fur Kulturanthropolgie und Europäische Ethnologie der Universität, 15–44.

Ronneberger, K. 1994: Zitadellenökonomie und soziale Transformation der Stadt. In P. Noller, W. Prigge and K. Ronneberger (eds), *Stadt–Welt*, Frankfurt/New York: Campus Verlag, 180–97.

Ronneberger, K. and Keil, R. 1993: Riding the tiger of modernization: a preliminary analysis of redgreen municipal reform politics in Frankfurt am Main. *Capital-*

ism, Nature, Socialism, 4 (2), 19–50.

Ronneberger, K. and Keil, R. 1995: Ausser Atem: Frankfurt nach der Postmoderne. In H. Hitz, R. Keil, U. Lehrer, K. Ronneberger, C. Schmid and R. Wolff (eds), *Capitales Fatales: Urbanisierung und Politik in den Finanzmetropolen Frankfurt und Zürich,* Zürich: Rotpunktverlag, 284–353.

Rosen, C.M. 1986: *The Limits of Power,* Cambridge: Cambridge University Press.

Rosen, J. 1999: Rehnquist's choice, annals of laws. *The New Yorker,* 11 January 1999.

Roth, R. 1991: Frankfurt am Main: Skizzen zu einer Bewegungsmetropole. In F.-O. Brauerhoch (ed.), *Frankfurt am Main: Stadt, Soziologie und Kultur,* Frankfurt: Vervuert, 149–68.

Ruderman, A.P. 1990: Economic adjustment and the future of health services in the Third World. *Journal of Public Health Policy,* 11 (4), 481–89.

Rushdie, S. 1991: *Imaginary Homelands: Essays and Criticism 1981–1991,* London: Granta.

Saboia, J. 1994: Tendências do mercado de trabalho metropolitano: (des) assalariamento da mão-de-obra e precarização das relações de trabalho. In *Globalização, Fragmentação e Reforma Urbana: o Futuro das Cidades Brasileiras na Crise,* Rio de Janeiro: Civilização Brasileira, 103–19.

Sanabria, H. 1997: The discourse and practice of repression and resistance in the Chapare. In M.B. Leons and H. Sanabria (eds), *Coca/Cocaine, and the Bolivian Reality,* Albany: State University of New York Press, 169–93.

Sansone, L. 1993: Pai preto, filho negro. *Estudos Afro-Asiáticos,* 25, 73–98.

Sansone, L. 1998: The new politics of black culture in Bahia, Brazil. In C. Grovers and H. Vermullen (eds), *The Politics of Ethnic Consciousness,* New York: Macmillan Press, 277–309.

Sassen, S. 1984: The new labor demand in global cities. In M.P. Smith (ed.), *Cities in Transformation: Class, Capital and the State,* Beverly Hills: Sage, 139–71.

Sassen, S. 1986: New York City: economic restructuring and immigration. *Development and Change,* 17, 85–119.

Sassen, S. 1988: *The Mobility of Labor and Capital,* Cambridge: Cambridge University Press.

Sassen, S. 1990: Economic restructuring and the American city. *Annual Review of Sociology,* 16, 465–90.

Sassen, S. 1991: *The Global City: New York, London, Tokyo,* Princeton NJ: Princeton University Press.

Sassen, S. 1994: *Cities in a World Economy,* Thousand Oaks: Pine Forge Press.

Sassen, S. 1994: The urban complex in a world economy. *International Social Science Journal,* 139, 43–62.

Sassen, S. 1996: *Losing Control: Sovereignty in an Age of Globalization,* New York: Columbia University Press.

Savage, M. and Warde, A. 1993: *Sociology, Capitalism and Modernity,* New York: Continuum.

Savitch, H.V. 1995: The emergence of global cities. *Urban Affairs Review,* 31 (1), 137–42.

Sayer, A. 1989: Post-Fordism in question. *International Journal of Urban and Regional Research,* 13, 666–95.

Schultz, J. 1985: *Steel City Blues. The Human Cost of Industrial Crisis,* Ringwood: Penguin Books.

Schwartz, A. 1992: Corporate service linkages in large metropolitan areas. *Urban Affairs Quarterly*, 28 (2), 276–96.

Seidman, G.W. 1994: Man*ufacturing Militance: Worker's Movements in Brazil and South Africa, 1970–1985*, Berkeley: University of California Press.

Sennett, R. 1970: *The Uses of Disorder: Personal Identity and City Life*, New York: Vintage.

Shefter, M. 1985: *Political Crisis, Fiscal Crisis: the Collapse and Revival of New York City*, New York: Basic Books.

Shefter, M. 1992: *Political Crisis, Fiscal Crisis: The Collapse and Revival of New York City*, New York: Columbia University Press.

Silver, H. 1993: National conceptions of the new urban poverty: social structural change in Britain, France and the United States. *International Journal of Urban and Regional Research*, 17 (3), 336–54.

Singh, A. 1994: Openness and the market friendly approach to development: learning the right lessons from development experience. *World Development*, 22 (12), 1811–23.

Skolnick, J.H. 1995: What not to do about crime; the American Society of Criminology's 1994 Presidential Address. *Criminology*, 33 (1), 1–15.

Smith, C. 1987: Land of make-believe: Tokyo property price 'madness' defies reason. *Far Eastern Economic Review*, 29 October, 98.

Smith, N. 1997: Social justice and the new American urbanism: the revanchist city. In A. Merrifield and E. Swyngedouw (eds), *The Urbanization of Injustice*, New York: New York University Press, 117–36.

Smith, S.J. 1993: Residential segregation and the politics of racialization. In M. Cross, and M. Keith (eds), *Racism, The City and the State*, New York: Routledge and Kegan Paul, 128–43.

Sonenshein, R.J. 1993: *Politics in Black and White*, Princeton (NJ): Princeton University Press.

Soja, E.W. 1990: Heterotopologies: a remembrance of other spaces in the citadel-LA. *Strategies*, 3, 16–39.

Soja, E. 1991: Poles apart: urban restructuring in New York and Los Angeles. In J. Mollenkopf and M. Castells (eds.), *Dual City: Restructuring New York*, New York: Russell Sage Foundation, 361–76.

Soja, E.W. 1997: Margin/Alia: social justice and the new cultural politics. In A. Merrifield and E. Swyngedouw (eds), *The Urbanization of Injustice*, New York: New York University Press, 180–99.

South Burlington County NAACP v Mt. Laurel, 336 A.2d. 713 (1975) and 450 A.2d 390 (1983).

Stapleton, C.M. 1980: Reformulation of the family life-cycle concept: implications for residential mobility, *Environment and Planning A*, 12, 1103–18.

Stegman, M. 1988: *Housing and Vacancy Report: New York City, 1987*, New York: New York City Department of Housing Preservation and Development.

Stein, H. and Nafzier, E.W. 1990: Structural adjustment, human needs, and the World Bank Agenda. *Journal of Modern African Studies*, 29 (1), 173–89.

Stephens, G.R. 1996: Urban underrepresentation in the U.S. Senate. *Urban Affairs Review*, 31 (3), 404–18.

Stilwell, F. 1996: *"Globalisation": Reshaping Australian Cities?* Paper for the Regional Meeting of the International Sociological Association (Research Committee 21,

Regional and Urban Development), Brisbane 2–5 July 1996.

Storper, M. 1991: *Industrialization, Economic Development and the Regional Question in the Third World: From Import Substitution to Flexible Production*, London: Pion.

Storper, M. 1994: *Capitalist Imperative: Territory, Technology, and Industrial Growth*, Oxford: Blackwell.

Storper, M. and Walker, R. 1989: *The Capitalist Imperative: Territory, Technology, and Industrial growth*, New York: Blackwell.

Straits Times, several issues, March 1988–July 1989.

Sulamis, D. 1990: *Rio de Todas as Crises*, Rio de Janeiro: Instituto Universitário de Pesquisa do Rio de Janeiro.

Sumida Ward 1989: *Sangyô shinkô jigyô gaido '89* (Guide to Industry-Promotion Operations 1989), Tokyo: Sumida Ward Office.

Sutcliffe, B. 1994: Migration, rights and illogic. *Index on Censorship*, 23 (3), 27–37.

Suttles, G.D. 1974: *The Social Order of the Slum; Ethnicity and Territory in the Inner City*, Chicago: The University of Chicago Press.

Swamy, D.S. 1994: *The Political Economy of Industrialization: From Self-reliance to Globalization*, New Delhi: Sage.

Swyngedouw, E. and Kesteloot, C. 1990: Le passage sociospatial du Fordisme à la flexibilité: une interprétation des aspects spatiaux de la crise et de son issue. *Espace et Sociétés*, 54/55, 243–68.

Syms, P.M. 1994: The funding of developments on derelict and contaminated sites. In R. Ball and A.C. Pratt (eds), *Industrial Property*, London: Routledge, 63–82.

Tai Ching Ling 1988: *Housing Policy and High-rise Living. A Study of Singapore's Public Housing*, Singapore: Chopmen Publishers.

Takahashi Yûetsu (ed). 1992: *Dai toshi shakai no risutorakucharingu: Tôkyô no innaa shitei mondai* (The restructuring of a metropolitan society: Tokyo's inner city problems), Tokyo: Nihon Hyôronsha.

Takaki, R.T. 1993: *A Different Mirror: The Making of Multicultural America*, Boston: Little, Brown & Company.

Tanaka Yasuo 1980: *Nantonaku, kurisutaru* (Somehow, crystal), Tokyo: Iwanami Shoten.

Tarrow, S. 1996: Making social science work across space and time: a critical reflection on Robert Putnam's Making Democracy Work. *American Political Science Review*, 90 (2), 389–97.

Telles, E. 1992: Residential segregation by skin color in Brazil. *American Sociological Review*, 57, 186–97.

Telles, Edward E. and Lim, Nelson 1998: Does it Matter Who Answers the Race Question? Racial Classification and Income Inequality in Brazil. *Demography*, 35 (4), 465–74.

Teo Siew Eng 1986: New towns planning and development in Singapore. *Third World Planning Review*, 8, 251–71.

Teo Siew Eng 1989: Patterns of change in public housing in Singapore. *Third World Planning Review*, 11, 373–91.

Teo Siew Eng and Kong, L. 1997: Public housing in Singapore: interpreting 'quality' in the 1990s. *Urban Studies*, 34 (3), 441–52.

Thrift, N. 1987: The fixers: the urban geography of international commercial capital. In J. Henderson and M. Castells (eds), *Global Restructuring and Territorial Development*, London: Sage, 203–33.

TMG (Tokyo Metropolitan Government) 1990a: *Planning of Tokyo 1990,* Tokyo: Tokyo Metropolitan Government.

TMG (Tokyo Metropolitan Government) 1990b: *Tôkyôto jûtaku seisaku kondankai hôkoku: Seikatsu no yutakasa o jikkan dekiru sumai o mezashite* (Report of the advisory group on housing policy in Tokyo: Aiming for homes that afford a feeling of a prosperous life), Tokyo: Tokyo Metropolitan Government.

TMG (Tokyo Metropolitan Government) 1989: *Tôkyô no sangyô '89* (Industry in Tokyo, 1989), Tokyo: Tokyo Metropolitan Government.

TMG (Tokyo Metropolitan Government) 1991: *Tôkyô toshi hakusho '91* (White paper for Tokyo, 1991), Tokyo: Tokyo Metropolitan Government.

TMG (Tokyo Metropolitan Government) 1993: *Tôkyô no sangyô '93* (Industry in Tokyo, 1993), Tokyo: Tokyo Metropolitan Government.

TMG (Tokyo Metropolitan Government) 1996a: *Tôkyô toshi hakusho '96* (White paper for Tokyo, 1996), Tokyo: Tokyo Metropolitan Government.

TMG (Tokyo Metropolitan Government) 1996b: *Planning of Tokyo 1996,* Tokyo: Tokyo Metropolitan Government.

Toh Mun Heng and Tay Boon Nga 1994: *Households and Housing in Singapore,* Singapore: Department of Statistics.

Tolchin, M. 1989: Richest got richer and poorest got poorer in 1979–87. *New York Times,* March 23.

Torres, A. 1995: *Between Melting Pot and Mosaic: African Americans and Puerto Ricans in the New York Political Economy,* Philadelphia: Temple University Press.

Troy, P.N. 1991: *The Benefits of Owner Occupation.* Urban Research Program Working Paper No. 29, Canberra: URP.

United Nations Development Program 1993: *Human Development Report,* New York: Oxford University Press.

US Department of Housing and Urban Development 1995: *The Clinton Administration's National Urban Policy Report,* Washington DC: Office of Policy Development and Research, HUD.

Vale, L.J. 1993: Beyond the problem projects paradigm: defining and revitalizing "severely distressed" public housing. *Housing Policy Debate,* 4 (2).

Van Criekingen, M. 1996: Processus de gentrification à Bruxelles: le cas du quartier 'Dansaert Saint-Géry'. *Tijdschrift van de Belgische Vereniging voor Aardrijkskundige Studies,* 2, 205–33.

Vanden Eende, M. and Martens. A. 1994: *De Noordwijk, de Herhuisvesting van de Uitgewezenen,* Berchem: EPO.

Vandermotten, C. 1994:, Le Plan Régional de Développement de la Région de Bruxelles-capitale. In C. Vandermotten (ed.), *Planification et stratégies de développement dans les capitales européennes,* Bruxelles: Editions de l'Université de Bruxelles, 195–206.

Vandermotten, C. and Collard, A. 1985: La péri-urbanisation bruxelloise: le début de la fin. *Tijdschrift van de Belgische Vereniging voor Aardrijkskundige Studies,* 2, 277–98.

Van der Haegen, H. 1992: De strijd van de huishoudens om de Brusselse woonruimte. *Acta Geographica Lovaniensia,* 33, 721–35.

Van Elteren, M. 1996: GATT and beyond: world trade, the arts and American popular culture in Western Europe. *Journal of American Culture,* 19 (3), 59–73.

Van Grunsven, L. 1986: Residential mobility and population change in a regulated housing market: the case of Singapore. *Netherlands Journal of Housing and Environmental Research*, 1 (4), 353–78.

Van Grunsven, L. 1990: *Veranderend Wonen in Singapore; Overheidsinterventie in Stedelijke Huisvesting in Macro- en Micro-perspectief*, Utrecht: Faculty of Geographical Sciences, Utrecht University (PhD dissertation).

Van Grunsven, L. 1991: Population dynamics and housing environment change in Singapore: recent trends and policy responses. *Netherlands Journal of Housing and the Built Environment*, 6 (3), 229–52.

Van Grunsven, L. 1992: Integration versus segregation: ethnic minorities and urban politics in Singapore. *Journal of Economic and Social Geography*, 83 (3), 196–215.

Van Kempen, R. 1994: Ruimtelijke segregatie, ruimtelijke concentratie en sociale marginalisering in de Nederlandse stad. *Planologisch Nieuws*, 14 (4), 367–77.

Van Kempen, R. 1997: Turks in the Netherlands: housing conditions and segregation in a developed welfare state. In A.Ş. Özüekren and R. van Kempen (eds), *Turks in European Cities: Housing and Urban Segregation*, Utrecht: European Research Centre on Migration and Ethnic Relations, 158–90.

Van Kempen, R. and Bolt, G.S. 1997: Turks in the Netherlands: urban segregation and neighborhood choice. *American Behavioral Scientist*, 41 (3), 367–88.

Van Kempen, R. and Marcuse, P. 1997: A new spatial order in cities? *American Behavioral Scientist*, 41 (3), 285–99.

Van Kempen, R. and Özüekren, A.Ş. 1998: Ethnic segregation in cities: new forms and explanations in a dynamic world. *Urban Studies*, 35 (10), 1631–56.

Van Kempen, R. and Priemus, H. 1997: *Undivided Cities in the Netherlands: Present Situation, Political Rhetoric, and the Research Agenda*. Paper for the NETHUR Seminar on "Undivided Cities", The Hague, 11 October 1997.

Van Kempen, R. and Priemus, H. 1999: *Revolution in Social Housing in the Netherlands: Changing Social Function and Legal Status of Housing Associations*. Paper for the ENHR–CECODHAS–NETHUR Workshop on Social Housing Policy, Nunspeet, The Netherlands, 18/19 February 1999.

Van Kempen, R. and Van Weesep, J. 1997: Segregation, housing and ethnicity in Dutch cities. *Tijdschrift voor Economische en Sociale Geografie*, 88, 188–95.

Van Kempen, R. and Van Weesep, J. 1998: Ethnic residential patterns in Dutch cities: backgrounds, shifts and consequences. *Urban Studies*, 35 (10), 1813–33.

Varady, D.P., Preiser, W.F.E. and Russell, F.P. (eds) 1998: *New Directions in Urban Public Housing*, New Brunswick, NJ.: Center for Urban Policy Research.

Vasconcellos, E. 1997: The making of the middle-class city: transportation policy in São Paulo. *Environment and Planning A*, 29, 293–310.

Veja (weekly news periodical) 1992: *Arruaça Na Areia*, October 28.

Vianna, H. (ed.) 1997: *Galeras Cariocas: Territórios de Conflitos e Encontros Culturais*, Rio de Janeiro: Universidade Federal de Rio de Janeiro.

Vietorisz, T., Goldsmith, W.W. and Grengs, J. 1998: *Air Quality, Urban Form, and Coordinated Urban Policies*, Ithaca: Cornell University, Department of City and Regional Planning (Working Papers in Planning).

Von Freyberg, Th. 1996: *Der gespaltene Fortschritt: Zur städtischen Modernisierung am Beispiel Frankfurt am Main*, Frankfurt/New York: Campus Verlag.

Wacquant, L.J.D. 1993: Urban outcasts: stigma and division in the Black American ghetto and the French urban periphery. *International Journal of Urban and Regional*

Research, 17 (3), 366–83.

Wacquant, L.J.D. 1996: The rise of advanced marginality: notes on its nature and implications. *Acta Sociologica*, 39 (2), 121–39.

Wacquant, L.J.D. 1997: Three pernicious premises in the study of the American ghetto. *International Journal of Urban and Regional Research*, 21 (2), 341–53.

Wada Kiyomi 1992: *Chiiki shakai no 'kokusaika' to chônaikai jichikai* (Neighbourhood associations and the "internationalisation" of local society). *Toshi mondai*, 83 (1), 51–68.

Wade, R.C. 1964: *Slavery in the Cities: The South 1820–1860*, Oxford: Oxford University Press. Extracted in J.H. Bracey, Jr., A. Meier and E. Rudwick (eds) 1971: *The Rise of the Ghetto*, Belmont, CA: Wadsworth Publishing Co., 11–12.

Waldinger, R. 1986–1987: Changing ladders and musical chairs: ethnicity and opportunity in post-industrial New York. *Politics and Society*, 15, 369–401.

Waley, P. 1997: Tokyo: patterns of familiarity and partitions of difference. *American Behavioral Scientist*, 41 (3), 390–429.

Walker, R. 1978: The transformation of the urban structure in the nineteenth century and the beginnings of suburbanization. In K.R. Cox (ed.), *Urbanization and Conflict in Market Societies*, London: Methuen, 165–211.

Waters, M.C. 1990: *Ethnic Options: Choosing Identities in America*, Berkeley: University of California Press

Webber, M.M. 1964: The urban place and the nonplace urban realm. In M.M. Webber, J.W. Dijckman, D.L. Foley, A.Z. Guttenberg, W.L.C. Wheaton and C. Bauer Wurster (eds), *Explorations into Urban Structure*, Philadelphia: University of Pennsylvania Press, 79–153.

Wegener, M.. 1994: Tokyo's land market and its impact on housing and urban life. In P. Shapira, I. Masser & D. Edgington (eds), *Planning for Cities and Regions in Japan*, Liverpool: Liverpool University Press, 92–112.

Wentz, M. 1991: Stadtplanung in Frankfurt. In M. Wentz (ed.), *Stadtplanung in Frankfurt: Wohnen, Arbeiten, Verkehr*, Frankfurt/New York: Campus Verlag, 11–22.

White, R. 1996: No-go in the fortress city: young people, inequality and space. *Urban Policy and Research*, 14, 37–50.

Whiteford, P. 1995: Does Australia have a ghetto underclass? *Social Security Journal*, June, 3–19.

Williams, C.J. 1998: Arson, racist attack feared in deadly Sweden disco fire. *The Buffalo News*, 31 October 1998.

Williamson, J. (ed.) 1994: *The Political Economy of Policy Reform*, Washington, DC: Institute for International Economics.

Wilson, W.J. 1987: *The Truly Disadvantaged: The Inner City, the Underclass, and Public Policy*, Chicago: University of Chicago Press.

Wilson, W.J. 1996: *When Work Disappears; The New World of the Urban Poor*, New York: Alfred Knopf.

Winter, I. and Bryson, L. 1996: *Economic and Political Restructuring in Holdenist Suburbia*. Paper for the Regional Meeting of the International Sociological Association (Research Committee 43, Housing and Built Environment), Brisbane, 2–5 July, 1996.

Wolman, H. and Marckini, L. 1998: Changes in central-city representation and influence in congress since the 1960s. *Urban Affairs Review*, 34 (2), 291–312.

Wong, A.K. and Yeh, S.H.K. (eds) 1985: *Housing a Nation, 25 Years of Public Housing in*

Singapore, Singapore: Maruzen Asia Press.

World Bank 1993: *The East Asian Miracle: Economic Growth and Public Policy*, New York: Oxford University Press.

World Bank 1997: *World Development Report 1997*, Oxford: Oxford University Press.

Yinger, J.M. 1995: *Closed Doors, Lost Opportunities: The Continuing Costs of Housing Discrimination*, New York: Russell Sage Foundation.

Yoong, C.P. 1990: *Foreign Investment in Singapore Property*, Singapore: National University of Singapore.

Zukin, S. 1991: *Landscapes of Power*, Berkeley: University of California Press.

Zukin, S. 1995: *The Cultures of Cities*, Oxford: Blackwell.

Index